D1569951

JOURNAL FOR THE STUDY OF THE NEW TESTAMENT
SUPPLEMENT SERIES
254

Executive Editor
Stanley E. Porter

The Gospel of Matthew's Dependence on the *Didache*

Alan J.P. Garrow

T & T CLARK INTERNATIONAL
A Continuum imprint
LONDON • NEW YORK

Copyright © 2004 T&T Clark International
A Continuum imprint

Published by T&T Clark International
The Tower Building, 11 York Road, London SE1 7NX
15 East 26th Street, Suite 1703, New York, NY 10010

www.tandtclark.com

British Library Cataloguing-in-Publication Data
A catalogue record for this book is available from the British Library

Library of Congress Cataloging-in-Publication Data
A catalogue record for this book is available from the Library of Congress

Typeset by ISB Typesetting, Sheffield
Printed on acid-free paper in Great Britain by MPG Books Ltd, Bodmin, Cornwall

ISBN 0-8264-6977-9

CONTENTS

Abbreviations   vii
A Supporting Website   viii
Preface   ix
A Parallel Text of the *Didache*   xi

Chapter 1
INTRODUCTION   1

Part I
THE COMPOSITIONAL HISTORY OF THE *DIDACHE*

Chapter 2
THE 'EUCHARISTIC' PRAYERS IN *DIDACHE* 9 AND 10   13

Chapter 3
THE INTEGRITY OF *DIDACHE* 16   29

Chapter 4
ELEMENTS WITHIN *DIDACHE* 1–5   67

Chapter 5
THE PERI LAYER: 6.1-3; 7.1a, c, e, 4a; 9.1-5a; 11.3a, 4-6;
16.1-6, 8-9   93

Chapter 6
THE PROPHET DOCUMENT: 10.1-7; 11.7-9, 12; 12.1-5   107

Chapter 7
THE MODIFYING TEACHER LAYER: 1.5a-6; 7.1b, d, 2-3, 4b;
8.1-2a, 2c-3; 9.5b; 11.1-2; 11.10-11; 13.11–15.2   113

Chapter 8
THE GOSPEL LAYER: 8.2b; 11.3b; 15.3-4   129

Chapter 9
THE FULL EXTENT OF THE PERI LAYER   142

Chapter 10
CONCLUSION: THE COMPOSITIONAL HISTORY OF THE *DIDACHE*   150

Part II
THE POINTS OF CONTACT BETWEEN THE *DIDACHE* AND
MATTHEW'S GOSPEL

Chapter 11
MATTHEW'S GOSPEL AND THE MODIFYING TEACHER LAYER   161

Chapter 12
MATTHEW'S GOSPEL AND THE PROPHET LAYER   186

Chapter 13
MATTHEW'S GOSPEL AND *DIDACHE* 16   190

Chapter 14
MATTHEW'S GOSPEL AND *DIDACHE* 1.1-6   216

Chapter 15
FURTHER POINTS OF CONTACT BETWEEN MATTHEW'S GOSPEL
AND THE PERI/BASE LAYER   238

Part III
CONCLUSION

Chapter 16
CONCLUSION   244

Bibliography   253
Index of References   261
Index of Authors   271

ABBREVIATIONS

AGJU	Arbeiten zur Geschichte des antiken Judentums und des Urchristentums
ATR	*Anglican Theological Review*
BNTC	Black's New Testament Commentaries
Const.	*The Apostolic Constitutions*, Book VII
HNT.E	Handbuch zum Neuen Testament. Ergänzungsband
HTR	*Harvard Theological Review*
Int	*Interpretation*
JQR	*Jewish Quarterly Review*
JSNT	*Journal for the Study of the New Testament*
JSNTSup	*Journal for the Study of the New Testament*, Supplement Series
JTS	*Journal of Theological Studies*
KAV	Kommentar zu den apostolischen Vätern
LCL	Loeb Classical Library
NovT	*Novum Testamentum*
NovTSup	*Novum Testamentum*, Supplements
NTS	*New Testament Studies*
RivAC	*Rivista di archeologia cristiana*
SBT	Studies in Biblical Theology
SJT	*Scottish Journal of Theology*
SNTSMS	Society for New Testament Studies Monograph Series
TU	Texte und Untersuchungen
VigChr	*Vigiliae christianae*
VigChrSup	*Vigiliae christianae* Supplement Series
WBC	Word Biblical Commentary
WUNT	Wissenschaftliche Untersuchungen zum Neuen Testament
ZNW	*Zeitschrift für die neutestamentliche Wissenschaft*

A SUPPORTING WEBSITE

Studies that attempt to demonstrate the dependence of one text upon another need to show how detailed, local analyses fit into the wider pattern of contacts between the two texts. The following discussion makes use of a number of diagrams and synopses to try to meet this requirement.

While the current volume stands on its own, it is nonetheless the case that the black and white printing process does not always allow the clearest possible presentation of diagrams. As an additional resource, therefore, a supporting website provides coloured and sometimes expanded versions of the volume's texts and diagrams, alongside additional features.

www.didache-garrow.info

This project began with a slight tug on a small loose thread. I have for some time believed that the writings of the New Testament bear a closer relation to the liturgical life of the early Church than is generally perceived. This conviction arose after trying to resolve the puzzle of the structure of the book of Revelation, and concluding that this text was designed to be read in six separate instalments possibly in the context of eucharistic worship. In search of information relevant to the further exploration of the latter part of this hypothesis, I turned to the *Didache*.

On beginning to study this short but enigmatic text I soon came to understand why it is frequently referred to but seldom relied upon. It has something to say about a great number of issues relevant to New Testament and early Christian studies, but it is difficult to know what value to place upon its contributions so long as it eludes placement within the wider context of early Christianity. This combination of features also explains the feverish interest shown in the *Didache* when the rediscovered version was published in 1883, as well as the waning of that interest through the course of the twentieth century. This brings me to my first vote of thanks. I am tremendously indebted to those scholars who have continued to publish on the *Didache* in recent years, in particular, Clayton Jefford, Kurt Niederwimmer and Jonathan Draper. Without the work of scholars such as these a novice such as myself would have had great difficulty gaining access to the stream of *Didache* studies.

Predictably, the original goal of my research soon raced to a far distant horizon. It became necessary to re-address the traditional preliminary questions associated with the *Didache* before its contents could be claimed as having any relevance to the pattern of first-century life, literature or worship. This was a daunting task given the lack of success encountered by those who had gone before. Closer examination of this question soon revealed, however, that early studies of the *Didache* had failed to address some foundational issues with full rigour.

The greater part of this book (Part I) is concerned to uncover the compositional history of the *Didache*. That this task has received limited attention in the past may be attributed to its reputation as a tedious means of producing inconclusive results. Certainly, I didn't expect to find it an intriguing and satisfying exercise but two factors helped me to persist with an initially unpromising programme. First, my initial encounter with the *Didache* was with the eucharistic prayers in *Did.* 9 and 10. A redactional explanation for the puzzling pattern of these prayers (presented in Chapter 2) revealed scope for fresh exploration of the compositional history of the whole. Second, I was at the same time convinced that a method for establishing Matthew's dependence on the *Didache* (presented in Part II) could be made to rest on strong evidence for a number of separate contributions to the *Didache*, even if the exact extent and number of those contributions could not always be precisely pinned down. From this 'one step at a time' approach a complete compositional analysis ultimately arose.

Seeing an initial research goal recede into the far distance can be frustrating. I hope that one day I will have opportunity to return to the question of the eucharistic setting of Revelation. In the meantime, however, I am glad to have been taken on a detour that has introduced me to a text so rich in implications for how the faith, worship and literature of the earliest Christians is understood. I am grateful too to all those people who have made these researches possible. First of all to Professor C.M. Tuckett, my supervisor during the latter stages of the DPhil, of which this volume is the result. His unfailing fairness while dealing with a student with whom he almost entirely disagrees consistently challenged and, I hope, refined my thinking. I would also like to thank Professor Christopher Rowland, who supervised the early stages of this project before it turned more particularly to the study of the relationship between the *Didache* and Matthew's Gospel, and the members of the New Testament Graduate Seminar at Oxford University, especially Dr Andrew Gregory and Pastor Reiner Behrens. The comments of Drs David Wenham and John Court, who examined the DPhil thesis, have also been very helpful in the preparation of the current text.

Thanks too to my extraordinarily supportive parents. To friends, colleagues and students at the St Albans and Oxford Ministry Course, and fellow worshippers in the Akeman Benefice. Finally, I would like to dedicate this book to my wife, Emma, who, amongst many other things, knows a great deal about a short early Christian text known as the *Didache*.

Oxford
November 2002

A PARALLEL TEXT OF THE *DIDACHE*

The following Greek text is based on the criticial edition of the Jerusalem manuscript published by Archbishop Bryennios in 1883. Variant readings, significant for the following discussion, are footnoted. The layout of the text, its verse sub-divisions and the reconstruction of *Didache* 16.8b-9 are my own, as is the English translation.

Column A indicates the redactional layer to which the accompanying text is attributed in the following discussion.

1 = the Peri or Base layer (also referred to in the ensuing text as P/B)
2 = the Prophet layer (also referred to in the ensuing text as PR)
3 = the Modifying Teacher layer (also referred to in the ensuing text as MT)
4 = the Gospel layer
5 = the Jerusalem addition

Column B indicates the presence of previously existing traditions incorporated into, or quoted by, one of the *Didache*'s five contributors.

AP = a self-contained Apocalypse or eschatological warning
BP = a tradition concerning Baptism and the baptismal fast
DG = a saying regarding Giving what is holy to Dogs
FF = a tradition regarding Firstfruits
GV = a saying on Giving, possibly from Sirach 12.1
LP = a version of the Lord's Prayer
LS = a Law Summary
ML = a quotation of Malachi 1.11
PR = the Prophet document (which constitutes the entirety of the Prophet layer)
SO = a Sayings Onion; SO.a-e represent five individual elements of that collection
TK = the so-called Teknon teaching, a wisdom tradition based on Ps. 36 (LXX)
TW = the Two Ways tradition

Where column B is vacant, this indicates a direct contribution by the editor of the layer whose number is indicated in column A.

Column C indicates those verses of Matthew's Gospel that contain conceptual and verbal similarities to the corresponding text of the *Didache*. Underlining of this text indicates a direct verbal parallel between the *Didache* and the verse indicated in Matthew's Gospel.

	A	B	C
Διδαχὴ κυρίου διὰ τῶν δώδεκα ἀποστόλων	1		28.16, 20
τοῖς ἔθνεσιν.			28.19
1.1 Ὁδοι δύο εἰσί, μία τῆς ζωῆς καὶ μία τοῦ θανάτου,	1	TW	7.13-14
διαφορὰ δὲ πολλὴ μεταξὺ τῶ δύο ὁδῶν.		TW	
1.2a Ἡ μὲν οὖν ὁδὸς τῆς ζωῆς ἐστιν αὕτη·	1	TW	
1.2b πρῶτον	1	LS	22.38
ἀγαπήσεις τὸν θεὸν τὸν ποιήσαντά σε,	1	TW	
1.2c δεύτερον τὸν πλησίον σου ὡς σεαυτόν·	1	LS	22.39
1.2d πάντα δὲ ὅσα ἐὰν θελήσῃς μὴ γίνεσθαί σοι,	1	LS	7.12
καὶ σὺ ἄλλῳ μὴ ποίει.	1	LS	
1.3a Τούτων δὲ τῶν λόγων ἡ διδαχή ἐστιν αὕτη·	1		
1.3b εὐλογεῖτε τοὺς καταρωμένους ὑμῖν	1	SO.a	
καὶ προσεύχεσθε ὑπὲρ τῶν ἐχθρῶν ὑμῶν,	1	SO.a	5.44
νηστεύετε δὲ ὑπὲρ τῶν διωκόντων ὑμᾶς·	1	SO.a	5.44
1.3c ποία γὰρ χάρις,	1	SO.b	
ἐὰν ἀγαπᾶτε τοὺς ἀγαπῶντας ὑμᾶς;	1	SO.b	5.46
οὐχὶ καὶ τὰ ἔθνη τὸ αὐτό[1] ποιοῦσιν;	1	SO.b	5.47
ὑμεῖς δὲ ἀγαπᾶτε[2] τοὺς μισοῦντας ὑμας	1	SO.b	
καὶ οὐχ ἕξετε ἐχθρόν.	1	SO.b	
1.4a ἀπέχου τῶν σαρκικῶν καὶ σωματικῶν[3] ἐπιθυμιῶν·	1	SO.c	
1.4b ἐάν τίς σοι δῷ ῥάπισμα εἰς τὴν δεξιὰν σιαγόνα,	1	SO.d	5.39
στρέψον αὐτῷ καὶ τὴν ἄλλην,	1	SO.d	5.39
1.4b(r) καὶ ἔσῃ τέλειος·	1		5.48; 19.21
ἐὰν ἀγγαρεύσῃ σέ τις μίλιον ἕν, ὕπαγε μετ᾽ αὐτοῦ δύο·	1	SO.d	5.41
ἐὰν ἄρῃ τις τὸ ἱμάτιόν σου, δὸς αὐτῷ καὶ τὸν χιτῶνα·	1	SO.d	5.40
ἐὰν λάβῃ τις ἀπὸ σοῦ τὸ σόν,	1	SO.d	
μὴ ἀπαίτει· οὐδὲ γὰρ δύνασαι.	1	SO.d	
1.5a παντὶ τῷ αἰτοῦντί σε δίδου καὶ μὴ ἀπαίτει·	1	SO.e	5.42
πᾶσι γὰρ θέλει δίδοσθαι ὁ πατὴρ ἐκ τῶν ἰδίων	1	SO.e	5.45
χαρισμάτων.	1	SO.e	

1. *Const.* reads τοῦτο.
2. *Const.* reads φιλεῖτε.
3. P.Oxy 1782 omits καὶ σωματικῶν in its long version of 1.4a.

	A	B	C
The Teaching of the Lord, by the Twelve Apostles,	1		28.16, 20
to the Gentiles.			28.19
1.1 There are two ways, one of life, the other of death,	1	TW	7.13-14
and there is a great difference between the two ways.		TW	
1.2a Now the way of life is this:	1	TW	
1.2b first ,	1	LS	22.38
1.2c you shall love the God who made you;	1	TW	
1.2d second, your neighbour as yourself,	1	LS	22.39
1.2e and everything that you would not have done to you, do	1	LS	7.12
not do to another.	1	LS	
1.3a The teaching of these words is this:	1		
1.3b Bless [pl. throughout v. 3] those that curse you and	1	SO.a	
pray for your enemies,	1	SO.a	5.44
fast for those that persecute you.	1	SO.a	5.44
1.3c For what merit is there	1	SO.b	
if you love those that love you?	1	SO.b	5.46
Do not even the Gentiles do the same?	1	SO.b	5.47
But love those who hate you	1	SO.b	
and you will not have any enemy.	1	SO.b	
1.4a Avoid the fleshly and bodily passions.	1	SO.c	
1.4b If someone strikes you on your right cheek,	1	SO.d	5.39
turn the other to him also,	1	SO.d	5.39
1.4b(r) and you will be perfect.	1		5.48; 19.21
If someone forces you to go one mile, go with him two.	1	SO.d	5.41
If someone takes your coat, give him your shirt also.	1	SO.d	5.40
If someone takes away from you what is yours,	1	SO.d	
do not ask for it back, since you cannot.	1	SO.d	
1.5a To everyone asking of you give, and do not ask for it back,	1	SO.e	5.42
for the Father wishes that gifts be given to all from his own	1	SO.e	5.45
bounty.	1	SO.e	

	A	B	C
1.5b Μακάριος ὁ διδοὺς κατὰ τὴν	3		
ἐντολήν· ἀθῷος γάρ ἐστιν. 1.5c οὐαὶ	3		
τῷ λαμβάνοντι· εἰ μὲν γὰρ χρείαν ἔχων λαμβάνει τις,	3		
ἀθῷος ἔσται· ὁ δὲ μὴ χρείαν ἔχων δώσει δίκην, ἱνατί ἔλαβε	3		
καὶ εἰς τί· ἐν συνοχῇ δὲ γενόμενος ἐξετασθήσεται περὶ ὧν	3		
ἔπραξε καὶ οὐκ ἐξελεύσεται ἐκεῖθεν, μέχρις οὗ <u>ἀποδῷ τὸν</u>	3		5.26
<u>ἔσχατον κοδράντην.</u>	3		5.26
1.6 ἀλλὰ καὶ περὶ τούτου δὲ εἴρηται·	3		
Ἱδρωσάτω ἡ ἐλεημοσύνη σου εἰς τὰς χεῖράς σου,	3	GV	
μέχρις ἂν γνῷς, τίνι δῷς.	3	GV	
2.1 Δευτέρα δὲ ἐντολὴ τῆς διδαχῆς·	1	LS	
2.2 <u>οὐ φονεύσεις,</u>	1	TW	5.21; 19.18
<u>οὐ μοιχεύσεις,</u>	1	TW	5.27; 19.18
οὐ παιδοφθορήσεις, οὐ πορνεύσεις,	1	TW	
<u>οὐ κλέψεις,</u> οὐ μαγεύσεις,	1	TW	19.18
οὐ φαρμακεύσεις,	1	TW	
οὐ φονεύσεις τέκνον ἐν φθορᾷ οὐδὲ γεννηθέντα ἀποκτενεῖς,	1	TW	
οὐκ ἐπιθυμήσεις τὰ τοῦ πλησίον.			
	1	TW	
2.3 <u>οὐκ ἐπιορκήσεις,</u>	1	TW	5.33
οὐ ψευδομαρτυρήσεις,	1	TW	
οὐ κακολογήσεις,	1	TW	
οὐ μνησικακήσεις.	1	TW	
2.4 οὐκ ἔσῃ διγνώμων οὐδὲ δίγλωσσος	1	TW	
παγὶς γὰρ θανάτου ἡ διγλωσσία.	1	TW	
2.5 οὐκ ἔσται ὁ λόγος σου ψευδής οὐ κενός,	1	TW	
ἀλλὰ μεμεστωμένος πράξει.	1	TW	
2.6 οὐκ ἔσῃ πλεονέκτης οὐδὲ ἅρπαξ οὐδὲ ὑποκριτὴς	1	TW	
οὐδὲ κακοήθης οὐδὲ ὑπερήφανος· οὐ λήψῃ βουλὴν	1	TW	
πονηρὰν κατὰ τοῦ πλησίον σου.	1	TW	
2.7 οὐ μισήσεις πάντα ἄνθρωπον, ἀλλὰ οὕς μὲν ἐλέγξεις,	1	TW	
περὶ δὲ ὧν προσεύξῃ, οὓς δὲ ἀγαπήσεις ὑπὲρ	1	TW	
τὴν ψυχήν σου.	1	TW	
3.1 Τέκνον μου, φεῦγε ἀπὸ παντὸς πονηροῦ	1	TK	
καὶ ἀπὸ παντὸς ὁμοίου αὐτοῦ.	1	TK	
3.2 μὴ γίνου ὀργίλος, ὁδηγεῖ γὰρ ἡ <u>ὀργὴ</u> πρὸς τὸν <u>φόνον,</u>	1	TK	5.21, 22
μηδὲ ζηλωτὴς μηδὲ ἐριστικὸς μηδὲ θυμικός·	1	TK	
ἐκ γὰρ τούτων ἁπάντων φόνοι γεννῶνται.	1	TK	

	A	B	C
1.5b Blessed is the one who gives according to the commandment,	3		
for he is guiltless. 1.5c Woe to	3		
the one who receives. For if he receives because he has need,	3		
he is guiltless, but if he does not have need, he shall stand trial	3		
as to why he received and for what, and being put in prison he	3		
will be examined about what he has done, and he will not come	3		
out of it until he pays the last penny.	3		5.26
1.6 But of this it was also said,	3		
'Let your charitable gift sweat in your hands	3	GV	
until you know to whom you give'.	3	GV	
2.1 The second commandment of the teaching means:	1	LS	
2.2 You shall not murder,	1	TW	5.21; 19.18
You shall not commit adultery.	1	TW	5.27; 19.18
You shall not corrupt boys. You shall not fornicate.	1	TW	
You shall not steal. You shall not practise magic.	1	TW	19.18
You shall not use sorcery.	1	TW	
You shall not murder a child by abortion or commit infanticide.	1	TW	
You shall not covet what belongs to your neighbour.			
	1	TW	
2.3 You shall not swear falsely.	1	TW	5.33
You shall not bear false witness.	1	TW	
You shall not speak evil.	1	TW	
You shall not harbour a grudge.	1	TW	
2.4 You shall not be double-minded, nor double-tongued,	1	TW	
for the double tongue is a snare of death.	1	TW	
2.5 Your word shall not be false or empty	1	TW	
but fulfilled by action.	1	TW	
2.6 You shall not be covetous, nor a swindler,	1	TW	
nor a hypocrite, nor ill-tempered, nor proud. You shall not plot	1	TW	
evil against your neighbour.	1	TW	
2.7 You shall not hate anyone. But some you shall reprove, and	1	TW	
for some you shall pray. And some you shall love more than	1	TW	
your own life.	1	TW	
3.1 My child, flee from all evil	1	TK	
and from everything like it.	1	TK	
3.2 Do not be angry, for anger leads to murder;	1	TK	5.21, 22
nor jealous nor contentious nor hot-tempered,	1	TK	
for all these things breed murder.	1	TK	

	A	B	C
3.3 τέκνον μου, μὴ γίνου ἐπιθυμητής,	1	ΤΚ	5.27
ὁδηγεῖ γὰρ ἡ ἐπιθυμία πρὸς τὴν πορνείαν,	1	ΤΚ	
μηδὲ αἰσχρολόγος μηδὲ ὑψηλόφθαλμος·	1	ΤΚ	
ἐκ γὰρ τούτων ἁπάντων μοιχεῖαι γεννῶνται.	1	ΤΚ	5.28
3.4 τέκνον μου, μὴ γίνου οἰωνοσκόπος,	1	ΤΚ	
ἐπειδὴ ὁδηγεῖ εἰς τὴν εἰδωλολατρίαν,	1	ΤΚ	
μηδὲ ἐπαοιδὸς μηδὲ μαθηματικὸς μηδὲ περικαθαίρων,	1	ΤΚ	
μηδὲ θέλε αὐτὰ βλέπειν·	1	ΤΚ	
ἐκ γὰρ τούτων ἁπάντων εἰδωλολατρία γεννᾶται.	1	ΤΚ	
3.5 τέκνον μου, μὴ γίνου ψεύστης,	1	ΤΚ	
ἐπειδὴ ὁδηγεῖ τὸ ψεῦσμα εἰς τὴν κλοπήν,	1	ΤΚ	
μηδὲ φιλάργυρος μηδὲ κενόδοξος·	1	ΤΚ	
ἐκ γὰρ τούτων ἁπάντων κλοπαὶ γεννῶνται.	1	ΤΚ	
3.6 τέκνον μου, μὴ γίνου γόγγυσος	1	ΤΚ	
ἐπειδὴ ὁδηγεῖ εἰς τὴν βλασφημίαν,	1	ΤΚ	
μηδὲ αὐθάδης μηδὲ πονηρόφρων·	1	ΤΚ	
ἐκ γὰρ τούτων ἁπάντων βλασθημίαι γεννῶντια.	1	ΤΚ	
3.7 ἴσθι δὲ πραΰς, ἐπεὶ οἱ πραεῖς κληρονομήσουσι τὴν γῆν	1	ΤΚ/ ΤW	5.5
3.8 Γίνου μακρόθυμος καὶ ἐλεήμων καὶ ἄκακος καὶ ἡσύχιος	1	ΤW	5.7
καὶ ἀγαθὸς καὶ τρέμων τοὺς λόγους διὰ παντός, οὕς	1	ΤW	
ἤκουσας.	1	ΤW	
3.9 οὐχ ὑψώσεις σεαυτὸν	1	ΤW	
οὐδὲ δώσεις τῇ ψυχῇ σου θράσος.	1	ΤW	
οὐ κολληθήσεται ἡ ψυχή σου μετὰ ὑψηλῶν,	1	ΤW	
ἀλλὰ μετὰ δικαίων καὶ ταπεινῶν ἀναστραφήσῃ.	1	ΤW	
3.10 τὰ συμβαίνοντά σοι ἐνεργήματα ὡς ἀγαθὰ προσδέξῃ,	1	ΤW	
εἰδώς, ὅτι ἄτερ θεοῦ οὐδὲν γίνεται.	1	ΤW	
4.1 Τέκνον μου, τοῦ λαλοῦντός σοι τὸν λόγον τοῦ θεοῦ	1	ΤW	
μνησθήσῃ νυκτὸς καὶ ἡμέρας, τιμήσεις δὲ αὐτὸν ὡς	1	ΤW	
κύριον· ὅθεν γὰρ ἡ κυριότης λαλεῖται, ἐκεῖ κύριός ἐστιν.	1	ΤW	
4.2 ἐκζητήσεις δὲ καθ' ἡμέραν τὰ πρόσωπα τῶν ἁγίων, ἵνα	1	ΤW	
ἐπαναπαῇς τοῖς λόγοις αὐτῶν.	1	ΤW	
4.3 οὐ ποθήσεις σχίσμα, εἰρηνεύσεις δὲ μαχομένους· κρινεῖς	1	ΤW	
δικαίως, οὐ λήψῃ πρόσωπον ἐλέγξαι	1	ΤW	
ἐπὶ παραπτώμασιν.	1	ΤW	
4.4 οὐ διψυχήσεις, πότερον ἔσται ἢ οὔ.	1	ΤW	
4.5 μὴ γίνου πρὸς μὲν τὸ λαβεῖν ἐκτείνων τὰς χεῖρας, πρὸς δὲ	1	ΤW	
τὸ δοῦναι συσπῶν.	1	ΤW	
4.6 ἐὰν ἔχῃς διὰ τῶν χειρῶν σου,	1	ΤW	
δώσεις λύτρωσιν ἁμαρτιῶν σου.	1	ΤW	
4.7 οὐ διστάσεις δοῦναι οὐδὲ διδοὺς γογγύσεις· γνώσῃ γάρ, τίς	1	ΤW	
ἐστιν ὁ τοῦ μισθοῦ καλὸς ἀνταποδότης.	1	ΤW	

	A	B	C
3.3 My child, do not be <u>lustful</u>,	1	TK	5.27
for lust leads to fornication;	1	TK	
nor should you use obscene speech or lustful gazes,	1	TK	
for all these breed acts of <u>adultery</u>.	1	TK	5.28
3.4 My child, do not be a soothsayer,	1	TK	
for this leads to idolatry;	1	TK	
nor an enchanter, nor an astrologer, nor a magician;	1	TK	
do not be willing to even look at such things,	1	TK	
for all these breed idolatry.	1	TK	
3.5 My child do not be a liar,	1	TK	
for lying leads to theft;	1	TK	
nor avaricious, nor vainglorious,	1	TK	
for all these breed theft.	1	TK	
3.6 My child, do not be a grumbler,	1	TK	
for this leads to blasphemy;	1	TK	
nor self-willed, nor evil-minded,	1	TK	
for all these breed blasphemy.	1	TK	
3.7 but be <u>meek</u>, since <u>the meek shall inherit the earth</u>.	1	TK/ TW	5.5
3.8 Be patient and <u>merciful</u>, and guileless, and quiet	1	TW	5.7
and good, and always revering the words	1	TW	
you have heard.	1	TW	
3.9 You shall not exalt yourself	1	TW	
or admit arrogance into your soul.	1	TW	
Your soul shall not associate with the lofty	1	TW	
but you shall walk with those who are righteous and humble.	1	TW	
3.10 Accept the things that happen to you as good,	1	TW	
knowing that nothing is done without God.	1	TW	
4.1 My child, be mindful night and day of the one who speaks	1	TW	
the word of God to you. You shall honour him as the Lord, for	1	TW	
wherever the Lord's nature is spoken of, there the Lord is.	1	TW	
4.2 You shall seek out daily the presence of the saints	1	TW	
to find support in their words.	1	TW	
4.3 You shall not cause division; instead you shall reconcile	1	TW	
those who quarrel. You shall judge righteously. You shall not	1	TW	
show partiality in reproving people for their faults.	1	TW	
4.4 You shall not doubt whether a thing shall be or not.	1	TW	
4.5 Do not be someone holding out your hands to receive,	1	TW	
but closing them when it comes to giving.	1	TW	
4.6 If you have earned something through the work of your	1	TW	
hands, you shall give something as a ransom for your sins.	1	TW	
4.7 You shall not hesitate to give, nor grumble when giving,	1	TW	
for you will know the good paymaster of your reward.	1	TW	

	A	B	C
4.8 οὐκ ἀποστραφήσῃ τὸν ἐνδεόμενον, συγκοινωνήσεις δὲ	1	TW	
πάντα τῷ ἀδελφῷ σου καὶ οὐκ ἐρεῖς ἴδια εἶναι·	1	TW	
εἰ γὰρ ἐν τῷ ἀθανάτῳ κοινωνοί ἐστε,	1	TW	
πόσῳ μᾶλλον ἐν τοῖς θνητοῖς;	1	TW	
4.9 Οὐκ ἀρεῖς τὴν χεῖρά σου ἀπὸ τοῦ υἱοῦ σου ἢ ἀπὸ τῆς	1	TW	
θυγατρός σου, ἀλλὰ ἀπὸ νεότητος διδάξεις τὸν φόβον	1	TW	
τοῦ θεοῦ.	1	TW	
4.10 οὐκ ἐπιτάξεις δούλῳ σου ἢ παιδίσκῃ,	1	TW	
τοῖς ἐπὶ τὸν αὐτὸν θεὸν ἐλπίζουσιν, ἐν πικρίᾳ σου,	1	TW	
μήποτε οὐ μὴ φοβηθήσονται τὸν ἐπ᾽ ἀμφοτέροις θεόν·	1	TW	
οὐ γὰρ ἔρχεται κατὰ πρόσωπον καλέσαι,	1	TW	
ἀλλ᾽ ἐφ᾽ οὓς τὸ πνεῦμα ἡτοίμασεν.	1	TW	
4.11 ὑμεῖς δὲ οἱ δοῦλοι ὑποταγήσεσθε τοῖς κυρίοις ὑμῶν	1	TW	
ὡς τύπῳ θεοῦ ἐν αἰσχύνῃ καὶ φόβῳ.	1	TW	
4.12 μισήσεις πᾶσαν ὑπόκρισιν καὶ πᾶν ὃ μὴ ἀρεστὸν	1	TW	
τῷ κυρίῳ. 4.13 οὐ μὴ ἐγκαταλίπῃς ἐντολὰς κυρίου,	1	TW	
φυλάξεις δὲ ἃ παρέλαβες, μήτε προστιθεὶς	1	TW	
μήτε ἀφαιρῶν. 4.14 ἐν ἐκκλησίᾳ ἐξομολογήσῃ τὰ	1	TW	
παραπτώματά σου καὶ οὐ προσελεύσῃ ἐπὶ προσευχήν	1	TW	
σου ἐν συνειδήσει πονηρᾷ. αὕτη ἐστὶν ἡ ὁδὸς τῆς ζωῆς.	1	TW	
5.1a Ἡ δὲ τοῦ θανάτου ὁδός ἐστιν αὕτη·	1	TW	
πρῶτον πάντων πονηρά ἐστι καὶ κατάρας μεστή·	1	TW	
5.1b <u>φόνοι, μοιχεῖαι,</u> ἐπιθυμίαι, <u>πορνεῖαι, κλοπαί,</u> εἰδωλολατρίαι,	1	TW	15.19
μαγεῖαι, φαρμακίαι, ἁρπαγαί,	1	TW	
<u>ψευδομαρτυρίαι,</u> ὑποκρίσεις, διπλοκαρδία, δόλος,	1	TW	15.19
ὑπερηφανία, κακία, αὐθάδεια, πλεονεξία, αἰσχρολογία, ζηλοτυπία,	1	TW	
θρασύτης, ὕψος, ἀλαζονεία.	1	TW	
5.2a διῶκται ἀγαθῶν, μισοῦντες ἀλήθειαν,	1	TW	
ἀγαπῶντες ψεῦδος, οὐ γινώσκοντες μισθὸν δικαιοσύνης,	1	TW	
οὐ κολλώμενοι ἀγαθῷ οὐδὲ κρίσει δικαίᾳ,	1	TW	
ἀγρυπνοῦντες οὐκ εἰς τὸ ἀγαθόν, ἀλλ᾽ εἰς τὸ πονηρόν·	1	TW	
ὧν μακρὰν πραΰτης καὶ ὑπομονή, μάταια ἀγαπῶντες,	1	TW	
διώκοντες ἀνταπόδομα, οὐκ ἐλεοῦντες πτωχόν,	1	TW	
οὐ πονοῦντες ἐπὶ καταπονουμένῳ οὐ γινώσκοντες τὸν	1	TW	
ποιήσαντα αὐτούς, φονεῖς τέκνων, φθορεῖς πλάσματος	1	TW	
θεοῦ, ἀποστρεφόμενοι τὸν ἐνδεόμενον, καταπονοῦντες τὸν	1	TW	
θλιβόμενον, πλουσίων παράκλητοι, πενήτων ἄνομοι	1	TW	
κριταί, πανθαμάρτητοι·	1	TW	
5.2b ῥυσθείητε, τέκνα, ἀπὸ τούτων ἁπάντων.	3		

	A	B	C
4.8 You shall not turn the needy away; but you shall hold	1	TW	
everything in common with your brother, and not say that	1	TW	
anything is your own, for if you share in what is immortal,	1	TW	
how much more in mortal things?	1	TW	
4.9 You shall not withhold your hand from your son or your	1	TW	
daughter, but from their youth you shall teach them the fear of	1	TW	
God.	1	TW	
4.10 You shall not command in bitterness your slave or your	1	TW	
maid who trusts in the same God, lest they stop revering the God	1	TW	
who is over you both.	1	TW	
For he comes not to call people according to their status	1	TW	
but he comes to those whom the Spirit has prepared.	1	TW	
4.11 And you slaves shall be subject to your masters,	1	TW	
as symbols of God, with reverence and fear.	1	TW	
4.12 You shall hate all hypocrisy and all that is not pleasing to	1	TW	
the Lord. 4.13 You shall not abandon the commandments	1	TW	
of the Lord but shall keep what you have received without adding or	1	TW	
subtracting anything. 4.14 In the assembly you shall confess	1	TW	
your faults, and you shall not approach prayer	1	TW	
with an evil conscience. This is the way of life.	1	TW	
5.1a And the way of death is this.	1	TW	
First of all, it is evil and full of accursedness;	1	TW	
5.1b <u>murder, adultery</u>, lust, <u>fornication, theft</u>,	1	TW	15.19
idolatry, magic, sorcery, robbery,	1	TW	
<u>false witness</u>, hypocrisy, doubleness of heart, treachery, pride,	1	TW	15.19
malice, stubbornness, covetousness, obscene speech, jealousy, insolence,	1	TW	
arrogance, boastfulness.	1	TW	
5.2a Those who are persecutors of the good, hating truth, loving	1	TW	
falsehood, not knowing the reward of the righteous, not adhering	1	TW	
to the good nor to righteous judgment,	1	TW	
lying awake not for what is good but for what is evil,	1	TW	
those who are far from being meek and patient, loving what is	1	TW	
futile, seeking repayment, not showing mercy to the poor,	1	TW	
not labouring for the oppressed, not recognizing him who made	1	TW	
them, murderers of children, corrupters of God's	1	TW	
creatures, who turn away from the needy, oppressing the afflicted, defenders of	1	TW	
the rich, unjust judges of the poor	1	TW	
and altogether sinful.	1	TW	
5.2b May you [pl.] be delivered, children, from all this.	3		

	A	B	C
6.1 Ὄρα, μή τίς σε πλανήσῃ ἀπὸ ταύτης τῆς ὁδοῦ τῆς	1		
διδαχῆς, ἐπεὶ παρεκτὸς θεοῦ σε διδάσκει.	1		
6.2 εἰ μὲν γὰρ δύνασαι βαστάσαι ὅλον τὸν ζυγὸν τοῦ	1		
κυρίου, τέλειος ἔσῃ· εἰ δ᾿ οὐ δύνασαι, ὃ δύνῃ, τοῦτο ποίει. 6.3	1		
περὶ δὲ τῆς βρώσεως, ὃ δύνασαι βάστασον· ἀπὸ δὲ τοῦ	1		
εἰδωλοθύτου λίαν πρόσεχε· λατρεία γάρ ἐστι	1		
θεῶν νεκρῶν.	1		
7.1a Περὶ δὲ τοῦ βαπτίσματος, οὕτω βαπτίσατε·	1		
7.1b ταῦτα πάντα προειπόντες,	3		
7.1c βαπτίσατε εἰς τὸ ὄνομα	1		28.19
7.1d τοῦ πατρὸς καὶ τοῦ υἱοῦ καὶ τοῦ ἁγίου πνεύματος	3	BP	28.19
7.1e ἐν ὕδατι ζῶντι.	1		
7.2a ἐὰν δὲ μὴ ἔχῃς ὕδωρ ζῶν,	3	BP	
εἰς ἄλλο ὕδωρ βάπτισον· 7.2b εἰ δ᾿ οὐ δύνασαι ἐν ψυχρῷ,	3	BP	
ἐν θερμῷ. 7.3 ἐὰν δὲ ἀμφότερα μὴ ἔχῃς, ἔκχεον εἰς τὴν	3	BP	
κεφαλὴν τρὶς ὕδωρ εἰς ὄνομα πατρὸς καὶ υἱοῦ καὶ ἁγίου	3	BP	
πνεύματος.	3	BP	
7.4a πρὸ δὲ τοῦ βαπτίσματος προνηστευσάτω ὁ βαπτίζων	1		
καὶ ὁ βαπτιζόμενος καὶ εἴ τινες ἄλλοι δύνανται·	1		
7.4b κελεύσεις δὲ νηστεῦσαι τὸν βαπτιζόμενον	3	BP	
πρὸ ἢ δύο.	3	BP	
8.1 Αἱ δὲ νηστεῖαι ὑμῶν μὴ ἔστωσαν μετὰ τῶν ὑποκριται·	3		6.16
νηστεύουσι γὰρ δευτέρᾳ σαββάτων καὶ πέμπτῃ·	3		
ὑμεῖς δὲ νηστεύσατε τετράδα καὶ παρασκευῇ	3		
8.2a μηδὲ προσεύχεσθε ὡς οἱ ὑποκριταί, ἀλλ᾿	3		6.2, 5, 16
8.2b ὡς ἐκέλευσεν ὁ κύριος ἐν τῷ εὐαγγελίῳ αὐτὸ,	4		
8.2c οὕτω προσεύχεσθε·	3		6.9
πάτερ ἡμῶν ὁ ἐν τῷ οὐρανῷ,	3	LP	6.9
ἁγιασθήτω τὸ ὄνομά σου,	3	LP	6.9
ἐλθέτω ἡ βασιλεία σου,	3	LP	6.10
γενηθήτω τὸ θέλημά σου ὡς ἐν οὐρανῷ καὶ ἐπὶ γῆς·	3	LP	6.10
τὸν ἄρτον ἡμῶν τὸν ἐπιούσιον δὸς ἡμῖν σήμερον,	3	LP	6.11
καὶ ἄφες ἡμῖν τὴν ὀφειλὴν ἡμῶν,	3	LP	6.12
ὡς καὶ ἡμεῖς ἀφίεμεν τοῖς ὀφειλέταις ἡμῶν,	3	LP	6.12
καὶ μὴ εἰσενέγκῃς ἡμᾶς εἰς πειρασμόν,	3	LP	6.13
ἀλλὰ ῥῦσαι ἡμᾶς ἀπὸ τοῦ πονηροῦ·	3	LP	6.13
ὅτι σοῦ ἐστιν ἡ δύναμις καὶ ἡ δόξα εἰς τοὺς αἰῶνας.	3	LP	
8.3 τρὶς τῆς ἡμέρας οὕτω προσεύχεσθε.	3		

	A	B	C
6.1 See that no one leads you astray from this way of teaching,	1		
since the one who does so teaches apart from God.	1		
6.2 If you are able to bear the whole yoke of the Lord,	1		
you will be perfect, but if you cannot, do what you can.	1		
6.3 Concerning food, bear what you can, but abstain strictly	1		
from food offered to idols, for it is worship of	1		
dead gods.	1		
7.1a Concerning baptism, baptize thus:	1		
7.1b (After you have repeated all these things)	3		
7.1c <u>Baptize in the name</u>	1		28.19
7.1d <u>of the Father, the Son and the Holy Spirit</u>	3	BP	28.19
7.1e in running water.	1		
7.2a If you [sing. through vv. 2-4] do not have running water,	3	BP	
baptize in other water; 7.2b if you cannot in cold,	3	BP	
then in warm. 7.3 But if you have neither, pour water on the	3	BP	
head three times in the name of Father, Son, and Holy	3	BP	
Spirit.	3	BP	
7.4a Before the baptism, let the one baptizing and the one being	1		
baptized, and any others who are able, fast.	1		
7.4b Command the one being baptized to fast for one or two days	3	BP	
beforehand.	3	BP	
8.1 Do not let your <u>fasts</u> coincide with those of the <u>hypocrites</u>.	3		6.16
They fast on Monday and Thursday;	3		
you, though, should fast on Wednesday and Friday.	3		
8.2a And do not <u>pray</u> as the <u>hypocrites</u>, but	3		6.2, 5, 16
8.2b as the Lord commanded in his gospel	4		
8.2c pray thus:	3		6.9
<u>Our Father in heaven</u>	3	LP	6.9
<u>Hallowed be your name</u>	3	LP	6.9
<u>Your kingdom come</u>	3	LP	6.10
<u>Your will be done on earth as it is in heaven</u>	3	LP	6.10
<u>Give us this day our bread for the morrow</u>	3	LP	6.11
<u>And forgive us our sin</u>	3	LP	6.12
<u>As we forgive those who sin against us</u>	3	LP	6.12
<u>And lead us not into temptation</u>	3	LP	6.13
<u>But deliver us from evil</u>	3	LP	6.13
For the power and glory are yours forever.	3	LP	
8.3 Pray this three times a day.	3		

	A	B	C
9.1 Περὶ δὲ τῆς εὐχαριστίας, οὕτως εὐχαριστήσατε·	1		
9.2 πρῶτον περὶ τοῦ ποτηρίου·	1		
εὐχαριστοῦμέν σοι, πάτερ ἡμῶν,	1		
ὑπὲρ τῆς ἁγίας ἀμπέλου Δαυὶδ τοῦ παιδός σου,	1		
ἧς ἐγνώρισας ἡμῖν διὰ Ἰησοῦ τοῦ παιδός σου·	1		
σοὶ ἡ δόξα εἰς τοὺς αἰῶνας.	1		
9.3 περὶ δὲ τοῦ κλάσματος·	1		
εὐχαριστοῦμέν σοι, πάτερ ἡμῶν,	1		
ὑπὲρ τῆς ζωῆς καὶ γνώσεως.	1		
ἧς ἐγνώρισας ἡμῖν διὰ Ἰησοῦ τοῦ παιδός σου,	1		
σοὶ ἡ δόξα εἰς τοὺς αἰῶνας.	1		
9.4 ὥσπερ ἦν τοῦτο κλάσμα	1		
διεσκορπισμένον ἐπάνω τῶν ὀρέων	1		
καὶ συναχθὲν ἐγένετο ἕν,	1		
οὕτω συναχθήτω σου ἡ ἐκκλησία	1		
ἀπὸ τῶν περάτων τῆς γῆς	1		
εἰς τὴν σὴν βασιλείαν·	1		
ὅτι σοῦ ἐστιν ἡ δόξα καὶ ἡ δύναμις	1		
διὰ Ἰησοῦ Χριστοῦ εἰς τοὺς αἰῶνας.	1		
9.5a μηδεὶς δὲ φαγέτω μηδὲ πιέτω ἀπὸ τῆς εὐχαριστίας	1		
ὑμῶν, ἀλλ' οἱ βαπτισθέντες εἰς ὄνομα κυρίου·	1		
9.5b καὶ γὰρ περὶ τούτου εἴρηκεν ὁ κύριος·	3		
μὴ δῶτε τὸ ἅγιον τοῖς κυσί.	3	DG	7.6
10.1 Μετὰ δὲ τὸ ἐμπλησθῆναι οὕτως εὐχαριστήσατε·	2	PR	
10.2 εὐχαριστοῦμέν σοι, πάτερ ἅγιε,	2	PR	
ὑπὲρ τοῦ ἁγίου ὀνόματός σου,	2	PR	
οὗ κατεσκήνωσας ἐν ταῖς καρδίαις ἡμῶν,	2	PR	
καὶ ὑπὲρ τῆς γνώσεως καὶ πίστεως καὶ ἀθανασίας,	2	PR	
ἧς ἐγνώρισας ἡμῖν διὰ Ἰησοῦ τοῦ παιδός σου·	2	PR	
σοὶ ἡ δόξα εἰς τοὺς αἰῶνας	2	PR	
10.3 σύ, δέσποτα παντοκράτορ,	2	PR	
ἔκτισας τὰ πάντα ἕνεκεν τοῦ ὀνόματός σου,	2	PR	
τροφήν τε καὶ ποτὸν ἔδωκας τοῖς ἀνθρώποις εἰς ἀπόλαυσιν,	2	PR	
ἵνα σοι εὐχαριστήσωσιν.	2	PR	
ἡμῖν δὲ ἐχαρίσω πνευματικὴν τροφὴν καὶ ποτὸν	2	PR	
καὶ ζωὴν αἰώνιον διὰ Ἰησοῦ[4] τοῦ παιδός σου.	2	PR	
10.4 πρὸ πάντων εὐχαπιστοῦμέν σοι, ὅτι δυνατὸς εἶ·	2	PR	
σοὶ ἡ δόξα εἰς τοὺς αἰῶνας.	2	PR	

4.   Ἰησου is omitted in the Jerusalem manuscript and Bryennios's edition, but occurs in the Coptic version.

	A	B	C
9.1 Concerning the eucharist, give thanks thus:	1		
9.2 First, concerning the cup:	1		
We give thanks to you, our Father,	1		
For the holy vine of David your servant	1		
which you have revealed to us through Jesus your servant.	1		
To you be glory for ever.	1		
9.3 And concerning the fragment:	1		
We give thanks to you, our Father,	1		
For the life and knowledge, which you have revealed to us	1		
through Jesus your servant.	1		
To you be glory for ever.	1		
9.4 As this fragment	1		
lay scattered upon the mountains	1		
and has been gathered to become one,	1		
so gather your Church	1		
from the ends of the earth	1		
into your kingdom.	1		
For the glory and power are yours,	1		
through Jesus Christ, forever.	1		
9.5a Let no one eat or drink of your eucharist	1		
but those baptized in the name of the Lord,	1		
9.5b For concerning this the Lord has said,	3		
'Do not give to dogs what is holy'.	3	DG	7.6
10.1 After you have had your fill, give thanks thus:	2	PR	
10.2 We give thanks to you holy Father	2	PR	
for your holy Name	2	PR	
which you have made to dwell in our hearts	2	PR	
and for the knowledge, faith and immortality	2	PR	
which you have revealed to us through Jesus your servant.	2	PR	
To you be glory for ever.	2	PR	
10.3 You Lord almighty	2	PR	
have created everything for the sake of your Name;	2	PR	
you have given human beings food and drink to partake with	2	PR	
enjoyment so that they might give thanks;	2	PR	
but to us you have given the grace of spiritual food and drink	2	PR	
and of eternal life through Jesus your servant.	2	PR	
10.4 Above all we give you thanks because you are mighty.	2	PR	
To you be glory for ever.	2	PR	

	A	B	C
10.5 μνήσθητι, κύριε, τῆς ἐκκλησίας σου τοῦ ῥύσασθαι αὐτὴν	2	PR	
ἀπὸ παντὸς πονηροῦ, καὶ τελειῶσαι αὐτὴν ἐν τῇ	2	PR	
ἀγάπῃ σου, καὶ σύναξον αὐτὴν ἀπὸ τῶν τεσσάρων	2	PR	
ἀνέμων, τὴν ἁγιασθεῖσαν, εἰς τὴν σὴν βασιλείαν,	2	PR	
ἣν ἡτοίμασας αὐτῇ·	2	PR	
ὅτι σοῦ ἐστιν ἡ δύναμις καὶ ἡ δόξα εἰς τοὺς αἰῶνας.	2	PR	
10.6 ἐλθέτω χάρις καὶ παρελθέτω ὁ κόσμος οὗτος.	2	PR	
Ὡσαννὰ τῷ υἱῷ⁵ Δαυίδ.	2	PR	
εἴ τις ἅγιος ἐστιν, ἐρχέσθω·	2	PR	
εἴ τις οὐκ ἔστι, μετανοείτω·	2	PR	
μαραναθά· ἀμήν.	2	PR	
10.7 τοῖς δὲ προφήταις ἐπιτρέπετε εὐχαριστεῖν,	2	PR	
ὅσα θέλουσιν.			
11.1 ὃς ἂν οὖν ἐλθὼν διδάξῃ ὑμᾶς ταῦτα πάντα τὰ	3		5.17, 19
προειρημένα, δέξασθε αὐτόν· 11.2 ἐὰν δὲ αὐτὸς ὁ διδάσκων	3		
στραφεὶς διδάσκῃ ἄλλην διδαχὴν εἰς τὸ καταλῦσαι,	3		5.17
μὴ αὐτοῦ ἀκούσητε· εἰς δὲ τὸ προσθεῖναι δικαιοσύνην	3		5.20
καὶ γνῶσιν κυρίου, δέξασθε αὐτὸν ὡς κύριον.	3		
11.3a Περὶ δὲ τῶν ἀποστόλων	1		
11.3b καὶ προφητῶν, κατὰ τὸ δόγμα τοῦ εὐαγγελίου	4		
οὕτω ποιήσατε.	4		
11.4 πᾶς δὲ⁶ ἀπόστολος ἐρχόμενος πρὸς ὑμᾶς δεχθήτω	1		
ὡς κύριος·	1		
11.5 οὐ μενεῖ δὲ εἰ μὴ⁷ ἡμέραν μίαν· ἐὰν δὲ ᾖ χρεία,	1		
καὶ τὴν ἄλλην· τρεῖς δὲ ἐὰν μείνῃ, ψευδοπροφήτης ἐστίν.	1		
11.6a ἐξερχόμενος δὲ ὁ ἀπόστολος μηδὲν	1		
λαμβανέτω εἰ μὴ ἄρτον, ἕως οὗ αὐλισθῇ·	1		
11.6b ἐὰν δὲ ἀργύριον αἰτῇ, ψευδοπροφήτης ἐστί.	1		
11.7 καὶ πάντα προφήτην λαλοῦντα ἐν πνεύματι	2	PR	12.31
οὐ πειράσετε οὐδὲ διακρινεῖτε· πᾶσα γὰρ ἁμαρτία	2	PR	12.31
ἀφεθήσεται, αὕτη δὲ ἡ ἁμαρτία οὐκ ἀφεθήσεται.	2	PR	12.31
11.8 οὐ πᾶς δὲ ὁ λαλῶν ἐν πνεύματι προφήτης ἐστιν,	2	PR	
ἀλλ᾽ ἐὰν ἔχῃ τοὺς τρόπους κυρίου. ἀπὸ οὖν τῶν τρόπων	2	PR	
γνωσθήσεται ὁ ψευδοπροφήτης καὶ ὁ προφήτης.	2	PR	

5.   Jerusalem manuscript reads θεῷ Δαυίδ: Coptic reads οἴκῳ Δαυίδ. Bryennios is probably mistaken in favouring υἱῷ Δαυίδ which is found in *Const.*

6.   δὲ is omitted by the Coptic and Ethiopic.

7.   εἰ μὴ is omitted in the Jerusalem manuscript and in Bryennios's edition but appears in the Ethiopic.

	A	B	C
10.5 Remember Lord your Church, to preserve	2	PR	
it from all evil and to make it perfect in	2	PR	
your love. And, sanctified, gather it from the four winds	2	PR	
into your kingdom	2	PR	
which you have prepared for it.	2	PR	
Because yours is the power and the glory for ever.	2	PR	
10.6 Let grace come and let this world pass away.	2	PR	
Hosanna to the son of David.	2	PR	
If anyone is holy let him come,	2	PR	
if anyone is not let him repent.	2	PR	
Maranatha. Amen.	2	PR	
10.7 Allow the prophets to give thanks	2	PR	
as much as they wish …			
11.1 Whoever <u>comes teaching</u> all the above,	3		5.17, 19
receive him. 11.2 But if the teacher himself turns away and	3		
teaches another teaching, to <u>destroy</u> them,	3		5.17
do not listen to him. But if it aims at promoting <u>righteousness</u>	3		5.20
and knowledge of the Lord, then receive him as the Lord.	3		
11.3a Concerning apostles	1		
11.3b and prophets, according to the directions in the gospel,	4		
act in this way.	4		
11.4 let every apostle who comes to you be received	1		
as the Lord.	1		
11.5 He shall stay only one day, or, if need be,	1		
another day too. If he stays three days, he is a false prophet.	1		
11.6a When the apostle leaves, let him receive nothing but	1		
enough bread to see him through until he finds lodging.	1		
11.6b If he asks for money he is a false prophet.	1		
11.7 … and every prophet speaking in the <u>Spirit</u>	2	PR	12.31
neither test nor judge; <u>every</u> <u>sin</u>	2	PR	12.31
<u>shall be forgiven</u>, but this sin <u>shall not be forgiven</u>.	2	PR	12.31
11.8 But not every one speaking in the Spirit is a prophet,	2	PR	
but only those whose behaviour is as the Lord's, by their actions	2	PR	
you can discern the false prophet from the prophet.	2	PR	

	A	B	C
11.9 καὶ πᾶς προφήτης ὁρίζων τράπεζαν ἐν πνεύματι,	2	PR	
οὐ φάγεται ἀπ' αὐτῆς, εἰ δὲ μήγε, ψευδοπροφήτης ἐστί.	2	PR	
11.10 πᾶς δὲ προφήτης διδάσκων τὴν ἀλήθειαν, εἰ ἅ	3		
διδάσκει οὐ ποιεῖ, ψευδοπροφήτης ἐστί. 11.11 πᾶς δὲ	3		
προφήτης δεδοκιμασμένος, ἀληθινός, ποιῶν εἰς	3		
μυστήριον κοσμικὸν ἐκκλησίας, μὴ διδάσκων δὲ ποιεῖν, ὅσα αὐτὸς	3		
ποιεῖ, οὐ κριθήσεται ἐφ' ὑμῶν· μετὰ θεοῦ γὰρ ἔχει τὴν	3		
κρίσιν· ὡσαύτως γὰρ ἐποίησαν καὶ οἱ ἀρχαῖοι προφῆται.	3		
11.12 ὃς δ' ἂν εἴπῃ ἐν πνεύματι· δός μοι ἀργύρια	2	PR	
ἢ ἕτερά τινα, οὐκ ἀκούσεσθε αὐτοῦ· ἐὰν δὲ περὶ	2	PR	
ἄλλων ὑστερούντων εἴπῃ δοῦναι,	2	PR	
μηδεὶς αὐτὸν κρινέτω.	2	PR	
12.1 Πᾶς δὲ ὁ ἐρχόμενος ἐν ὀνόματι κυρίου	2	PR	
δεχθήτω· ἔπειτα δὲ δοκιμάσαντες αὐτὸν γνώσεσθε,	2	PR	
σύνεσιν γὰρ ἕξετε δεξιὰν καὶ ἀριστεράν.	2	PR	
12.2a εἰ μὲν παρόδιός ἐστιν ὁ ἐρχόμενος, βοηθεῖτε	2	PR	
αὐτῷ, ὅσον δύνασθε· 12.2b οὐ μενεῖ δὲ πρὸς ὑμᾶς εἰ μὴ δύο	2	PR	
ἢ τρεῖς ἡμέρας, ἐὰν ᾖ ἀνάγκη. 12.3 εἰ δὲ θέλει πρὸς ὑμᾶς	2	PR	
καθῆσθαι, τεχνίτης ὤν, ἐργαζέσθω καὶ φαγέτω.	2	PR	
12.4 εἰ δὲ οὐκ ἔχει τέχνην, κατὰ τὴν σύνεσιν ὑμῶν	2	PR	
προνοήσατε, πῶς μὴ ἀργὸς μεθ' ὑμῶν ζήσεται χριστιανός.	2	PR	
12.5 εἰ δ' οὐ θέλει οὕτω ποιεῖν, χριστέμπορός ἐστι·	2	PR	
προσέχετε ἀπὸ τῶν τοιούτων.	2	PR	
13.1 Πᾶς δὲ προφήτης ἀληθινός, θέλων καθῆσθαι πρὸς	3		
ὑμᾶς, ἄξιός ἐστι τῆς τροφῆς αὐτοῦ. 13.2 ὡσαύτως	3		
διδάσκαλος ἀληθινός ἐστιν <u>ἄξιος</u> καὶ αὐτός ὥσπερ	3		10.10
<u>ὁ ἐργάτης τῆς τροφῆς αὐτοῦ</u>.	3		10.10
13.3a πᾶσαν οὖν ἀπαρχὴν	3	FF	
γεννημάτων ληνοῦ καὶ ἅλωνος,	3	FF	
βοῶν τε καὶ προβάτων	3	FF	
λαβὼν δώσεις τὴν ἀπαρχὴν τοῖς προφήταις·	3	FF	
13.3b αὐτοὶ γάρ εἰσιν οἱ ἀρχιερεῖς ὑμῶν. 13.4 ἐὰν δὲ μὴ	3		
ἔχητε προφήτην, δότε τοῖς πτωχοῖς.	3		
13.5 ἐὰν σιτιαν ποιῇς,	3	FF	
τὴν ἀπαρχὴν λαβὼν δὸς κατὰ τὴν ἐντολήν.	3	FF	
13.6 ὡσαύτως κεράμιον οἴνου ἢ ἐλαίου ἀνοίξας, τὴν	3	FF	
ἀπαρχὴν λαβὼν δὸς τοῖς προφήταις·	3	FF	
13.7 ἀργιρίου δὲ καὶ ἱματισμοῦ καὶ παντὸς κτήματος	3	FF	
λαβὼν τὴν ἀπαρχὴν ὡς ἄν σοι δόξῃ, δὸς κατὰ τὴν	3	FF	
ἐντολήν.	3	FF	

	A	B	C
11.9 Every prophet calling for a table of food in the Spirit	2	PR	
will not eat of it. If he does he is a false prophet.	2	PR	
11.10 And every prophet teaching the truth who does not do	3		
what he teaches is a false prophet. 11.11 But every	3		
prophet tested and found true who lives 'the mystery of the	3		
church in the world' and does not teach others to do the same—	3		
do not judge him. His judgment is with God.	3		
For the prophets of old also lived/acted in this way.	3		
11.12 If any prophet, speaking in the Spirit says, 'Give me	2	PR	
money', or anything else, do not listen to him. On the other hand,	2	PR	
if he calls you to give it to someone who is in need,	2	PR	
do not judge him.	2	PR	
12.1 Let everyone who comes in the name of the Lord be	2	PR	
received, after that, when you have tested him, you will know	2	PR	
what he is like—for you will have right and left perception.	2	PR	
12.2a If the one who comes is a traveller, help him as much as	2	PR	
you can, 12.2b but he shall not stay with you more than two	2	PR	
or three days if this is necessary. 12.3 But if he wants to settle	2	PR	
with you, and he is a craftsman, let him work and so eat.	2	PR	
12.4 If he has no craft, see to it in your own understanding that	2	PR	
no one lives among you in idleness because he is a Christian.	2	PR	
12.5 If he is unwilling to do this, he is trading on Christ.	2	PR	
Be on your guard against such people.	2	PR	
13.1 But every true prophet, who wants to settle with	3		
you is worthy of his food, 13.2 In the same way,	3		
a true teacher is <u>worthy</u>, just as	3		10.10
<u>the worker is worthy of his food</u>.	3		10.10
13.3a Therefore, when you [sing.] take any firstfruits	3	FF	
of what is produced by the wine press and the threshing floor,	3	FF	
by cows and by sheep,	3	FF	
you [sing.] shall give the firstfruits to the prophets,	3	FF	
13.3b for they are your [pl.] High Priests. 13.4 If, however,	3		
you [pl. through v. 4] have no prophet, give them to the poor.	3		
13.5 If you [sing. through vv. 5-7] make bread, take the firstfruits	3	FF	
and give them according to the commandment.	3	FF	
13.6 Likewise, when you open a jar of wine or oil, take the	3	FF	
firstfruits and give them to the prophets.	3	FF	
13.7 Take the firstfruits of money and clothing and whatever	3	FF	
you own as you think best and give them according to the	3	FF	
commandment.	3	FF	

	A	B	C
14.1 Κατὰ κυριακὴν δὲ κυρίου συναχθέντες κλάσατε ἄρτον	3		
καὶ εὐχαριστήσατε, προσεξομολογησάμενοι	3		
τὰ παραπτώματα ὑμῶν, ὅπως καθαρὰ ἡ θυσία ὑμῶν ᾖ.	3		
14.2 πᾶς δὲ ἔχων τὴν ἀμφιβολίαν μετὰ τοῦ ἑταίρου αὐτοῦ	3		
μὴ συνελθέτω ὑμῖν, ἕως οὗ <u>διαλλαγῶσιν</u>,	3		5.24
ἵνα μὴ κοινωθῇ ἡ <u>θυσία</u> ὑμῶν.	3		5.24
14.3 αὕτη γάρ ἐστιν ἡ ῥηθεῖσα ὑπὸ κυρίου·	3		
ἐν παντὶ τόπῳ καὶ χρόνῳ προσφέρειν μοι θυσίαν καθαράν·	3	ML	
ὅτι βασιλεὺς μέγας εἰμί, λέγει κύριος,	3	ML	
καὶ τὸ ὄνομά μου θαυμαστὸν ἐν τοῖς ἔθνεσι.	3	ML	
15.1 Χειροτονήσατε οὖν ἑαυτοῖς ἐπισκόπους καὶ διακόνους	3		
ἀξίους τοῦ κυρίου, ἄνδρας πραεῖς καὶ ἀφιλαργύρους καὶ	3		
ἀληθεῖς καὶ δεδοκιμασμένους· ὑμῖν γὰρ λειτουργοῦσι καὶ	3		
αὐτοὶ τὴν λειτουργίαν τῶν προφητῶν καὶ διδασκάλων.	3		
15.2 μὴ οὖν ὑπερίδητε αὐτούς· αὐτοὶ γάρ εἰσιν οἱ τετιμημένοι	3		
ὑμῶν	3		
μετὰ τῶν προφητῶν καὶ διδασκάλων.	3		
15.3 ἐλέγχετε δὲ ἀλλήλους μὴ ἐν ὀργῇ, ἀλλ᾽ ἐν εἰρήνῃ,	4		
ὡς ἔχετε ἐν τῷ εὐαγγελίῳ·	4		
καὶ παντὶ ἀστοχοῦντι κατὰ τοῦ ἑτέρου μηδεὶς λαλείτω	4		
μηδὲ παρ᾽ ὑμῶν ἀκουέτω, ἕως οὗ μετανοήσῃ.	4		
15.4 τὰς δὲ εὐχὰς ὑμῶν καὶ τὰς ἐλεημοσύνας καὶ πάσας	4		
τὰς πράξεις οὕτω ποιήσατε, ὡς ἔχετε ἐν τῷ εὐαγγελίῳ	4		
τοῦ κυρίου ἡμῶν.	4		
16.1 <u>Γρηγορεῖτε</u> ὑπὲρ τῆς ζωῆς ὑμῶν. οἱ λύχνοι ὑμῶν	1		24.42; 25.13
μὴ σβεσθήτωσαν, καὶ αἱ ὀσφύες ὑμῶν μὴ ἐκλυέσθωσαν,	1		
ἀλλὰ γίνεσθε ἕτοιμοι· <u>οὐ</u> γὰρ <u>οἴδατε τὴν ὥραν</u>, ἐν ᾖ	1		24.42; 25.13
<u>ὁ κύριος</u> ἡμῶν <u>ἔρχεται</u>.	1		24.42
16.2 πυκνῶς δὲ συναχθήσεσθε ζητοῦντες τὰ ἀνήκοντα ταῖς	1		
ψυχαῖς ὑμῶν· οὐ γὰρ ὠφελήσει ὑμᾶς ὁ πᾶς χρόνος τῆς	1		
πίστεως ὑμῶν, ἐὰν μὴ ἐν τῷ ἐσχάτῳ καιρῷ τελειωθῆτε.	1		
16.3 ἐν γὰρ ταῖς ἐσχάταις ἡμέραις <u>πληθυνθή</u>σονται οἱ	1	AP	24.11
<u>ψευδοπροφῆται</u> καὶ οἱ φθορεῖς,	1	AP	24.12
καὶ στραφήσονται τὰ πρόβατα εἰς λύκους	1	AP	
καὶ <u>ἡ ἀγάπη</u> στραφήσεταιμ εἰς μῖσος·	1	AP	24.12
16.4a Αὐξανούσης γὰρ τῆς <u>ἀνομίας</u>,	1	AP	24.12
<u>μισήσουσιν ἀλλήλους</u> καὶ διώξουσι καὶ <u>παραδώσουσι</u>.	1	AP	24.10

	A	B	C
14.1 Assembling on every Sunday of the Lord, break bread	3		
and give thanks, confessing	3		
your faults besides so that your sacrifice may be clean.	3		
14.2 Let no one engaged in a dispute with his comrade	3		
join you until they have been <u>reconciled</u>,	3		5.24
lest your <u>sacrifice</u> be profaned.	3		5.24
14.3 This is the sacrifice of which the Lord has said:	3		
" 'to offer me a clean sacrifice in every place and time, because I	3	ML	
am a great king,' says the Lord,	3	ML	
'and my name is wonderful among the nations.' "	3	ML	
15.1 Elect, then, for yourselves bishops and deacons	3		
worthy of the Lord, meek men who are not lovers of money,	3		
who are true and have proved themselves, for they too	3		
perform the functions of prophets and teachers for you.	3		
15.2 So do not disregard them, for they are persons	3		
who hold a place of honour among you,	3		
together with the prophets and teachers.	3		
15.3 Correct one another not in anger but in peace,	4		
as you have it in the gospel;	4		
and let no one speak to anyone who wrongs another,	4		
let him not hear a word from you, until he has repented.	4		
15.4 Perform you prayers and your almsgiving and everything	4		
you do as you have it in the gospel	4		
of our Lord.	4		
16.1 <u>Watch</u> over your life. Let your lamps	1		24.42; 25.13
not go out and let your loins not be ungirded but be ready,	1		24.42; 25.13
for <u>you do not know the hour</u> at which	1		24.42
our <u>Lord is coming</u>.	1		
16.2 You shall assemble frequently, seeking what your souls	1		
need, for the whole time of your faith will be of no profit to you	1		
unless you are perfected at the final hour.	1		
16.3 In the last days shall be <u>multiplied</u>	1	AP	24.11
<u>false prophets</u> and corruption	1	AP	24.12
and shall turn the sheep into wolves	1	AP	
and <u>love</u> shall turn into hate	1	AP	24.12
16.4a For with the increase of <u>lawlessness</u> they shall	1	AP	24.12
<u>hate</u> <u>one another</u> and shall persecute and <u>betray.</u>	1	AP	24.10

	A	B	C
16.4b καὶ τότε φανήσεται ὁ κοσμοπλανὴς ὡς υἱὸς θεοῦ	1	AP	
καὶ ποιήσει σημεῖα καὶ τέρατα,	1	AP	
καὶ ἡ γῆ παραδοθήσεται εἰς χεῖρας αὐτοῦ,	1	AP	
καὶ ποιήσει ἀθέμιτα,	1	AP	
ἃ οὐδέποτε γέγονεν ἐξ αἰῶνος.	1	AP	
16.5 <u>τότε</u> ἥξει ἡ κτίσις τῶν ἀνθρώπων εἰς	1	AP	24.10
τὴν πύρωσιν τῆς δοκιμασίας,	1	AP	
καὶ <u>σκανδαλισθήσονται πολλοὶ</u> καὶ ἀπολοῦνται,	1	AP	24.10
οἱ δὲ ὑπομείναντες ἐν τῇ πίστει αὐτῶν σωθήσονται	1	AP	
ὑπ' αὐτοῦ τοῦ καταθέματος.	1	AP	
16.6 <u>καὶ τότε φανήσεται</u> τὰ <u>σημεῖα</u> τῆς ἀληθείας·	1	AP	24.30
πρῶτον σημεῖον ἐκπετάσεως <u>ἐν οὐρανῷ,</u>	1	AP	24.30
εἶτα σημεῖον φωνῆς <u>σάλπιγγος,</u>	1	AP	24.31
καὶ τὸ τρίτον ἀνάστασις νεκρῶν·	1	AP	
16.7 οὐ πάντων δέ, ἀλλ' ὡς ἐρρέθη·	5		
ἥξει ὁ κύριος καὶ πάντες οἱ ἅγιοι μετ' αὐτοῦ.	5		
16.8 τότε ὄψεται ὁ κόσμος τὸ κύριον	1	AP	
<u>ἐρχόμενον ἐπάνω τῶν νεφελῶν τοῦ οὐρανοῦ,</u>	1	AP	24.30
[Jerusalem MS breaks off here]			
<u>καὶ πάντες οἱ</u> ἅγιοι <u>μετ' αὐτοῦ,</u>	1	AP	25.31; 16.27
<u>ἐπὶ θρόνου</u> βασιλείας	1	AP	25.31; 16.27
κατακρῖναι τὸν κοσμοπλάνον	1	AP	
καὶ <u>ἀποδοῦναι ἑκάστῳ κατὰ τὴν πρᾶξιν αὐτοῦ.</u>	1	AP	16.27
16.9 τότε <u>ἀπελεύσονται</u> οἱ μέν πονηροὶ	1	AP	25.46
<u>εἰς αἰώνιον κόλασιν,</u>	1	AP	25.46
<u>οἱ δὲ δίκαιοι</u> πορεύσονται <u>εἰς ζωὴν αἰώνιον,</u>	1	AP	25.46
<u>κληρονομ</u>οῦντες ἐκεῖνα,	1	AP	25.34
ἃ ὀφθαλμὸς οὐκ εἶδεν	1	AP	
καὶ οὖς οὐκ ἤκουσεν	1	AP	
καὶ ἐπὶ καρδίαν ἀνθρώπου οὐκ ἀνέβη,	1	AP	
ἃ <u>ἡτοίμασ</u>εν ὁ θεὸς τοῖς ἀγαπῶσιν αὐτόν.	1	AP	25.34

	A	B	C
16.4b And then shall appear the world-deceiver as a son of God	1	AP	
and he shall do signs and wonders	1	AP	
and the earth shall be betrayed into his hands	1	AP	
and he shall do godless things	1	AP	
that have not been done since the beginning of the age.	1	AP	
16.5 <u>Then</u> human creation shall pass into	1	AP	24.10
the fire of testing	1	AP	
and <u>many shall be caused to stumble</u> and be lost	1	AP	24.10
but those who persevere in their faith shall be saved	1	AP	
by the curse itself.	1	AP	
16.6 <u>And then shall appear</u> the <u>signs</u> of truth	1	AP	24.30
first the sign of extension <u>in heaven</u>	1	AP	24.30
next the sign of the <u>trumpet</u> call	1	AP	24.31
and third the resurrection of the dead	1	AP	
16.7 not of all the dead, but, as it says,	5		
'the Lord shall come, and all his holy ones with him'.	5		
16.8 Then the world shall see the Lord	1	AP	
<u>coming</u> up<u>on the clouds of heaven</u>, …	1	AP	24.30
[Jerusalem MS breaks off here]			
<u>and all</u> his holy ones <u>with him,</u>	1	AP	25.31; 16.27
<u>on</u> his royal <u>throne,</u>	1	AP	25.31; 16.27
to judge the world-deceiver	1	AP	
and to <u>reward each according to his deeds.</u>	1	AP	16.27
16.9 Then <u>shall go away</u> the evil	1	AP	25.46
<u>into eternal punishment</u>	1	AP	25.46
<u>but the righteous</u> shall enter <u>into life eternal</u>	1	AP	25.46
<u>inheriting</u> those things	1	AP	25.34
which eye has not seen	1	AP	
and ear has not heard	1	AP	
and which has not arisen in the heart of man.	1	AP	
Those things which God <u>has prepared</u> for those who love him.	1	AP	25.34

Chapter 1

INTRODUCTION

Recently I went for a walk in woods adjoining a conference centre. I was familiar with the encompassing area but not with the woods themselves and so, after wandering for a while, I was glad to come across a notice-board with a map which, on initial encounter, seemed likely to provide useful guidance. However, there was no red spot saying 'You are here' and no indication of where the conference centre lay in relation to the wooded area. I had no idea where I was in terms of the map, or where I would emerge if I travelled north, south, east or west. The map that promised to assist me turned out to be useless.

When Archbishop Bryennios stumbled on a manuscript of the *Didache* in 1873[1] he did not at first appreciate the enormity of his discovery. However, by the time the first critical edition was published, in 1883, its potential significance had become startlingly apparent; it created a first class literary sensation (Schaff 1885: 10-12). New editions, translations and commentaries appeared almost instantly as scholars hurried to devour a text that promised to reveal otherwise unknown details of worshipping life and organization of the very early Church.

Initial excitement turned to frustration and then disinterest. In the second half of the twentieth century the *Didache* became a text often referred to in passing but very seldom considered in detail. The discovery that

---

1. Bryennios discovered this manuscript within a volume belonging to the library of the Monastery of the Holy Sepulcre ('Jerusalem Monastery'). It was published by him in 1883 and was moved, in 1887, to the Greek patriarchate of Jerusalem where it remains under the reference Κῶδ. πατρ. 54. The manuscript is variously known by the names, Bryennios, Constantinople, H. 54 or Jerusalem. Hereafter, I shall refer to it as the Jerusalem manuscript. Van de Sandt and Flusser (2002: 16–24) give a positive assessment of the quality of this manuscript. They suggest that 'Despite the late date of its origin [1056 CE], the Jerusalem codex in some respects measures up to the Alexandrinus and Sinaiticus' (p. 18), and suggest that 'it may have originated in the patristic period' (p. 23).

promised so much could not be made to deliver on that promise because it proved all but impossible to determine its geographical, historical and literary context: was it a mainstream document or the rule of a backwater community? Did it belong to the late first or to the mid second century? Did it follow in the Matthean tradition or was it a much earlier text than that? Without some means of establishing these types of bearings the *Didache* remains as useless as the noticeboard I found in the woods.

The aim of this volume is to present a detailed map of the relationship between Matthew's Gospel and the *Didache*. Widespread acceptance of *some* form of connection between these two texts[2] makes this a logical starting point for any attempt to locate the *Didache* within the wider web of early Christian life and literature. However, recognition that a relationship exists between these texts is by no means the same as agreement regarding the nature of that relationship.

Historically, scholars have been divided between those who explain the connection as a product of the *Didache*'s direct dependence on, or allusion to, Matthew's Gospel,[3] and those who see this as resulting from the dependence of both texts on common tradition(s).[4] In what follows I shall argue for the further possibility that the author of Matthew's Gospel depended

---

2.   All the scholars listed in nn. 3, 4 and 7, immediately below, perceive some form of link between Matthew's Gospel and the *Didache*.

3.   'The earliest commentators on the text usually assumed the use of Matthew's gospel, especially since the *Didache* itself four times refers to "the gospel" in 8:2; 11:3; 15:3,4. Representative of those who affirm such a dependence is E Massaux' (Draper 1996a: 16). Layton (1968), Köhler (1987: 19–56, esp. 29-30), Wengst (1984: 25–30, 61–63), Luz (1989: 93), Butler (1960 and 1961), Vielhauer (1965), Giet (1970) and Tuckett (1989 reproduced 1996) also support this view. Tuckett, being the most recent and thorough exponent of the *Didache*'s presupposition of Matthew's Gospel will be my chief dialogue partner, with respect to this view, in the following discussion.

4.   'The debate was thrown wide open with the publication of the important study of Helmut Köster in 1957, which argued that although the reference to εὐαγγέλιον might point to a knowledge of a written gospel by the "compiler" of the *Didache*, the latter did not himself use such a source. The *Didache* did not stand after the gospel writers but alongside them, utilizing the same traditions' (Draper 1996a: 17). Scholars who similarly see the *Didache* and Matthew's Gospel as dependent on shared common traditions include: Audet (1958: 166–86), Glover (1958 and 1985: 234–51), Rordorf and Tuilier (1978: 83–91), Rordorf (1981), Mees (1971), Kloppenborg (1979), Draper (1996b) and Jefford (1989: esp. 91, 160–61). This understanding of the relationship between Matthew's Gospel and the *Didache* has been in the ascendant since Köster's 1957 volume, although severely questioned by Tuckett and others mentioned in n. 3 above.

directly upon a version of the *Didache* essentially similar to that rediscovered by Bryennios, except for the absence of *Did.* 8.2b;[5] 11.3b; 15.3-4
and 16.7.[6] This view has not previously received detailed consideration.[7]

The lack of scholarly interest in the possibility that Matthew directly
depended on the *Didache* invites, at the start of a book on the subject,
some explanation. Two features of the *Didache* may account for a widespread assumption that it does not pre-date Matthew's Gospel, and thus
cannot have been used in the creation of that text. First, the single 'full'
manuscript of the *Didache* was rediscovered within a collection of writings from the Apostolic Fathers.[8] Consciously or otherwise this context
may have led some of the earlier students of the text to see it as secondary
to the witness of the gospels. A small initial assumption of this kind can, if
repeated sufficiently often, lead to the establishment of a widespread scholarly consensus.[9]

A second argument against a pre-Matthean dating of the *Didache* is the
presence of four references to 'the gospel' (8.2b; 11.3b; 15.3-4) amid, in
the case of 8.2b especially, passages that relate closely to Matthean material. These references have been understood by some scholars[10] as

---

5.   A full text of the *Didache*, which shows the verse sub-divisions referred to here
and elsewhere, may be found at the beginning of this volume.

6.   In the following text, wherever the proposed dependence of Matthew's Gospel
on the *Didache* is discussed, then *Did.* 8.2b; 11.3b; 15.3-4 and 16.7 should always be
understood as excluded from the text of the *Didache* that (I argue) was known by
Matthew.

7.   Draper (1996a: 18-19) suggests that both texts evolved in the same community
so that, 'the influence, then, could run in either direction, depending on the redactional
layer of the text'. Draper stops short, however, of straightforwardly proposing the direct
dependence of Matthew on the *Didache*, especially with respect to *Did.* 1.3-6; 8.1-3;
15.3-4, which he sees (1996c: 227 and 1996b: 76) as belonging to the latest redactional
layer of the *Didache*. In Draper 1996d: 347, *Did.* 1.2-6 and chapters 8 and 15 are seen
as later insertions. (Three of the above-mentioned articles were first published prior to
Draper's 1996 edited collection of articles. Thus, 1996b first appeared in 1985; 1996c
in 1992; 1996d in 1991. Full details may be found in the bibliography.)

8.   Jefford (1989: 18) notes that the *Didache* has been largely accepted 'into the
informal canon of early Christian literature, i.e., the Apostolic Fathers'.

9.   Not all of the earliest generation of *Didache* scholars assumed its post-apostolic
date. For example, Sabatier (1885) considered it to be extremely early, but their views
were largely ignored by contemporary and later scholarship. Some advocates of a very
early date for certain parts of the *Didache* have reappeared in the latter half of the
twentieth century. For example, Audet (1958) and Mazza (1995).

10.   Streeter (1924: 507) claimed that the Didachist seemed 'not only to have read

demonstrating knowledge of a written and authoritative Gospel of Matthew.[11] This, in turn, may be taken as suggesting a post-Matthean date for the whole text.

The essential flaw in this latter observation lies in its assumption that what may be true for *Did.* 8.2b; 11.3b; 15.3-4, must also be true for the whole of the remainder of the text. This assumption rests on a highly dubious foundation given that the *Didache* is widely recognized as having a complex compositional history.[12] This feature allows the possibility that the four references to 'the gospel' are among one of the later contributions to the whole,[13] in which case earlier elements could theoretically have been known and used by the author of Matthew's Gospel.

Despite these logical flaws it is understandable that, all other things being equal, the references to 'the gospel' and the patristic context of the Jerusalem manuscript have favoured a post-Matthean consensus. However, as is often the case, all things are not equal.

The combined implication of two widely accepted factors has been consistently overlooked in previous studies of the relationship between the *Didache* and Matthew's Gospel. These two factors are: the complex compositional history of the *Didache* and the large number of points of similarity between the two texts. Taken together these lead, as I shall argue in detail below, towards a relatively simple explanation of the two texts' relationship; namely, that various elements (disparate in terms of style, origin

Matthew, but also, like Ignatius, to refer to it under the title of "The Gospel"'. Carrington (1957: 500) described the *Didache* as 'an appendix to Matthew, to which [its] readers…are explicitly referred no less than four times'. See also n. 3 above.

11. I accept the view that Matthew's Gospel is likely to be the text behind the *Didache*'s references to 'the gospel'. This question is discussed in Chapter 8, § 1.3.

12. 'The *Didache* cannot, of course, be considered a homogenous text. Even those who attempt to attribute it to a single author must unhesitatingly grant that older material is used in it. This is especially true in the first five chapters' (Rordorf 1991: 396). '[T]he text shows signs of considerable redactional activity, which defies any theory of unity of composition, even allowing for the activity of an interpolator. The *Didache* is a composite work, which has evolved over a considerable period' (Draper 199b: 74–75). 'It is almost universally agreed that the present text is, in some sense at least, "composite"' (Tuckett 196: 93). See also scholars noted in the introduction to Part I, below.

13. There is every reason to suppose that this is the case since references to 'the gospel' are embedded in elements of the *Didache* that are generally, and justifiably, recognized as being among the younger strata of the text. A full analysis of the compositional history of the *Didache*, including the relative age of the four references to 'the gospel', is conducted through the course of Part I.

and age) were incorporated into the *Didache* over time and that, at a later date, Matthew drew on the resulting text in the construction of his gospel. Later still, I shall propose, referrals to 'the gospel' were inserted into the *Didache* (at 8.2b; 11.3 and 15.3-4) to abrogate certain teachings in favour of the similar, but now more developed,[14] instructions also to be found in Matthew's Gospel.

Given that the composite nature of the *Didache* is all but universally acknowledged, it is striking that none of the scholars who argue for the *Didache*'s use of Matthew's Gospel address the difficulties this creates for their conclusions. For example, Massaux (1993: 176) ignores the issue entirely, and so is capable of concluding that

> All these remarks lead me to recognize and affirm that the *Didache* has come under a very profound literary influence from Mt., to the point of wondering sometimes whether it is a tracing of the first gospel.

If Massaux had considered the possibility that the *Didache* was composed by more than one person, then his conclusion would require these different contributors to have worked together, in some remarkable way, to achieve such a 'tracing'. However, Massaux makes no attempt to explain how this could have happened.

Tuckett (1996: 93), unlike Massaux, is not guilty of entirely ignoring the issue of the *Didache*'s compositional history. He makes this very important observation:

> Any discussion of the problem of synoptic tradition in the *Didache* must take note of the question of the unity of the text… It is almost universally agreed that the present text is, in some sense at least, 'composite'. *Didache* 1–6 incorporates an earlier Two Ways tradition attested also in the *Epistle of Barnabas* 18–20, *Doctrina Apostolorum* and elsewhere; further, within this Two Ways tradition, the section 1.3–2.1 is probably a secondary, Christianising addition. Other seams within our text have been suggested: for example, chapters 8 and 15 may be secondary additions to an earlier

---

14.   The concept of 'development' is fraught with difficulties in that traditions do not always 'develop' in uniform or predictable ways. For this reason developmental arguments are used sparingly in what follows. It is nonetheless the case, however, that the standard indicators of development speak for the antiquity of the *Didache*'s traditions relative to those in Matthew's Gospel. This has been an important factor for those scholars who see the *Didache* as preserving traditions that were also used, and developed, by Matthew. Thus, van de Sandt (2002: 229) is not alone in expressing the view that, for example, in the cases of *Did.* 8.1 and Mt. 6.16; *Did.* 8.2 and Mt. 6.9-13; *Did.* 9.5 and Mt. 7.6; *Did.* 11.7 and Mt. 12.31, 'The *Didache*…witnesses to an earlier stage of the Matthean tradition'.

Vorlage. The precise number of stages of redaction which one should postulate is much debated. Nevertheless it is clear that any theories about the origins of synoptic tradition in one part of the *Didache* will not necessarily apply to the *Didache* as a whole. Each part of the text must therefore be examined separately and, to a certain extent, independently.

However, despite noting this crucial point, Tuckett proceeds to over-look its implication. He thus argues, 'separately and, to a certain extent, independently', that the *Didache* alludes to Matthew's Gospel at each point where they share parallel material. However, what this conclusion requires is that the authors of the Two Ways, the section 1.3–2.1, chs. 8 and 15, and so on, all behaved in a remarkably similar manner in their use of Matthew's Gospel, despite the widely differing style, origin and content of the various sections involved. This circumstance invites an explanation. Such is not offered by Tuckett.

Scholars who propose that the *Didache* and Matthew's Gospel are principally related via the use of shared common traditions[15] have also ignored the full implications of the *Didache*'s compositional history. For example, Köster (1957: 239) believes that five separate units were incorporated into the *Didache*, four of which drew upon sources such as Jewish paranesis, liturgical modes of expression, Old Testament sayings, Jewish rules, meschalim and completely enclosed pieces of Jewish tradition, which were also used by the author of the Matthew's Gospel. This type of theory relies on very high levels of coincidence in that Matthew's Gospel and the *Didache* must both happen to draw on the *same* selection of Jewish paraneses, liturgical modes of expression, Old Testament sayings, and so on. This problem is exacerbated when it is noted, with John Court (1981: 111), that the majority of the material shared by the two texts is 'from Matthew's special material or from the synoptic traditions at points where Matthew's distinctive rendering is preferred'. This means that Matthew and the Didachist are required, not only to share a varied collection of common sources, but also repeatedly to take from them *uniquely* similar selections. The levels of coincidence rise still further when questions are asked regarding the adequacy of Köster's extremely brief, though confident, analysis of the compositional history of the *Didache*.[16] In the discussion

15. It is significant that this view, introduced by Köster in 1957, arose to take account of the observation that, although it was thought impossible that the *Didache* could pre-date Matthew's Gospel the *Didache* nonetheless frequently appears to preserve a more ancient version of traditions shared with Matthew.

16. Köster devotes just two pages to this complex question (1957: 159–60). Here he states that five separate units of previously existing tradition, more or less accurately

that follows I aim to show that it is highly unlikely that the complex and sometimes self-contradictory text of the *Didache* was put together at one time by a single compiler. If the text was compiled by more than one author over a period of time, as most scholars suppose,[17] then Köster's theory requires yet another layer of coincidence. Thus, two or more contributors to the *Didache* are required, over a period of time, to have quarried uniquely similar material from diverse previously existing traditions also selected by Matthew.

My contention is not that the above pattern of events is strictly impossible; simply that it is a highly improbable explanation for the presence of 26 points of similarity between the two texts.[18] It is more credible to propose that Matthew used the *Didache*, a composite text containing all the 'shared traditions' required to explain their several points of distinctive similarity.

In the chapters that follow I shall explore the possibility that Matthew knew and used a version of the *Didache* to which the references to 'the gospel' had not yet been added. The hypothesis of Matthew's use of some parts of the *Didache* requires only that the *Didache* is composite to a degree that is already widely accepted. However, an attempt to identify precisely which parts of the *Didache* were used by Matthew invites a full compositional analysis. The first stage of my argument therefore involves a detailed exploration of the compositional history of the *Didache*.

Past experience of this type of exercise will persuade most readers that this endeavour is unlikely to prove either successful or especially interesting. However, this case offers more than usual cause for optimism on both counts. The *Didache* is a text in which the joins between various

---

reproduced by the compiler, may be identified 'Ohne Schwierigkeiten' – without difficulty.

17. Kraft (1965: 1-4) describes the *Didache* as 'evolved literature' which is the product of a community and not an individual. Giet (1970) takes a similar view in seeing the text as responding to changing circumstances in a process of organic development. This type of view is endorsed, with some reservations, by Draper (1996a: 19-22). Jefford (1989: 20) suggests that Kraft's view is representative of a consensus among more recent scholarship. Jefford (1989: 21 n. 60) states his assumption that the text of the *Didache* developed in three basic stages. The first led to the creation of 1.1-3a; 2.2–6.1a. To this text was then added 7–15 (added to the original materials of 1.1–6.1a by one hand in two phases [7–10 and 11–15]). At a third stage a 'final redactor' added 1.3b–2.1, most of chapter 16 and probably 6.1b-3.

18. A list of the points of contact discussed in the ensuing text may be found at the end of Chapter 15.

sources may, in a significant number of cases, be relatively simply identified. Further, because the *Didache* contains several interpretative puzzles
that are bound up with compositional questions, there is interest to be had
in the need to wrestle with some of the *Didache*'s infamous riddles while
engaging in the study of its history.

Part I

THE COMPOSITIONAL HISTORY OF THE *DIDACHE*

That the *Didache* was not composed by one author at one time is almost universally acknowledged. However, scholars differ widely in their precise understanding of how the text was put together. Some see the whole as the product of one compiler who drew upon, or incorporated, a selection of different traditions.[1] Others see the whole as the product of several redactional layers and accretions by different authors.[2] Others see a single author adding to the text over a period of time, with additional redactors making further contributions.[3]

Each of these assessments sees the *Didache*, directly or indirectly, as the product of multiple authors. To this extent any of these proposals may be used to challenge the view either that the *Didache* depended on Matthew's Gospel, or that both texts shared common traditions (as argued in Chapter 1). However, a thorough understanding of the *Didache* and its relationship to Matthew's Gospel invites a detailed analysis of the *Didache*'s compositional history.

Given the great variety of previous such analyses it may seem unrealistic to expect a more convincing study in this case. It is worth remembering, however, that the reluctance of most readers to read studies of this type is mirrored by the reluctance of many scholars to write them. It is not correct to suppose, therefore, that scores of detailed studies have consistently

1.   E.g. Harnack (1884: 24–63); Knopf (1920); de Halleux (1996: 301–302); Nautin (1959: 209–214); Alfonsi (1972: 480–81); Wengst (1984: 18–20); Schöllgen (1996: 67). Köster (1957: 159–160) suggests that five units were taken up by the Didachist. Niederwimmer (1998: 43–46) sees four sources so used.

2.   See n. 7 in Chapter 1.

3.   Audet (1958: 119–20) sees one 'apostolic' (in a broad sense) author as responsible for two stages of development. First 'D1', consisting of 1.1-3a; 2.2–5.2; 7.1a; 8.1–11.2, written before the emergence of the gospel tradition. Second 'D2', consisting of 11.3–13.2; 14.1–16.8 written with knowledge of, but not directly quoting, the gospel tradition. Audet then proposes further interpolations by a different hand at 1.3b-c; 1.4b–2.1; 6.2-3; 7.2-4 and 13.3, 5-7. He then sees 1.4a, 7.1b and 13.4 as subsequent glosses. Rordorf and Tuilier (1978: 49, 63, 92–94) suggest that *Didache* 1–13 was created by one author who added his own contributions (1.3b–2.1; 6.2-3; 7.2-3, 4b) to a selection of primitive teachings. *Didache* 14–15 and 16 were then, they propose, added by a second redactor.

No more extensive *Forschungsbericht* of previous attempts to describe the compositional history of the *Didache* is offered here because of the infinite variety of such schemes. Instead, the specific views of particular scholars will be noted as part of the ongoing analysis of individual elements of the *Didache*.

arrived at equivocal results. Rather, a good number of analyses, on which later theories have also been built, are founded on very limited prior discussion (as reference to volumes mentioned in footnotes 1-3, above, will show). This means that there is, in reality, plenty of scope for progress in what is a surprisingly under-ploughed field.[4]

The study that follows is a detailed and lengthy one. This is an unavoidable necessity if some of the shortcomings of its predecessors are to be overcome. An unfortunate by-product is that this approach requires the pursuit of a number of threads whose relevance to the wider project is not always immediately apparent. This problem can be mitigated, to some extent, by providing a preview of the conclusion towards which the various strands of Part I ultimately contribute. Thus, Figure 1 at the end of Chapter 10 (p. 155) describes a text put together in five stages:

- First, a base document concerning baptism, eucharist and visitors was formed, into which several previously existing traditions were incorporated (e.g. an augmented Two Ways tradition, a collection of sayings concerning the avoidance of fleshly passions and an ancient eschatological discourse).
- Separately and subsequently, a reframing of the base text's rulings on the conduct of the eucharist and the accommodation of visitors was created. Following the formation of this separate 'prophet document', it was divided in two and inserted alongside material in the base text also concerned with the eucharist and visitors.
- Third, a modifying teacher inserted alternative instructions at various points and quoted external authorities in support of these modifications. In addition, this teacher sought to make a clear distinction between the practice of Christians and Jews and introduced differentiating traditions to this end.
- After the creation of Matthew's Gospel, in an effort to abrogate certain teachings to the similar but now more developed sayings in Matthew's Gospel, referrals to 'the gospel' were inserted by a fourth contributor.
- Finally, *Did.* 16.7 was inserted to repair a theological deficiency created by the disappearance of the last few lines of the textual tradition preserved by the Jerusalem manuscript.

---

4.   'Surprising' in the sense that this work is foundational to the study of basic questions such as the *Didache*'s dates, provenances and authorships.

The individual strands of argument, with which the next few chapters are concerned, often have relevance to fields of study beyond the question of the *Didache*'s compositional history. For example, the next chapter addresses the puzzle of the curious sequence of 'eucharistic' prayers recorded in *Did.* 9 and 10. Progress here not only serves the goal of Part I, but also provides information relevant to the study of early Christian worship.

Chapter 2

The 'Eucharistic' Prayers in *Didache* 9 and 10

Since Bryennios's publication of the *Didache* in 1883, scholars have strug-
gled to present a coherent understanding of chs. 9–10. These chapters have
been variously understood as referring to:

1. An agape.[1]
2. A eucharist.[2]
3. A satisfying eucharist.[3]
4. A fellowship meal followed by a eucharist.[4]

1. The term 'agape' is used throughout this discussion to denote a fellowship meal
that is intended to satisfy hunger as well as to symbolize the fellowship of the community. Mazza's (1996: 285–86) criticism of the anachronistic use of this term is justified.
However, 'agape' provides a convenient term that is widely used to denote one of the
possible meal types in *Did.* 9 and 10. Jeremias (1966: 118) lists the following representatives of the view that *Did.* 9 and 10 describe only an agape: Ladeuze, Kattenbusch,
Drews, Ermoni, van Crombrugghe, Baumgärtner, Cagin, Knopf, Ferris, Goossens,
Brinktrine, Connolly, Dölger, Cirlot, Dix. Of these authors the most recent appears to
be Dix (1945). To this list may be added Vokes (1938: 197–207) and Gero (1977: 82).
2. The term 'eucharist' is used throughout to describe the meal of bread and wine
instituted by Jesus. Jeremias (1966: 118) lists the following representatives of this view:
Batiffol, Völker in 1927, Casel, Greiff in 1932 and Bricout. To this list may be added:
Middleton (1935: 259–61), Creed (1938: 374, 386–87) and Glover (1958: 26–27).
Bouley (1981: 89–99) is a more recent supporter of this type of view. His reading is
unusual, supposing that *Did.* 9.2 is non-sacramental, while *Did.* 9.3-4 represents a sacramental thanksgiving over the bread and *Did.* 10.2-5 a sacramental thanksgiving over the
wine. Bouley also allows for a full meal between these two events. Riggs (1984) proposes an understanding of the development of the prayers in *Did.* 9 and 10 that leads to
their ultimate use for a eucharist only (see § 2.2 in this chapter).
3. This type of eucharist supposes that the enjoyment of a meal in a community is
also experienced as a eucharist. J. Betz (1996: 247) cites Reicke and Lilje as exponents
of this view. Mazza (1995: 12–41) also proposes this solution.
4. Jeremias (1966: 118) who subscribes to this view himself lists: Zahn, Dibelius,
von de Goltz, Hennecke, Stapper, Hupfeld, Quasten, Arnold, Bultmann, Schneider and

5.   A eucharist followed by an agape.[5]
6.   Simple table prayers, reworked out of eucharistic prayers, used in ascetic circles.[6]

J. Betz (1996: 247) sums up this range of options by remarking, 'This large number of interpretations shows the uncertainty of the state of the research, the hypothetical character of the explanations and the difficulty of the question'. Mazza (1996: 283) concurs, 'On the meaning of... *Didache* 9-10, there have been many interpretations, none of which are outstanding'.

The unsatisfactory nature of these conclusions is caused by an apparently unresolvable tension within the evidence. The situation is similar to that of someone trying to cover all four corners of a mattress with an insufficiently large fitted sheet. Although three corners may be covered satisfactorily the inclusion of the fourth may only be achieved at the expense of one of the others.

In the case of *Did.* 9 and 10 there are five liturgical actions located within 9.2-4, 9.5, 10.1, 10.2-5 and 10.6. When these verses are considered independent of their context within *Did.* 9 and 10, the actions described may be identified relatively straightforwardly. However, as the following two sections aim to show, confusion arises when attempts are made to combine all five actions within one liturgical event.

1. *The Five Actions of* Didache *9 and 10*

1.1. Didache *10.1: A Full Meal*

> After you have had your fill (ἐμπλησθῆναι), give thanks thus:

With respect to the action referred to in *Did.* 10.1 there is almost universal agreement among scholars that this verse should be seen as referring back to a literally filling meal.[7] There are two powerful arguments in

perhaps without complete justification, Audet. J. Betz (1996: 247), who also subscribes to a version of this view, lists: Lessig, Stählin, Jungmann, Batley, Goppelt, Daniélou and Adam.

5.   Lietzmann (1953–64: 192) is isolated in this view.

6.   Peterson (1951). This view, a product of the sceptical American school, is not currently influential.

7.   Bouley (1981: 96) interprets Quasten (1975: 31–32) as supposing that an actual meal is *not* referred to here. Other opponents of the literal interpretation of ἐμπλησθῆναι include the small number of earlier scholars mentioned by Jeremias in n. 2, above.

favour of a literal interpretation of ἐμπλησθῆναι. One is expressed by J. Betz (1996: 249):

> The expression ἐμπλησθῆναι in 10:1…is a rubric, and so cannot be taken in an extended sense, but must rather be understood literally…it then points to the preceding food and drink as a genuine meal.

A second important observation is made by Mazza (1995: 16–17):

> The verb 'to satisfy fully'…immediately recalls the expression – one that is almost a technical term – from Deuteronomy 8.10: 'kai fage kai emplesthese'.[8]

The level of overall support for a literal interpretation of ἐμπλησθῆναι may be measured by observing that only one of the interpretations of *Did.* 9 and 10, listed in the introduction above, contemplates the absence of a full meal within the overall liturgy of *Did.* 9 and 10.[9]

1.2. Didache *10.6: An Invitation to a Eucharist*

> Let grace come and let this world pass away.
> Hosanna to the God of David.
> If anyone is holy let him come,
> if anyone is not let him repent.
> Maranatha. Amen.

Before attempting to assess the function of this verse it is necessary to consider whether or not the phrase, 'If anyone is holy, let him come. If anyone is not let him repent', should be taken as a liturgical proclamation or as a rubric.

The fact that every other line of this verse has a proclamatory character suggests that it is highly likely that the invitation to the holy would also have been spoken aloud. This is the view taken by the majority of scholars.[10] The opposing view must argue, with Bouley (1981: 95), that 'The admonition of 10.6 may well be another of the general directives awkwardly inserted by the author in the midst of liturgical formulas'. Bouley's own admission that the insertion of a rubric in the midst of spoken liturgical formulas is 'awkward' confirms that it is more natural to accept the orality of the whole of *Did.* 10.6. If, for the time being, *Did.* 10.6 is taken

---

8.   Mazza (1995: 17) goes on to give other examples of the technical use of this term in Deuteronomy.

9.   Audet (1958: 430–31) argues for a literal interpretation. For the list of scholars who actively or passively accept this view see references in nn. 1, 2, 4, 5 and 6, above.

10.   See those listed in n. 4, above.

independent of its context,[11] then the conclusion that the whole verse was intended to be spoken aloud, perhaps as a responsive dialogue (Lietzmann 1953–64: 192), is difficult to avoid.

As a proclaimed liturgy *Did.* 10.6 issues three invitations, two of which appear to carry a dual force. As J. Betz (1996: 271) states:

> The community implores: 'Let grace come and let the world pass away!' Further 'Maranatha!' These prayers/cries relate primarily to the future event of the fulfilment of salvation, but nevertheless still have a second dimension of meaning, which even though it is not overt should still not be mistaken: they indicate that the future Parousia event, the future coming of Jesus, experiences a foretaste and anticipation here and now in the event of the Lord's Supper.[12]

The inherent ambiguity in the force of *Maranatha*[13] means that it is possible to interpret this cry as focusing on the Parousia, a future event that lies beyond the boundaries of the service. This allows for the possibility that *Did.* 10.6 acts as a closing liturgy that sends the congregation out into the world.[14] However, this interpretation is extremely difficult to sustain so long as the invitation to the holy to 'come' is accepted as part of this spoken liturgy. In this circumstance it is necessary to suppose that the holy were invited to 'come' in the sense of 'go into the world'. This interpretation is not only contrary to the obvious reading of 'come', it also creates an awkward situation for those who are not holy, but who may not 'come' until they have repented. Must they stay behind until they are holy enough to leave?

It has also been suggested that the invitation to the holy, and the ban on the unholy, refers back to a preceding meal.[15] However, in this case,

---

11. Bouley (1981: 95) recognizes that an oral invitation to the holy in 10.6 provides a strong indication of a following eucharist. Because he perceives a eucharist as already described in *Did.* 9.3–10.5, Bouley must propose his awkward reading of this invitation.

12. Concerning the force of *Maranatha*, J. Betz (1996: 272) follows Lietzmann (1953–64: 193), Dibelius (1938: 40) and Cullmann (1963: 208–216) in perceiving, in combination with a call for the ultimate Parousia, a eucharistic focus in this acclamation. Moule (1961: 44) also considers this possibility, although he is ultimately more sceptical.

13. Moule (1961: 70–71) and J. Betz (1996: 271–72) both consider the alternative grammatical possibilities within *Maranatha*. These allow for the indicative, 'Our Lord has come', as well as for the more common imperative reading.

14. In an informal conversation, Jonathan Draper appeared to support this view.

15. This is the force of Bouley's argument (1981: 95). However, Bouley recognizes that this is only feasible if the invitation and prohibition were not spoken aloud.

because the prohibitions of *Did.* 9.5 appear within a rubric, the invitation and prohibition would only have been publicly announced after the event in question had already taken place.

In conclusion, the three invitations of *Did.* 10.6 strongly indicate a forthcoming event. This eschatologically significant event is one to which the Lord and the holy are invited. In these circumstances J. Betz (1996: 249) is justified in concluding, in line with several other scholars,[16] that

> The command in 10:6, that only the holy should come while the unholy do penance, presents the eucharist as only now happening, not as already having happened.

Similarly, Jeremias (1966: 118) concludes:

> The liturgical ejaculations in 10.6, which greet the coming Lord, and the warning 'if anyone is holy, let him come; if he is not let him repent' are meaningful only as the introduction to the Eucharist (not as the conclusion of an Agape or a Eucharist).

1.3. Didache *10.2-5: Thanksgiving After a Meal*

Did. 10.2-5 is commonly accepted as a prayer of thanksgiving after a meal akin to the Jewish *Birkat Ha-Mazon*.[17] The fact that scholars who espouse very different understandings of *Did.* 9 and 10 all agree on this point is a powerful argument in its favour. Mazza (1995: 17) notes that 'Since the studies of Finkelstein, Dibelius, and Hruby the connection between the *Birkat Ha-Mazon* and *Didache* 10 no longer requires demonstration'. Finkelstein (1928–29: 215–16) seeks to illustrate the relationship between *Did.* 10.2-5 and the *Birkat Ha-Mazon* by providing parallel translations:

---

16. See those listed in n. 4, above. In addition, Riggs (1984: 97) and Niederwimmer (1998: 143), 'If we allow the text to stand as it has been handed down we have scarcely any other choice but to suppose that 10.6 is the invitation to the Lord's Supper, which follows immediately thereafter'.

17. Riggs (1984: 91) cites several supporters of this view: Oesterley; Finkelstein; Dibelius; Middleton; Baumstark; R. Grant and C. Richardson; Audet; Bouyer; Köster; Vööbus; Talley; Verheul; Rordorf and Tuilier. Among those disagreeing with this view Riggs cites Peterson, J. Betz and Kilmartin. Draper (1996a: 26) also mentions Taylor and Turner, von der Goltz and Klein. Mazza (1995: 4, 17), himself a supporter of this connection, also cites Bouyer and Hruby.

Birkat Ha-Mazon	*Did.* 10
I	II
Blessed art Thou, O Lord, our God, King of the Universe, Who feedest the whole world with goodness, with grace and with mercy.	(10.3a) Thou, Master Almighty, didst create all things for Thy name's sake: both food and drink Thou didst give to men for enjoyment in order that they might give thanks to Thee, (10.3b) but to us Thou hast graciously given spiritual food and drink and eternal life through Thy servant. (10.4) Before all things, we thank Thee that Thou art mighty.
Blessed art Thou, O, Lord, Who feedest all.	To Thee be the glory forever.
II	I
We thank Thee, O Lord, our holy God, that Thou hast caused us to inherit a goodly and pleasant land, the covenant, the Torah, life and food. For all these things we thank Thee and praise Thy name for ever and ever.	(10.2) We thank Thee, Father for Thy holy name, which Thou hast caused to dwell in our hearts and for the knowledge and faith and immortality which thou hast made known to us through Jesus Thy servant;
Blessed art Thou, O, Lord, for the land and for the food.	To Thee be glory forever.
III	III
Have mercy, O Lord, our God, on Thy people Israel, and on Thy city Jerusalem, and on Thy Temple and Thy dwelling-place and on Zion Thy resting-place, and on the great and holy sanctuary over which Thy name was called, and the Kingdom of the dynasty of David mayest Thou restore to its place in our days, and build Jerusalem soon.	(10.5) Remember, Lord, Thy church, to deliver it from every evil and to make it perfect in Thy love and gather it from the four winds, it, the sanctified, into Thy kingdom which Thou hast prepared for it;
Blessed art Thou, O, Lord, who buildest Jerusalem.	For Thine is the power and the glory forever.
	(10.6) Let grace come and this world pass away.
	Hosanna to the son of David.
	Whoever is holy, let him come: whoever is not let him repent.
	Maranatha. Amen.

These two prayers undoubtedly exhibit common structural and conceptual similarities. Further, if the content of *Did.* 10.1, with its reference to a filling meal may be taken into account, then there is little doubt that *Did.* 10.2-5 acts, at least in part, as a thanksgiving after a meal. However, a certain degree of caution is necessary before drawing more detailed conclusions from the supposed relationship between these two prayers. First, although they may reflect ancient tradition, it is not possible to be certain of the exact content of this type of prayer at the time of *Did.* 10's composition. Mazza (1995: 19) also invites caution when he suggests that

> We can show that the *Didache* has not inverted the first two strophes of the *Birkat Ha-Mazon* [as Finkelstein portrays]. The transition between the Jewish and the Christian prayer-texts has been more complicated than that. The *Didache* has eliminated the first strophe of the *Birkat Ha-Mazon* and has substituted another text that at once expresses…Christian tidings.

Mazza (1995: 28) also suggests that '*Didache* 10.5 departs from the *Birkat Ha-Mazon* in order to draw from other Jewish prayers, such as the tenth blessing of the *Amidah* prayer or from the *Ahabhah Rabbah*'.[18]

In addition to these variations there is a clear discrepancy between the *Birkat Ha-Mazon* and *Did.* 10.3b, where spiritual food and drink are mentioned. This apparent addition to the standard structure of the prayer suggests, if the proximity of *Did.* 10.6 may be taken into account, that *Did.* 10.2-5 acts, not only as a prayer after a meal, but also as a transitional prayer from physical food (10.1, 3a) to the eating of spiritual food and drink (10.3b, 6) at a following eucharist.

In summary then, the essential and agreed action described in *Did.* 10.2-5 is a prayer of thanksgiving after a satisfying meal. However, the addition of *Did.* 10.3b implies that this prayer also serves as a prayer before the spiritual meal indicated by the invitatory liturgy of *Did.* 10.6.

1.4. Didache *9.1-5: Preparation for a Eucharist*
An overwhelming weight of evidence suggests that *Did.* 10.1 refers to a filling meal. This is taken as fact, with strong justification, by the vast majority of scholars. The effect of this consensus is to skew the way in which *Did.* 9.1-5 is read. That is to say that, because *Did.* 10.1 refers to a full meal, and the adjacent *Did.* 9.5 refers to a meal, then the meal in *Did.* 9.5 must be the same full meal that is mentioned in *Did.* 10.1. While this reasoning is understandable it seriously distorts the evidence provided by *Did.* 9.1-5. For the time being, therefore, the shadow of *Did.* 10.1 should

---

18. A reference to the *Amidah* in *Did.* 9 and 10 is also suggested in Riggs (1984: 92).

be removed from the consideration of *Did.* 9.1-5 so that evidence of the actions described by these verses may be evaluated on its own terms.

When *Did.* 9.1-5 is considered independently of its proximity to *Did.* 10 it gives no indication that it serves as a prelude to a filling meal. An important obstacle to such an understanding of these prayers is the fact that the second thanksgiving is said over a fragment of bread. An extraordinary violation of Jewish practice would be required to allow the breaking of bread to precede the opening *Berakah*. However, the fact that the term κλάσματος rather than ἄρτος[19] is used here suggests that a single fragment was all that was on offer. A very large fragment would be required to satisfy the hunger of even the smallest congregation.[20]

A meal prayer concerning a cup and a fragment of bread is already suggestive of a eucharist. This suggestion is further emphasized by the technical language, parallel to the language concerning baptism (*Did.* 7.1), of *Did.* 9.1: 'Concerning the eucharist, eucharistize in this way'. While this title could be taken to apply to a eucharist beyond *Did.* 9 it is nonetheless the case that this title certainly also embraces *Did.* 9.

Concerning *Did.* 9.2-4, J. Betz (1996: 249) notes that

> The sayings in these verses offer a pronounced eucharistic colour which can hardly be ignored. Thus the fact that the bread and cup, the specific eucharistic elements, are blessed, though not conclusive in itself, is nevertheless noteworthy. If, however, the text speaks of the holy 'vine' of David, of klasma, of life and immortality, of spiritual food and (likewise) drink, then it not only alludes distantly to the eucharist which only appears in 10.6, but reveals a close and immediate reference to such a kind of sacramental Lord's meal.

J. Betz (1996: 250) thus concludes:

> If one considers the texts as isolated units, in terms of their content and development, not according to their external place in the framework of the

---

19.   Niederwimmer (1998: 148), after wrestling with this problem prefers ἄρτος to κλάσματος. However, the fact that κλάσματος presents the more difficult reading provides strong evidence in its favour. Further, Niederwimmer's amendment creates its own syntactical difficulties; see Niederwimmer (1998: 150).

20.   Bauer *et al.* (1957: 433) note that κλάσματος refers to 'fragment, piece, crumb' or 'the remains of a meal' in every other instance where it appears in the New Testament and early Christian literature. Van de Sandt (2002: 223) notes that the elements blessed are merely symbolic of the whole meal and do not necessarily constitute the entire menu. This observation would be fair if the thanksgiving were over a loaf. However, the presence of a fragment poses a larger puzzle. A specific explanation for the presence of a 'fragment' is offered below in § 3.1 in this chapter.

Didache's celebration, then it leads to the conclusion that they are genuine eucharistic prayers and that the meal ordered by them is a genuine Lord's meal. They have also been evaluated in this way by a row of reputable researchers for a long time.[21]

This conclusion is all the more compelling because it is inconvenient for Betz's ultimate thesis, in which he suggests that these eucharistic prayers were downgraded to serve as a rule for an agape (1996: 251). That this reading of *Did.* 9.1-5 is also inconvenient for the majority of interpreters[22] provides some explanation for why this evidence has not been more widely considered.

1.5. *Five Incompatible Actions*

The above interpretations of the actions described in *Did.* 9 and 10 have sought to evaluate the evidence, as far as possible, independent of the influence of the surrounding context. The reason for this approach is not to suggest that this context should not be allowed to influence these interpretations but simply to make plain the nature of the challenge that faces scholars who seek to make sense of the whole of *Did.* 9 and 10.

In summary then, the five actions so far considered in *Did.* 9 and 10 include:

1. *Did.* 9.2-4: thanksgivings prior to a eucharist.
2. *Did.* 9.5: the eating of a eucharist (implied).
3. *Did.* 10.1: a filling meal (implied).
4. *Did.* 10.2-3a, 4-5: a thanksgiving after a filling meal.
5. *Did.* 10.3b, 6: preparation for, and invitation to, a eucharist.

These five actions, including two eucharists, cannot all take place within one continuous liturgy. This perhaps explains the 'large number of interpretations…the uncertainty of the state of the research, the hypothetical character of the explanations and the difficulty of the question' (J. Betz 1996: 247). As the following review seeks to show scholars have, in the main, sought to overcome the problem of two eucharists by seeking an alternative interpretation of either *Did.* 9.2-5, or *Did.* 10.6.

---

21. J. Betz (1996: 250) lists: Rauschen, Batiffol, Völker, Ruch, Casel, Goguel, Snape, Quasten, Rietschel and Graff, Reicke, Cayré, Lilje, Lietzmann (1953–64: 189–94). This interpretation was first taken up by the author of *Apostolic Constitutions* VII.

22. This interpretation causes difficulties for almost every scholar except the small minority who perceive only one meal within *Did.* 9 and 10.

2. *Attempts to Modify the Five Actions of* Didache *9 and 10*

2.1. *Alternative Readings of* Didache *10.6*

Scholars who favour a eucharist between *Did.* 9.5 and 10.1 face the challenge of explaining the presence of *Did.* 10.6. Bouley claims that the invitation to the holy to 'come', is an awkwardly inserted rubric that refers to the foregoing eucharist rather than a future one. However, the proclamatory character of *Did.* 10.6 makes this alternative very unlikely.[23] Draper favours an interpretation that sees *Did.* 10.6 as a liturgy of dismissal. However, it is difficult to read 'come' in an opposite sense, and problems are created as to the fate of the unholy, who may not 'come'.[24] A further option, adopted by Lietzmann (1953–64: 192), is simply to relocate *Did.* 10.6. By locating this verse between *Did.* 9.4 and 9.5, Lietzmann neatly co-ordinates both sets of verses that lead into a eucharist. Unfortunately, the challenge in hand is to account for the text as it stands. The fact that Lietzmann is alone in his eccentric solution is an indication of its unsatisfactory nature.[25] However, it should be recognized that this undesirable action was forced upon a highly respected scholar by the quality of the evidence for two eucharists in one liturgy. A similar approach is taken by the author of the *Apostolic Constitutions* VII, who re-places the offending invitation to the holy after the final 'Amen' of *Did.* 10.6. In this location it may better serve, as Bouley would also like it to, as a reflexive rubric. However, like Lietzmann, this solution fails to explain the authentic, difficult text. Finally the option adopted by Mazza (1995), who sees a satisfying eucharist at *Did.* 9.5/10.1,[26] is simply to ignore the question altogether.[27]

In summary, attempts to ignore or re-place *Did.* 10.6 do not provide

23. See § 1.2 in this chapter.
24. See § 1.2 in this chapter.
25. J. Betz (1996: 247) emphasizes Lietzmann's complete isolation, despite the otherwise revered status of *Mass and Lord's Supper*. See also Dibelius's (1938) critique of Lietzmann.
26. This is in itself a difficult, though not impossible, thesis to sustain. While the concept of sacral full meals is strong in Judaism, the idea of a full *eschatological* meal is more problematic. Mazza's view is also unsupported by New Testament evidence of the full incorporation of the eucharist within the full meal that accompanied it.
27. Mazza might be expected to refer to 10.6, either after his consideration of *Did.* 10.5 (1995: 29), or after his consideration of *Did.* 9 (1995: 40); it occurs in neither. Interestingly, the only reference that Mazza makes to *Did.* 10.6, in an article first published in 1979 (reproduced in 1996: 279), is one agreeing with Audet's method for dating this verse before the fall of Jerusalem.

satisfactory explanations for its content and location. The most uncontrived interpretation of this verse remains, therefore, that it introduces a further liturgical event, which, in context, is most likely to be a eucharist.

2.2. *Alternative Readings of* Didache *9.2-5*

The great majority of scholars are persuaded by the strong arguments, recited above, that *Did.* 10.1 refers to a filling meal, that *Did.* 10.2-5 acts as a thanksgiving after a meal, and that *Did.* 10.6 serves as an introduction to a eucharist.[28] Taken together these three actions form a coherent flow of events, which also echo the snippets of evidence regarding eucharistic practice to be found in the New Testament.[29] As soon as this flow of events is assumed it becomes infeasible to consider the possibility that *Did.* 9.2-5 also introduces a eucharist. Alternative explanations for the presence of these thanksgivings must be found.

By far the most common interpretation of *Did.* 9.2-5, in these circumstances, is to treat them as prayers before a filling meal. However, this solution fails to take account of the eucharistic character of these prayers, and the fact that the second blessing is made over a fragment, not a whole loaf.[30]

Audet's solution to this difficulty is to propose a new, semi-eucharistic service that he names 'the breaking of bread' or 'the minor eucharist'. This theory has found no supporters and is derided by Vööbus (1968: 64) as having 'not one shred of evidence in its support'. However, it should be noted, as with Lietzmann, that Audet's theory is not the result of a crazed fancy, but the response of a respected scholar to a very puzzling circumstance. Audet's response is unsatisfactory, but it does at least attempt to deal with the evidence, rather than forcing it into the convenient mould of an 'agape'.

J. Betz and Riggs are two more recent scholars who have sought to deal justly with the evidence of two eucharists within *Did.* 9 and 10. Betz (1996: 274) argues that *Did.* 9.2-4 had its origins in a primitive eucharist that became redundant in the course of developing eucharistic theology. Rather than discard these outdated prayers, Betz proposes, they were downgraded to serve as a formal introduction to the agape. Betz further suggests that *Did.* 10.3a was added to the overall liturgy at this point so as to refer back to the satisfying nature of the preceding agape.

Betz's theory is commendable in that it at least addresses the problem

28. See n. 4, above.
29. The eucharist follows a full meal in Mk 14, Mt. 26 and 1 Cor. 11.
30. See § 1.4 in this chapter.

of the eucharistic character of *Did.* 9. However, his thesis is highly con-jectural, in that it supposes a process of 'downgrading' for which there is no evidence. Further, Betz must argue that, although these prayers were put to a new use, they were not adapted in the most obvious detail so as logically to suit that use. That is to say that the term κλάσματος survived such a supposed downgrading, when a change to ἄρτος (a change made by *Apostolic Constitutions* in its paraphrase of *Did.* 9.4) would have clari-fied an otherwise confusing detail. Further, Betz's addition of 10.3a to the following thanksgiving violates, as Riggs points out, one of the most secure parallels between *Did.* 10.2-5 and the *Birkat Ha-Mazon.*

Riggs (1984) critiques Betz's solution, but his own alternative requires an even more unlikely turn of events. Riggs suggests that *Did.* 9 and 10 record several stages in a developing liturgy. Thus the oldest prayer is *Did.* 10.2-5 (less the διά phrases), which was used as a restructured *Birkat Ha-Mazon* by the Christian community. At a later stage *Did.* 9.2-3 was used to pray over the bread and wine before the meal. At this stage also *Did.* 9.4 was added to parallel 10.5, and the Christian phrases from *Did.* 9 were added to *Did.* 10. At a third stage Riggs (1984: 101) claims that 'The bread and cup prayers, as well as a Thanksgiving prayer, occur before the cultic event. The meal has dropped out, and the elements themselves have become something sacred.'

Riggs's explanation is ingenious in that it explains the inherent tensions between the various parts of the liturgy as a product of its successive developments. However, Riggs fails to explain the continued existence of the extant text. The most pressing problem in this regard is why a redun-dant and confusing reference to a full meal should have been retained in a set of instructions for a rite from which the full meal has 'dropped out'.

In summary, attempts to explain the eucharistic character of *Did.* 9.2-5 by ignoring the problem, inventing new services, or suggesting a multiple layering of the text, all fail to explain its surviving form. The considerable difficulty experienced by scholars who seek to avoid a eucharistic inter-pretation of these verses serves to reinforce the case for their relationship to a eucharist.

2.3. *Conclusion*
This section began by suggesting that trying to fit all of the actions described by *Did.* 9 and 10 into one liturgy was like trying to cover a large mattress with a small sheet. Creative solutions to the problem posed by *Did.* 9 and 10 have included rearrangements of the text and the invention of new services. However, the fact that so many solutions have been

offered, while none has proved satisfactory, suggests the impossibility of the task. In these circumstances an entirely new approach to the problem is invited.

3. *An Alternative Solution: Two Separate Liturgies*

Before presenting my solution to the problems posed by *Did.* 9 and 10 it is helpful to note one further action within these chapters that has been universally overlooked by scholars, for understandable reasons.

3.1. *A Sixth Action*

Up until this point the assumption has been maintained that there are only five actions described or implied by *Did.* 9 and 10. However, there is evidence to suggest that there are in fact six.

The presence of the term κλάσματος implies the existence of a further action, one that is not considered even by scholars who see *Did.* 9.2-4 as preparations for a eucharist. The presence of broken bread at this point in a meal is highly unusual. That is to say that a Jewish table blessing would almost always precede the fraction of the bread rather than follow it.[31] This is also the case in each of the New Testament accounts of the meal prayers of Jesus.[32] The presence of a 'fragment' before the thanksgiving therefore suggests an action of breaking the bread *before* the beginning of the meal. Such a bread breaking would be most likely to happen at a full meal. The sixth action is therefore, according to this reading, the sharing of a full meal before the thanksgiving over the cup and the fragment.[33]

3.2. *Two Parallel Liturgies*

A previously unconsidered solution to the problems posed by the collection of incompatible actions in *Did.* 9 and 10 is that they represent two separate accounts of the same liturgical event. Thus, following the consensus, the pattern of events in *Did.* 10 is a full meal followed by a prayer that creates a connection between the past full meal and the forthcoming

31. Alon (1996: 186) mentions a possible exception to this rule in Rabbi Hiyya bar Ashi.

32. For example: Mt. 14.19; 15.36; Mk 6.41; 14.22; Lk. 22.19; 24.30; Jn 6.11; 1 Cor. 11.24.

33. This pattern presents an interesting parallel with the progress of events in Jn 6. In Jn 6.12, when the crowd are described as filled (ἐνεπλήσθησαν), the disciples then gather up the fragments (κλάσματα), and Jesus goes on to deliver the most strongly eucharistic discourse in the whole of John's Gospel (Jn 6.53–58).

eucharistic meal. At the same time *Did.* 9 describes precisely the same pattern of events. The presence of a fragment at the beginning of the liturgy may be accounted for as the remains of a preceding filling meal, which are then prayed over in preparation for a eucharist consisting of one cup and one fragment.

The parallels between the actions described in both prayers is emphasized by the striking level of similarity between the structure and wording of each chapter.

In the table below, verbal and conceptual similarities occurring in parallel strophes are underlined, while similarities that appear in different strophes are italicized. References to the eucharistic elements are in bold type. Recognition that the rubrics of *Did.* 9.2 and 9.3 would not have been spoken aloud increases the similarity between the opening sequences of both sets of prayers.

Did. 9	*Did.* 10
9.1 Concerning the eucharist, give thanks thus:	10.1 After you have had your fill, give thanks thus:
9.2 First, concerning the **cup**: We give thanks to you, our Father, for the holy vine of David your servant which you have revealed to us through Jesus your servant.	10.2 We give thanks to you holy Father for your holy Name which you have made to dwell in our hearts and for the knowledge, faith and immortality which you have revealed to us through Jesus your servant.
To you be glory for ever.	To you be glory for ever.
9.3 And concerning the **fragment**: We give thanks to you, our Father,	10.3a You Lord almighty have created everything for the sake of your Name; you have given human beings food and drink to partake with enjoyment so that they might give thanks; 10.3b but to us you have given the grace of **spiritual food and drink** and of eternal life
For the life and knowledge, which you have revealed to us through Jesus your servant.	through Jesus your servant. 10.4 Above all we give you thanks because you are mighty.
To you be glory for ever.	To you be glory for ever.

Did. 9	Did. 10
9.4 As this fragment was scattered upon the mountains and has been gathered to become one,	10.5 Remember Lord your <u>Church,</u> to preserve it from all evil and to make it perfect in your love. And, sanctified,
<u>so gather your Church from the four corners of the earth into your kingdom.</u>	<u>gather it from the four winds into your kingdom</u> which you have prepared for it.
<u>For yours is the glory and the power</u> through Jesus Christ <u>for ever.</u>	<u>For yours is the power and the glory for ever.</u>
	10.6 Let grace come and let this world pass away. Hosanna to the God of David.
9.5 Let no one eat or drink of your eucharist save those <u>baptized</u> in the name of the Lord,	If anyone is <u>holy</u> let him come, if anyone is not let him repent.
For the saying of the Lord applies, 'Do not give to dogs what is holy'.	
	Maranatha. Amen.

The two prayers correspond structurally, verbally and conceptually. In both cases there is a three strophe pattern.[34] In both cases there are exact verbal parallels and parallel imagery. In both cases a full meal is followed by a transitional prayer leading into a eucharist of spiritual food and drink, or cup and fragment. In both cases there is a prohibition with respect to the members of the community who may or may not take part in the following event.

This similarity not only provides evidence of their common function, but also presents a fresh challenge to those scholars who perceive a eucharist at 9.5/10.1. In this case it must be argued that a Jewish type of meal is preceded and followed by almost identical thanksgivings, a feature that has no precedent at any stage in known Jewish history.[35] Similarly, scholars who propose two meals, one after 9.5 and the other after 10.6, must ex-

---

34. Mazza (1995: 30) states that 'The tripartite structure of *Didache* 9 should never be confused with that of *Didache* 10'. However, this bald assertion is not supported by any accompanying explanation.

35. An important element of arguments such as Mazza's (see, for example, 1996: 277), is the supposed parallel between *Did.* 9 and 10 and contemporary Jewish practice, of which almost nothing is directly known.

plain why the supposed theological differences between these two meals is not more strongly reflected in the preparatory prayers in each case.

The parallel liturgy theory is, of course, also open to criticism. The remarkably similar language in both chapters is taken by several scholars as an indication that the parallel sections of these chapters were written at the same time by the same author(s). While such similarity of language might usually be taken as an indication of common authorship this is not necessarily the case with liturgical texts. That is to say that liturgical language forms are often preserved by a sequence of authors who wish to maintain, and express their membership of, the stream of liturgical tradition.

It is undoubtedly the case that, had these prayers been found in separate first-century Christian liturgies, they would be seen as performing identical functions. However, the most obvious objection to a two liturgy hypothesis is that it does not take the text as it stands. That is to say that it is necessary to show how *this* text was used, rather than how its component parts may have been used. However, there is evidence to suggest (considered in Chapter 6 below),[36] that *Did.* 9 and 10 belonged to two separate layers of tradition which, when joined together in the *Didache*, were juxtaposed by subject. It is therefore possible that, during the period when these liturgies were in regular use, such a juxtaposition would not have caused any confusion. However, as this form fell out of use it is understandable that these chapters came to be seen as a continuous whole. This is clearly the interpretation made in *Apostolic Constitutions* VII where, however, those aspects of *Did.* 9 and 10 that make such a running together impractical have been modified.[37]

In conclusion then, I have sought to demonstrate that *Did.* 9 and *Did.* 10 represent two separate, alternative accounts of a prayer that creates a transition between a full meal and a symbolic meal. Seen as two separate texts, the notorious difficulties associated with the order of events envisaged by *Did.* 9–10 are resolved.

---

36. This discussion will conclude that *Did.* 9 belongs to a layer that also includes 6.1-3; parts of 7.1-4; and 11.3-6, less references to prophets and the gospel. This layer, it will be proposed, was interwoven with a layer consisting of at least 10.1-7; 11.7-12.

37. Hence κλάσματος is omitted and the invitation to the holy (10.6) is moved to a position where it may feasibly function as a retrospective rubric.

Chapter 3

The two most significant collections of points of contact between the *Didache* and Matthew's Gospel occur in *Did.* 16 and *Did.* 1. For this reason two substantial chapters are now devoted to *Did.* 16 and *Did.* 1–5 in turn.

The first part of the present chapter focuses on the interpretation of the enigmatic phrase 'those who persevere in their faith shall be saved by the curse itself' (16.5). The answer given is pivotal to discussion of a second classic problem associated with the *Didache*'s final chapter; the extent and content of the text's original ending. In the course of this latter debate it will also be necessary to consider the history and function of *Did.* 16.7.

The preparatory elements of this chapter take a long time to reach their conclusion. However, once completed, they not only assist the process of reconstructing the compositional history of *Did.* 16, but also contribute to crucial elements in the ensuing case for Matthew's use of the *Didache*'s closing eschatological discourse.[1]

1. *The Curse that Saves*

A number of interpretations of 'the curse that saves' in 16.5 have been offered since the rediscovery of the *Didache*. By far the most popular among these is an equation of the 'curse' with Jesus.[2]

The grammar of the sentence in question may be read in one of two ways. Αὐτοῦ may be seen as a masculine or neuter third person singular

---

1. This latter factor need not directly occupy the reader's attention at this stage. The discussion to which the reconstruction of the lost ending of the *Didache* is relevant takes place in Chapter 13.

2. See Milavec (1995: 139–42) for a discussion of the history of this mainstream position. Scholars cited as supporting this line include: Taylor (1886: 100); Harris (1887: 68); Harnack and von Gebhardt (1886: 62); Wengst (1984: 99); Schöllgen (1991: 78–79); Giet (1970: 252) and Niederwimmer (1989: 265).

pronoun so that 'οἱ δὲ ὑπομείναντες ἐν τῇ πίστει αὐτῶν σωθήσονται ὑπ' αὐτοῦ τοῦ καταθέματος' is read as, 'but those who persevere in their belief will be saved by [agency of] him, the curse'. However, in this case, there should be a masculine or neuter noun to which αὐτοῦ refers. The likely candidates are eliminated, since κτίσις (creation), πύρωσις (burning process) and πιστίς (faith) are feminine nouns. Given the absence of a suitable referent, it is preferable, therefore, to read αὐτοῦ as an intensive adjectival pronoun agreeing with the neuter noun καταθέματος, thus, 'saved by [the agency of] the curse itself'.

To read the phrase 'the curse itself' as a covert reference to Jesus requires an already established association between Jesus and 'the curse' in the mind of the author/hearers. Such a connection is not made in the preceding (or following) text. To read 'the curse' as another name for Christ it is necessary, therefore, to propose that Christ was so well known as 'the curse' by the *Didache*'s intended hearers that this interpretation did not need to be spelt out in the *Didache* itself.

Scholars who wish to see 'the curse' as a reference to Jesus generally rely, as evidence for an association between these two terms in early Christianity, on Gal. 3.13, 'Christ redeemed us from the curse (κατάρα) of the Law by becoming a curse for us – for it is written, "Cursed is every one who hangs on a tree."' On this basis, and with additional reference to 1 Cor. 12.3, Rordorf and Tuilier (1978: 198) conclude: 'The notion of curse was therefore so widely dispersed in the early church that one will not be surprised that the noun κατάθεμα might here designate Christ himself'.[3]

There are, however, a number of difficulties with this view. An initial group of problems lies in the assumption that Gal. 3.13 provides a basis for the common association of Jesus with 'τό κατάθεμα'. First, if 1 Cor. 2.9 contains a quotation of *Did.* 16.9[4] (as reconstructed in section 4 below), and if Galatians was written after 1 Corinthians, then Gal. 3.13 cannot be used to interpret *Did.* 16.5. Second, even if *Did.* 16.5 is, contrary to my argument in Chapter 13, a post-Pauline text, then it is unclear why κατάθεμα should be used in *Did.* 16.5 if it depended on an idea expressed in Gal. 3.13, where κατάρα is used. Third, if *Did.* 16.5 does rely on a Paul-

---

3.   This translation appears in Milavec 1995: 143. The original text reads, 'La notion de malédiction était donc très répandue dans l'Eglise primitive, et on ne s'etonnera pas que le substantif κατάθεμα puisse désigner ici le Christ lui-même'.

4.   Observations regarding the antiquity of *Did.* 16.3-6, 8-9 may be found in the excursus on the relationship between Mk 13 and *Did.* 16 in Chapter 13. For a specific reference to the relationship between *Did.* 16.9 and 1 Cor. 2.9 see n. 2 at the end of this excursus in Chapter 13.

ine interpretative key, then it is surprising that a closer relation to the Pauline tradition is not more evident in the remainder of the text. As Milavec (1995: 142) notes:

> The resolution of the obscure meaning of Did 16.5 through an appeal to Paul (e.g., Gal 3:13; 1 Cor 12:3) is considerably weakened when one notes that the *Didache* originated within a community which exhibited no dependence upon Pauline theology or Pauline letters.

Categorical statements regarding the relationship between Paul and the *Didache* should perhaps be avoided at this stage. That said, Milavec's point is fair inasmuch as the *Didache* does appear to be remarkably free from the influence of distinctively Pauline theology.[5]

An additional appeal to 1 Cor. 12.3 does nothing to support the equation of curse and Christ in common Christian usage. All that this verse shows, if anything, is that opponents of Christianity may have called Christ ἀνά-θεμα. It does not follow that Christians are then likely to have taken up this type of insult as a suitable name for their saviour. If the sign of those who do not speak in the Spirit is that they can say 'Jesus be cursed' (1 Cor. 12.3), then is it likely that Christians would use such a term to describe their Lord?

The idea of a commonly understood association between 'κατάθεμα' and 'Christ' is made particularly problematic by the appearance of the very rare term κατάθεμα[6] in Rev. 22.3. Here it cannot be interpreted as a covert reference to Christ, since the verse declares that in the New Jerusalem there will 'no longer be any curse'. This suggests that even if some Christians did, however perversely, refer to Christ as 'the curse' this was not a description that was so 'widely dispersed' (as Rordorf and Tuilier would have it [1978: 198]) that it had reached the circles in which Revelation was read.

Finally, even if in some very particular circumstance Jesus was known as 'the curse', it is unclear why this appellation should be used in *Did.* 16.5. That is to say, 'Lord' is used to describe Christ on every other occasion where he may be seen as referred to within the *Didache*, so why might 'the curse' be used in *Did.* 16.5? 'Those who persevere in their faith shall be saved by the Lord himself' would appear to adequately express the meaning favoured by those who see 'the curse' as a reference to Jesus. No

---

5.   Particularly starkly, Paul's view of the centrality of the crucifixion is entirely absent from the *Didache*. The *Didache* does not even mention the cross in its two eucharistic prayers (*Did.* 9 and 10).

6.   This noun occurs in Rev. 22.3 and *Did.* 16.5, but nowhere else in early Christian literature, according to Bauer *et al.* (1957).

special service is apparently performed by this metaphor, since it does not illuminate the mode of salvation. For example, it is not as if anyone has been saved from the curse of the testing fire by Christ's taking that curse upon himself, because only those who don't fall away in the *course* of the fire and who persevere in their faith will be saved. Thus, it is not only unlikely that Jesus was *ever* described by Christians as 'τὸ κατάθεμα', but also, there are no unusual circumstances which might explain or justify the use of this metaphor in this particular instance.

In summary, multiple problems arise from equating 'τὸ κατάθεμα' with Christ: not only is it difficult to envisage a concrete circumstance where this equivalence might safely be assumed of a Christian audience, but also, it is difficult to find textual evidence of any kind to support such a notion, least of all evidence that bears a tangible connection to the *Didache*. Why then has *Didache* scholarship maintained such a firm stance on this issue? I suspect that the reason is not because Christ is genuinely seen as likely to have been commonly known as 'the curse', but because he is commonly understood, from our present day perspective, as the one who saves. Thus, if *Did.* 16.5 had read, 'but those who persevere in their faith shall be saved by the kitchen sink itself', then the assumption would be made that, because Jesus is the one who saves, 'the kitchen sink' must have been a 'widely dispersed' metaphor for Christ (who washes us of our sins?). This type of automatic interpretative move could perhaps be justified if it were possible to show that Jesus is the *only* possible agent of the salvation that could be referred to in *Did.* 16.5. In the following discussion of Milavec's work it will be argued that this is not the case. First of all, however, it is appropriate to note two other interpretations of the enigmatic phrase.

Bryennios suggested that there may be a textual error in *Did.* 16.5 and that ὑπ' should read ἀπ', so that salvation is from the curse rather than by it. This view, quoted and endorsed by Funk (1887: 48) has been almost entirely ignored in subsequent discussion.[7] Such a dismissal is justified inasmuch as this emendation is entirely arbitrary, does nothing to explain the difficult form of the extant text and still provides scant explanation as to why the verse should have been written in this way.

Jonathan Draper (1996d: 362) offers the unique opinion that

> [T]he phrase ὑπ' αὐτοῦ τοῦ καταθέματος is a polemic against Paul and refers to the 'curse of the Law'. This may have been a proverbial expression... The instruction of the *Didache* would then remind the community that they are saved by the very thing which they find brings a curse on

7.   See Pardee (1995: 173 n. 49).

them, namely the Torah. It is to this that they must hold fast if they are to be perfect on the last day.

Draper's interpretation of the 'curse' is dependent on his view that Paul is the one who teaches another teaching, as mentioned in *Did.* 11.2a. However, as I argue in Chapter 7, section 3, the force of *Did.* 11.1-2 is located in its final clause. Thus, the reference to turn-coat teachers is part of a declaration of orthodoxy prior to the introduction of the possibility, in 11.2b, that an alternative teaching may after all be acceptable. It is an unjustified step, therefore, to see a specific engagement with Paul in the reference to teachers who turn to teach another doctrine.

A third view, and one worthy of detailed consideration, is that of Aaron Milavec, who argues that the saving 'curse' is the burning process itself. Vital to Milavec's argument is his observation of the linguistic parallelism of *Did.* 16.5. Thus he writes (1995: 137):

> The term πύρωσις (burning process) is a derivative of πῦρ (fire) and is only found once in the NT (1 Pet 4:12). The word δοκιμασία (verb δοκιμάζω) has the sense of 'testing,' normally with the prospect of approving something... The phrase εἰς τὴν πύρωσιν τῆς δοκιμασίας (through the burning process of testing), therefore, aptly signals that both positive and negative results could be anticipated. In Did 16.5, accordingly, two divergent results are indeed forthcoming:
>
> A. Negative results of burning
> For whom?   'many' (unspecified; includes false prophets, the world-deceiver, etc.)
> *Effect?*   *'entrapped and destroyed [by the burning]'*
>
> B. Positive results of the burning
> For whom?   'the faithful' (those who are not corrupted or deceived as explained in Did 16.4)
> *Effect?*   *'saved [by the burning=curse]'*

Milavec goes on to show that in prophetic and apocalyptic literature of the period this dual role of the eschatological fire is a recurring feature. Thus, Milavec argues that that which destroys God's enemies is what simultaneously saves and purifies those who remain faithful to him. He concludes (1995: 154):

> When the text is examined on its own grounds, the term δοκιμασία (testing) would appear to suggest that both positive and negative results are anticipated. Furthermore, when the metaphor of fire is investigated in the prophetic and apocalyptic literature, multiple instances appear which support the notion that a dual effect was being assigned to the eschatological fire. Given the linguistic parallelism within the text, therefore, the possibility

remains that the *Didache* had in mind that the elect were to be 'saved by the accursed [burning process] itself' (*Did.* 16.5).

It was observed above that if Jesus may be seen as the only possible agent of salvation, then it is reasonable, if ungainly, to interpret the saving curse as a reference to Christ. What Milavec succeeds in showing is that the 'burning process' may also be seen as an agent of salvation for those who, by their perseverence, survive it. The immediate question is, therefore, which of these two possible agents of salvation is most likely to be in view in *Did.* 16.5? The several difficulties with interpreting the curse as a reference to Christ have already been listed above. By contrast, these difficulties do not apply in the case of the burning process. First, there is nothing curious in the description of the burning process as 'the curse'.[8] Second, the grammar of the phrase in question, which presupposes the hearers' knowledge of what 'the curse itself' refers to, is unproblematic if this phrase refers back to the burning process that has just been mentioned. By this means Milavec's solution avoids having to appeal to a Pauline interpretative key.

In a response to Milavec's proposal Pardee raises two objections (1995: 174). First, she notes that

[T]he overall context of Did 16.5, specifically the use of σωθήσονται followed by the preposition ὑπό, speaks against this theory, since elsewhere σώζω and ὑπό together indicate a personal, most likely divine, agent. (In the accompanying footnote she writes, 'In all of the examples which I have checked, σώζω + ὑπό is only found with animate agents, i.e., persons or personified entities...')

The fact that Pardee found, in the examples she checked, that the agents of salvation were always animate and usually divine is not surprising, since the act of saving generally requires animation. Further, the phrase 'usually divine' indicates that the texts Pardee consulted were primarily religious, and in religious literature the agent of salvation is, of course, most likely to be divine. What is at issue here is not whether σώζω + ὑπό usually conforms to the pattern Pardee describes, but whether this construction *must* indicate an animate saviour. To make this case Pardee has to show that a *different* construction would have been used if salvation by the 'non-human' burning process were intended. Pardee cannot meet this requirement because no such construction exists.[9]

8. This issue is discussed more fully below.
9. Perhaps surprisingly, Milavec (1995: 136) appears to accept Pardee's observation as a potentially valid argument against his position.

Pardee's second objection is very much more substantial and revolves around the semantic range of καταθεματος and the likelihood that this word would be used to describe the fiery test as conceived by Milavec. There are some difficulties with Milavec's view of the nature of the test. It is necessary to consider his conception in greater detail before returning to Pardee's second objection.

Milavec understands the burning process of *Did.* 16.5 to be the fire of *final* judgment. Thus he can say 'The eschatological fire of the *Didache* functions "to utterly destroy" (ἀπόλλυμι being used as an emphatic form of ὄλλυμι) and only takes effect during the last days' (1995: 137 n. 15). It is because Milavec sees the 'false prophets, world-deceiver, etc.' as all utterly destroyed by this process that he is willing to argue (1995: 151–54) against majority opinion (cf. section 2 in this chapter), that lines describing final judgment have *not* been lost from the end of *Did.* 16. This view is also necessary to Milavec's ultimate thesis that the *Didache* bears witness to the ancient roots of the doctrine of purgatory.

There are, however, considerable difficulties with the equation of the burning process with the final judgment. For this judgment to fall *before* the arrival of the Lord on the clouds (16.8) is, to say the least, surprising. Milavec (1995: 151) attempts to address this problem by suggesting that

> The final coming of the Lord in glory to gather the elect into the kingdom (*Did* 16.8 supported by 9.4 and 10.5) needs to occur unimpeded by the world-deceiver and his followers. Accordingly, the *Didache* envisions the Lord's judgment coming upon the earth, first, to break the power of the world-deceiver and to destroy all hindrances to the kingdom.

Milavec's understanding of events is not impossible, but the idea that the Lord stands in the wings while some other agent executes the final judgment so that he may come 'unimpeded' is not paralleled in any other Jewish or Christian text.

Further, Milavec overstates the case when he reads ἀπόλλυμι as an emphatic form of ὄλλυμι meaning 'to utterly destroy'. The phrase used to describe those who succumb to the fiery text is 'σκανδαλισθήσονται πολλοὶ καὶ ἀπολοῦνται'. Ἀπολοῦνται uses the middle voice of ἀπόλλυμι, which may also be translated as 'lost'. This word for lost is used to describe the sheep and son that are lost and then found in Lk. 15.4, 6, 24. It also applies to sheep gone astray in Mt. 10.6; 15.24 and remnants of bread in Jn 6.12. If ἀπόλλυμι may be taken in this way then the preceding 'σκανδαλισθήσονται' may be read in the more usual sense of 'shall cause to stumble/lead into sin', rather than Milavec's somewhat strained 'will be entrapped' (Milavec 1995: 137 n. 15). In all, the line 'σκανδαλισ-θήσονται πολλοὶ καὶ ἀπολοῦνται' is most easily read as inferring that the test causes some Christians[10] to fall into sin and thus to be lost/ separated from the faithful flock. This is a process which precedes the final judgment, it does not coincide with it.

These difficulties with Milavec's view do not arise if, instead of assuming that the purifying fire is that of the final judgment, the fire is seen as representing persecution. As quoted above, Milavec himself notes: 'The term πύρωσις (burning process) is a derivative of πῦρ (fire) and is only found once in the New Testament (1 Pet 4:12)'. This unique recurrence of πύρωσις deserves close attention. 1 Pet. 4.12-13 reads:

> Beloved, do not be surprised at the fiery ordeal (πυρώσει) that is taking place among you to test (πειρασμὸν) you, as though something strange were happening to you. But rejoice insofar as you are sharing Christ's sufferings, so that you may also be glad and shout for joy when his glory is revealed.

Thus, the 'burning process' in this text is used to describe a time of persecution (which ultimately leads to salvation) and not the final fire.

If πύρωσις is seen as a time of persecution prior to the final judgment, then several details of the *Didache*'s apocalypse[11] fall into place. First, the flow from *Did.* 16.4 to 16.5 makes sense. Thus, the appearance of the world-deceiver does not simply end in his being thrown into the fire before the Lord has even arrived (16.8). Rather, the arrival of the world-deceiver provides the *means* by which Christians will be subjected to a purifying fire of persecution.[12] In the course of this persecution some will fall away and be lost from the community, but others will be proved true, and thus will be saved to rejoice when Christ's glory is revealed (cf. 1 Pet. 4.12-13). The curse by which the latter are saved, therefore, represents persecution at the hands of the world-deceiver. Thus, paradoxically, the agent of their salvation is the persecution which reveals the persevering faith of those who, thereby, are saved.

I return now to Pardee's second objection to Milavec's thesis. Pardee contests that the semantic range of κατάθεματος is unlikely to stretch to the burning fire of testing, as conceived by Milavec. This objection is justi-

---

10. Niederwimmer (1998: 221) notes: 'The continuation (v.5b) shows that in fact it is not the whole human creation that is in view, but only the Christians. Thus it is probably the threat of persecution that is being presented here.'
11. The use of the term 'apocalypse' to describe *Did.* 16.3-6, 8-9 is one of convenience. A more accurate description would be 'eschatological discourse'.
12. See n. 10, above.

fied in that Milavec offers no explanation as to why 'κατάθεματος' should be used to describe the eschatological fire. The difficulties here are some-what similar to those associated with calling Jesus 'the curse'. First, there are no other examples of such a designation, a point made by Pardee (1995: 174). Second, it is not immediately clear why 'the curse' should be chosen as a suitable means of describing an act initiated by God for the ultimate salvation of his faithful people.

If, on the other hand, the 'burning process' refers to a persecution of Christians initiated by the world-deceiver, then 'κατάθεματος' is an entirely feasible means of describing this event. Pardee (1995: 174) notes: 'when ἀνάθεμα can be translated as "curse" it is virtually always in the sense of a pronouncement and not of its ramifications'. This observation causes Pardee (1995: 175) to conclude: 'It is...likely that the reference is to Jesus as an "accursed person"'. By the same logic, however, the pro-nouncement of cursed status could be directed at Jesus' followers. If the cursing of Christians was an element of the persecution anticipated by *Did.* 16.5, then the description of this event as 'the curse' (meaning 'the reli-gious anathema laid on us by others')[13] creates no difficulties.

The interpretation of 'the curse that saves' as a reference to testing persecution, which ultimately reveals those who are worthy of salvation, is supported by the presence of this idea in several other early Christian eschatologies. For example: Mk 13.9-13a speaks of the various persecu-tions prior to the End and then notes (in v. 13b): 'But the one who endures to the end shall be saved'; Lk. 21.19 and Mt. 10.22; 24.13 are parallel to Mark's text and express the identical idea; 2 Thess. 1.4-6 speaks of perse-cutions and afflictions making Christians worthy of the kingdom of God; 1 Pet. 4.12-13, as already noted, speaks of purifying endurance under per-secution as the precursor of glorification; Revelation's constant theme is that of salvation through steadfast endurance under religious persecution, for example Rev. 2.10; 3.9-10; 6.9-10; 7.14-17; 12.11; 20.4; 21.7. Reve-lation's vision of the New Jerusalem where every κατάθεμα will be no longer is entirely consistent with the *Didache*, when κατάθεματος is un-derstood as referring to religious persecution. In each of these cases, with the exception of 1 Peter, there is an association between this persecution and the coming of a figure parallel to the *Didache*'s 'world-deceiver' who comes 'as a son of God' (*Did.* 16.5). In all three Synoptic Gospels, per-

---

13. As, for example, the Jews are said to do in Justin, *Dial.* 47.4.11. Evidence that this experience is anticipated, or is already being experienced, may perhaps be found in 1 Cor. 12.3.

secution is mentioned in association with the coming of false Christs (Mt. 24.23-24; Mk 13.21-22; Lk. 21.8); in Mt. 24.15-16 and Mk 13.14-15 tribulation is closely associated with the appearance of the abomination of desolation. An equivalent figure may also be found in Paul's 'man of lawlessness' (2 Thess. 2.3) and Revelation's 'beast who makes war on the saints' (Rev. 13.7).

In conclusion, the interpretation of the paradoxical idea 'the curse that saves' as a reference to the world-deceiver's testing persecution is here preferred to previously proposed alternatives for the following reasons. (1) The extant text, 'ὑπ' αὐτοῦ τοῦ καταθέματος', may be taken without speculative amendment to 'ἀπ' αὐτοῦ τοῦ καταθέματος'. (2) The grammar of *Did.* 16.5 may be read in the most conventional way; namely, as referring to 'by the curse itself', rather than 'by him who is a curse'. (3) No appeal to a very specific, external (and possibly anachronistic) Pauline interpretative key is required. (4) If the very rare term 'τὸ κατάθεμα' is interpreted as referring to persecution, then this use may be seen as consistent with, rather than directly contradictory to, its use in Rev. 22.3. (5) This solution does not necessitate the curious proposal that 'the curse' was widely used by Christians as a reverent appellation for Christ. (6) The dual effect of the purifying fire in *Did.* 16.5 (for both salvation and exclusion) is taken into account. (7) The semantic range of 'καταθέματος' is not breached. (8) this interpretation causes *Did.* 16 to express the idea that faithful endurance under anathematizing persecution leads to salvation; this concept is consistent with eschatological expectation expressed in all three Synoptic Gospels, 2 Thessalonians, 1 Peter and Revelation.

2. *The Lost Ending of the* Didache

Tuckett (1996: 99) observes that 'it is universally agreed that the text at the end of the *Didache* here is in some disarray and that some further text has probably got lost'.[14]

---

14. Scholars who perceive a lost ending include: Aldridge (1999); Audet (1958: 73–74); Rordorf and Tuilier (1978: 107, 199); Draper (1983: 326) and Wengst (1984: 20). Wengst is unusual in speculating as to the content of the final clause which he proposes (p. 91) to be 'ἀποδοῦναι ἑκάστῳ κατὰ τὴν πρᾶξιν αὐτοῦ', on the basis of the longer and more complex parallel text in the *Apostolic Constitutions* (see Tuckett 1996: 99 n. 34). Aldridge (1999: 7) states (without naming the scholars concerned) that 'Some *Didache* editions and commentaries attempt to justify chapter 16's ending at the words "the clouds of heaven" (a truncation of Dan. 7:13) by presenting parallel quotations which stop at the same words (such as Matt 26:64, Mk 14:62, or Justin

Four observations suggest that the Jerusalem manuscript of the *Didache* does not contain a complete version of chapter 16. First, the abrupt closure at 16.8 is narratologically unsatisfactory. The difficulty lies in the incomplete convergence of the two central characters: the world-deceiver and the Lord. As the text stands, according to the above interpretation of the curse that saves, the world-deceiver persecutes humanity in 16.5 and then remains on stage. In 16.8 the dramatic arrival on the clouds brings the Lord onto the same stage but with no apparent consequence for the drama. The situation left by the abrupt ending of the Jerusalem manuscript is that of two archetypal protagonists forever prevented from bringing their meeting to a conclusion.[15]

Second, a number of Christian eschatological narratives depict the arrival of the Lord followed by a scene of judgment. Thus, in Mt. 25.31-46 the Son of man comes in his glory and separates the sheep from the goats, sending the latter to eternal punishment and the former to eternal life. In 2 Thess. 2.3-11 Paul is explicit about the fate of the lawless one; he is doomed to destruction (2.3) and will be destroyed by the Lord Jesus (2.8). This specific judgment is also accompanied by the kind of general judgment and salvation envisaged by Matthew (2 Thess. 2.12 and 13-14 respectively). Revelation provides a fuller account of a similar storyline. In Rev. 19.11 the Messiah figure arrives from heaven, engages in battle with and defeats the beast (19.19-21), and a scene of final judgment ultimately ensues where all are either punished or rewarded according to their deeds (20.11-15). Inasmuch as *Did.* 16 should be seen as parallel to these texts, therefore it may be expected that the arrival of the Lord on the clouds will be followed by, now lost, scenes of judgment and reward.

The particular format of the Jerusalem manuscript also suggests that its scribe wished to indicate the absence of final lines from the text. This point is made by Aldridge (1999: 2–4):

Martyr's *Dialogue with Trypho*, 120)'. However, as Aldridge (1999: 7–8) points out, the fact that *Did.* 16 is an eschatological text means that the parallels to be examined should not be Jesus' trial but the eschatological discourses such as Mt. 24.30. Milavec (1995: 151–54) argues against the existence of a lost ending. His reasoning is, however, strongly influenced by his desire to see the test in 16.5 as the act of final judgment. The weaknesses of this case have been considered in the immediately preceding section.

15. Mk 13 offers no account of a direct conflict between the abomination of desolation and the Son of man. As such this appears to present an example of another occasion where 'narratological expectation' is violated. It is not within the scope of this volume to explain this phenomena; however, I aim to do so in a further study.

The Jerusalem manuscript contains seven early Christian writings (plus two other short compositions), extending for 120 folia (240 pages) almost without a break. Each new work begins on the next line following the end of the previous work, with no intervening space, and is indicated only by a *quadrupunctum* before the title and a great initial before the text proper... The work's single scribe, Leon, wrote in small, neat script, abbreviating heavily, using all available space... There is no unused space in the Jerusalem manuscript.

Except for in the *Didache*, that is, which ends in the middle of fol. 80b, with the entire half-page being left blank – an extraordinary omission! ... Leon also punctuates the end of the *Didache* with the lower point used to terminate sentences (except at the end of a work), omitting the *bipunctum cum obelo* which he normally uses in the manuscript to indicate the end of a literary work. This point is of considerable importance since Leon was highly conscious of properly formatting the various elements of a work and there are no other such 'errors' in the photographed portions of the manuscript. It is therefore probable that Leon knew his exemplar was defective and left space accordingly.

The incomplete nature of the Jerusalem manuscript is further indicated by the appearance of additional material, beyond 16.8, in texts that appear to depend on *Did.* 16. The continuation of *Did.* 16 provided by the *Apostolic Constitutions* Book VII (hereafter, *Const.*) is set out below.[16]

Did. 16	*Const.* VII
16.3 Ἐν γὰρ ταῖς ἐσχάταις ἡμέραις πληθυνθήσονται οἱ ψευδοπροφῆται καὶ οἱ φθορεῖς, καὶ στραφήσονται τὰ πρόβατα εἰς λύκους καὶ ἡ ἀγάπη στραφήσεταιμ εἰς μῖσος·	32.1 Ἐν γὰρ ταῖς ἐσχάταις ἡμέραις πληθυνθήσονται οἱ ψευδοπροφῆται καὶ οἱ φθορεῖς τοῦ λόγου, καὶ στραφήσονται τὰ πρόβατα εἰς λύκους καὶ ἡ ἀγάπη εἰς μῖσος·
16.4a Αὐξανούσης γὰρ τῆς ἀνομιας, μισήσουσιν ἀλλήλους	πληθυνθείσης γὰρ τῆς ἀνομιας, ψυγήσεται ἡ ἀγάπη τῶν πολλῶν, μισήσουσιν γὰρ ἀλλήλους οἱ ἄνθρωποι
καὶ διώξουσι καὶ παραδώσουσι.	καὶ διώξουσι καὶ προδώσουσι.
16.4b καὶ τότε φανήσεται ὁ κοσμοπλανὴς ὡς υἱὸς θεοῦ καὶ ποιήσει σημεῖα καὶ τέρατα, καὶ ἡ γῆ παραδοθήσεται εἰς χεῖρας αὐτοῦ, καὶ ποιήσει ἀθέμιτα, ἃ οὐδέποτε γέγονεν ἐξ αἰῶνος.	32.2 καὶ τότε φανήσεται ὁ κοσμοπλανος,

16. The Greek text is taken from Metzger (1987: 62, 64). The lettered verse divisions are my own and are intended to assist the discussion in § 4, below.

Did. 16	*Const.* VII
	ὁ τῆς ἀληθείας ἐχθρός, ὁ τοῦ ψεύδους προστάτης, ὃν ὁ Κύριος Ἰησοῦς ἀνελεῖ τῷ πνεύματι τοῦ στόματος αὐτοῦ ὁ διὰ χειλέων ἀναιπῶν ἀσεβῆ·
16.5 Τότε ἥξει ἡ κτίσις τῶν ἀνθρώπων εἰς τὴν πύρωσιν τῆς δοκιμασίας, <u>καὶ σκανδαλισθήσονται πολλοὶ</u> καὶ ἀπολοῦνται, <u>οἱ δὲ ὑπομείναντες</u> ἐν τῇ πίστει αὐτῶν <u>σωθήσονται</u> ὑπ᾽ αὐτοῦ τοῦ καταθέματος.	<u>καὶ σκανδαλισθήσονται πολλοὶ</u> ἐπ᾽ αὐτῳ, <u>οἱ δὲ ὑπομείναντες</u> εἰς τέλος, οὗτοι <u>σωθήσονται</u>.
16.6 <u>Καὶ τότε φανήσεται</u> τὰ σημεῖα τῆς ἀληθείας· πρῶτον <u>σημεῖον</u> ἐκπετάσεως <u>ἐν</u> <u>οὐρανῳ</u>, <u>εἶτα</u> σημεῖον <u>φωνῆς</u> <u>σάλπιγγος</u>, καὶ τὸ τρίτον ἀνάστασις νεκρῶν·	32.3 <u>Καὶ τότε φανήσεται</u> τὸ <u>σημεῖον</u> τοῦ Υἱοῦ τοῦ ἀνθρώπου <u>ἐν</u> τῷ <u>οὐρανῳ</u>, <u>εἶτα</u> <u>φωνὴ</u> <u>σάλπιγγος</u> ἔσται δι᾽ ἀρχαγγέλου καὶ μεταχὺ ἀναβίωσις τῶν κεκοιμημένων.
16.8 <u>Τότε</u> ὄψεται ὁ κόσμος τὸ <u>κύρ</u>ιον ἐρχόμενον <u>ἐπάνω τῶν νεφελῶν</u> τοῦ οὐρανοῦ ...	32.4a Καὶ <u>τότε</u> ἥξει ὁ <u>Κύρ</u>ιος καὶ πάντες οἱ ἅγιοι μετ᾽ αὐτοῦ ἐν συσσεισμῷ <u>ἐπάνω τῶν νεφελῶν</u> μετ᾽ ἀγγέλων δυνάμεως αὐτοῦ 32.4b ἐπὶ θρόνου βασιλείας, 32.4c κατακρῖναι τὸν κοσμοπλάνον διάβολον 32.4d καὶ ἀποδοῦναι ἑκάστῳ κατὰ τὴν πρᾶξιν αὐτοῦ. 32.5a Τότε ἀπελεύσονται οἱ μὲν πονηροὶ εἰς αἰώνιον κόλασιν, οἱ δὲ δίκαιοι πορεύσονται εἰς ζωὴν αἰώνιον, 32.5b κληρονομοῦντες ἐκεῖνα, 32.5c ἃ ὀφθαλμὸς οὐκ εἶδεν καὶ οὖς οὐκ ἤκουσεν καὶ ἐπὶ καρδίαν ἀνθρώπου οὐκ ἀνέβη, ἃ ἡτοίμασεν ὁ θεὸς τοῖς ἀγαπῶσιν αὐτόν, 32.5d καὶ χαρήσονται ἐν βασιλείᾳ τοῦ θεοῦ τῇ ἐν Χριστῷ Ἰησοῦ.

A longer ending was also apparently recorded in the Georgian version of the *Didache*.[17] This translation is from Aldridge (1999: 7):

> Then the world will see our Lord Jesus Christ, the Son of Man who is [simultaneously] Son of God, coming on the clouds with power and great glory in His holy righteousness to repay every man according to his works before all mankind and before the angels. Amen.

Aldridge (1999: 8–10) draws attention to a third witness to a longer ending of the *Didache* which has been largely overlooked. This text is the *De abrenuntiatione in baptismate* ('Baptismal Renunciation', hereafter *Renunciation*) of St Boniface. Aldridge (1999: 8–9) notes that this text is 'an eighth century catechetical sermon of St Boniface, reminding new conerts of their baptismal vows in connection with the approaching Advent season, and clearly based on the *Didache*.[18] *Renunciation* opens with the "way of death", summarises the *Didache*'s middle chapters into a list of Christian duties, and continues [with a scene of final judgment and reward].'[19]

17. The Georgian version of the *Didache*, apparently written in the early nineteenth century, was found and copied by Simon Pheikrishvili in 1923. It has subsequently been lost and thus no verification of the text can take place. For this reason the value of the text as a witness to the content of the ending of the *Didache* should not be given any weight. However, the fact that the text appears to have had some continuation beyond *Did.* 16.8 may be taken as evidence, however insignificant, of a continuation of some kind in the original *Didache*.

18. Aldridge's claim that *Renunciation* is 'clearly based on the *Didache*' requires some expansion. The widespread nature of the Two Ways tradition means that it may not automatically be assumed that Boniface derived his 'way of death' from the original text of the *Didache*. However, there are a number of points of contact between *Renunciation* and the *Didache*. First, they are both explicitly presented as pre-baptismal catechesis. Second, they both preserve the negative form of the golden rule. Third, they both include reference to the return of Christ/the Lord and the resurrection of the dead. It is also striking that both *Renunciation* and *Const.* should combine this type of material with almost identical visions of the final judgment and reward – despite the lack of any other sign that Boniface had knowledge of *Const.* On balance, therefore, Aldridge's claim should perhaps be modified to the claim that *Renunciation* is 'probably', rather than 'clearly', based on the *Didache*.

19. Aldridge (1999: 8 n. 20) notes the various editions of this text: '*Renunciation* comes from a manuscript in the Abbey of St Hilary in Melk, Austria (where it is entitled *Ammonitio sive praedictio sancti Bonifacii episcopi de abrenuntiatione in baptismate*) and is given in Bernhard Pez' *Thesaurus anecdotorum novissimus* (1721–29; vol. 4), Edmond Martène's *Veterum scriptorum* (1724–33), Martin Kropff's *Bibliotheca Mellicensis* (1747), and J.-P. Migne's *Patrologia Latina* (1844–55; vol. 89, col. 87, Sermon 15).'

The striking similarities between the ending of Boniface's *Renunciation* and *Const.*'s version of the end of the *Didache* is highly unlikely to be the product of Boniface's dependence on *Const.* since none of that work's extensive additions to the rest of the text of the *Didache* also appear in Boniface's sermon.

In conclusion, the belief that the *Didache* originally extended beyond 16.8a is supported by narratological study, by comparison with some New Testament eschatological storylines, by evidence from the punctuation and layout of the Jerusalem manuscript, and by comparison of the Jerusalem manuscript with the versions of *Did.* 16 preserved in *Const.*, the Georgian version and the *Renunciation* of Boniface. A detailed reconstruction of the content of this lost ending is offered in section 4, below.

3. *The Redactional Status of* Didache *16.7*

The attempted reconstruction of the closing lines of the *Didache* will be assisted if the history of *Did.* 16.7 may first be established.

Niederwimmer (1998: 225 n. 27) observes that 'Verse 7 is a gloss… Verse 8 follows well after v.6.' Niederwimmer's point is entirely justified. In the absence of *Did.* 16.7 the eschatological discourse exhibits a well-ordered narrative structure. *Did.* 16.3-5 consists of three paragraphs. The first describes signs leading up to the arrival of the world-deceiver. The second (introduced by καὶ τότε) describes that arrival. The third (introduced by τότε) describes the critical consequence of that arrival. Correspondingly 16.6 (introduced by καὶ τότε) depicts signs leading up to the arrival of the Lord, 16.8 (introduced by τότε) depicts that arrival, and the lost ending may be expected to show some consequence of that arrival. The presence of the explanatory aside at *Did.* 16.7 disrupts this build-up to the arrival of the Lord by focusing attention away from the signs that precede his coming and onto the identity of his companions.

If, as discussed above, it is likely that the original text of the *Didache* continued into a scene of judgment, then the superfluity of *Did.* 16.7 is further emphasized. The addition of 16.7 creates a situation where the only characters capable of appearing in the heavenly court are those who have *already* been judged holy enough to enjoy resurrection. Without the intervention of *Did.* 16.7, however, the flow of expected story events is entirely conventional. Thus, all the dead are raised at the coming of the Lord (as, for example, in Rev. 20.11-15 and Mt. 25.31-46); they are then judged by him and sent to their punishment or reward.

The possibility that the full version of *Did.* 16 would have made narrative sense without the inclusion of 16.7 provides a clue as to why this verse may have been added in the extant shorter text. That is to say, once the scene of final judgment is lost from the manuscript a difficulty in the theology of the storyline appears. Without the insertion of 16.7 the shortened text could be taken as making no differentiation between the fate of the just and the unjust, since all, according to 16.6, are apparently resurrected without discrimination. *Did.* 16.7 introduces a means of creating an element of differentiation by stating that not all the dead will be raised, but only the holy ones.

If it may be concluded that the inclusion of *Did.* 16.7 makes best sense if the original ending of the *Didache* had *already* been lost, then this interpolation should be seen as separate from every other contribution to the *Didache* and unique to one particular manuscript tradition, of which the Jerusalem manuscript is a member.

4. *A Reconstruction of the Lost Ending of the* Didache

Textual reconstructions generally offer few solid results in return for the considerable energies they consume. It is perhaps for this reason that few scholars have attempted to reconstruct the lost ending of the *Didache*.[20] This caution obscures the possibility, however, that there may be sufficient evidence to allow a more thorough investigation of this question than has thus far been considered.

As observed in section 2, above, there is good reason to suppose, from a narratological point of view, that the missing text contained some mention of a meeting between the world-deceiver and the Lord. In this section it was also noted that a narrative pattern in some contemporary apocalypses suggests that a scene of general judgment is likely to have followed the arrival of the Lord.

In addition to these general expectations there is also evidence, of a kind, for the ending of the *Didache* in *Const.* VII.32.1-5. It is certainly the case that *Const.* frequently adds to, and omits from, the text of the *Didache*, as well as introducing assimilations to the text of the New Testament. However, the fact that the text of *Const.* does, as independently expected, describe a meeting of the two protagonists and a scene of general judgment suggests that this version of the ending bears some relation to the

---

20. As noted above, Wengst attempts a short conclusion on the basis of *Const.* Aldridge (1999) attempts to show that *Const.*'s conclusion is at least approximately correct.

original. The precise nature of that relationship cannot always be established, but certain clues do suggest that some parts of the *Const.* ending are close to the original ending of the *Didache*.

A further element of external evidence for the origin of the *Const.* ending is provided by the *Renunciation* of Boniface. Both the *Renunciation* and *Const.* appear to depend upon the *Didache*,[21] but Boniface shows no knowledge of *Const.* It is significant, therefore, that these two texts agree on two elements that might come from the proposed lost ending of the *Didache*.

> *Const.* '…and render to every one according to his deeds.
> 32.5 Then shall the wicked go away into everlasting punishment,
> but the righteous shall enter life eternal,
> inheriting those things which eye has not seen,
> and ear has not heard,
> and which has not arisen in the heart of man
> those things which God has prepared for those who love him…'
>
> *Renunciation* '… Believe in Christ's coming, the resurrection of the flesh,
> and the judgment of all men.
> Evil men will be assigned to eternal fire
> and righteous men to eternal life. …
> there the righteous shall shine like the sun,
> since eye has not seen,
> and ear has not heard,
> nor has arisen in the heart of man
> that which God has prepared for those that love him…'[22]

The agreement between *Renunciation* and *Const.* regarding a scene of general judgment that leads to a separation of the evil and the righteous (expressed in slightly different terms), with an identical, triadic description of the final reward of the just, is striking. This level of agreement suggests that these elements have a viable claim to inclusion in a reconstruction of the lost ending of the *Didache*.

The principal point that counts against this conclusion is, however, the observation that *Const.* sometimes assimilates its text to New Testament parallels, or simply incorporates New Testament material. It is possible therefore that, despite the apparently independent agreement between Boniface and *Const.*, these elements of *Const.* are dependent on close parallels

---

21. This dependence is more readily apparent in the case of *Const.* (see n. 18, above).

22. Aldridge (1999: 8 n. 20) provides information about Boniface and bibliographical references to copies of the full *Renunciation*.

in Mt. 16.27; 25.46 and 1 Cor. 2.9. However, arguments against this possibility may be made in each case.

4.1. *The Immediate Continuation of* Didache *16.8*

> Then the world shall see the Lord coming
> upon the clouds of heaven *and all his holy ones with him*

Before venturing to analyse those parts of *Const.* that are supported by Boniface's *Renunciation*, it is necessary to consider the content of the line immediately continuing from the end of *Did.* 16.8, as preserved in the Jerusalem manuscript.

The interpolation at *Did.* 16.7 provides an initial indication that *Did.* 16.8 may originally have read, 'Τότε ὄψεται ὁ κόσμος τὸ κύριον ἐρχόμενον ἐπάνω τῶν νεφελῶν τοῦ οὐρανοῦ *καὶ πάντες οἱ ἅγιοι μετ᾽ αὐτοῦ*. It was suggested in section 3.3 that this interpolation served to make good a theological deficiency in the truncated text. It is, of course, possible that the interpolator gained inspiration for this move from Zech. 14.5, independent of any prompting from the *Didache*. However, it is also possible that this quotation was seen as relevant to the case because it was present in the *Didache* itself, in text beyond the extant 16.8 and just before the damaged manuscript broke off. Thus, if this verse originally read: 'Then the world shall see the Lord coming upon the clouds of heaven and all his holy ones with him...', then the interpolator of 16.7 may have calculated that the 'holy ones' were with the Lord because it was they who had been raised in the resurrection of 16.6. This provides a rationale for the quotation inserted at 16.7, which ensures that the selective nature of the resurrection is made explicit. The resulting text would then read:

> ...and third, resurrection of the dead – 16.7 not of all, however, but as it has been said, 'The Lord shall come and all his holy ones with him.' – 16.8 Then the world shall see the Lord coming upon the clouds of heaven and all his holy ones with him [original damage occurs after this point].

The closing repetition prompted, I propose, the cropping of the damaged text so that it appears as we now know it in the Jerusalem manuscript.

The inclusion of a mention of accompanying 'holy ones' in the original text of *Did.* 16.8 is also attractive because it provides an answer to a question posed by the interpretation of *Did.* 16.5 offered above. Here it was argued that the 'testing fire' of 16.5 referred to persecution at the hands of the world-deceiver. If it may be assumed that such an ultimate persecution would have resulted in death, then the question of what it means to be 'saved' in this context is raised. One possibility is that these faithful martyrs are 'saved', through death, to join the heavenly army of 'holy ones' who accompany the Lord at his final coming. This possibility arises because of the presence of a similar pattern of events in 1 Thessalonians and Revelation. In 1 Thess. 4.14 Paul expresses his belief that God will bring with him at his coming those who have died.

The parallel between the *Didache* and Revelation is particularly extensive. Both feature an antichristian figure who claims divinity and who persecutes God's holy ones:

Didache's World-Deceiver	Revelation's Beast
• acts as son of God (16.4)	• utters blasphemous words (13.5)
• performs signs and wonders (16.4)	• signs performed by the second beast deceive the inhabitants of the earth (13.14)
• the earth is betrayed into his hands (16.4)	• all the inhabitants of the earth worship it (13.8)
• performs ultimate blasphemies (16.4)	• utters blasphemies against God and his dwelling (13.6)
• creates testing fire of persecution (16.5)	• makes war on the holy ones and conquers (13.7)

The Christian response called for by both texts is also similar:

Didache	Revelation
• but the one enduring in the faith shall be saved (16.5)	• Here is a call for the endurance of the holy ones, those who keep the commandments of God and the faith of Jesus (14.12; cf. also 2.10; 3.9-10; 6.9-10; 7.14-17; 12.11; 20.4; 21.7)

Beyond this point the extant text of the *Didache* provides no further information regarding the fate of those who remain faithful during the world-deceiver's persecution. Revelation, on the other hand, does describe their progress. Thus, in Revelation, the martyrs who pass through the tribulation are caught up to heaven after the pattern of their Lord (cf. 7.9-17). There they gather to form an eschatological army on Mount Zion (Rev. 14.1-5; cf. 6.9-11). Then, at the last, they accompany the warrior Messiah as he comes to earth for the final judgment of the beast and false prophet (Rev. 19.14).[23] If Revelation and *Did.* 16 may be seen as parallel expressions of a similar eschatological scheme,[24] then a mention of accompanying

23. For an attempt to expound this storyline in full see Garrow (1997).
24. That Revelation and the *Didache* belong to a similar stream of tradition is

'holy ones' in the lost section of *Did.* 16.8 is consistent with a continuation of this parallel.

More specific support for the originality of the line, 'and all his holy ones with him', may be found in the version of *Did.* 16.8 recorded in *Const.* 32.4a:

> *Did.* 16.8   Then the world shall see the Lord coming upon the clouds of heaven…
>
> *Const.* 32.4a   And then shall come the Lord, and all his holy ones with him, with great concussion upon the clouds, with the angels of this power.

A comparison of these two texts shows that, for some reason, the Constitutionist chose to change the word order of his original source. A motive for such a change may be proposed if the original text read, 'Then the world shall see the Lord, coming on the clouds of heaven *and all his holy ones with him*'. This line invites an interpretation, since the precise identity of the 'holy ones' is unclear (especially given the omission of the fiery testing in *Const.*'s version of *Did.* 16.5). The Constitutionist appears to offer an interpretation of the 'holy ones' by presenting the event of the Lord's coming in two parallel versions.

The first line is thus reordered by removing the reference to the Lord's coming 'on the clouds'. An image of an arrival on the clouds is then used to open the next line. This arrival is unlikely to refer to the following angels because angels are never described as travelling on the clouds in the biblical texts; this is a divine mode.[25] This means that the re-use of the phrase 'on the clouds' effectively redescribes the arrival of the Lord so that, 'with great concussion upon the clouds' serves as a restatement of 'And then shall come the Lord'. The two halves of *Const.* 32.4a may thus be seen as two descriptions of the same event:

καὶ τότε ἥξει ὁ Κύριος…………………… καὶ πάντες οἱ ἅγιοι μετ᾽ αὐτοῦ
ἐν συσσεισμῷ ἐπάνω τῶν νεφελῶν ……… μετ᾽ ἀγγέλων δυνάμεως αὐτοῦ.

suggested by Barr (1986: 253–55). The links between the broader Johannine tradition, in the shape of John's Gospel, and the *Didache* are considered, albeit briefly, in J. Betz (1996: 255–56).

25. Dan. 7.13 could be interpreted otherwise; however, even here the rider is not angelic. God is described as coming or riding on the clouds in: Exod. 19.9; 2 Sam. 22.10; Pss. 18.9-12; 68.4; 104.3; Ezek. 1.4; Nah. 1.3. Cloud is theophanic in: Exod. 13.21; 1 Kgs 8.10 and Ezek. 10.4.

If the same event is described in both lines, then the 'holy ones' who accompany the Lord in the first line are apparently interpreted, by the Constitutionist, as angels in the second.

The fact that *Const.* preserves a reference to 'holy ones' even though these figures are immediately interpreted as angels, suggests that a reference to 'holy ones' was present in its source. This is the case simply because it is unlikely that the Constitutionist would have introduced ambiguous characters such as 'holy ones' only to have to immediately clarify their identity.

The original status of 'and all his holy ones with him' is supported by one further detail. The phrase, 'coming upon the clouds of heaven' in *Did.* 16.8 alludes to Dan. 7.13. It is surprising, therefore, that the one who is seen so coming is neither Daniel's 'one like a son of man', nor even the evangelist's 'Son of man', but rather, 'the Lord'. It is possible that the Didachist simply changed 'Son of man' to 'Lord' for some unknowable reason; however, another explanation is suggested if the original text contained a reference to accompanying 'holy ones'. In this circumstance *Did.* 16.8 may be seen as owing a debt to both Dan. 7.13 *and* Zech. 14.5 (LXX). If the Didachist sought to combine these two established visions of the coming Judge/King, then the *Didache*'s use of κύριος, rather than ὡς υἱὸς ἀνθρώπου, is explicable:

Zech. 14.5	Dan. 7.13
Καὶ ἥξει <u>κύριος</u> ὁ θεός μου,	... ἐπὶ τῶν νεφελῶν τοῦ οὐρανοῦ
<u>καὶ πάντες οἱ ἅγιοι μετ' αὐτοῦ</u>	ὡς υἱὸς ἀνθρώπου ἤρχετο,

Did. 16.8 τότε ὄψεται ὁ κόσμος
τὸν <u>κύριον</u> ἐρχόμενον ἐπάνω τῶν νεφελῶν τοῦ οὐρανοῦ,
<u>καὶ πάντες οἱ ἅγιοι μετ' αὐτοῦ</u>

In summary, a reconstruction of *Did.* 16.8 which includes the words, '...καὶ πάντες οἱ ἅγιοι μετ' αὐτοῦ', serves to explain two features of the Jerusalem manuscript. First, it provides a rationale for the wording of the interpolation at *Did.* 16.7. Second, it provides an explanation for the use of κύριος rather than ὡς υἱὸς ἀνθρώπου, in the *Didache*'s version of Dan. 7.13. This reconstruction also provides a reason for the Constitutionist's rearrangement of *Did.* 16.8 in the composition of *Const.* 32.4a. Finally, this version of *Did.* 16.8 explains the fate of the faithful ones of *Did.* 16.5, and thereby conforms to the pattern of eschatological expectation expressed in 1 Thessalonians, and more specifically, in Revelation.

4.2. *The Authenticity of* Const. *32.5a*

> Then shall go away the evil into eternal punishment
> but the righteous shall enter into life eternal

Having made an assessment of the likely continuation of *Did.* 16.8 it is possible to return to the question of how much of *Const.* 32 derives directly from the original text of the *Didache*. It was noted above that although there is apparently independent agreement between Boniface and *Const.* with regard to the *Didache*'s final lines, it is possible that these elements of the *Const.* are in fact assimilations to close parallels in Mt. 16.27; 25.46 and 1 Cor. 2.9. This section focuses on this issue with respect to the relationship between *Const.* 32.5a, *Did.* 16 and Mt. 25.46.

A comparison of *Const.* 32.5a and Mt. 25.46 shows that, while the vocabulary is almost identical, the word order reversals in *Const.* create a poetic balance between the two parallel lines, while Matthew's version is more straightforward.

Const. 32.5a

| τότε | ἀπελεύσονται | οἱ μέν πονηροὶ | εἰς | αἰώνιον | κόλασιν, |
| | οἱ δὲ δίκαιοι | πορεύσονται | εἰς | ζωὴν | αἰώνιον, |

Mt. 25.46

| καὶ | ἀπελεύσονται | οὗτοι | εἰς | κόλασιν | αἰώνιον, |
| | οἱ δὲ δίκαιοι | | εἰς | ζωὴν | αἰώνιον |

If *Const.* 32.5a were dependent on Mt. 25.46, then why was Matthew's straightforward wording not simply copied? It is unlikely that the Constitutionist altered Matthew's word order to suit a preference for this more elaborate style, since the Constitutionist chose not to preserve a similar parallelism while copying *Did.* 16.3b.

Did. 16.3b

| καὶ | στραφήσονται | τὰ πρόβατα | εἰς | λύκους |
| | ἡ ἀγάπη | στραφήσεται | εἰς | μῖσος· |

Const. 32.1

| καὶ | στραφήσονται | τὰ πρόβατα | εἰς | λύκους |
| καὶ | | ἡ ἀγάπη | εἰς | μῖσος· |

If the Constitutionist is unlikely to have *created* the pattern of wording in 32.5a, and if this pattern is not derived from Mt. 25.46, then the possibility remains that these words were taken, in this order, from the original ending of the *Didache*. This possibility is made stronger by the presence of a similarly arranged pair of parallel lines earlier in the *Didache*'s closing apocalypse, in 16.3b. It is probable, therefore, that rather than borrowing from Mt. 25.46, *Const.* 32.5a preserves wording from the lost ending of the *Didache*.

4.3. *The Authenticity of* Const. *32.5c*

> which eye has not seen,
> and ear has not heard,
> and which has not arisen in the heart of man,
> Those things which God has prepared for those who love him.

Despite the close support for this reading provided by Boniface's *Renunciation* the exact parallel to these lines in 1 Cor. 2.9 presents the possibility that *Const.* is not here dependent upon the *Didache*, but has instead incorporated Paul's quotation as a conclusion to the apocalypse. The following section assesses the case for the originality of these lines to the *Didache*, before considering the alternative possibility that they were taken from 1 Cor. 2.9.

To make a case for the originality of the lines recorded in *Const.* 32.5c it must be shown that they are of a piece with the compositional method used in the creation of the rest of the *Didache*'s apocalypse. This process has two stages. First, it is necessary to consider whether the lines preserved in *Const.* 32.5c are likely to be reworking of Isa. 64.4. Second, if they do appear to be such a reworking, then it will be possible to assess whether the pattern of redaction is consistent with the compositional method exhibited in the rest of the apocalypse.

The possibility that the lines preserved in *Const.* 32.5c are a reworking of Isa. 64.4 is initially suggested by similarities of wording:

Isa. 64.4
ἀπὸ τοῦ αἰῶνος
οὐκ ἠκούσαμεν
οὐδὲ οἱ ὀφθαλμοὶ ἡμῶν εἶδον
θεὸν πλὴν σοῦ καὶ τὰ ἔργα σου ἃ ποιήσεις τοῖς ὑπομένουσιν ἔλεον

Const. 32.5c
ἃ ὀφθαλμὸς οὐκ εἶδεν
καὶ οὖς οὐκ ἤκουσεν
καὶ ἐπὶ καρδίαν ἀνθρώπου οὐκ ἀνέβη,
ἃ ἡτοίμασεν ὁ θεὸς τοῖς ἀγαπῶσιν αὐτόν

However, to conclude that *Const.* 32.5c feasibly represents a direct reworking of Isa. 64.4 it is necessary to show that the Didachist was willing to rework Old Testament texts, and was likely to have sought to rework Isa. 64.4.

The first of these two tests is satisfied inasmuch as the Didachist was evidently willing to allude to Dan. 7.13 in *Did.* 16.8a. In section 4.1, above, it was further argued that *Did.* 16.8 contains a conflation of Dan. 7.13 with Zech. 14.5.

Given that the Didachist was willing to rework Old Testament material, then it remains to ask why Isa. 64.4 might have caught the author's attention. This question may be answered by considering why Dan. 7.13 and Zech. 14.5 were chosen as suitable resources. These two passages are notable in that they can be taken (with some reworking in the case of Dan. 7.13) as descriptions of the personal in-breaking of God from heaven. This event is the subject of *Did.* 16.8, and so it is not surprising that relevant Old Testament texts should have been referred to in the construction of this verse. Isa. 64.4 is also relevant to this subject because it occurs in the context of the prophet's appeal to God to 'open the heavens and come down' (64.1a), display his power (64.1b-2a) and consume his enemies (64.2b-3).

Two factors therefore suggest that the lines preserved in *Const.* 32.5c are a reworking of Isa. 64.4. First, the texts exhibit parallel images of neither seeing nor hearing something to do with God, and of benefiting from his actions towards those who love him/wait for him. Second, Isa. 64.4 occurs in the context of a description of God's personal in-breaking to earth from heaven which, alongside other Old Testament texts similarly used, may be seen as a suitable resource for the Didachist's portrayal of this event.

If the lines preserved in *Const.* 32.5c may be credibly understood as a direct reworking of Isa. 64.4, then it is possible to ask whether the adaptations made show signs of being original to the *Didache*'s apocalypse.

There are three important differences between Isa. 64.4 and the lines preserved in *Const.* 32.5c: a reversal of references to not seeing or hearing, so that seeing comes first; the addition of a line about what has not arisen in the heart of man, to make a set of three senses that are surpassed by God's action; a change in the beneficiaries of God's action from 'those who wait for his mercy' to 'those who love him'. These changes are consistent with the type of alternations made to Old Testament sources in the creation of *Did.* 16.8.

As noted above, the image of the Lord who comes on the clouds accompanied by his holy ones is created by the combination and re-ordering of the LXX of Zech. 14.5 and Dan. 7.13:

Zech. 14.5

Καὶ ἥξει <u>κύριος</u> ὁ θεός μου,
<u>καὶ πάντες οἱ ἅγιοι μετ᾽ αὐτοῦ</u>

Dan. 7.13

... *ἐπὶ τῶν νεφελῶν τοῦ οὐρανοῦ*
ὡς υἱὸς ἀνθρώπου ἤρχετο,

Did. 16.8 τότε ὄψεται ὁ κόσμος
τὸν <u>κύριον</u> *ἐρχόμενον ἐπάνω τῶν νεφελῶν τοῦ οὐρανοῦ,*
<u>καὶ πάντες οἱ ἅγιοι μετ᾽ αὐτοῦ</u>

By inserting 'τότε ὄψεται ὁ κόσμος' and repositioning the verb after the subject the Didachist creates an oppositional parallel between 'and then shall appear the world-deceiver as a son of God' (16.4b) and 'then shall see the world the Lord' (16.8):[26]

| 16.4b καὶ | τότε | φανήσεται | ὁ κοσμοπλανὴς, | ὡς υἱὸς θεοῦ |
| 16.8 | τότε | ὄψεται | ὁ κόσμος | τὸν κύριον |

This treatment, in *Did.* 16.8, of Dan. 7.13 and Zech. 14.5 illustrates the Didachist's willingness to conform Old Testament texts to a particular structural agenda, in this case one which sets up an oppositional parallel between the world-deceiver and the Lord.

A similar redactional formula may be seen in the lines preserved by *Const.* 32.5c. Thus, the reversal of the references to hearing and sight, in Isa. 64.4, creates a parallel to the ordering of the first two signs of truth (*Did.* 16.6):

a sign which may be seen (the sign of extension in heaven)
is followed by a sign that may be heard (the sign of the trumpet).

The relationship between the reordered and augmented text of Isa. 64.4 and the three signs of truth in *Did.* 16.6 goes beyond the parallel ordering of sight and hearing. The *addition* of a reference to 'in the heart of man has not arisen', in the text preserved in *Const.* 32.5c, creates a group of three entities:

πρῶτον σημεῖον ἐκπετάσεως ἐν οὐρανῷ,	see	ἃ ὀφθαλμὸς οὐκ εἶδεν
εἶτα σημεῖον φωνῆς σάλπιγγος	hear	καὶ οὓς οὐκ ἤκουσεν
καὶ τὸ τρίτον ἀνάστασις νεκρῶν	imagine/ hope	καὶ ἐπὶ καρδίαν ἀνθρώπου οὐκ ἀνέβη,

The first two signs may be relatively easily paired with sense responses that are surpassed by the future inheritance. Thus, the first sign can be

---

26. As will be shown in § 4.8, these patterns of opposition are an important structural characteristic of the *Didache*'s apocalypse.

seen; the new order that these signs precede contains that which cannot be seen. The second sign can be heard; that which it announces is beyond hearing. The third sign is of a different order. What 'sense' is fired by the sign of the resurrection of the dead? Resurrection is the greatest hope conceivable by the human mind, or to put it in Hebraic idiom, the greatest hope that has arisen in the heart of man. If the first two dimensions of the future inheritance go beyond what can be seen or heard, the third goes beyond what humans have ever imagined or hoped for, even resurrection. Thus, a pattern of 'see, hear, imagine' is created out of Isa. 64.4 (in *Const.* 32.5c's version of the end of *Did.* 16) which reflects the 'see, hear, imagine' pattern in *Did.* 16.6.

It may observed at this stage, therefore, that the treatment of Isa. 64.4 found in *Const.* 32.5c is similar to the treatment of Dan. 7.13 and Zech. 14.5 in *Did.* 16.8; both have been reordered and augmented and thus fit a structural pattern within the *Didache*'s apocalypse. This suggests that the version of Isa. 64.4, preserved in *Const.* 32.5c, was created by the same author who also wrote *Did.* 16.6 and 16.8.

A further alteration to Isa. 64.4 preserved in *Const.* 32.5c is also suggestive of the original hand of the Didachist. This change occurs in the final lines of the passages in question:

Isa. 64.4:   θεὸν πλὴν σοῦ καὶ τὰ ἔργα σου ἃ ποιήσεις τοῖς ὑπομένουσιν ἔλεον
Const. 32.5c: ἃ ἡτοίμασεν ὁ θεὸς .... τοῖς ἀγαπῶσιν αὐτόν.

The replacement of 'τοῖς ὑπομένουσιν' with 'τοῖς ἀγαπῶσιν' is explicable when it is noted that in *Did.* 16.5 οἱ ὑπομείναντες refers specifically to those who persevere in their faith during the persecution initiated by the world-deceiver. The retention of τοῖς ὑπομένουσιν in the *Didache*'s version of Isa. 64.4 could, therefore, lead to the impression that only those who die in the course of persecution can inherit the final blessing. If, however, as *Const.* 32.5a suggests, the more general category of 'the righteous' will receive the final inheritance, then a change to another term is necessary. The phrase 'those who love him' is a particularly apt description of the righteous in this context, since 'Πρῶτον ἀγαπήσεις τὸν θεὸν τὸν ποιήσαντά σε' stands at the head of the *Didache*'s presentation of the Law that leads to righteousness (*Did.* 1.2).

On the basis of the above evidence, therefore, it may be concluded that the version of Isa. 64.4 preserved in *Const.* 32.5c shows signs of having been selected, re-ordered and augmented by the author who also wrote *Did.* 16.3-6, 8. That is to say, at this stage in the discussion, *Const.* 32.5c appears to credibly preserve original wording from a putative *Did.* 16.9.

This supposition is not complete, however, because a further factor must be discussed; namely, the relationship between *Const.* 32.5c and 1 Cor. 2.9.

The version of Isa. 64.4 found in *Const.* 32.5c is identical to a quotation, presented by Paul as Scripture, in 1 Cor. 2.9. The standard explanation for this is that, rather than taking these lines from the full text of the *Didache*, the Constitutionist used 1 Cor. 2.9 to complete the *Didache*'s eschatological chapter.[27] This view requires, however, that, centuries after *Did.* 16 was written, the Constitutionist succeeded in adding a quotation from a Pauline discussion of wisdom which happened to neatly complete the *Didache*'s apocalypse. It should be noted that it is the *Didache*'s apocalypse which is neatly completed by this addition (cf. section 4.8, below) and not the Constitutionist's paraphrase of that text.[28] The completion brought about was not only at the level of the balanced structure of the text, but also in terms of completing the *Didache*'s extended debt to Isa. 64.1-4. Thus, with the addition of *Const.* 32.5a, c, the *Didache*'s apocalypse follows Isaiah's event line in its vision of the God who breaks into earth from heaven (*Did.* 16.8/Isa. 64.1a), displays his power (*Did.* 16.8/Isa. 64.1b-2a), judges his enemies (*Const.* 32.5a/Isa. 64.2b-3) and surpassingly rewards those who persevere in faithfulness (*Const.* 32.5c/Isa. 64.4).

In conclusion, Boniface's witness to the authenticity of the final lines of the *Didache* preserved in *Const.* 32.5c is supported by a common willingness, in both *Did.* 16.8 and *Const.* 32.5c, to re-order and augment Old Testament sources so as to conform them to the structural patterns of this short apocalypse. For such structural unity to result from the paraphrasing activity of a fourth-century writer requires an extraordinary coincidence. It is preferable, therefore, to suppose that *Const.* 32.5c faithfully records the redaction of Isa. 64.4 with which the *Didache*'s apocalypse originally concluded.

4.4. *The Likely Authenticity of* Const. *32.4d*

> and to reward each according to his deeds

The final element of the *Const.* version of the *Didache*'s ending that receives support from Boniface's *Renunciation* is the reference to the Lord's rewarding each according to their deeds. Boniface's version is

---

27. The possibility that Paul's curious version of Isa. 64.4 is the result of his quotation of *Did.* 16.9 is considered in n. 2 at the close of the excursus in Chapter 13.

28. See § 2, above for the text of *Const.* 32. Here it may be seen that the Constitutionist's uneven additions to, and omissions from, *Did.* 16 are not concerned with preserving the passage's carefully balanced structure.

limited to 'the judgment of all men' and so provides evidence for a line of this type, but not necessarily one exactly as preserved in *Const.* 32.4d.

Additional evidence for the likely authenticity of a line of this type may be found in *Did.* 16.2, which warns that the whole time of a person's faith will be of no profit unless they are 'perfected' in the final hour. This implies that the 'perfection' or otherwise with which they have kept the community's *halakah* will be assessed at some final test.

The structure of the extant part of the *Didache* apocalypse is also supportive of the existence of such a line inasmuch as the pattern of a dividing test, followed by two consequences of that division, is mirrored in the presentation of the world-deceiver's persecution of humanity:

> *Did.* 16.5: The world-deceiver's test of humanity
> DIVIDING TEST:
> Then human creation shall pass into the fire of testing
> CONSEQUENCE FOR THE EVIL:
> and many will be caused to stumble and shall be lost
> CONSEQUENCE FOR THE RIGHTEOUS:
> but those who persevere in their faith shall be saved by the curse itself.

> *Const.* 32.4c-5a/(*Did.* 16.8-9?): The Lord's test of humanity
> DIVIDING TEST:
> to judge the world-deceiver and to reward each according to his deeds
> CONSEQUENCE FOR THE EVIL:
> Then shall go away the evil into eternal punishment
> CONSEQUENCE FOR THE RIGHTEOUS:
> but the righteous shall enter into life eternal.

There is a very close parallel between *Const.* 32.4d, 'καὶ ἀποδοῦναι ἑκάστῳ κατὰ τὴν πρᾶξιν αὐτου', and Mt. 16.27, 'καὶ τότε ἀποδώσει ἑκάστῳ κατὰ τὴν πρᾶξιν αὐτοῦ'. This invites the possibility that *Const.* has assimilated a similar line in its original source to this text from the gospel. This question will be discussed further in Chapter 13, section 2.3. For the time being it may simply be observed that a line recording judgment according to actions is likely to have been part of the original ending of the *Didache*'s apocalypse.

4.5. *The Partial Authenticity of* Const. *32.5c*

> To judge the world-deceiving devil

The flow of the narrative within *Did.* 16.3-8a suggests, as assessed in section 2, above, that a reference to a conflict between the Lord and the world-deceiver is very likely to have formed part of the original text of the

Didache. However, given that this character is portrayed as a human persecutor in *Did.* 16.4-5, it may be supposed that the original ending described the judgment of the world-deceiver (cf. 16.4b) and not of the world-deceiving devil.

The extreme rarity of the term κοσμοπλανής, which occurs only here in the New Testament and early Christian literature, means that assimilation to another text is not a likely explanation for the presence of this line in the text of the *Const.*

4.6. *An Interim Summary of the Process of Reconstruction*
By inserting the start of *Did.* 16.8 into the reading provided by *Const.*, and removing the interpretative additions concerning the holy ones and the world-deceiver, an interim reconstruction of the original ending of the *Didache* may be presented. Underlining denotes where arguments for the authenticity of a particular line, if not always its exact wording, have been discussed.

> Τότε ὄψεται ὁ κόσμος τὸν κύριον ἐρχόμενον
> ἐπάνω τῶν νεφελῶν τοῦ οὐρανοῦ
> καὶ πάντες οἱ ἅγιοι μετ' αὐτοῦ
> ἐπὶ θρόνου βασιλείας,
> κατακρῖναι τὸν κοσμοπλάνον καὶ ἀποδοῦναι ἑκάστῳ κατὰ τὴν
> πρᾶξιν αὐτοῦ.
> Τότε ἀπελεύσονται οἱ μέν πονηροὶ εἰς αἰώνιον κόλασιν,
> οἱ δὲ δίκαιοι πορεύσονται εἰς ζωὴν αἰώνιον,
> κληρονομοῦντες ἐκεῖνα,
> ἃ ὀφθαλμὸς οὐκ εἶδεν
> καὶ οὖς οὐκ ἤκουσεν
> καὶ ἐπὶ καρδίαν ἀνθρώπου οὐκ ἀνέβη,
> ἃ ἡτοίμασεν ὁ θεὸς τοῖς ἀγαπῶσιν αὐτόν,
> καὶ χαρήσονται ἐν βασιλείᾳ τοῦ θεοῦ τῇ ἐν Χριστῷ Ἰησοῦ.

4.7. The Status of the Three Remaining Lines:
> 1. ἐπὶ θρόνου βασιλείας,
> 2. κληρονομοῦντες ἐκεῖνα,
> 3. καὶ χαρήσονται ἐν βασιλείᾳ τοῦ θεοῦ τῇ ἐν Χριστῷ Ἰησοῦ.

The phrase 'ἐπὶ θρόνου βασιλείας' is likely to be original if the reconstruction of the immediately preceding line is correct. This is the case because its inclusion overcomes a potential ambiguity as to whether it is the Lord or the holy ones who judge of the world-deceiver. Additional support for this view may be found in the absence of the particular description of the Lord's throne as 'βασιλείας' in any New Testament text, despite the appearance of a throne, otherwise described, prior to judgment in both Matthew's Gospel and Revelation. A final point in favour of the authenticity of this line is the assistance it gives to the creation of a fuller oppositional parallel to the appearance of the world-deceiver in *Did.* 16.4b. Thus, the appearance of the world-deceiver as a son of God is followed by three badges of his power: sign and wonders, the handing over of the world into his hands, and the doing of godless things. In opposition to this the son of man figure (implicit in the reference to Dan. 7.13) comes as the Lord with three badges of his power: he rides on the clouds, is accompanied by an army, and is seated on a throne. Without the reference to a throne the power of the Lord in opposition to the world-deceiver would not be so clearly expressed. It is likely, therefore, that this line was also taken by the Constitutionist from the original ending of the *Didache*.

The linking phrase, 'κληρονομοῦντες ἐκεῖνα', has a good claim to authenticity for purely practical reasons. Without some form of connection between 'οἱ δὲ δίκαιοι πορεύσονται εἰς ζωὴν αἰῶνιον', and 'ἃ ὀφθαλμὸς οὐκ εἶδεν' the sentence would not make sense. It is not possible to depend upon the exact wording of this link because *Const.* is capable of retaining the sense of the original while changing its precise vocabulary. That said, the presence of a connective phrase of this kind is highly likely.

The last line of the eschatological story, 'καὶ χαρήσονται ἐν βασιλείᾳ τοῦ θεοῦ τῇ ἐν Χριστῷ Ἰησοῦ', is unlikely to have closed the original text of the *Didache*. First, it is not attested by Boniface's *Renunciation*. Second, the addition of superfluous lines using references to Χριστῷ Ἰησοῦ is consistent with the style of the Constitutionist. For example, a similar addition is made to the end of the *Didache*'s 'way of life'. The original (*Did.* 4.14) reads, 'Αὕτη ἐστὶν ἡ ὁδὸς τῆς ζωῆς'. The Constitutionist's paraphrase, in Book VII chapter 17, presents this line as, 'Αὕτη ἐστὶν ἡ ὁδὸς τῆς ζωῆς – ἧς γένοιτο ἐντὸς ὑμᾶς εὑρεθῆναι διὰ Ἰησοῦ Χριστοῦ τοῦ Κυρίου ἡμῶν'.

In the reconstruction of the *Didache*'s apocalypse, therefore, the Constitutionist's reference to the Lord coming 'ἐπὶ θρόνου βασιλείας', is retained, as is the linking line, 'κληρονομοῦντες ἐκεῖνα'. However, 'καὶ χαρήσονται ἐν βασιλείᾳ τοῦ θεοῦ τῇ ἐν Χριστῷ Ἰησοῦ' is removed.

The full text of the *Didache*'s eschatological discourse, with the ending reconstructed above, is as follows:

16.3 Ἐν γὰρ ταῖς ἐσχάταις ἡμέραις
πληθυνθήσονται οἱ ψευδοπροφῆται καὶ οἱ φθορεῖς,
καὶ στραφήσονται τὰ πρόβατα εἰς λύκους
καὶ ἡ ἀγάπη στραφήσεταιμ εἰς μῖσος·
16.4a Αὐξανούσης γὰρ τῆς ἀνομίας,
μισήσουσιν ἀλλήλους καὶ διώξουσι καὶ παραδώσουσι.

16.4b καὶ τότε φανήσεται ὁ κοσμοπλανὴς ὡς υἱὸς θεοῦ
καὶ ποιήσει σημεῖα καὶ τέρατα,
καὶ ἡ γῆ παραδοθήσεται εἰς χεῖρας αὐτοῦ,
καὶ ποιήσει ἀθέμιτα, ἃ οὐδέποτε γέγονεν ἐξ αἰῶνος.

16.5 Τότε ἥξει ἡ κτίσις τῶν ἀνθρώπων εἰς τὴν πύρωσιν τῆς
δοκιμασίας, καὶ σκανδαλισθήσονται πολλοὶ καὶ ἀπολοῦνται,
οἱ δὲ ὑπομείναντες ἐν τῇ πίστει αὐτῶν σωθήσονται ὑπ᾽ αὐτοῦ τοῦ
καταθέματος.

16.6 Καὶ τότε φανήσεται τὰ σημεῖα τῆς ἀληθείας·
πρῶτον σημεῖον ἐκπετάσεως ἐν οὐρανῷ,
εἶτα σημεῖον φωνῆς σάλπιγγος,
καὶ τὸ τρίτον ἀνάστασις νεκρῶν·

16.8 Τότε ὄψεται ὁ κόσμος τὸ κύριον
ἐρχόμενον ἐπάνω τῶν νεφελῶν τοῦ οὐρανοῦ,
[καὶ πάντες οἱ ἅγιοι μετ᾽ αὐτοῦ,
ἐπὶ θρόνου βασιλείας
κατακρῖναι τὸν κοσμοπλάνον καὶ ἀποδοῦναι ἑκάστῳ κατὰ τὴν
πρᾶξιν αὐτοῦ.

16.9 τότε ἀπελεύσονται οἱ μέν πονηροὶ εἰς αἰώνιον κόλασιν,
οἱ δὲ δίκαιοι πορεύσονται εἰς ζωὴν αἰώνιον,
κληρονομοῦντες ἐκεῖνα,
ἃ ὀφθαλμὸς οὐκ εἶδεν
καὶ οὖς οὐκ ἤκουσεν
καὶ ἐπὶ καρδίαν ἀνθρώπου οὐκ ἀνέβη,
ἃ ἡτοίμασεν ὁ θεὸς τοῖς ἀγαπῶσιν αὐτόν.]

4.8. *A Structural Evaluation of the Reconstruction*

The above process of reconstruction has been like piecing together a broken part of a pottery vase. Each small fragment has been examined individually until a collection of 'original' elements has been gathered. An important test of this type of exercise, however, is the overall result that is created. That is to say, does the addition of the reconstructed part create a completed item that functions successfully as a whole?

The addition of *Did.* 16.8b-9 fulfils this requirement inasmuch as the resulting eschatological discourse is one that not only contains a completed narrative, but also carries that narrative within a simple and elegantly structured whole.

The discourse has six units which, with the exception of the introductory unit, are introduced by a τότε or καὶ τότε. Each unit, with the exception of 16.8, is devoted to one subject:

16.3-4a   Events presaging the coming of the world-deceiver
16.4b   The arrival of the world-deceiver
16.5   The occurrence and consequences of the deceiver's persecution
16.6   Events presaging the coming of the Lord
16.8   The arrival of the Lord and the occurrence of judgment
16.9   The consequences of the Lord's judgment

These six units fall into two groups of three. The first group of three is concerned with the world-deceiver; the second group, by contrast, with the Lord. This division bisects the full discourse into two halves of 89 and 90 words each.

Within these two groups, three types of event are set in oppositional parallel: the build-up to the arrival of each of the two central characters; the arrival of that central character; the testing consequences for the hearers of that arrival:[29]

BUILD-UP TO ARRIVAL OF WORLD-DECEIVER:

16.3 In the last days shall be multiplied false prophets and corruptors

and shall turn	the sheep	into	wolves
and love	shall turn	into	hate

16.4a For with the increase of lawlessness they will
      hate one another
      and persecute
      and betray.

BUILD-UP TO THE ARRIVAL OF THE LORD:

16.6 And then shall appear the signs of truth
      first the sign of extension in heaven
      next the sign of the trumpet call
      and third the resurrection of the dead.

---

29. Cf. the observation made in § 4.4, above. Because structural considerations were taken into account in the evaluation of the lost ending of the *Didache*, there is an apparent circularity in observing the same structural balance at this stage of the discussion. However, it is not the case that any element of the lost ending was *created* on the grounds that a structural parallel with the extant text could thereby be achieved. Rather, it was simply noted that the lines preserved in *Const.* 32.4-5 already exhibited such parallels.

ARRIVAL OF THE WORLD-DECEIVER:

16.4b And then shall appear the world-deceiver as a son of God
 and he will do signs and wonders
 and the earth shall be betrayed into his hands
 and he will do godless things which have never been since the beginning of the age.

ARRIVAL OF THE LORD:

16.8 Then the world shall see the Lord coming
 upon the clouds,
 and all his holy ones with him,
 on the throne of his kingdom,

WORLD-DECEIVER'S TEST OF HUMANITY:

16.5 Then human creation shall pass into the fire of testing
 and many shall be caused to stumble and be lost
 but those who persevere in their faith shall be saved by the curse
  itself.

LORD'S TEST OF HUMANITY:

 to judge the world deceiver and to reward each according to his
 deeds.

16.9 Then shall go away   the evil   into   eternal punishment
 but the righteous   shall enter   into   life eternal
 inheriting those things
 which eye has not seen
 and ear has not heard
 and which has not arisen in the heart of man.
 Those things which God has prepared for those who love him.

This ABC/A'B'C' pattern serves to set up an oppositional parallel between the world-deceiver and the Lord.

Alongside this structural pattern there is also a concentric ABC/C'B'A' scheme that focuses around the moment of choice faced by the hearers (16.5) with respect to their willingness to participate in the transition from a state of evil to a state of good.

The 'before' and 'after' pictures presented in the slightly longer units one and six are set in opposition to one another, so that the transformations from good to bad (unit one) are reversed into transformations from bad to surpassingly good (unit six). There are also structural parallels between these two units: each contains a open/closing line, a crossover pair (cf. section 4.2, above), a linking line, and a triad of consequences.

UNIT ONE – A

16.3 In the last days shall be multiplied false prophets and corruptors (open line)

and   shall turn   the sheep   into   wolves (crossover pair)
and   love   shall turn   into   hate

16.4a For with the increase of lawlessness they will, (link line)

1. hate
2. and persecute
3. and betray one another.

UNIT SIX – A'

16.9 Then

shall go away   the evil   into   eternal punishment (crossover pair)
but the righteous   shall enter   into   life eternal
inheriting those things (link line)
1. which eye has not seen
2. and ear has not heard
3. and which has not arisen in the heart of man
Those things which God has prepared for those who love him.
(close line)

As noted above, B and B' oppose the world-deceiver and the Lord.

UNIT TWO – B

16.4b And then shall appear the world-deceiver as a son of God
and he shall do signs and wonders
and the earth shall be betrayed into his hands
and he shall do godless things which have never been since the beginning of the age.

UNIT FOUR – B'

16.8 Then the world shall see the Lord
coming upon the clouds,
and all his holy ones with him,
on the throne of his kingdom,
to judge the world-deceiver and to reward each according to his deeds,

The C and C' sections lead up to and proceed from the transformational crux of the text which is the statement that those who persevere in their faith through the persecution shall be saved.

UNIT THREE – C

16.5 Then human creation shall pass into the fire of testing
and many shall be caused to stumble and be lost
but those who persevere in their faith shall be saved by the curse itself.

UNIT FOUR – C'
16.6   And then shall appear the signs of truth
        first the sign of extension in heaven
        next the sign of the trumpet call
        and third the resurrection of the dead.

These two structural patterns convey a sense of a choice between good and evil with a mid-way point of decision. However, a third structural pattern makes plain that transformation is effected by the agency of the Lord, and not by the perseverence of his faithful people.

This third pattern is shaped by the three triads within units two, four and six:

UNIT TWO
16.4b and he shall do signs and wonders
        and the earth shall be betrayed into his hands
        and he shall do godless things that have not been done since the
            beginning of the age.

UNIT FOUR
16.6   first the sign of extension in heaven
        next the sign of the trumpet call
        and third the resurrection of the dead.

UNIT SIX
16.9   which eye has not seen
        and ear has not heard
        and which has not arisen in the heart of man.

The first triad describes the state of the world during the world-deceiver's reign where his power and godlessness surpasses all that has been known before. The second triad signals the transition from the reign of the world-deceiver to the reign of the Lord. The third triad describes the state of the new order under the reign of the Lord, and that it surpasses everything known, or conceivable, in the past.

This third pattern prevents a simple symmetrical opposition between good and evil where the world-deceiver and the Lord are described in equivalent terms, which might imply their similar status. Instead, the 'evil', 'transition', 'good', pattern of triads, within units two, four and six, introduces a progressive dynamic which ensures that the whole discourse is weighted towards its conclusion, and the action of the Lord.

To express the subjective opinion that the *Didache* apocalypse is a small literary gem is to expose one of the inherent dangers of structural analyses such as the one above; their subjectivity. This factor means that the eye of faith can detect nuances, relationships and parallels where no dispassionate onlooker would otherwise find them. In concluding this structural analysis, therefore, I draw attention once again to the simplest feature of the reconstructed text; its oppositional presentation of the arrival of the world-deceiver and the arrival of the Lord. This feature, which creates narrative completeness as well as structural elegance, arises only when the proposed *Did.* 16.8b-9 is added to the damaged text. If a valid test of a reconstruction is that it reveals an elegant and functional whole where such was not previously evident, then the above reconstruction achieves a remarkably high level of success.

4.9. *Summary and Conclusion*

It was noted first of all that manuscript and narratological evidence indicates the incomplete nature of the Jerusalem manuscript. It was further noted that *Apostolic Constitutions* VII, the *Renunciation* of Boniface and the Georgian version of the *Didache* all contain some form of continuation of the *Didache* apocalypse, although with incomplete agreement as to its precise contents.

The process of reconstruction began with an examination of the words immediately following the extant version of *Did.* 16.8. On the basis of information from the interpolation at *Did.* 16.7, parallel eschatological expectation in 1 Thessalonians and Revelation, the interpretation of 'holy ones' as angels in *Const.* 32.4a, and the presence of 'Lord' instead of 'son of man' in *Did.* 16.8 it was concluded that the original text is likely to have read: 'And then the world shall see the Lord, coming on the clouds of heaven, and all his holy ones with him'.

The succeeding sections began by considering those parts of the *Const.*'s version of the lost ending that are supported by Boniface's *Renunciation*. Here it was noted that the Constitutionist reproduced textual and redactional features that also appear in the surviving verses of the *Didache*'s apocalypse, and which are difficult to attribute to the Constitutionist or the New Testament authors.

A concluding analysis of the structure of the whole eschatological discourse sought to show that, with the addition of the reconstructed ending, the *Didache*'s eschatological discourse appears to function as a carefully structured whole.

The structural unity of the completed discourse favours the accuracy of the general pattern and extent of the above reconstruction. That said, the tendency of the Constitutionist, exhibited elsewhere, to assimilate the

Didache to similar New Testament texts means that the precise vocabulary of every element of the reconstruction can not be identified with full certainty.

5. *The Integrity of* Didache *16*

This chapter, and hence this conclusion, is concerned with the relationships between the constituent elements of *Did.* 16.

Three elements of *Did.* 16 have been identified.

- First, the structurally and conceptually unified eschatological discourse recorded in *Did.* 16.3-6, 8-9.[30]
- Second, the interpolation at *Did.* 16.7, added to the manuscript tradition (preserved in the Jerusalem manuscript) from which the final lines of the discourse had been lost.
- Third, by a process of elimination, *Did.* 16.1-2 must have been written at a time separate from the initial composition of *Did.* 16.3-6, 8-9 because these verses do not conform to the symmetry of that unified discourse.

Given the separate status of 16.1-2 and 16.3-6, 8-9, there are three possible sequences in which these two sections could have been added to the *Didache*. Either 16.1-2 was added and then 16.3-6, 8-9, or 16.1-2 was inserted after the addition of 16.3-6, 8-9, or 16.1-2 and 16.3-6, 8-9 were added at the same time.

The first of these options implies that 16.3-6, 8-9 was written as a means of expanding upon and re-framing the briefly expressed expectations in 16.1-2. The difficulty with this view is that 16.3-6, 8-9 appears to represent an original and structurally self-contained reworking of Old Testament eschatological expectation. To this extent the discourse does not bear the marks of a reactive text struggling to make good the inadequacies of 16.1-2. It is possible that the eschatological discourse was composed separately and then added to the *Didache* at a later date, but this requires coincidences in shared references to 'the faith' (16.2 and 16.5), 'the coming of the Lord' (rather than the Son of man) (16.1 and 16.8), and

---

30. Niederwimmer (1998: 46) writes: '…it is immediately obvious that 16.3-8, which represent a little apocalypse, are a separate unit. I believe that here, too, the Didachist is quoting an older tradition (probably written). Thus I consider 16.3-6, 8 the quotation of an old, predidachistic apocalypse, and 16.7 an addition by the didachistic redaction.'

the expectation of judgment according to actions (16.2[31] and 16.8). Thus, this solution is neither impossible, nor especially convincing.

The second option, where 16.1-2 is inserted after the inclusion of 16.3-6, 8-9, is less credible than the first.[32] This requires that, in the initial instance, the self-contained discourse preserved in 16.3-6, 8-9 was appended to the *Didache* without any introduction. And that later, such an introduction was inserted. There is nothing to be said in favour of this view beyond the fact that it is a theoretical possibility.

The third option, where both parts were added to the *Didache* at the same time, is the most satisfactory. In this case *Did.* 16.3-6, 8-9 may be seen as a separately existing eschatological discourse which was quoted by the author of *Did.* 16.1-2 as a means of concluding the whole text. The message of 16.1-2 may be summed up as a call to constant vigilance in preparation for the final judgment, a message that is consistently reinforced by the quotation of 16.3-6, 8-9. This solution accounts for the links between 16.1-2 and what follows, without violating the self-contained and independent character of 16.3-6, 8-9.

31. Cf. discussion of the significance of τέλειος in Chapter 5, § 4.

32. Kloppenborg (1979: 57) firmly endorses the view of Bartlet (1921: 247) that 16.1 represents a later interpolation.

Chapter 4

ELEMENTS WITHIN *DIDACHE* 1–5

This chapter is concerned to isolate the various elements that comprise the *Didache*'s pre-baptismal catechism. At its simplest *Did.* 1–5 is a Two Ways tractate into which a number of previously existing traditions have been incorporated. The first step in isolating these traditions is to compare *Did.* 1–5 with the very similar Two Ways tradition found in *Barnabas* 18–20. Two sections of the *Didache*'s opening chapters immediately stand out by virtue of their absence from *Barnabas* 18–20; namely, *Did.* 1.3-6 and 3.1-6. This suggests that these two sections have a separate status with respect to the Two Ways.

1. *The Separate Status of* Didache *1.3-6*

The presence of an addition to the Two Ways tradition beginning in *Did.* 1.3 is not at all controversial.[1] This separate status is generally suggested by a lack of connection with the Two Ways tradition of *Barnabas* 18–20 and by the more distinctively Christian content of these verses in comparison to the uniformly Jewish character of the surrounding text.

However, the *precise* extent of this interpolation is far from straightforward. The difficulty arises because of the presence of a Latin text, parallel to *Did.* 1–6, which omits *Did.* 1.3b–2.1. This *Doctrina apostolorum* is commonly viewed as recording a stage in the process of the *Didache*'s composition prior to the insertion of the so-called *sectio evangelica* (seen by most as comprising 1.3b–2.1). At this stage only a very minor issue is at stake; namely, should the *sectio* be described as 1.3-6 or 1.3b–2.1? However, the question of whether the *Didache* depends on a source represented by the *Doctrina apostolorum* will be important in later discussion. An excursus to consider this question is therefore appropriate at this point.

---

1. 'Without any doubt, 1.3b–2.1 represents a subsequent interpolation in the text of the "basic document" ' (Niederwimmer 1998: 68).

Excursus: The Didache *and the* Doctrina apostolorum

Kloppenborg (1995: 90) states: 'In the case of the *Didache* and the *Doctrina apostolorum* the extremely high degree of agreement both in wording and order makes a literary relationship between the two virtually inescapable'.

If there is a literary relationship between the two texts, as seems highly likely,[2] then one of two options presents itself. The first, adopted by a majority of scholars, is that the *Didache* is dependent on the *Doctrina*. This position is confidently asserted by Audet (1996: 134–35):

> When one compares the so-called Latin version (i.e. the *Doctrina apostolorum* of Schlect) attentively with the Greek text which it is supposed to translate (i.e. the *Duae viae* of the *Didache*), one is faced with a fact which is very strange for a translation: whereas the (Christian!) translator would naturally have manipulated the text he had to translate, it would appear, on the contrary, that he has worked hard to make it hark back to the distant origins, in such a way that the alleged translation of the *Duae viae* of the *Didache* seems still more strongly coloured by Judaism than the *Duae viae* of the *Didache* itself. This sounds very unlikely.

At first sight Audet's point sounds compelling, and he certainly has some weighty scholarly support (Layton 1968: 379; Draper 1996a: 9; Kloppenborg 1995: 90; Rordorf 1991: 400; 1996a: 149; Niederwimmer 1998: 31, 50). Draper (1996a: 13) even goes so far as to say that 'Audet…established beyond dispute that the *Doctrina apostolorum* could not be an abbreviation of the *Didache*'. However, Audet's claim that a translator would have had to 'work hard' to produce the *Doctrina* from the *Didache* is overstated. That is to say, almost the only significant difference between the two texts is the omission of *Did.* 1.3b–2.1 and *Did.* 7–16 in the *Doctrina*. This would not have been difficult to achieve given that *Did.* 1.3-6 is very different in style and tone from the Two Ways material that surrounds it. Of course, a motive for such an omission must be provided if this possibility is to be taken seriously. Such a motive will be considered in due course.

Before simply accepting Audet's analysis of the relationship between the *Doctrina* and the *Didache* it is worth observing the peculiar circumstances that this conclusion creates. First, Audet's thesis demands that

---

2.   Goodspeed (1945: 228–47) supposes that both *Didache* and *Barnabas* are directly dependent on the *Doctrina*. This is not generally accepted in the case of *Barnabas*. Cf. Kloppenborg (1995: 90).

1.3b–2.1 was interpolated into the *Didache*. This requires very unusual behaviour on the part of the interpolator. Any text is profoundly influenced by the way in which it is introduced.[3] An interpolator is therefore likely to create a new heading to introduce new material. According to Audet, however, the interpolator chose to set new material under an element of the base text (1.3a) that had previously served as a heading for the continuing base (namely, 2.2-7). Having done so Audet's interpolator must then provide a *replacement* heading for 2.2-7 at the *end* of the interpolation. Niederwimmer (1998: 86-87) accepts this pattern of events but admits that it creates certain difficulties:

> The compiler of the *Didache* interrupted the text of his source (the 'basic document') at 1.3a in order to introduce the *sectio evangelica*, as we call it. Now, having completed the interpolation, he saw himself faced with the task of creating a transition to the source. This is accomplished by 2.1. The Didachist was apparently inspired by the final clause of the source… (1.3a). In the source this refers to the series of prohibitions that follows (2.2-7). It now occurred to the compiler that he could describe the commandments in the *sectio* and the series of prohibitions in the basic document as two successive concretions of the fundamental commandment (1.2). Therefore he writes δευτέρα δὲ ἐντολὴ τῆς διδαχῆς (2.1) and thus implicitly makes the commandments of the *sectio* the πρώτη ἐντολή, and the following commandments the δευτέρα ἐντολή (but without any thought of such a thing as the double love commandment). One cannot call this arrangement particularly skillful. This division thus created remains an emergency construction behind which there is no deeply reflective theological conception but simply a literary principle of order.

According to Niederwimmer, the interpolator was 'inspired' by the line, 'Here is the teaching that flows from these words' (1.3a) in writing 'The second commandment of the teaching means' (2.1) and referred therein to a second commandment 'without any thought' of the double love command mentioned in 1.2. The result, he admits, is not skilful. This is something of an understatement. The effect of this interpolator's forgetfulness of the significance of 'δευτέρα' is to create, by means of 2.1, considerable confusion regarding the status of 1.3b-6. Does the interpolation interpret the first commandment while 2.2-7 expands the second (Harnack 1884: 45-47; Hüntermann 1931: 195-96), or is it a primary interpretation of the second commandment, while 2.2-7 is a secondary one (Niederwimmer 1998: 86)?

---

3.   A striking example of how headings influence the interpretation of ensuing text may be found in Brown and Yule (1983: 139–40). This example is reproduced by Court (1997: 57–58) and Garrow (1997: 3).

Thus, the view that 1.3b-6 was inserted by someone who also added the linking line at 2.1 requires two curious actions on their part. First, a surprising unwillingness to provide a tailor-made heading for the new material, preferring instead to borrow an existing one. Second, a hurried ineptitude in referring to the 'second commandment' when creating a new heading for the ensuing base text.

If, on the other hand, the interpolation began at 1.3**a**, then 'Here is the teaching that flows from these words' introduces the insertion in a wholly conventional way. Further, if the base text into which the interpolation was made *already* contained 2.1, then its reference to the second commandment is, in its original context, entirely logical: a statement of the double love commandment (1.2) flows through the linking line, 'The second commandment of the teaching means' (2.1), into an interpretation of that second commandment (2.2-7).

If it is likely that *Did.* 1.3a provided the original heading for the ensuing interpolation, then the presence of this line in the *Doctrina* speaks in favour of the Doctrinist's knowledge of *Did.* 1.3a, and the interpolation that it introduced, rather than the reverse.

A second problem for the view that the *Didache* depends on the *Doctrina* is the repetition of another element from the section *Did.* 1.3-6 later in the *Doctrina*. The line in question resembles *Did.* 1.5a: 'The Father wishes us to give from his gifts to all', and appears in *Doctrina* 4.8: 'The Lord wishes to give to all from his gifts'. Niederwimmer (1998: 82 n. 93) comments on this feature as follows:

> Irritatingly, this single sentence from the *sectio christiana* [*sic*] (1.3b–2.1) has a parallel in *Doctrina*, but in a different place – 4.8… One may suppose that this sentence was also in the *Didache*'s source, at the same place (i.e. after 4.8). The Didachist omitted it there (at 4.8), understandably enough, in order to avoid having a doublet.

Niederwimmer's explanation of the omission of *Doctrina* 4.8 (end) in *Did.* 4.8 is dependent on his thesis that the Didachist composed the whole *Didache* by combining, at one sitting, a collection of previously existing sources.[4] In this circumstance he proposes that it is possible that the

---

4.   Few scholars concur with Niederwimmer's assertion that *Did.* 1.3b–2.1 was not a later interpolation into a previously existing version of the *Didache*. For example, Draper (1996d: 342) responds to Niederwimmer's hypothesis of a single author using various resources, by saying, 'This seems to fly in the face of the way a community rule evolves by trial and error, by erasing words or phrases, by inserting new words or phrases above the line or in the margin, which are later incorporated into the text. This

Didachist might, having written 1.5a, have chosen to omit the line in question when it reappeared in his source at *Doctrina* 4.8 (end). However, this assumes a somewhat sudden interest in avoiding doublets on the part of the Didachist. Repetitions of almost identical instructions occur elsewhere in *Did.* 1–5. This is the case in that elements of the 'way of death' are exactly antithetical to elements of the 'way of life'. As a result there are multiple condemnations of murder, adultery, theft, magic and equivocation. There is a double call to treasure the words that have been heard (3.8 and 4.1). And on the smallest scale, there is a doublet within two verses that could easily have been avoided:[5]

> 1.4b If someone takes away from you what is yours, do not ask for it back,
> 1.5a Give to everyone what he asks of you, and do not ask for it back.

Thus, Niederwimmer must suppose that his Didachist was disinterested in all these repetitions, however closely juxtaposed, and yet chose, curiously, to avoid a doublet created by verses three chapters apart. Given the unsatisfactory nature of Niederwimmer's explanation for the 'irritating' re-emergence of *Did.* 1.5a in *Doctrina* 4.8 (end) a different solution may be preferable.

An alternative explanation for the absence of 'The Lord wishes to give to all from his gifts' from the *Didache*'s version of 4.8, despite the appearance of this line in the parallel verse in the *Doctrina*, is that the Doctrinist took this line from *Did.* 1.5a and incorporated it into *Doctrina* 4.8. According to this solution the Doctrinist must have known a version of the *Didache* that contained 1.5a, and, by implication, the insertion of which this line is a part.

In voicing the possibility that the *Doctrina* depends on the *Didache* my first duty is to explain the omission of *Did.* 1.3b–2.1 and *Did.* 7–16. I aim to do this by suggesting that the *Doctrina* is the product of a conflation of a version of the Two Ways similar to that found in the *Epistle of Barnabas* and the Two Ways within the *Didache*.[6]

---

process is graphically displayed in the manuscript of the *Community Rule* from Qumran. Certainly whole new sections may have been added from time to time, but one should not hypothesize a wholesale, consistent composition for every change.' My own view of the composition of *Did.* 1–5 does, however, come close to Niederwimmer's inasmuch as I think that these chapters at least (with the exception of 1.5b-6) were put together at one time using various previously established sources. This process is discussed in Chapter 9.

    5.   Niederwimmer himself (1998: 78) explicitly notes the presence of this doublet.

    6.   Vokes (1938: 17–21) argues that the *Doctrina* corrected the Two Ways to be

I propose that the author of the *Doctrina* wanted to write a discrete version of the Two Ways, on the basis that this was the teaching of the Apostles and therefore valuable for instruction, possibly of catechumens. The fact that *Did.* 7–16 is omitted is not surprising given that these chapters were clearly not for the instruction of the individual (they are omitted in later texts that also appear to be dependent on the *Didache* such as the *Apostolic Church Order* and *Epitome*). The resources available to the Doctrinist for the creation of this edition of the Two Ways were a copy of the *Didache* and a version of the Two Ways similar to that used in *Barnabas* 18–20.

The opening verses show distinct signs of the conflation of the *Didache*'s 'way of life and death' and *Barnabas*'s 'way of light and darkness'. Thus *Doctrina* 1.1a reads: 'There are two ways in the world, that of life and that of death, of light and of darkness'. Audet (1996: 145 n. 24) admits that conflation may be the cause of this doubling, although he proposes that 1QS and an unknown text are the conflated sources:[7]

> It is not absolutely impossible…that the double qualification, 'life and death, light and darkness,' which characterises the Latin *Duae viae* among all the recensions, is the result of the encounter of two distinct currents in the transmission which carry the one or the other.

If, as Audet allows, a combination of two separate strands took place before the *Didache* came to depend on the *Doctrina*, then the Didachist is required to *reverse* that process by choosing to include only the 'life and death' strand in his work. The need for this regressive move is avoided if the *Doctrina*'s unique double qualification was created by the simple conflation of *Did.* 1.1a and a text such as *Barnabas* 18.

In *Doctrina* 1.1b the influence of a '*Barnabas*' Two Ways may be seen in the reference to an angel of good and an angel of iniquity; *Barnabas* has one angel who is Lord from all eternity to all eternity, and another who stands paramount over this present age of iniquity.

After this conflationary opening I propose that the Doctrinist chose to follow the *Didache* for the lines leading up to 1.3a. However, at this point the Doctrinist noted that the following sayings were absent from the '*Barnabas*' version, and furthermore, that they had the appearance of material from the gospels that had been interpolated into the original apostles' text.

---

found in *Didache* in the light of *Barnabas* 18–20. Similarly Robinson (1920: 73–83). See Niederwimmer (1998: 32 n. 17).

7.   Few scholars support Audet's contention that the *Doctrina* is dependent on 1QS (Draper 1996a: 13–14).

The Doctrinist therefore omitted this section and went on to pick up the thread of the Two Ways at 2.2.[8] (The order of the commandments against murder and adultery being changed under the influence of the LXX.)

For almost all of the rest of the copying process the Doctrinist followed the *Didache*, choosing to incorporate 3.1-7, despite its absence from *Barnabas*, perhaps because it was not obviously parallel to the gospels. However, in the extant *Doctrina* the 'τέκνον μου' phrase, so distinctively repeated in *Did.* 3.1-7, is reduced to just one introductory instance (*Doctrina* 3.1).

On reaching *Did.* 4.3: 'You shall judge justly. You shall not show partiality in calling people to task,' the Doctrinist writes. 'You shall judge justly, knowing that you will be judged', an addition that may betray the influence of Mt. 7.

A very close adherence to *Did.* 4.8 is then interrupted by the insertion, by the Doctrinist, of a portion of *Did.* 1.5a (indicating the presence in his source of *Did.* 1.3b–2.1) as discussed above.

At the end of the Two Ways, further interesting features occur. Thus *Did.* 5.2b–6.2 reads:

> 5.2b May you (pl.) be delivered, children [τέκνα], from all this. 6.1 See to it that no one leads you (sg. and following) astray from this way of the teaching, since the one who does so teaches apart from God. 6.2 For if you are able to bear the whole yoke of the Lord, you will be perfect, but if you cannot, do what you can.

The parallel passage in *Doctrina* 6.1-4 reads:

> 6.1 Abstain, my son [*fili*], from all these things, and see that no one leads you astray from this Teaching; otherwise you will be taught outside true instruction. 6.4 If you do these things daily with reflection, you will be near the Living God, but if you do not do them, you will be far from the truth…

The first noteworthy point is the use of τέκνα in *Did.* 5.2b despite the use of τέκνον in *Did.* 3.1, 2, 3, 4, 5, 6 and 4.1. This variation does not

8.   Connolly (1923: 152) '…the witness of [the *Doctrina apostolorum*, the *Apostolic Church Order* and the *Life* of Schnudi], (to the omission of 1.3b–2.1) is of doubtful value owing to the character of the documents themselves: for reasons can be adduced why the authors of these documents might purposely have omitted the passage'. Interestingly the *Apostolic Church Order* Statute 52 appears to know the *Didache*'s references to 'the gospel' although it omits a good deal of the *Didache* which was almost certainly present in any version that contained these references. Niederwimmer (1998: 13–14) thinks that *Apostolic Church Order* and *Epitome* cannot be dependent on the *Didache* because of the omission of 1.3b–2.1 in them also.

occur in the *Doctrina*, where *fili* is used in 3.1, 4.13 and, significantly, in 6.1. This difference between the two texts is most readily explained if the *Didache*'s erratic use of the terms τέκνον and τέκνα was homogenized on being copied by the Doctrinist.

A second observation concerns the surprisingly non-dualistic closure of the *Doctrina*. In other extant examples, the Two Ways teaching ends with straightforward and sometimes graphic damnation for those who follow the 'way of death' (1QS 3 is particularly gruesome). In the *Doctrina*, however, failure to keep the instruction merely results in being 'far from the truth', implying that a journey towards the truth is still possible. An explanation for this unusual conclusion might be provided if the *Doctrina* was influenced by *Did.* 6.2 where the call to perfection is combined with an acceptance that perfection may only be acquired over time. The *Doctrina* appears to take a similar stance, while incorporating more familiar language regarding the destination of those who follow one way or the other, such as can be found in *Barnabas* 21. Here again, therefore, the distinctive shape of the *Doctrina* can be explained in terms of its conflation of the *Didache* and a '*Barnabas*' Two Ways.

This conflation theory provides an explanation for the omission of *Did.* 1.3b–2.1 from the *Doctrina* and for differences in content between the two texts. Further, it challenges those who espouse the *Didache*'s dependence on the *Doctrina* to explain the omission of the '*Barnabas*' elements of the *Doctrina* from the *Didache*'s version of the Two Ways, for example, the additional references to light, dark and angels.

So, did the Doctrinist omit 1.3b–2.1 from a text of the *Didache* that already contained these verses, or did the *Didache* depend on the shorter *Doctrina*? At first sight the second option seems more likely. However, closer inspection exposes some problems with this view. First, it requires the interpolator to add a heading at the end of the insertion rather than, as would be more normal, at the beginning. Second, it is difficult to account for the presence of *Did.* 1.5a in *Doctrina* 4.8 (end) if the Doctrinist knew nothing of *Did.* 1.3b–2.1. Third, the relative smoothness and consistency of the *Doctrina*, when compared with jagged edges in the *Didache*, poses an awkward question of Audet's view. Finally, I have sought to challenge the central positive element of Audet's case by showing that the *Doctrina*'s omission of *Did.* 1.3a–2.1 is credibly the product of the Doctrinist's conflation of the *Didache* with a '*Barnabas*' Two Ways. In the light of these combined factors it is probable that the *Doctrina* depends on the *Didache*, rather than the reverse. At the very least, it is unsafe to construct any hypothesis on the basis of the *Didache*'s dependence on the *Doctrina*.

If the *Doctrina* is not relevant to the pre-history of the *Didache*, then where does this leave the question of the existence, or extent, of any insertion into *Did.* 1? This question is best answered by examining the text itself.

It was noted above that there is a natural flow from *Did.* 1.2 straight into 2.1 in the use of the term δευτέρα. There is another sequence of sense in the *negative* form of the golden rule (1.2) leading into the negative admonitions of *Did.* 2.2-7. Both these elements of continuity are disturbed by the presence of *Did.* 1.3-6. First, as discussed above, 1.3-6 confuses the status of the reference to a 'second' commandment in 2.1. Second, the introduction of a set of positive admonitions in 1.3-5a sits uneasily with the negative form of the immediately preceding golden rule. This suggests that, while 1.2 and 2.1 are likely to have been added to the *Didache* by the same hand at the same time, it is unlikely that 1.3-6 was also contributed at the same point in the text's evolution. I conclude, therefore, that *Did.* 1.3-6 represents an addition, of at least one layer, to the basic Two Ways document. In the following discussion I shall therefore use the term 1.3-6 to describe the interpolation that is usually referred to as 1.3b–2.1.

2. *Two Layers within* Didache *1.3-6*

While scholars have universally identified *Did.* 1.3-6 (or 1.3b–2.1) as separate from the rest of *Did.* 1–5, there has been less consideration of evidence that two or more layers may exist within this short section. However, Rordorf (1991: 410–11) notes that:

> The passage is composed of two units, which have already been joined together before the Didachist came to use them. *Did.* 1.3-4 speaks of the attitude of the Christian to those who wish him ill, with regard to whom he has no freedom of movement. *Did.* 1.5-6 speaks of the attitude of the Christian to those who wish to take advantage of him, and here he has the possibility of thrusting their attempts aside.

I intend to dispute Rordorf's view that 1.3-6 was a complete unit prior to addition to the *Didache* in due course. At this stage, however, I wish to consider his observation that there is a distinct change of key between the first and second halves of this section. Rordorf identifies this change as occurring between 1.4 and 1.5. I believe, however, that it should be located between, 'Give to everyone what he asks of you, and do not ask for it back, for the Father wants people to share with everyone the gifts that have been freely granted to them' (1.5a), and 'Blessed is the one who gives according to the commandment, for he is guiltless. Woe to the one who receives' (1.5b).[9]

Did. 1.5a clearly states that, following the example of the Father's generosity, its readers should give to everyone who asks without expecting repayment. By contrast, 1.5b-6[10] not only suggests that repayment should be sought, but that an unworthy receiver deserves to be imprisoned until repayment is achieved.[11]

This contradiction is best explained if *Did.* 1.5b-6 were added at some point after the teaching of 1.5a had been received, implemented and subsequently abused.[12] If the instruction to give without asking repayment was adhered to in any measure, then the opportunity for abuse, and the need for a defence against such abuse, is readily apparent. *Did.* 1.5b-6 functions as a suitable defence against abuse of the commandment by making clear that only those in genuine need may ask for assistance and that if their request is found to be false, then they should be forced to repay their debt. The saying in *Did.* 1.6, possibly from a version of Sirach 12.1,[13] further suggests that the author is here reflecting bitterly on the experience of the command's abuse. The use of a piece of old Jewish wisdom reminds readers that giving should not be naive, as it appears to have been in the

---

9.   Manuscript evidence from the Georgian version and the *Apostolic Constitutions* might suggest that there is a break after 1.4 or after 1.5a, respectively. However, neither of these texts provide a strong basis for conclusions of this type; the Georgian text is now lost, and the *Apostolic Constitutions* sometimes omits material that is inconvenient or confusing (e.g. *Did.* 6.2 and a shortening of *Did.* 11–12).

10.   The unity of *Did.* 1.5b-6 is sometimes disputed. Layton (1968: 369) says: 'the…possibility of contradiction between verses 1.5 and 1.6, makes [1.6] liable to suspicion as a gloss which has crept into the text from the margin of some manuscript'. Layton has failed to note, however, that the point of contradiction is not between 1.5 and 1.6 but between 1.5a and 1.5b-6. Kirk (1998: 91) observes that 'a proverb can be appended to an admonition or prohibition as a motive or rationale'. Since 1.6 is entirely supportive of the force of 1.5b, it is natural to see 1.5b-6 as a unity.

11.   Robinson (1920: 52–53) notes the contradiction between 1.5a and 1.5c. However, he attributes this to 'the Didachist's eagerness to appear original [which has] lead him into futility'.

12.   Rordorf (1991: 411) notes: '…the progressively more cautious reflections on almsgiving [1.5a-6] which must reflect unpleasant experiences in this connection'. Niederwimmer (1998: 87): 'The Didachist is already aware of some bad experiences: the Christian obligation to give support can also be misused and exploited. Through the addition of v.6 the Didachist seeks to protect the Christian willingness to give alms (which he affirms, and to which neophytes are invited) against exploitative misuse.'

13.   Niederwimmer (1998: 83–86) expresses uncertainty regarding the precise origin of this saying.

earlier experience of the community. Niederwimmer (1998: 86) notes: 'One receives the impression that the Didachist wanted, by quoting the aphorism [1.6], to restrict the appeal to unconditional almsgiving that existed in his tradition'. Niederwimmer supposes that the whole of 1.3-6 was laid down at the same time. However, this suggests that the Didachist was prepared to state a tradition and then contradict it in a single breath. It is perhaps easier to imagine that 1.5b-6 represents a modification of a version of the *Didache* that already existed prior to the addition of 1.5b-6.

Further indications that *Did.* 1.5a and 1.5b-6 belong to different layers may be found in the stylistic differences between 1.3-5a and 1.5b-6. The former consists of pithy sayings set out in regular and easily memorized patterns, while the latter is more laboured and discursive.

A temporal gap between these two sections is also suggested by the use of the term 'commandment' in 1.5b. Layton (1968: 365–66) suggests: '"The" (τὴν) commandment can only be the one given immediately prior'. In the context, this conclusion seems highly likely.[14] This in turn suggests that the teaching on giving laid down in 1.5a had achieved a fixed status prior to the addition of 1.5b-6. Thus the author of 1.5b-6 was required to modify the thrust of 1.5a by means of a further addition, rather than by simply altering 1.5a itself. This modification is achieved by first affirming the validity of the existing text: 'Blessed is the one who gives according to the commandment' (1.5b), and then proceeding to present circumstances under which the 'commandment' should be disregarded. This rhetorical manoeuvering does not suggest that the whole of 1.3-6 was added to the *Didache* by one author at one time.

On the basis of these contradictions of style and content it may be concluded that a temporal gap existed between the inclusion of the instructions in *Did.* 1.3-5a and the composition of a modifying response to those instructions in *Did.* 1.5b-6.

3. Didache *1.3b-5a: A Collection of Independent Sayings*

Having sought to establish that *Did.* 1.3-5a and *Did.* 1.5b-6 belong to different layers of the *Didache* it is now possible to consider the history of *Did.* 1.3-5a.

---

14. Alternatively, Niederwimmer (1998: 82–83) comments: '[κατὰ τὴν ἐντολήν] probably refers to a commandment of the Lord, but it is not clear which concrete commandment the Didachist has in mind. Is the reference here to the word of the Lord quoted just before (in v.5a)? Or does it simply mean "in the right way, as the Lord has commanded us," without any thought of a specific saying?'

At the heart of these verses is *Did.* 1.4a. This awkward line is often considered a later interpolation. For example, Niederwimmer (1998: 76) writes:

> In my opinion, the history of the interpolation [1.4a] can be reconstructed as follows: (1) At an early time a glossator intervened in the traditional text, because he missed the motif of resistance of fleshly desires in the previous lines, and this was one of the fundamental motifs of early Christian catechesis. Compare, for example... 1 Pet 2:11... Titus 2:12. I think, then, that this motif was introduced by means of a gloss (in some such form as ἀπέχου τῶν σαρκικῶν ἐπιθυμιῶν, 'avoid the fleshly passions').

The uncomfortable location of 1.4a rightly inspires questions regarding its origins. However, that same awkwardness demands a clear answer to two further questions. First, given the wealth of injunctions against every kind of passion of the flesh elsewhere in *Did.* 1–5, why was the inclusion of 1.4a thought necessary at all? Second, if there was such a necessity, why was this line inserted in such an awkward position?[15] Given that these questions are not easily answered by those who propose that 1.4a is a later interpolation, it is worth considering the possibility that this line was original, even pivotal, to a previously existing group of sayings (1.3b–5a) which was later inserted into the *Didache* as a whole.

I propose that *Did.* 1.4a provides the hub, or central gnomic saying, that holds together the whole of *Did.* 1.3b-5a. Kirk (1998: 163) observes: 'a gnomic saying by nature is hermeneutically open and...as a result will always form a highly interactive hermeneutical relationship with its rhetorical context'. He goes on to give examples of how a line that can seem odd in context is actually deliberately reshaped by that context as a means of developing its meaning. An instance can be found in the golden rule from Lk. 6.31. Kirk (1998: 163) notes: 'Verse 31...has long been a bone of contention in exegesis of the passage, for it seems to advocate a mild reciprocity ethic present in most everyday social relations and thus in collision with the radical ethic of the sayings flanking it'. He goes on to argue, however, that because the golden rule is hermeneutically open it can be interpreted in terms of the radical sayings with which it is juxtaposed. A similar observation may be made regarding the notoriously awkward

---

15. That the position was felt to be awkward in the history of the text is demonstrated by P.Oxy 1782. Connolly (1923: 153) notes that in this manuscript the variant reading of 1.4 may be because '"Abstain from fleshly lusts" come[s] in somewhat abruptly...and the person responsible for our little book seems to have felt they called for a word of introduction'. The version of 1.4a in P.Oxy 1782 reads: 'ἄκουε τί σε δεῖ ποιοῦντα σῶσαι σοῦ τὸ πνεῦμα. π[ρ]ῶτον πάντων ἀπόσχου τῶν σαρκε[ι]κῶν ἐπιθυμειῶν'.

Mt. 7.6: 'do not give what is holy to dogs; and do not throw your pearls before swine, or they will trample them under foot and turn and maul you'. The imagery of this verse is highly susceptible to the hermeneutical influence of its context. Thus it is generally interpreted as in some way related to judging and giving, because of its context, even though this is quite far from the meaning that might be attributed to it in another circumstance. I suggest that the same type of compositional technique is at work in the placement of *Did.* 1.4a. In this I agree with Draper (1996b: 83) who notes: 'In [1.4a], the *Didache* contrasts the desires of the flesh with the way of perfection, which is that of turning the other cheek'. Draper goes on to describe this as a 'sophisticated setting' for the line in question. That sophistication can be found in the way that a simultaneously limited and general instruction such as 'avoid the fleshly passions' is stretched and interpreted by its context. The fleshly response to being cursed is to retaliate in like manner, but *Did.* 1.3b teaches that the non-fleshly (or spiritual) response is rather to bless, pray and fast for our adversaries. The pattern of the flesh is to love only those who love us; to avoid this passion we must love those who hate us (1.3c). The fleshly response to being struck is to retaliate; this passion is avoided by offering the other cheek, going the extra mile, and so on. Thus, by arranging four sets of sayings around the central gnome, its generalities are made specific and its limitations are broken down.

The status of *Did.* 1.4a is not vital to the discussion of the compositional history of *Did.* 1.3b-5a, but it does make one valuable contribution. If *Did.* 1.4a is original to *Did.* 1.3b-5a then this indicates, by virtue of the awkwardness of 1.4a, that this section was not composed as a seamless original discourse. In the case of 1.4a, at least, a saying with an external existence has been brought into the text and has been shaped by juxtaposition with other material, rather than by means of internal changes to the saying itself. This suggests, in turn, that the material with which 1.4a has been juxtaposed may also not be the original composition of the compiler. A closer examination of these sayings points in this direction.

Didache 1.3b is a closely contained triplet.

> 1.3b Εὐλογεῖτε τοὺς καταρωμένους ὑμῖν
> καὶ προσεύχεσθε ὑπὲρ τῶν ἐχθρῶν ὑμῶν,
> νηστεύετε δὲ ὑπὲρ τῶν διωκόντων ὑμᾶς·

The structure and sense of this 'three rules' saying is capable of operating entirely satisfactorily outside the context of the *Didache*. 'Bless', 'pray' and 'fast' are all terms associated with prayer. 'Those who curse you', 'your enemies' and 'those who persecute you' are similarly all means of describing an opponent. 'Three rules' sayings of this type, although usually referring to prayer, fasting and alms, are a common feature of the Jewish wisdom tradition, as in Tobit 12.8, and appear in early Christian writings such as *Gospel of Thomas* 6a, 14a (cf. Jefford 1989: 44). There is therefore no reason why this three rules saying should have been composed specifically for inclusion in the *Didache*. Further, there is no connection between the prayer emphasis of these three rules and any other part of 1.3b-5a.

Didache 1.3c is presented, in the context, as an expansion of 1.3b:

1.3c ποία γὰρ χάρις,
ἐὰν ἀγαπᾶτε τοὺς ἀγαπῶντας ὑμᾶς;
οὐχὶ καὶ τὰ ἔθνη τὸ αὐτὸ ποιοῦσιν;
ὑμεῖς δὲ ἀγαπᾶτε τοὺς μισοῦντας ὑμᾶς
καὶ οὐχ ἕξετε ἐχθρόν.

While there is every reason to suppose that *Did.* 1.3b could have existed outside the *Didache*, this conclusion is less certain in the case of 1.3c. The connective 'γὰρ' seems to point towards composition for the setting, although this could have been inserted later as a means of connecting 1.3c to 1.3b. The saying itself is not so self-contained that an independent life immediately suggests itself. However, this does not preclude the possibility that it has been adapted or separated from a different setting in order to be included here. The absence of any reference to prayer and a repeated focus instead on love may suggest an originally separate context for the saying relative to 1.3b, but these features are not conclusive.

While it is not possible to determine whether *Did.* 1.3c existed prior to its inclusion in 1.3b-5a, what may be said about these lines with some confidence is that their history is *different* from that of *Did.* 1.3b. This is indicated not only by the self-contained nature of 1.3b, but also by the differing attitude to enemies (the one concrete connection between the two sayings) that is portrayed in each case. In *Did.* 1.3c the love of those who hate you is presented as an investment in one's own reputation and ease of life. This is not the stark radicality of 1.3b, where the hearer is enjoined to pray, even to the point of fasting, for those who oppose them without any indication of benefit for the intercessor. This difference in attitude between 1.3b and 1.3c, whether the consequence of the location-specific composition of 1.3c, or the result of a juxtaposition of two previously existing sayings, suggests the same result; namely, that 1.3c and 1.3b were not composed by the same hand at the same time. This is not to suggest that 1.3b and 1.3c were added to the *Didache* separately, simply that their form in the *Didache* shows that their individual histories may be ultimately traced to different origins.

The separate origin of *Did.* 1.4a, with respect to the sayings that surround it, has already been considered above. This separate status is further confirmed by the reversion of the addressee from second person plural (1.3b-c) to second person singular (1.4a–5.2a). Some scholars argue that this type of change of addressee provides no indication of a seam in the redaction history of a text. For example, Kirk (1998: 160) states (while referring to this phenomenon in the gospels): 'The switch from plural to singular second person address is a rhetorical technique aimed at arresting attention, not a redaction history indicator'. It is certainly true that this type of rhetorical device can be found in homogenous texts. However, it is just as mistaken to assume that this phenomenon always has a rhetorical function as it is to assume that it always indicates a change of source. In *Did.* 1.3b-5a there are other indicators, such as the discrete structure and content of the sets of sayings concerned, that point to separate points of origin. Further, the rhetorical force of the switch from singular to plural (rather than the reverse) in *Did.* 1.3b-c is far from obvious.

The effect of the change in number between 1.3b-c and what follows, is not only to separate 1.4a from this group of sayings, but also to suggest that 1.4b-5a has a history separate from that of the commands to pray for enemies and to love those who hate you.

The separate history of 1.4b is further indicated by its uniform and self-contained structure.

> 1.4b ἐάν τίς σοι δῷ ῥάπισμα εἰς τὴν δεξιὰν σιαγόνα, στρέψον αὐτῷ
> καὶ τὴν ἄλλην,
>   1.4b(r) καὶ ἔσῃ τέλειος·
> ἐὰν ἀγγαρεύσῃ σέ τις μίλιον ἕν, ὕπαγε μετ᾽ αὐτοῦ δύο·
> ἐὰν ἄρῃ τις τὸ ἱμάτιόν σου, δὸς αὐτῷ καὶ τὸν χιτῶνα·
> ἐὰν λάβῃ τις ἀπὸ σοῦ τὸ σόν, μὴ ἀπαίτει·
>   οὐδὲ γὰρ δύνασαι.

This structure is disturbed by 'καὶ ἔσῃ τέλειος', which Niederwimmer (1998: 79), with some justification, believes may be a later addition (see also Chapter 9, sections 1 and 4, below). At the end of this group, the saying 'οὐδὲ γὰρ δύνασαι' is difficult to interpret, which may be the consequence of a textual error or a destructive change of context from this line's previous location to its present situation. Despite these difficulties, however, the unity of this group is clear. This is particularly true of the first three lines, each of which are concerned with an event that would bring shame or humiliation on the recipient. It is possible, in view of the tight unity of these lines, that they were not originally attached to the final line, which may have been added by catchword at a later date. However, for the purposes of this discussion it is sufficient to allow that they may all have the same origin. I am therefore in agreement with Niederwimmer (1998: 78) when he says: 'The first four logia belong together both formally and in content (cf. the fourfold ἐαν..., στρέφον, ὕπαγε, δός, μὴ ἀπαίτει)'.

Two features suggest the separate origin of *Did.* 1.5a with respect to 1.4b.

1.5a παντὶ τῷ αἰτοῦντί σε δίδου καὶ μὴ ἀπαίτει·
πᾶσι γὰρ θέλει δίδοσθαι ὁ πατὴρ ἐκ τῶν ἰδίων χαρισμάτων.

First, there is a doublet of 1.4b in 1.5a (Niederwimmer 1998: 78). If a continuous discourse were being recorded here, then it may be expected that this repetition would be avoided. As Glover (1958: 15) observes: 'Each synoptic avoids the clumsy repetition of ἀπαίτει'. Second, there is a change of subject from forced giving (1.4b) to voluntary giving (1.5a). These two factors combine to suggest that 1.5a existed as a separate saying that has been juxtaposed to 1.4b on the basis of the catchwords, μὴ ἀπαίτει.

4. *Summary: The Textual History of* Didache *1.3-6*

The foregoing analysis of the different elements that comprise *Did.* 1.3b-5a suggests that each of the sets of sayings in this section had a separate history prior to their inclusion in this collection.[16] At the same time the current organization of these separate sayings suggests that they were consciously arranged so as to expand upon and reinterpret the command, 'avoid the fleshly and bodily passions' (1.4a):

εὐλογεῖτε τοὺς καταρωμένους ὑμῖν
καὶ προσεύχεσθε ὑπὲρ τῶν ἐχθρῶν ὑμῶν,
νηστεύετε δὲ ὑπὲρ τῶν διωκόντων ὑμᾶς·

ποία γὰρ χάρις, ἐὰν ἀγαπᾶτε τοὺς ἀγαπῶντας ὑμᾶς;
οὐχὶ καὶ τὰ ἔθνη τὸ αὐτὸ ποιοῦσιν;
ὑμεῖς δὲ ἀγαπᾶτε τοὺς μισοῦντας ὑμας καὶ οὐχ ἕξετε ἐχθρόν.

---

16. This conclusion overlaps to some extent with the conclusion of Niederwimmer (1998: 87) who states, 'The Didachist is not formulating freely here [*Did.* 1.3b–2.1], but is making use of a variety of materials whose origins are uncertain. In vv. 3, 4b-5a and 5d there is reliance on logia from the Jesus traditions, but we cannot point with certainty to the source from which the Didachist derived them...'

1.4a ἀπέχου τῶν σαρκικῶν καὶ σωματικῶν ἐπιθυμιῶν·

ἐάν τίς σοι δῷ ῥάπισμα εἰς τὴν δεξιὰν σιαγόνα,
 στρέψον αὐτῷ καὶ τὴν ἄλλην,
 καὶ ἔσῃ τέλειος·
ἐὰν ἀγγαρεύσῃ σέ τις μίλιον ἕν, ὕπαγε μετ᾽ αὐτοῦ δύο·
ἐὰν ἄρῃ τις τὸ ἱμάτιόν σου, δὸς αὐτῷ καὶ τὸν χιτῶνα·
ἐὰν λάβῃ τις ἀπὸ σοῦ τὸ σόν, μὴ ἀπαίτει·
 οὐδὲ γὰρ δύνασαι.

Παντὶ τῷ αἰτοῦντί σε δίδου καὶ μὴ ἀπαίτει·
πᾶσι γὰρ θέλει δίδοσθαι ὁ πατὴρ ἐκ τῶν ἰδίων χαρισμάτων.

The balance of this collection suggests that it existed as a complete and self-contained 'sayings onion' prior to its insertion into the *Didache*. This assessment has the advantage of explaining how *Did.* 1.4a, which is incongruous in its current setting within the *Didache*, came to find its central place in the collection.

This conclusion suggests, therefore, that the whole of *Did.* 1.3-5a should be treated as part of the same redactional layer of the *Didache*. However, it should be recognized that this section also exhibits a prehistory where five different elements, each with its own previous and separate existence (with the possible exception of 1.3c), have been brought together to expand the meaning of 'avoid the fleshly passions'.

The above analysis has the additional effect of emphasizing the break between *Did.* 1.3-5a and 1.5b-6. Whereas the former is made up of sayings that show signs of each having had an independent life prior to inclusion in this collection, the material in the latter makes sense only in response to the preceding text. For the remainder of this discussion 1.3-5a ('sayings onion') and 1.5b-6 (modification of 'sayings onion') will therefore be treated as belonging to two separate stages in the compositional history of the *Didache*.

5. Didache *3.1-7: The Teknon Unit*

A second block within *Did.* 1–5 that it generally accepted as having been added, at some point, to the original Two Ways tractate, is *Did.* 3.1-6.[17] This passage has a distinctive style, very different in content and structure from the Two Ways teaching in *Barnabas* 18–20, which marks it out as a self-contained unit. Kloppenborg (1995: 104–105) notes:

---

17. See Niederwimmer (1998: 94).

The repetitive use of the phrase τέκνον μου...places this section squarely within the idiom of sapiential discourse. The symmetry in the construction of this section has been noted by many scholars and is often taken as an indication of independent origin. R.H. Connolly [1932: 241–42] observed, moreover, that of the twenty-five terms that are used for vices or faults in *Did* 3.1-6, fully nineteen do not appear elsewhere in the *Didache*.

The different vocabulary and grammar of *Did.* 3.1-6 is especially accentuated by the rhythmical and carefully structured repetitions of this section, in contrast to the comparatively loose organization of the Two Ways instructions.

While there is every reason to suppose that *Did.* 3.1-6 was inserted into the original Two Ways tractate, the same level of certainty does not apply in the case of *Did.* 3.7. This verse contains the term πραΰς, which also appears in *Barnabas* 18. Almost all of *Barnabas* 18–20 appears in *Did.* 1–5, so it is likely that a call to be meek also appeared at some point in the *Didache*'s Two Ways. However, it is also the case that a call to be meek provides a fitting conclusion to the Teknon teaching. This is the case structurally in that the Teknon teaching begins with a positive call, in the present imperative active, to flee from all evil. *Did.* 3.7 uses the same tense, otherwise unusual in the context, for the positive instruction to be meek. The content of *Did.* 3.7 also rounds off the Teknon teaching in that meekness is opposite to the anger, zeal, quarrelsomeness, hot-temper, passion, obscene speech, bold gazes, soothsayings, lies, theft, avarice, vainglory, grumbling, slander and stubborn wilfulness censured in the preceding lines. Further, and perhaps most significantly, the promise that 'the meek shall inherit the earth' (cf. Ps. 36.11 LXX) provides a positive consequence to endorsed behaviour to balance the negative consequences of the proscribed behaviours (murderous acts, adultery, idolatry, theft, slander), all of which wickedness leads to disinheritance and banishment (cf. Ps. 36.9, 18, 20, etc.). Draper (1985: 272) adds: '3:7 forms part of the "Tugendkatalog" from the earliest stratum of the Way of Life (cf. 1QS 4:3) which has been embellished from Psalm 36:11'.[18]

There is a case, therefore, for suggesting that the Teknon teaching (in its exposition of Ps. 36), and the Two Ways tractate (insofar as it is parallel to the Two Ways found in *Barnabas*), *both* contained a reference to meekness. Such a sharing provides an attractive explanation for the insertion of the Teknon teaching just before *Did.* 3.7 in the Two Ways. Thus, it may

---

18. Audet (1958: 320) thinks that *Did.* 3.7 records an independent saying, but this is unlikely given its links with both Ps. 36 and *Barnabas* 18.

be supposed that, because the tail of the Teknon unit shared a reference to meekness with the Two Ways, this point of similarity was seen as a suitable anchorage point for its insertion. Anchorage from the tail, rather than the head, would explain why the flow of the Two Ways teaching (2.2-7) into the head of the Teknon teaching, at 3.1, is so abrupt and apparently random.[19]

In conclusion, therefore, the Teknon teaching appears to represent a sapiential exposition of Ps. 36 which had a life independent of the *Didache* prior to its insertion into the Two Ways. The style and content of this addition has little in common with either *Did.* 1.3-5a or 1.5b-6, and is therefore likely to be the work of a different author.

6. *Other Additions to the Base Two Ways*

The discrete character of *Did.* 1.3-6 and 3.1-6/7 clearly identifies them as later additions to the Two Ways teaching. However, this does not necessarily mean that the remainder of *Did.* 1–5 is free from other additions. It is not possible to trace the minutiae of each potential insertion, but there are two points, *Did.* 1.2 and 5.2, where evidence of minor additions will have significance for subsequent discussion.

6.1. Didache *1.2*
In the case of *Did.* 1.2 there is an overlap with the Two Ways tradition as found in *Barnabas* in that the first command of the 'way of light' is to 'love your maker'. However, the double love command and golden rule in the *Didache* are notably absent from *Barnabas*.[20] This omission, despite the memorable character of these teachings, suggests that they were not present in the version of the Two Ways available to *Barnabas*. Consequently, it is likely that this teaching was not a standard feature of the Two Ways tradition, and thus, at some stage in the life of the Two Ways text used in the *Didache* these summaries of the Law were added to the whole. Thus Niederwimmer (1998: 65) suggests:

19. The Oxyrynchus papyrus 1782 illustrates that at least one copyist perceived a radical break between *Did.* 2.7 and 3.1; a series of black and red chevrons are used to separate the two chapters.

20. 'The Didachist did not construct *Didache* 1.2a-b with the assistance of the Two Ways source alone, since the wording of the "double love commandment" in *Barnabas* does not indicate a knowledge of materials that could have led to the more complete rendering of the "double love commandment" that appears in the *Didache*' (Jefford 1989: 35).

> We must apparently imagine that the Two Ways tractate, in its introduc-
> tion, originally spoke only of the commandment to love God (*Barn*. 19.2).
> At some point a redactor expanded the command to love God by adding the
> commandment to love one's neighbour, and so constructed the double com-
> mandment. In doing so, he made the doubling explicit by inserting 'first'
> and 'second'.

Niederwimmer seems to suggest here that the *Didache* represents the creation of the double love command. However, it is not fanciful to suppose that the double love commandment could have functioned as a complete unit in itself. As Hultgren (quoted in Jefford 1989: 34) comments:

> Two reasons can be given [in justification that this commandment could
> have functioned as a unit]. First, the double commandment of love would
> have been a characteristic and rather important teaching (whether of Jesus,
> or attributed to him). We have other examples in which Jewish teachers of
> the period summarised the Torah, and one can expect that the same would
> have been done by Jesus or the teachers of the primitive community (as
> Rom 13.9 gives evidence for the latter). Furthermore, this summary could
> be used on various occasions and in several connections. We have indepen-
> dent traditions in which it is used, viz., Mark and Q.

It is possible, therefore, that the double love command and the negative golden rule were known as important teachings independent of the Two Ways. Their insertion into the Two Ways may be credibly accounted for by the overlap between 'Love the God who made you' (*Did.* 1.2) and the first half of the double love command. This overlap creates a suitable point at which the double love command may be woven into the text of the *Didache*. Thus, where the two traditions essentially overlap, as in 'Love the God who made you' and 'Love the Lord God', the version in the host text is preserved. Where this overlap does not occur the incoming text is played out in full.

The inclusion of the negative golden rule may be by virtue of its association with the double love command in the experience of the interpolator, or because it was similarly seen as a summary of the Torah, important for Christians, which deserved a place at the start of the Two Ways exposition of the commandments.

If it is the case that 1.2b, d-e was added to an existing form of the Two Ways then one of the linking devices in either 1.3a or 2.1 may also be attributed to this interpolator. This is the case since the insertion of an initial summary of the Law requires a means of showing that the follow-ing instructions are subsequent details, which fill out the broad cloth pain-ted by the opening commands. Either 'Here is the teaching that flows from these words', or 'The second commandment of the doctrine' would serve this function equally well. However, as argued above, it is more likely that the second of these two options was used (cf. section 1, above).

None of the following discussions are affected by the question of whether or not *Did.* 1.2b, d-e was copied from the Two Ways source or not. The question of significance here is whether or not these verses formed an additional part of the collection of sayings quoted in *Did.* 1.3b-5a. Three factors suggest that this is not the case. First, 1.3b-5a stands alone as a balanced set of sayings concerned with what it means to 'avoid the fleshly passions' (according to the discussion in section 3, above) and 1.2b, d-e does not fall easily within the structure of this unit. Second, there is a disjunction between the negative form of the golden rule in 1.2e and the positive instructions of 1.3b-5a which does not suggest that they originally belonged together. Third, as noted in section 1, above, the flow from 1.2b, d-e straight into 2.1 is disturbed by the intrusion of 1.3-6. It is not likely, therefore, that both 1.2b, d-e and 1.3-6 were added to the whole at one time.

With regard to the status of 1.2b,d-e. It is possible to gather the following pieces of evidence: these verses do not appear in the Two Ways teaching in *Barnabas* and so it is likely that they do not belong to the Two Ways tradition used in the *Didache*. The likelihood of their later addition is further enhanced by the case for the independent existence of these Law summaries, and the credible basis for their inclusion in the *Didache* provided by the overlap between the double love command and the opening command of the Two Ways. The use of 'second' in both 1.2 and 2.1 suggests that the latter verse may also have been added with the double love command and the golden rule as a means of restoring the flow of sense from the interpolation back into the host text. In concluding that 1.2b, d-e and 2.1 are likely to have been added to an older version of the Two Ways it is crucial to note that this addition appears not to have been made at the same time as the insertion of *Did.* 1.3-5a, since the latter interrupts the flow from *Did.* 1.2 into 2.1.

6.2. Didache *5.2*
At the end of the Two Ways teaching there is a further detail of the history of the text that will be important in subsequent discussion. This is the point at which a free-standing version of the Two Ways teaching could have ended.

Three possible end-points of a free-standing Two Ways document may be proposed: 5.2a, 5.2b or 6.1.[21]

21. Niederwimmer (1998: 120); Kloppenborg (1995: 97); Audet (1958: 352) and Rordorf (1996a: 153 n. 36) favour 6.1 as a closing point.

To establish which of these potential end-points is the most likely it is necessary to note, first of all, that 5.2a, 5.2b and 6.1 were added to the text at three different times, either singly or as part of larger elements.

Thus, *Did.* 5.2a is almost identical to the parallel 'way of darkness' in *Barnabas* 20 and so there can be little doubt that this verse forms part of the original Two Ways tractate.

Did. 5.2b, on the other hand, does not appear in *Barnabas*, and further, it introduces a form of address, 'τέκνα', which is contrary to the preceding text in that neither this word, nor the plural form of address, occur elsewhere in the Two Ways material.[22] It is unlikely, therefore, that 5.2b was originally written by the same hand as 5.2a.

The reversion in *Did.* 6.1 to the singular form of address suggests the possibility that 5.2a and 6.1 belonged together in an original version of the Two Ways. However, two factors indicate that 6.1 did not follow on directly from 5.2a in the original Two Ways source. First, 6.1 is absent from the *Barnabas* account of the Two Ways. Second, the expression, 'See that no one leads you astray from this way of the teaching', implies that, in the conception of the author of 6.1, the Two Ways is a complete and established entity of which the author has an objective view. Otherwise the call to adhere to 'this way of the teaching' could be taken as referring to the way of the teaching that has just been mentioned, namely, the 'way of death'.

If *Did.* 5.2a, 5.2b and 6.1 were all added to the *Didache* at different times, then the question of which verses could have closed the Two Ways document arises.

Two factors suggest that 5.2b could never have formed the end of a free-standing document. First, the most likely motivation for adding additional material to the Two Ways teaching would be to enjoin readers to keep the teaching therein. It is surprising, therefore, that 5.2b contains only half of what might be expected. That is to say that rather than finishing the text with parallel injunctions to live the 'way of life' and reject the 'way of death', only the latter point is emphasized.

Second, a superior motivation for the addition of 5.2b may be found in the presence, rather than the absence, of 6.1. In this circumstance the text would run (picking it up towards the end of the 'way of death'):

---

22. There is one exception in that the plural form of address is also used in *Did.* 4.11.

> 5.2a … Those…who are murderers of children, corrupters of God's crea-
> tures, who turn away from the needy, who oppress the afflicted, defenders
> of the rich and unjust judges of the poor, altogether sinful.

> 6.1 See that no one leads you astray from this way of teaching, since the
> one who does so teaches apart from God.

This juxtaposition could take place if the author of 6.1 were commend-
ing the whole of the Two Ways teaching much as someone might say,
'Don't stray from what it says in this book', while handing over the
volume in question. A later reader of the resultant combined text might,
however, perceive an unhelpful ambiguity, since it could be taken that the
readers are being enjoined to let no one lead them astray from the 'way of
death'! In this circumstance the insertion of 5.2b, while clumsy, does
serve a feasible purpose in that it clarifies the potential ambiguity:

> 5.2a … Those…who are murderers of children, corrupters of God's
> creatures, who turn away from the needy, who oppress the afflicted, defen-
> ders of the rich and unjust judges of the poor, altogether sinful.

> 5.2b May you (pl.) be delivered, children, from all this.

> 6.1 See that no one leads you astray from this way of teaching, since the
> one who does so teaches apart from God.

If it may be concluded that 5.2b was unlikely ever to have been the last
line of a free-standing Two Ways document, then one of the other two
options for this function, 5.2a or 6.1, may be preferred. The case for *Did.*
6.1 is very much dependent on the presence of a parallel to *Did.* 6.1 (and
5.2b) in the *Doctrina apostolorum*. It is certainly the presence of 6.1 in the
Doctrina apostolorum that causes Niederwimmer (1998: 45, 120), Kloppenborg (1995: 97) and Audet (1958: 352) to suppose that this verse
belonged to the Didachist's Two Ways source. However, as discussed in
the *excursus* above, the inconsistency of the sequence *Did.* 5.2a–5.2b–6.1,
when compared with the relatively smooth parallel in the *Doctrina*, suggests that the *Doctrina* is a later document, and thus that it does not provide evidence of the presence of *Did.* 6.1 in the version of the Two Ways
known to the Didachist. Without the support of the *Doctrina* the case for
Did. 6.1 as an end-point to the base Two Ways collapses entirely.

Given that, in the absence of evidence from the *Doctrina*, *Did.* 6.1 shows
few signs of acting as a postscript to the Two Ways teaching[23] it is prefer-

---

23. As a later postscript to the Two Ways teaching, *Did.* 6.1 could only have functioned as an attempt to bolster the authority of the preceding text. However, the long
established and highly orthodox basis of the Two Ways teaching means that it is

able to consider the possibility that it served a different function as part of a larger addition to the *Didache*. In Chapter 5, section 2, below, it will be argued that 6.1 serves as a linking verse that provides a smooth transition from the Two Ways into the ensuing baptismal liturgy (7.1). Without this verse, it will be argued, the following instructions could not have made sense. If this conclusion is justified, then it is likely that *Did.* 6.1 was added as part of a larger layer of Christian instruction, rather than as an additional support to the authority of the Two Ways.

If neither 6.1 or 5.2b serve as credible end-points for the free-standing Two Ways document, then it may be concluded that any further layers that were added to the Two Ways were appended to the end of 5.2a. That this verse is the most likely end-point of the Two Ways document is strongly supported by the exactly parallel ending in the version of this teaching found in *Barnabas* 20.

7. *The Two Ways:* Didache *1.1-2a, c; 2.1-7; 3.8–5.2a*

With the removal of *Did.* 1.3-6; 3.1-7; 1.2b, d-e; 2.1 and 5.2b the base Two Ways may be limited to: 1.1-2a, c; 2.2-7 and 3.8–5.2a. The presence of parallels to almost all of this material in *Barnabas* 18–20 suggests that these verses record a Two Ways tractate into which additional elements, outlined above, were incorporated.

8. *Summary: Elements within* Didache *1–5*

This chapter has been solely concerned with the isolation of the various elements that comprise the *Didache*'s pre-baptismal catechism. This is not the same as attempting to identify when these elements were added to *Didache*; a question addressed in Chapter 7 with respect to *Did.* 1.5b-6, and in Chapter 9 with respect to the remaining verses. All that is required

---

unlikely to have needed support against generalized attacks; no such defence is provided in *Barnabas*. If *Did.* 6.1 was specially added in response to a specific challenge, then it is remarkable that this response is no more pointed than the general, 'See to it that no one leads you astray from this way of the doctrine'. In addition, as noted above, such an addition creates a curious ambiguity in the absence of 5.2b, thus requiring the addition of this insert also. The complications involved in the addition of these final lines as the end of a free-standing Two Ways document would therefore be so great, relative to the benefit gained, that it is hard to imagine that such a course could ever have been taken.

at this preparatory stage is the identification of elements in *Did.* 1–5 that derive from different points of origin.

8.1. *Two Ways*
The similarity of *Did.* 1.1-2a, c; 2.2-7 and 3.8–5.2a to the Two Ways material in *Barnabas* 18–20 and the distinct difference in style and content between these verses and *Did.* 1.2b, d-e; 1.3-6 and 3.1-7 suggests that *Did.* 1.1-2a,c; 2.2-7 and 3.8–5.2a represents a Two Ways source separate from the surrounding material.[24]

8.2. *Law Summary Unit*
Did. 1.2b, d-e and 2.1 contains the double love command and a negative version of the golden rule that links back, at *Did.* 2.1, into the continuing Two Ways. This distinctive expansion of the Two Ways instruction to 'love the God who created you' is not present in the *Barnabas* Two Ways and so is taken as an additional separate element.

8.3. *Sayings Onion*
The collection of sayings at *Did.* 1.3-5a expand the command to love the neighbour and interrupt the flow, both in terms of content and style, from the negative golden rule (1.2c) into the negative instructions following *Did.* 2.1. While generally recognized as an addition to the Two Ways, scholars have overlooked the crucial possibility that this unit contains five elements, themselves of separate origin.

8.4. *Modification of Sayings Onion*
If *Did.* 1.5b-6 seeks to modify the immediately preceding call to 'give without asking back', then it is highly unlikely to have been written by the person who also contributed *Did.* 1.3-5a. In addition, within *Did.* 1.5b-6, a further saying of separate origin is quoted in 1.6b, 'Let your charitable gift sweat in your hands until you know to whom you give'.

---

24. The origins of this unit cannot be traced precisely. For some time it was believed that *Barnabas* was the direct source for these verses. However, the more recent scholarly consensus supposes that *Didache* and *Barnabas* were both dependent on a common written document. This is the view of Glover (1958: 22); Rordorf (1991: 396); Layton (1968: 379); Draper (1996a: 10, 13, 16); Kloppenborg (1995: 88–92) and Niederwimmer (1998: 31). The widespread extent of this type of tradition in the Old Testament and Apocrypha (Niederwimmer 1998: 59–62) suggests that the tradition expressed in *Did.* 1.1-2a, c; 2.2-7 and 3.8–5.2a may well be pre-Christian.

In summary, this chapter has argued that *Did.* 1–5 contains work derived from nine points of origin: a Two Ways tractate, a summary of the Law, a collection of five sayings arranged around a central gnome, and a modification of those sayings which itself appeals to an external authority.

The end of this chapter marks the completion of three major preparatory tasks concerning the prayers in *Did.* 9–10, the integrity of *Did.* 16 and the elements within *Did.* 1–5. It is now possible to progress to a more direct consideration of the compositional history of the *Didache*.

Chapter 5

THE PERI LAYER:
6.1-3; 7.1a, c, e, 4a; 9.1-5a; 11.3a, 4-6; 16.1-6, 8-9

This chapter takes up a loose thread left at the end of Chapter 2, where it was concluded that the eucharistic prayers within *Did.* 9 and 10 belong to two separate redactional layers. The first aim of this chapter is to identify those parts of the *Didache* that belong to the same redactional layer as *Did.* 9. (This layer will be referred to, for the time being, as the 'Peri' layer because of the recurrence of the formula 'περὶ δὲ' within it.) Towards the close of this chapter, one further thread, made available by Chapter 3, will also be addressed; namely, the redactional status of *Did.* 16 in relation to the Peri layer.

1. *The Peri Layer Baptism:* Didache 7.1a,[1] c, e, 4a

One verse that has several strong connections with *Did.* 9.1-5 is *Did.* 7.1.[2] At a stylistic level this verse follows the distinctive pattern of introduction that is used in *Did.* 9.1:

9.1   Περὶ δὲ τῆς εὐχαριστίας, οὕτως εὐχαριστήσατε·
7.1a   Περὶ δὲ τοῦ βαπτίσματος, οὕτω βαπτίσατε·

Did. 7.1 also has strong functional coherence in relation to the eucharist of *Did.* 9. The fact that *Did.* 9.5 states that only the baptized may partake of the eucharist, suggests that instructions concerning the means by which such eligibility may be achieved are likely to have been included along with instructions regarding the eucharist.[3]

There is, therefore, good reason to suppose that the Peri layer contained instructions concerning baptism followed by instructions concerning the

1.   The redactional status of 7.1b, d will be considered in Chapter 7, §§ 6 and 9.
2.   Niederwimmer 1998: 144.
3.   Baptism is immediately followed by the eucharist in the account provided by Justin, *First Apology* 65–66.

eucharist. However, the identification of the extent of those instructions is not straightforward. In their present form the rules for baptism show strong signs of having been amended. To establish the extent of the original Peri layer, therefore, it is necessary to consider the nature and effect of that amendment.

Two signs suggest both the presence and the extent of an addition made to *Did.* 7. First, the threefold formulae for baptism in 7.1 (with articles) and 7.3 (without articles), are inconsistent with the reference to baptism 'in the name of the Lord' to be found in *Did.* 9.5. Draper (1996b: 78) expresses the view that 'The trinitarian baptismal formula in 7:1 is probably a later redactional retouch, since a slightly different formula is given in 7:3, and the earlier formula εἰς ὄνομα κυρίου has survived in 9:5'.[4]

A second sign that *Did.* 7 is not the work of one hand can be found in the change of addressee that takes place, without rhetorical purpose, in the course of the baptismal instructions. Rordorf (1996b: 214) says:

> I do not believe that one could deny an important change of perspective between *Didache* 7:1 and 7:2ff, which is expressed precisely in the fact that the beginning of the chapter is addressed to a plurality of persons, whereas what follows is addressed to one person only. This fact alone proves that the chapter could not have been written by the same hand.

Rordorf goes on to suggest that 7.1, being plural, addresses a more primitive situation than 7.2-3. This, he argues, is indicative of a change from a primitive situation, where many members of a church may baptize, to a later one where only an authorized individual may do so. While this is possible, Rordorf's point is perhaps overplayed, since 7.1 could simply be addressed to more than one community. However, even if Rordorf may be on uncertain ground regarding this particular basis for the supposed antiquity of 7.1 relative to 7.2-3, his point regarding the change in addressee (and therefore of author) still stands.

If the change of addressee is indicative of an amendment, then the identification of text addressed to plural recipients should reveal what remains, in these instructions, of what may be traced back to the Peri layer. Rordorf (1996b: 215) observes, with respect to *Did.* 7.4a and 7.1:

> …the same situation [plural addressees] is reflected in *Didache* 7:4a, where the term ὁ βαπτίζων to designate the one who administers baptism

---

4.   Rordorf (1996b: 217) is certain that the text of 9.5 is a more ancient baptism formula. Wedderburn (1987) suggests that the formula 'into the name of the Lord' (9.5) may be even more ancient than baptism 'into the name of the Lord Jesus', as commonly found in the New Testament (cf. Hartman 1997).

indicates the absence of a specific minister; for this reason, it seems to me that *Didache* 7:4a is drawn from the same source as *Didache* 7:1. *Didache* 7:2-3,4b, in turn, is addressed directly to the one who administers baptism.

Niederwimmer (1998: 125) agrees:

> In my opinion 7.2-3 is also redactional, in contrast to the original and more rigorous demand to baptize 'with living water'... I also consider 7.4a to be old tradition, and 7.4b to be redactional.

The picture that emerges, therefore, is one where the original Peri text reads something approximating to:

> Concerning baptism, baptize thus:
> [After you have repeated all these things][5]
> Baptize in the name of the Lord
> in running water.
> Before the baptism, let the one baptizing and the one being baptized, and others who are able, fast.

This text, addressed to unknown plural recipients, is then altered by the addition of instructions addressed to an individual. The fact that these additions show no concession to their new context, both in the different addressee and in the apparent absence of any need to describe how long the baptizer and others should fast, suggest that the amendment has been made by inserting a text with a previously separate existence. As Schöllgen (1996: 48) observes: 'With vv.2,3,4b, which differ from the context in their use of the second person singular address, the author may well have worked in pre-existent traditional material'.[6]

A further indication that the changes in *Did.* 7 are the product of an insertion, rather than poor editorial retouching (so Draper 1996c: 226), may be found in the fact that the baptismal formula in *Did.* 9.5 has escaped amendment.

The inserted text, addressed to a singular addressee, may be approximately reconstructed as follows:

> Baptize in the name of the Father, the Son and the Holy Spirit
> in running water.
> If you do not have running water baptize in other water; if you cannot in cold, then in warm,

---

5.   Later discussion will conclude that 7.1b is likely to have been added as part of the third layer of the *Didache* (cf. Chapter 7, § 10). This line is removed, therefore, in the immediately following discussion.

6.   Vööbus (1968: 34) is sceptical of this.

But if you have neither, pour water on the head thrice
in the name of Father, Son, and Holy Spirit.
Command the one being baptized to fast for one or two days beforehand.

The similarities and differences between the Peri instructions for baptism and this 'trinitarian' text provides a strong rationale for the insertion of the latter into the former. The two texts overlap in their treatment of baptism, in their reference to living water and their consideration of baptismal fasting. The point where there is direct contradiction is in the baptismal formula itself. The interpolator therefore meshes the texts as follows; where the 'original' text is on the left and the interpolated 'trinitarian' text is on the right. Underlining indicates the wording that ultimately appears in the Jerusalem manuscript.

Peri Layer Baptism	*Inserted Baptismal Tradition*
7.1a περὶ δὲ τοῦ βαπτίσματος, οὕτω βαπτίσατε·	
7.1c βαπτίσατε εἰς τὸ ὄνομα	7.1c βαπτίσατε εἰς τὸ ὄνομα
7.1d κυρίου	7.1d τοῦ πατρὸς καὶ τοῦ υἱοῦ καὶ τοῦ ἁγίου πνεύματος
7.1e ἐν ὕδατι ζῶντι.	7.1e ἐν ὕδατι ζῶντι.
	7.2a ἐὰν δὲ μὴ ἔχῃς ὕδωρ ζῶν, εἰς ἄλλο ὕδωρ βάπτισον· 7.2b εἰ δ' οὐ δύνασαι ἐν ψυχρῷ, ἐν θερμῷ. 7.3 ἐὰν δὲ ἀμφότερα μὴ ἔχῃς, ἔκχεον εἰς τὴν κεφαλὴν τρὶς ὕδωρ εἰς ὄνομα πατρὸς καὶ υἱοῦ καὶ ἁγίου πνεύματος.
7.4a πρὸ δὲ τοῦ βαπτίσματος προνηστευσάτω ὁ βαπτίζων καὶ ὁ βαπτιζόμενος καὶ εἴ τινες ἄλλοι δύνανται·	
	7.4b κελεύεις δὲ νηστεῦσαι τὸν βαπτιζόμενον πρὸ ἢ δύο.

The point at which 7.1d, 2-3, 4b was interpolated into the *Didache* will be considered in due course (cf. Chapter 7, section 6).

It is unlikely that the Peri layer instructions continue into *Did.* 8.1-3. This is the case not only because there is no 'περὶ δε' formula, but also because the connection between 8.1 and 7.4 is by catchword only, and does not follow a progressive development. That is to say, the fasts of 7.4 are specifically addressed to the situation prior to baptism – before which an unbroken fast would be logical. The fast in 8.1, however, is something regular and not specifically associated with baptism.[7]

In summary, instructions regarding baptism are likely to have belonged to the same layer as *Did.* 9.1-5. This is indicated by the strikingly parallel introductory formulae of 7.1 and 9.1, and by the logical sequence of baptism followed by eucharist. These instructions have been changed by the interpolation of a separate text, and by the insertion of 7.1b, 'ταῦτα πάντα προειπόντες' (cf. Chapter 7, section 10). Thus, the proposed wording of the original baptismal instructions of the Peri layer is:

περὶ δὲ τοῦ βαπτίσματος, οὕτω βαπτίσατε·
βαπτίσατε εἰς τὸ ὄνομα κυρίου ἐν ὕδατι ζῶντι.
πρὸ δὲ τοῦ βαπτίσματος προνηστευσάτω ὁ βαπτίζων καὶ ὁ βαπτιζόμενος καὶ εἴ τινες ἄλλοι δύνανται·

2. *Link between the Two Ways and Baptism:* Didache *6.1-3*

Thus far an element of the Peri layer has been traced as far forward as *Did.* 7.1. However, two factors suggest that *Did.* 7.1 cannot have served as the opening verse of a free-standing 'Peri document'.

First, it would be highly unconventional to open a discourse with a piece of specific meta-language such as 'concerning baptism' if the text concerned were not solely to do with this subject. This is the case because, as Brown and Yule (1983: 139) note:

> …the expectation-creating aspect of thematisation, especially in the form of a title, means that thematised elements provide not only a starting point around which what follows in the discourse is structured, but also a starting point which *constrains our interpretation of what follows*.[8] [emphasis added]

This means that a discourse entitled 'Concerning Baptism' creates the expectation that the interpretation of what follows should be limited to, or constrained to, the subject of baptism. In the case of the Peri document it has already been concluded that this text contains instructions on eucharist as well as baptism (in section 3, below, it will be argued that the Peri layer also addresses the subject of apostles). The presence of sections on the

7. The timing and purpose of the insertion of *Did.* 8.1-3 will be considered in Chapter 7, § 7.

8. Similarly, Sperber and Wilson (1986: 216) state: '…the classic discourse topics are titles and picture captions, whose role is precisely to give access to encyclopaedic information crucial to the comprehension of the accompanying texts or pictures'.

eucharist and apostles, in a text headed 'Concerning Baptism', may only be explained if the latter instructions could be seen as a sub-section of 'Concerning Baptism'. This requires an unnatural understanding of eucharist and apostles. Further, the similar style in which the paragraphs on baptism, eucharist and apostles are introduced suggests that they are sub-sections which are each intended to carry equal weight. This parity requires the three sections to be equally subordinate to a main heading of some kind.[9]

Second, if 7.1 were the opening verse of a free-standing Peri document, then the process of baptism would be remarkably undemanding for the initiate. That is to say, the newcomer would only be required to receive a washing in running water, presumably 'in the name of the Lord' (cf. 9.5), in order to be transformed from an outsider (9.5; cf. 10.6) into a person worthy of participating in the eschatological feast. Given this mismatch it is preferable to suppose that 7.1 was originally preceded by some mechanism to show that the initiate had stepped into a new state of membership. Rordorf (1996a: 156) notes (having previously argued that the *Didache* was addressed to a Gentile audience): 'The situation of those first converts from Paganism seeking baptism [meant that] it was necessary to instruct them, prior to their baptism, in the rudiments of ethical behaviour in accordance with faith in one God'.[10] This suggests that *Did.* 7.1 is likely to have been preceded by a set of requirements to be laid on the initiate prior to baptism. Such a requirement is amply described by the Two Ways tradition recorded in *Did.* 1–5.

That *Did.* 7.1 was indeed designed to follow from the *Didache*'s augmented Two Ways tradition is indicated by a number of factors. First, the curious juxtaposition of two distinctly different types of text (a traditional Jewish ethical exposition and a manual of Christian liturgical instruction), requires an explanation. The 'principle of relevance', a linguistic phenomenon noted by Sperber and Wilson (1986), notes that each succeeding part of any discourse, however constructed, must contain some element that makes it relevant to that discourse at the point of introduction. This means, for example, that, even in a collection of unrelated aphorisms, each new saying may be seen as relevant simply because it belongs to the common

---

9.   The nature and location of this main heading will be discussed in Chapter 9.

10.   That pre-baptismal catechesis was a feature of Gentile conversion from the earliest times is intimated by the remarks of Pliny the Younger in his letter to Trajan, 10.96.7 regarding the ethical promises made by Christians prior to their sharing in a common meal.

genre 'aphorism'. Similarly, as occurs elsewhere in the *Didache*, a new layer of text may be considered relevant to the preceding text because it contains common subject matter or a common catchword. In the case of *Did.* 1–5 and *Did.* 7.1, however, there is almost no overlap of wording or genre that explains their combination. However, the fact that they *are* combined suggests that the person responsible for their juxtaposition considered one to be relevant to the other. The location of such relevance may be found in the fact that *Did.* 1–5 invites initiates to step from the 'way of death' to the 'way of life', thus providing a suitable preamble to baptism. As N. Mitchell (1995: 250) notes:

> There can be little doubt, in the opinion of most contemporary scholars,[11] that the materials of *Did* 1.1–6.1a should be understood as instructions which are designed primarily for catechumens. The very structure of the Two Ways schema in 1.1–6.1a invites decision.

The functional logic of the relationship between *Did.* 1–5 and *Did.* 7 is supported by evidence of the use of Two Ways types of instruction in baptismal catechesis in the early Christian centuries. As Rordorf (1996a: 158–59) notes:

> There was, without doubt, an uninterrupted tradition of prebaptismal ethical instruction in the Christian church of the first two centuries, a tradition which has its roots in Judaism, which has its *Sitz im Leben* in the context of the initiation of Gentile converts, and which led to the instruction of the Christian catechumens at the end of the second century. The *duae viae* has its place in this tradition.

Further, Rordorf (1996a: 152) notes the longstanding appreciation (even before the discoveries made at Qumran) of the relationship between Jewish proselyte catechetical instruction and the *duae viae*. He continues: 'Although we might be poorly informed of the baptism of Jewish prose-lytes in the primitive Christian epoch, the parallels which it presents to Christian baptism are undeniable'. Records of Jewish proselyte baptism from the end of the first century CE show that the Law was recited prior to the washing. While it is possible that this practice developed in imitation of the Christian baptism this nonetheless suggests that that which was imi-tated contained a recitation of an ethical code prior to baptism, as is found in the *Didache*.

If *Did.* 1–5 did indeed provide a suitable preamble to baptism, then *Did.* 7.1 must always have been preceded by linking lines that explain the role

---

11. Mitchell cites Niederwimmer (1989: 88); Draper (1991: 359) and Rordorf (1972b: 503).

of the ancient Two Ways teaching in relation to the baptismal rite. Without such intervening material a spoken liturgy that drove straight through from 5.2a (the end of the Two Ways, cf. Chapter 4, section 6) into 7.1 would sound ridiculous and would be potentially misleading; the impression could be given that initiation was into the 'way of death', rather than the 'way of life'.

The intervention of *Did.* 6.1 between 5.2a and 7.1a is vital to the transition between the two texts. This verse presents the Two Ways as a valid expression of the community rule to which initiates should seek to adhere. The vital service performed by 6.1, in binding the Two Ways and the baptismal liturgy together, suggests that it formed an original element of the Peri layer.

The inclusion of *Did.* 6.1 as part of the Peri layer still leaves a question mark over the status of 6.2-3. From a liturgical point of view these verses are a little clumsy. That is to say that it would be neater to pass straight from the summarizing statement of 6.1 into the baptism without the added details of 6.2-3. However, this clumsiness does not in itself disqualify 6.2-3 from the Peri layer since, if these instructions were considered important for initiates at the time at which the Peri layer was composed, it is difficult to see where else they could have been included. A factor which suggests that these two verses *were* added as part of the Peri layer is the parallel use of the 'περὶ δὲ' formula in *Did.* 6.3 and 7.1 (περὶ δὲ τῆς βρώσεως …περὶ δὲ τοῦ βαπτίσματος…).[12]

The strong connection between 6.3 and 6.2, in terms of their shared interest in 'doing what you are able' with respect to the 'yoke of the Lord',[13] leads towards the further conclusion that 6.2 and 6.3 were written by the same author. These considerations mean that, although the section 6.2-3 is liturgically untidy, it is likely to have been added at the same time as 6.1 and the instructions regarding baptism, eucharist (and apostles).

The beginning of this section argued that 7.1 is unlikely ever to have been the opening verse of a free-standing document. This position was taken because of the need for a preamble to baptism, and for a main heading under which sub-sections on baptism, eucharist and apostles could sit. The former of these requirements was satisfied by *Did.* 1–5, thus creating a need for linking verses between *Did.* 1–5 and 7.1, which, it has been argued, is satisfied by *Did.* 6.1 (along with 6.2-3). I therefore conclude

---

12. So Kraft (1965: 161–63).
13. Flusser (1996: 199) and Draper (1995: 290) take 'the yoke of the Lord' to refer to the Torah.

that *Did.* 6.1-3 formed part of the Peri layer that linked *Did.* 1–5 to 7.1a, c, e, 4a and 9.1-5a.[14]

3. *Apostles:* Didache *11.3a, 4-6*

Thus far, the Peri layer has shown a logical progression. *Did.* 6.1-3 sums up the legal requirements incumbent upon initiates and adds details concerning food, *Did.* 7.1a, c, e, 4a describes the initiation ritual itself, and *Did.* 9.1-5a orders the eucharist to which only the baptized may be admitted. In combination with *Did.* 1–5, therefore, these elements of the Peri layer appear to constitute a complete and practical document. However, there is one further section that presents a strong claim for inclusion in the Peri layer: *Did.* 11.3a, 4-6.

Before attempting to argue for the inclusion of *Did.* 11.3a, 4-6 it is necessary to show that these verses do not belong to the same layer as the immediately following or preceding text.

The case for the separation of 11.3-6 from 11.7-12 has two strands. First, there is disjunction between the style, subject matter and structure of the two paragraphs. Thus, 11.4-6 contains clearly ordered instructions regarding the arrival, stay and departure of an apostle:

ARRIVAL | 11.4 Let every apostle who comes to you be received as the Lord.
STAY | 11.5 He shall stay only one day, or, if need be, another day too. If he stays three days, he is a false prophet.
DEPARTURE | 11.6 When the apostle leaves, let him receive nothing but enough bread to see him through until he finds lodging. If he asks for money he is a false prophet.

Didache 11.7-12,[15] on the other hand, is an ambiguously introduced, loosely arranged and repetitive set of statements devoted to the issue of how the community should respond to prophetic speech. These two issues are not unrelated, but it is nonetheless surprising that they are not treated in a more integrated manner if one author is responsible for both paragraphs.

---

14. One possibility that has not been considered here is that the Peri layer was a free-standing document, opening at either 6.1 or 6.2, that was later appended to *Did.* 1–5. This pattern is unlikely given that 6.1 must be preceded by a description of what 'this way of the teaching' might be. *Did.* 6.2 cannot open a free-standing document because the use of 'γὰρ' presupposes some preceding text, namely 6.1. In addition, neither 6.2 or 6.3 provide a suitable heading under which all the subsequent 'περὶ δὲ' subheadings may be set.

15. In Chapter 7, § 1 it will be argued that *Did.* 11.10-11 do not belong to the same layer as *Did.* 11.7-9,12.

A possible explanation for the awkward relationship between 11.3-6 and 11.7-12 is signalled by the close continuity between *Did.* 10.7 and 11.7:

> 10.7 Allow the prophets to give thanks as much as they wish 11.7 and (καὶ) every prophet speaking in the Spirit neither test nor judge; every sin shall be forgiven, but this sin shall not be forgiven.

In contrast to the awkward join between 11.6 and 11.7, the flow from 10.7 to 11.7 is remarkably smooth. These two sentences are a perfect grammatical match. Most notably, this sequence avoids having a grammatically unattractive 'καὶ' at the introduction to the subject of prophetic speech, and places it instead between two sentences of related subject. Since the non-interruption of prophetic speech is not addressed anywhere else in the *Didache*, it is particularly noteworthy that 10.7 and 11.7 both focus on this subject. Thus, 10.7 commands that prophetic thanksgiving over the eschatological meal should be allowed to continue for as long as the prophet wishes; while 11.7 rules, in the strongest possible terms, that the speech of a prophet should not be tested in mid-prophesy.

The quality of the connection between 10.7 and 11.7 suggests that these two lines originally formed one sentence in the previously existing document to which they belonged. Their split location in the *Didache* may be accounted for on the basis that the material concerned with the eucharist was inserted after the eucharistic instructions in *Did.* 9, and verses concerned with church leaders was paired with teaching on a similar subject in *Did.* 11.3-6. This type of spliced interpolation can also be seen in *Did.* 7, where a previously existing document was added to the host in two parts. Thus, teaching on baptism (7.1b, d, 2-3) was added after the host text's teaching on baptism (7.1a, c, e), and rules for the baptismal fast (7.4b) were inserted after the host's rules for the baptismal fast (7.4a).[16]

The relationship between 10.7 and 11.7 has implications for a number of further aspects of this study. In the meantime, however, it affects the question in hand in that, if 10.7 and 11.7 are adjacent verses in the same layer, then they cannot also belong to the same layer as 11.1-6. If this point may be accepted, then it is possible to go on to consider the status of 11.3-6 with respect to the Peri layer. (Conclusions regarding this connection will then assist in the consideration of the status of 11.1-2; see Chapter 7, section 3. below.)

The isolation of *Did.* 11.1-6 in relation to *Did.* 10.7 and 11.7 assists in the identification of 11.3-6 with the Peri layer because of the effect that this has on the heading in 11.3.

---

16. Cf. § 1, above.

Did. 11.3 operates as a heading that introduces the subject of apostles and prophets. However, if, as the foregoing analysis has argued, 11.4-6 (concerning apostles) was not originally followed by 11.7-9, 12 (concerning prophetic speech), then the heading that originally introduced 11.4-6 is unlikely to have mentioned prophets as well as apostles. Further, it will be argued below (Chapter 8), that in the developing community the curious instructions regarding apostles and prophets required subordination to the teaching of the later mainstream tradition. This requirement could have been achieved by adding 'κατὰ τὸ δόγμα τοῦ εὐαγγελίου οὕτω ποιήσατε', as a means of abrogating the difficulties and contradictions of the ensuing instructions. The version of 11.3 that is most likely to have originally appeared in combination with 11.4-6 is therefore: 'περὶ δὲ τῶν ἀποστόλων'. This short heading shows striking similarities with the introductions to baptism and eucharist in the Peri layer; not only in the characteristic use of 'περὶ δὲ', but also in the repetition of the subject word immediately after the heading:

9.1	Περὶ δὲ	τῆς εὐχαριστίας,	οὕτως	εὐχαριστήσατε·
7.1a	Περὶ δὲ	τοῦ βαπτίσματος,	οὕτω	βαπτίσατε·
11.3a, 4	Περὶ δὲ	τῶν ἀποστόλων,	πᾶς [δὲ][17]	ἀπόστολος.

This parallel form of subheading, in combination with the same pithy and direct style of the following instructions in each case, suggests that *Did.* 11.3-6 represents a further element of the Peri layer. The lack of any further uses of the formula 'περὶ δὲ' suggests that this layer does not continue into the ecclesial instructions of *Did.* 12–15.

My conclusion regarding the status of 11.3-6 (less the reference to prophets and the gospel in 11.3) is very largely in accordance with, and is sometimes dependent on, those of Jonathan Draper (1996d: 343-44):

> [The] instruction concerning apostles corresponds to the form of the instructions which precede it. Each set of instructions is prefaced by the same formula: περὶ δὲ τῶν...οὕτω ποιήσατε. Only one subject appears in the title of each section introduced in this way, with the exception of 11:3, where the introduction of prophets into the title seems to be a redaction made at a time when instructions concerning prophets were added. The reference to the δόγμα τοῦ εὐαγγελίου also marks this as a later interpolation, as we have seen. The original title probably read περὶ δὲ τῶν ἀποστόλων, οὕτω ποιήσατε. The instruction of 11:3-6 show the same casuistic development

17. Draper (1996d: 345) believes the δὲ here is inauthentic and that the title did not originally include a reference to prophets. Δὲ is absent from the Coptic and Ethiopic.

and the same brevity as the other instructions in the section 6:2–10:6.[18] The instructions on prophets are in marked contrast: detailed, self-contradictory[19] in places and vivid. The instructions concerning prophets have tended, for this reason, to dominate discussion on the *Didache*.

Nevertheless, there are signs of controversy surrounding the institution of apostles in the *Didache* too. Here I wish to focus particularly on 11:1-2. K. Niederwimmer sees this passage as a composition of the 'Didachist', connecting the liturgical tradition of 9–10 with further traditional material concerning apostles. However, the form of *instructions* does not require such connecting links between sections, which are simply introduced by περὶ δέ. Thus 11:1-2 should not be seen as a connecting link but as a later redaction, modifying the instructions on apostles in 11:3-6 in the light of new circumstances in the community.

In summary then, Draper sees 11.3-6, less the references to prophets and the gospel, as originally part of the Peri layer. I am in almost complete agreement with this conclusion. The following discussion of the redactional status of 11.1-2; 11.3b; 11.7-12, and so on, will offer further reasons for supporting Draper's position.

4. *The Peri Layer and* Didache *16.1-6, 8-9*

The aim of this section is to consider the possibility that *Did.* 16.1-6, 8-9 formed an additional element of the Peri layer.

In Chapter 3 it was argued that *Did.* 16 consists of two main elements. The older part, *Did.* 16.3-6, 8-9, records a previously existing eschatological scheme that is coherent, whole and apparently free from later amendment (with the exception of the interpolation at *Did.* 16.7, which is set aside in the following discussion). The younger part, *Did.* 16.1-2, appears to have been written in the light of *Did.* 16.3-6, 8-9 and serves to bind the older eschatological discourse onto the end of the *Didache*. The linking function of *Did.* 16.1-2, with respect to 16.3-6, 8-9, means that neither of these two elements is likely to have been added to the *Didache* without the other. Thus, the point at which *Did.* 16.1-2 was written is very likely also to be the point at which *Did.* 16.3-6, 8-9 was added to the whole.

The process of identifying a redactional location for 16.1-2 (and thereby also of 16.3-6, 8-9) will be undertaken in two stages. In Chapter 9, during

18.   An observation that is even more accurate if *Did.* 9.1-5 alone carries the eucharistic instruction of the Peri layer; cf. Chapter 2.

19.   I shall present a redactional explanation for these self-contradictions in Chapter 7, § 1.

the study of the full extent of the Peri layer, further evidence will be offered to suggest that *Did.* 16 formed part of this layer. At this stage, however, it is already possible to note some points of connection between *Did.* 16.1-2 and *Did.* 6.1-3 which, according to the case presented in section 2 above, belongs to the Peri layer.

> 6.1 See that no one leads you astray from this way of the teaching, since this one teaches apart from God. 6.2 If you are able to bear the whole yoke of the Lord, you will be perfect, but if you cannot, do what you can. 6.3 Concerning food, bear what you can, but abstain strictly from food offered to idols, for it is worship of dead gods.

> 16.1 Watch over your life. Let your lamps not go out and let your loins not be ungirded but be ready, for you do not know the hour at which our Lord is coming. 16.2 You shall assemble frequently, seeking what your souls need, for the whole time of your faith will be of no profit to you unless you are perfected at the final hour.

These two passages serve a common function in that they both exhort the reader to adhere to a comprehensive standard of behaviour. The threat to compliance in both cases is that they will be led astray by false teaching. Thus, in the eschatological discourse following 16.1-2 the readers are warned of the approach of one who will lead the world astray (ὁ κοσμο-πλανὴς) with the result that some will be lost (16.4b-5). In 6.1 the fear is expressed that the reader will be led astray (πλανήσῃ) from the preceding way of teaching by one who teaches apart from God. The goal of compliance is also similar in each case. Thus, in 6.2 the baptismal candidates are told that if they keep the whole yoke of the Lord they will become perfect (τέλειος ἔσῃ).[20] This goal of perfection is also held up before the readers of 16.1-2 where they are told that, although incomplete adherence to the 'yoke of the Lord' may be initially acceptable, at the end it is perfection that is required, 'for the whole time of your faith will be of no profit to you unless you are perfected (τελειωθῆτε) at the final hour'. These common themes of resisting deception while seeking perfection suggest that the linking material in 6.1-3 and 16.1-2 were both written by the same author. If this is the case, then *Did.* 16.1-6, 8-9 may initially be seen as belonging to the Peri layer alongside 6.1-3; 7.1a, c, e, 4a (baptism); 9.1-5a (eucharist); and 11.3a, 4-6 (apostles). As mentioned above, further reasons for assigning *Did.* 16.1-6, 8-9 to the Peri layer will be considered in Chapter 9, section 4.

---

20. 'The word τέλειος (perfect) is a technical term which refers to the fulfilment of Torah according to the *halakah* of a particular group' (Draper 1995: 290). See also n. 13.

5. *Sub-Summary: The Peri Layer*

A discussion of the full extent of the Peri layer must wait until Chapter 9, after the status of the rest of the text has been evaluated. At this stage, however, the following portions of the extant text have been identified as belonging to the Peri layer:

6.1-3: A commendation of the Two Ways teaching to those being baptized, with additional instructions not covered by the Two Ways.

7.1a, c, e, 4a: Rules for the administration of baptism and preparatory fasting associated with that rite.

9.1-5a: Rules for the administration of the eucharist to which only the baptized may be admitted.

11.3a, 4-6: Rules governing the treatment of apostles.

The possibility has also been raised (and will be pursued further in Chapter 9) that 16.1-6, 8-9 formed an eschatological warning at the conclusion to the Peri layer.

Chapter 6

THE PROPHET DOCUMENT: 10.1-7; 11.7-9, 12; 12.1-5

The purpose of the preceding chapter was to identify those parts of the *Didache* that belong to the same redactional layer as the eucharistic prayer recorded in *Did.* 9.1-5a. The aim of this chapter is to find those parts of the text that belong to the same layer as the parallel eucharistic prayer recorded in *Did.* 10.1-6.

1. Didache *10.7 and 11.7-9, 12*

In Chapter 5 it was noted that *Did.* 11.6 and 11.7 are roughly juxtaposed, while *Did.* 10.7 and 11.7 form a cohesive whole when placed together. This invites the possibility that *Did.* 10.7 and 11.7 were joined prior to their addition to the *Didache*. This in turn suggests that these two verses were part of a previously existing document, separate from the *Didache*, which was divided at 10.7/11.7 and inserted into the host text in two separate parts.[1]

Did. 10.7 shows a strong affinity to 10.1-6 in that both are concerned with the practice of giving thanks. This suggests that 10.1-6 formed an additional part of the separate document to which 10.7 and 11.7 belonged. The abrupt division of *Did.* 10.7 and 11.7 provides a clue to the possible continuing extent of this separate document. If 11.7 were the final element of this document, then it is surprising that the interpolator did not simply include 11.7 after 10.7, rather than detaching it from 10.7 and placing this defence of the sanctity of prophetic speech after a discussion of how apostles may be identified as false prophets. However, if 11.7 was always followed by 11.8, then the extant arrangement makes better sense. In this circumstance the means of recognizing apostles who are false prophets (11.5, 6), coheres with the test for false prophets provided in 11.8. It is likely, therefore, that 11.8 always followed 11.7 as part of the interpolated

---

1. A motive for this action is offered in § 3, below, and Chapter 10, § 2.

document (hereafter referred to as the Prophet document, because of its concern for prophets and prophecy).

Did. 11.8 teaches: 'But not every one speaking in the Spirit (ἐν πνεύ-ματι) is a prophet, but only those whose behaviour is as the Lord's, by their actions you can discern the false prophet from the prophet'. *Did.* 11.9 goes on to give a concrete example of an action that betrays the false prophesy of a false prophet. Thus, if someone claims to be 'in the Spirit' and uses this to gain food for themselves, then their claim to inspiration is false. In the same way, and using similar language, *Did.* 11.12 explains that if someone uses the cover of inspired speech to gain money or posses-sions, then they are a false prophet issuing false prophecy.

> 11.7 ...and every prophet speaking in the Spirit (ἐν πνεύματι) neither test nor judge; every sin shall be forgiven, but this sin shall not be forgiven.
> 11.8 But not every one speaking in the Spirit (ἐν πνεύματι) is a prophet, but only those whose behaviour is as the Lord's, by their actions you can discern the false prophet from the prophet.
> 11.9 Every prophet calling for a table of food in the Spirit (ἐν πνεύματι) will not eat of it. If he does he is a false prophet...
> 11.12 If any prophet, speaking in the Spirit (ἐν πνεύματι) says, 'Give me money', or anything else, do not listen to him. On the other hand, if he calls you to give it to someone who is in need, do not judge him.

The shared use of the expression 'ἐν πνεύματι' in 11.7, 8, 9, 12, and the structural coherence of teaching that moves from the general (11.8) to the specific (11.9, 12), suggests that these four verses belong together, and thus belong to the Prophet document, along with *Did.* 10.1-7.

The structural and stylistic coherence of this programme is disrupted by the inclusion of *Did.* 11.10-11. In Chapter 7, section 1 below, I will argue that these two verses were inserted as part of a later layer written in response to a possible misinterpretation of *Did.* 11.9.

The addition of *Did.* 10.7; 11.7-9, 12 to the eucharistic prayer of *Did.* 10.1-6 has the effect of revealing a document with a particular relationship to the Peri layer. As was noted in Chapter 2, the eucharistic prayer in *Did.* 10.1-6 is closely parallel to the eucharistic prayer in the Peri layer (9.1-5a). The level of similarity between these two prayers points to the direct dependence of one upon the other. That *Did.* 10.1-6 is a later development of *Did.* 9.1-5 is likely in the light, for example, of the differences between the calls for eucharistic exclusion in *Did.* 9.5 and 10.6. In the former this rubric is silent, while in the latter a public statement is made. Thus, in 9.5, there is a presupposition of the eucharistic president's knowledge of each member of the congregation, while 10.6 implies the presence of a larger, more anonymous gathering, suggestive of a later development in the Church's life.

The addition of 10.7; 11.7-9, 12 to the Prophet document's eucharistic teaching creates a set of instructions that build upon, but go beyond, that which is set down in the Peri layer. Thus, the basic teaching of the Peri layer with regard to the eucharistic prayer itself (9.1-5a) is largely adhered to by the Prophet document. However, where the Peri layer fails to address an issue, in this case the boundaries that should be placed on prophets when they give thanks at the eschatological meal, this deficiency is made good by a further elaboration in the Prophet document (10.7; 11.7-9, 12).

2. Didache *12.1-5*

Just as *Did.* 10.1-7; 11.7-9, 12 is closely dependent on *Did.* 9.1-5, while being willing to additionally respond to circumstances created by the presence of wandering prophets, so also *Did.* 12.1-5 pays consistent homage to *Did.* 11.3a, 4-6, while adapting those instructions to accommodate the ministry of itinerant prophets:

> THE WELCOME:
> 11.4 Let every apostle who comes to you be received as the Lord.
> 12.1 Let every one who comes in the name of the Lord be received,
> after that, when you have tested him, you will know what he is like—for you will have right and left perception.

The language and sentiment of the welcome in each case is remarkably similar. *Did.* 12.1, however, appears to address a situation where 'apostle' is no longer a suitable description for the type of visitor that is apparently in mind. This term is replaced by 'those who come in the name of the Lord'. This expression suggests individuals engaged in service on behalf of the Lord. A clue to their specific identity may be found in 12.2-3, where it is implied that these visitors adopt a perpetually wandering lifestyle, although the option to settle was apparently open to them. The immediate juxtaposition of 12.1-5 to 11.7-9, 12, combined with the parallel references to evaluation of prophets (11.8-9, 12) and evaluation of visitors (12.1), also suggest that those 'who come in the name of the Lord' are synonymous with the prophets mentioned in 10.7; 11.7-9, 12. It may be concluded, therefore, that the author of the Prophet document took the Peri layer's teaching concerning apostles and reapplied it to the situation of wandering prophets. These prophets, like the apostles, are to be welcomed, although the visitors must then be subjected to the tests outlined in *Did.* 11.8-9, 12.

THE STAY:
11.5 He shall stay only one day, or, if need be, another day too. If he stays three days, he is a false prophet.
12.2b He shall not stay with you more than two or three days if this is necessary.

Despite the similarity of subject and vocabulary the seemingly direct discrepancy between these two verses may give the impression that the latter cannot have been directly influenced by the former. However, the situation of the apostles referred to in 11.5 may have been very different from those of the wandering prophets. The apostles mentioned here are likely to have been envoys sent from and returning to a home base, rather than permanent wanderers.[2] While the two-day limit may have been feasible for an occasional traveller of this type, it would have been a disabling restriction for a permanent itinerant. The very fact that the Prophet document, which appears to hold prophetic ministry in high regard (cf. 10.7; 11.7), preserves a harsh limit of three days suggests that the continuing influence of the Peri layer instructions may indeed be seen here. That the Prophet document goes on in 12.3-5 to provide a means by which wanderers may settle (implicitly disallowed by 11.5), further indicates that the priority of this author is to create a viable situation for prophets. Overall then, the Prophet document's treatment of residence shows an awareness of the strictures of the Peri layer instructions, at the same time as wishing to work beyond those previously imposed limits to create viable conditions for travelling prophets, both those who wish to continue travelling and those who wish to settle.

THE DEPARTURE:
11.6a When the apostle leaves, let him receive nothing but enough bread to see him through until he finds lodging.
12.2a If the one who comes is a traveller, help him as much as you can,

Once again the Prophet document tackles a question also addressed by the Peri layer. A similar pattern persists. The principle of providing for the ongoing journey of the traveller is taken from the Peri layer and augmented in favour of the itinerant in the Prophet document's version of the teaching.

---

2.   Draper (1995: 295) sees the apostles mentioned in *Did.* 11 as envoys sent from Jerusalem who were expected to return home after delivering their message.

THE ISSUE OF MONEY:

11.6b If he asks for money he is a false prophet.

11.12 If any prophet, speaking in the Spirit says, 'Give me money', or anything else, do not listen to him. On the other hand, if he calls you to give it to someone who is in need, do not judge him.

The issue of money does not need to be explicitly tackled in *Did.* 12.1-5 because it has already been covered in 11.12. According to the Peri layer asking for money is the sign of a false prophet, this is echoed by the Prophet document in 11.12. The issue of money is also implicitly tackled, in line with the teaching of 11.6b, in the instructions of 12.3-5, where a prophet is not permitted to use Christ to make a living.

In conclusion, the faithfulness of *Did.* 12.1-5 to the Peri teaching in 11.4-6, combined with a willingness to expand on the earlier teaching to serve a new situation, suggests that these verses were written by the author who also wrote *Did.* 10.1-7; 11.7-9, 12, where a similar relationship to the Peri layer's eucharistic prayer (9.1-5a) may be found.

3. *Conclusion: The Prophet Document*

The aim of Chapter 6 has been to identify as much of the extant text of the *Didache* as was written by the author of *Did.* 10.1-6. It was noted that *Did.* 10.7 appears to belong to the same discourse as both *Did.* 10.1-6 and 11.7, and that the message and style of *Did.* 11.7 are continued into 11.8-9, 12. The unit *Did.* 10.1-7; 11.7-9, 12 was then noted as appearing to build directly upon *Did.* 9.1-5a at the same time as expanding the teaching of the earlier text to address the situation of wandering prophets; a pattern repeated in *Did.* 12.1-5[3] in relation to 11.4-6. It was concluded, therefore, that *Did.* 12.1-5 was written by the same hand as *Did.* 10.1-7; 11.7-9, 12.

The material so identified is here labelled the 'Prophet document'. This text is referred to as a document, rather than a layer, because the rough separation of 10.7 from 11.7 suggests that this text had a life prior to its insertion into the *Didache* (at which point it became, of course, an additional layer). The dependence of the Prophet document on the Peri materials offers an explanation, not only for the shape of the Prophet teaching, but also for the fact of its insertion and the way in which it was inserted into the Peri text. That is to say that the person responsible for this interpolation may have done so precisely because the document's teachings are so

---

3.   *Did.* 13.1-7 cannot belong to the Prophet document because it reacts against the teaching of 12.3-5. See Chapter 7, § 2.

similar to those of the Peri layer. Further, the fact that the Prophet document addresses two separate subjects also addressed by the Peri text provides a rationale for the rough separation of the Prophet document at 10.7/ 11.7. Thus, rather than disrupt the order of the Peri layer's teaching on the eucharist and apostles, the Prophet document was divided and its two halves inserted alongside the parallel materials in the host text.

In conclusion, the content of the Prophet document may be found in the *Didache* in 10.1-7; 11.7-9, 12; 12.1-5. As such it forms a redactional layer of the *Didache* and so may also be referred to as the Prophet layer.

Chapter 7

THE MODIFYING TEACHER LAYER:
1.5a-6; 7.1b, d, 2-3, 4b; 8.1-2a, 2c-3; 9.5b;
11.1-2; 11.10-11; 13.1–15.2

As can be seen from the string of references in the chapter title, the layer now to be considered is a complex one. Its analysis is best undertaken in small stages which can progressively be built up into a whole. The first section to be considered is *Did.* 11.10-11.

1. Didache *11.10-11*

In the preceding analysis of the Prophet layer it was noted that *Did.* 11.10-11 appears to have been inserted into the Prophet layer in response to a potential misunderstanding of *Did.* 11.9. This statement requires explanation at this point.

Did. 11.7-9, 12, it was observed, is uniformly concerned with the regulation of prophetic speech 'ἐν πνεύματι'. The instructions begin with the general points that prophetic speech should never be interrupted for testing, and that when testing becomes possible it may be done on the basis of the prophet's actions and their consistency with the manner of the Lord. *Did.* 11.9 and 11.12 then provide specific examples of how false inspiration, used to gain food, money or things, may be recognized.

Did. 11.10-11 interrupts the flow of these instructions with material that differs from the immediate context in two respects. First, there is no mention of what a prophet says 'ἐν πνεύματι'; rather, there is an interest in what the prophet teaches (διδάσκω is used three times in 11.10-11 and not at all in 11.7-8, 12) and does (ποιέω is used five times in 11.10-11 but never in 11.7-9, 12). In addition there is an emphasis on the 'true' status of an acceptable prophet in 11.10-11 ('διδάσκων τὴν ἀλήθειαν' in 11.10 and 'δεδοκιμασμένος ἀληθινός' in 11.11) which does not occur in 11.7-9, 12. This change of focus from what a prophet says (11.7-9, 12) to what a 'true' prophet does (11.10-11), as well as the disruption to the unity of

11.7-9, 12 caused by the inclusion of 11.10-11, suggests that the latter was interpolated into the former.

Before attempting to attribute this interpolation to a redactional layer of the *Didache* it is necessary to identify a motive for its inclusion in the extant text. The most important evidence in this regard is provided by the location of the insertion. *Didache* 10.9 informs its readers that a prophet who eats food called for 'in the Spirit' is a false prophet. This invites the possibility that the insertion at 11.10-11 represents an attempt to respond to this teaching. An itinerant who depended on the hospitality of local congregations may have had such a motive, since, if asking for food 'in the Spirit' could be taken as the mark of a false prophet, then it is possible that asking for food in any circumstance could be treated with circumspection. The presence of *Did.* 12.1-5 further exacerbates the prophet's difficulty since this contains a call to be on guard against those who 'trade on Christ'. I offer the possibility that the obscure interpolation at *Did.* 11.10-11 was inserted as part of an itinerant's defence of the right to a living without manual work.

I suggest that the strategy of modification was as follows. First, the interpolator affirms the preceding teaching by offering an unexceptionable method for identifying false prophets (11.10), namely, failure to do what they teach. Then a single exception to this rule is introduced: a prophet may be one who 'ποιῶν εἰς μυστήριον κοσμικὸν ἐκκλησίας', without teaching others to do the same. This is certainly an enigmatic saying. Two interpretations are commonly offered by scholars. Either, the 'worldly mystery of the church' is a prophetic action, or it refers to spiritual marriage. The former was clearly favoured by the author of the Ethiopic *Apostolic Church Order* (Statute 52), and is the view held by Draper (1995: 297 n. 36):

> Many commentators on the *Didache* take this as a reference to 'spiritual marriage,' for which there is not a single piece of evidence. It is better understood from the perspective of Mt 13:10-17, where Matthew greatly expands the material in Mk 4:10-12. The disciples have been given the power 'to know the mysteries of the kingdom of God.' This is then specifically related by him to the call of Isaiah to prophesy in Is 6:9-10, which is cited. The theme of prophecy is then repeated: 'Blessed are your eyes that see and your ears that hear. For truly I say to you that many prophets and righteous people have yearned to see the things that you see, and to hear the things which you hear and did not hear.' In other words, the 'mysteries' are both seen and heard by Matthew's community. This is probably the situation that lies behind the *Didache* text also.

The difficulty with this view is not only that it is somewhat tenuous in itself, but also that it provides no obvious explanation as to why this particular modification should be inserted into the Prophet layer at all. Further, Niederwimmer (1998: 180–81) makes some valid points against the prophetic action interpretation in his defence of the spiritual marriage alternative:

> the text…can be understood still more concretely if one thinks not of a symbolic action, but of the whole of the prophet's way of life, namely a *matrimonium spirituale* in which the prophet lives with his companion. The marriage (as the key phrase μυστήριον κοσμικὸν ἐκκλησίας would suggest) is ecclesiologically motivated; that is, it represents the union of *Kyrios* with his bride, the church. The advantage of this interpretation is that it achieves a focused meaning for an otherwise baffling text; the disadvantage is that it requires us to locate the beginnings of the institution of spiritual marriage relatively early.

Niederwimmer has a strong point when he suggests that the phrase refers to the prophet's whole way of life, and that this action is ecclesiologically motivated. However, the conclusion that spiritual marriage is therefore referred to is extremely dubious. For one thing, a crucial detail of the writer's defence is that this is a practice that has a precedent in the behaviour of the ancient prophets, in other words those of the Old Testament period. Also, as has already been noted in the preceding quotation from Draper, there is not a single piece of evidence for the spiritual marriage interpretation.

Given the apparent impasse over the interpretation of 'the mystery of the church in the world' it may seem preferable to agree with Schöllgen (1996: 55) that v. 11 has 'not yet been satisfactorily explained'. However, there is one avenue of approach that has yet to be considered.

Thus far a number of minor pieces of evidence regarding the meaning of 11.11 has been collected: (1) the context (after 11.9) suggests that this interpolation may be concerned with the prophet's right to ask for food; (2) the phrase appears to refer to the prophet's whole way of life; (3) this lifestyle expresses something about the nature of the church's relationship to the world; (4) this lifestyle is not to be copied by ordinary Christians; and finally (5) this lifestyle was also adopted by the ancient prophets.

These clues combine to suggest that *Did.* 11.10-11 presents a defence of prophets' right to food without work because of their unique lifestyle, described as 'ποιῶν εἰς μυστήριον κοσμικὸν ἐκκλησίας'. The phrase may refer to prophets' special experience of heaven even while still located on the earth. The picture painted is then of someone whose feet are still in the world but whose head is already in the heavenly experience, from whence prophesy may be given. This exalted spiritual state is possibly meant to imply that the prophet in question should not be expected to engage in such earthly pursuits as manual work to earn a wage. In the absence of such a source of income they must, like the ancient prophets, rely on the hospitality of communities of the faithful. This is a lifestyle that they cannot teach others to copy, but it is very much in their interests to argue that this particular inconsistency between action and teaching should not be regarded as a sign of falsity.

In this interpolation the modifying prophet/teacher begins to show some trademark concerns and techniques of operation: (1) the affirmation of an agreed principle (11.10); (2) the offering of a modification, in the interests of a prophet's lifestyle, to the established norm (11.11); (3) this modification is justified by a reference to some external authority, in this case, the practice of the ancient prophets (11.11).

2. Didache *13.1-7*

Before considering the relationship of *Did.* 13.1-7 to 11.10-11 it is necessary to examine the possibility that 13.1-7 contains a piece of integrated external tradition.

Clues to the fact that 13.1-7 is not a homogenous text may be found in the presence of features common to 13.1-2, 3b-4, which cannot be found in 13.3a, 5-7. The former verses address plural recipients and consider the treatment of the individual prophet or teacher whom this audience might encounter (the reference to plural high priests in v. 3b is necessitated by the sense of the preceding clause). By contrast, 13.3a, 5-7 addresses the receiver in the singular, apparently assumes the presence of many prophets and makes no reference to teachers at all.[1]

Schöllgen (1996: 56-57) argues that this pattern is created by the author's concern with the prophets and teachers' traditional claim to provision. Schöllgen (1996: 57) thus suggests that

> To address this question [of provision], the author [of 13.1, 2] had at his disposal a clearly identifiable piece of traditional material. It is clearly discernible, for one thing, in that it is in the Second Person Singular, in contrast to the context; in addition it forms a stylistic and material unity:
>
> 3a. Every firstfruit of the product of the vine and of the threshing floor, of the cattle and of the sheep, take now and give the firstfruit to the prophets.
> 5. If you make dough, take the firstfruit and give it according to the law.

---

1. Niederwimmer (1998: 191) says: 'it is striking that now [13.3-7] the text speaks explicitly and solely of the prophets as the recipients of these benefits'.

6. In the same way, if you open a jug of wine or oil, take the firstfruit and give it to the prophets.

7. But of gold and of clothes and of every possession take the firstfruit, as it seems appropriate to you, and give it according to the law.

In terms of content, all four verses are concerned with how the ἀπαρχή is to be provided. Formally they are constructed according to the same schema: τὴν ἀπαρχήν (with concrete specification) λαβὼν δός τοῖς προφήταις and κατὰ τὴν ἐντολήν, alternating according to an ABAB-Scheme.

That this piece of previously existing tradition was incorporated by the author of 13.1, 2, rather than having been added on at a later date, is suggested by the presence of 13.3b-4. These lines are written in direct response to 13.3a, and yet they show strong affinity with 13.1-2. Not only does 13.4 revert to the plural addressee, but it also uses 'prophet' in the singular. With respect to 13.3b Schöllgen (1996: 58 n. 88) notes: 'V.3b, which betrays that it belongs with vv.1-2,4 through the ὑμῶν, clearly indicates that the traditional piece of material 3a, 5-7 cannot be a later interpolation'.[2] At the risk of confusing rather than clarifying the issue, this means that 13.3a, 5-7 could not have been added to the *Didache* without the presence of 13.1-2; *Did.* 13.3b-4 could not have been added without the presence of 13.3a, 5-7, while 13.3b-4 belongs to the same layer as 13.1-2. In consequence, all of these verses must have been added to the *Didache* at the same time.

At this stage, therefore, 13.1-7 may be seen as a section concerned with the right of prophets and teachers to provision. In support of that right the author of 13.1, 2 refers to, integrates and modifies (by means of 13.3b-4) a previously existing piece of tradition now recorded in *Did.* 13.3a, 5-7.

Before going on to compare 13.1-7 with 11.10-11, a detail of the way in which the tradition about firstfruits is modified by 13.3b-4 is worthy of note. Niederwimmer (1998: 191-92) observes:

> with the term ἀπαρχή (awkwardly used twice), the Didachist deliberately adopts a term from Old Testament cultic language. He decrees that the cultic demand of Scripture (the OT) that the ἀπαρχη be surrendered as an offering is now translated into an obligation towards the Christian prophets active in the community. To *them* is due the ἀπαρχη of what God gives to humanity, and this is because they, the prophets, take the place in the Christian community that belonged to the high priests in Israel. Indeed the prophets *are* 'your' high priests (*Did* 13.3b).

---

2.   Audet (1958: 105, 110) and Rordorf and Tuilier (1978: 190 n. 5) think vv. 3b-4 provide a later expansion. However, Schöllgen's case is strengthened by the link between 13.3b and 11.11, as noted in the continuing discussion.

The thrust of *Did.* 13.1-7 is, therefore, that prophets should be treated in the same way as the ancient priests.

Having considered the structure and purpose of 13.1-7, it is now possible to consider the links between this section and 11.10-11.

Did. 13.1-2 shares with 11.10-11 two conceptual links expressed in common vocabulary that is exclusive to the modifying contributor. First, there is a concern for the treatment of prophets who are decribed as 'true' (11.10 and 13.1). Second, there is also a common interest in those who teach (11.10 and 13.2). Both passages also share a similar context, being located after verses which could be taken as threatening a prophet's right to food/support (11.9 and 12.5).

Both 11.10-11 and 13.1-7 appeal to an external authority or precedent in an attempt to justify their modification of the host text. Thus 11.11 appeals to the practice of the ancient prophets, while 13.1-2 is supported by the external authority quoted in 13.3a, 5-7.

The equation of prophets with priests in 13.3 may also throw further light on the enigmatic 'μυστήριον κοσμικὸν ἐκκλησίας' in 11.11. This equation allows 11.11 to be read as referring to the practice of the ancient *priests.* These priests, as is pointed out in 13.1-7, received the people's firstfruits. Thus, it may be argued, the prophets of the present day, who also have an apparently priestly function with respect to the eucharist (10.7, also 14.1-2), should not be judged for living by the same means.

In conclusion, the similarities of language, context and rhetorical method suggest that *Did.* 11.10-11 and 13.1-7 were added to the *Didache* by the same modifying author.

3. Didache *11.1-2*

Before considering the relationship of 11.1-2 to the work of the modifying contributor it will be helpful to consider more precisely the identity of this author. One of the features of this writer's contributions to the *Didache* is a grouping together of the terms 'prophet' and 'teacher'. Thus, there is reference to 'any prophet *teaching* the truth who does not do what he *teaches*' (11.10), and prophets and teachers are expected to receive equal treatment in 13.1, 2. Eugene Boring (1982: 79) observes that this connection between prophets and teachers is also a feature of the New Testament:

> Prophets and teachers are often closely associated in our [NT] sources … Among recent writers there seems to be a fresh perception of the way the functions of prophecy and teaching shade into each other, with the result that the prophet is now seen as much more of a teaching figure than

formerly. All the above discussion indicates that the picture of teachers who hand on the firmly-guarded tradition of the sayings of Jesus in one context, while charismatic prophets deliver their inspired, ephemeral revelations from the risen Jesus on the other, is based on fantasy. The horizontal, traditioning function of the churches ministry operated conjointly with the vertical, revelatory aspect. Prophets and tradents[3] were partners engaged in a complementary and mutually-enriching ministry of the word; prophet and tradent were sometimes the same person.

Boring's analysis of the New Testament sources introduces the possibility that a prophet may also be a teacher. It is in the interests of the author of 11.10-11 and 13.1-7, however, to be seen as a prophet more than a teacher because in this role the support due to prophets, according to the tradition cited in 13.3a, 5-7, may be demanded. At root, however, what this so-called prophet does is teach. Thus the way in which prophets should be measured, according to 11.10, is not by the accuracy of their prophecy, but by what they teach.

This prophet/teacher ambiguity also explains the inclusion of 13.2 within the argument. If the author who introduced 11.10-11 and 13.1, 3-7 was purely and obviously a prophet, then an appeal to the lifestyle of the ancient prophets and the tradition expressed in 13.3a, 5-7 could have been enough to justify their claim to support. If, however, this character was more obviously a teacher, then an equation between 'prophet' and 'teacher' must also be drawn to ensure that that which applied to prophets also applied to the modifying author. The equation between prophets and teachers is subtly introduced in 11.10 and then made explicit in 13.2. This evidence suggests that whoever wrote 11.10-11 and 13.1-7 saw themselves, at the very least, as a teacher.

At this stage, therefore, it is possible to deduce certain difficulties faced by the modifying teacher, and the technique by which they are overcome. At the centre of the teacher's unease lay the *Didache*'s strict instructions regarding the feeding, paying and settlement of itinerants. In an attempt to circumvent these rules the teacher appeals to alternative directives from alternative sources of authority, which offer loopholes in the *Didache*'s strictures (hence 11.10-11 and 13.1-7). However, the introduction of alternative teaching, especially when it directly contradicts the existing *Didache*, requires prior legitimation. This is the role performed by the insertion of *Did.* 11.1-2.

---

3.   Draper (1995: 302) remarks, with respect to this passage from Boring, 'Boring's subtle transition from the use of the title "teacher" to that of "tradent"...must be challenged in important aspects. It is better to retain the term teacher.'

Didache 11.1-2 once again bears some trademark features of the modifying teacher. It begins with a resounding affirmation of the authority of the existing text. Thus, those who teach the above are to be received and those who turn to an alternative doctrine are to be ignored (11.1-2a). This statement serves a parallel purpose to that performed by 11.10, in that it confirms the unimpeachable orthodoxy of the author. In 11.2b, however, comes the real purpose of the insertion. After the disarming affirmation of the established text comes the introduction of the possibility that an alternative teaching might, after all, be acceptable: 'but if [the other doctrine] aims at promoting righteousness and knowledge of the Lord, receive him as the Lord'.

That this final line is the goal of the insertion is betrayed not only by the fact that it is at the end of the insertion, but also by the inclusion of the command to 'receive him as the Lord'. This instruction is not included with reference to those who are simply orthodox (11.1), and yet those who teach another doctrine are to be given this ultimate honour. In *Did.* 11.1-2, therefore, it appears that a teacher who wished to introduce alternative teaching was preparing the ground for later innovations. These changes allow the teacher to be supported by the community and also to settle there. A permanent teaching presence would, it could be argued, lead to a greater knowledge of the Lord, thus affording the right to be received 'as the Lord'.

4. Didache *1.5b-6*

Thus far a pattern in the modifying teacher's approach to the host text has been noted: the modifier affirms the existing teaching (11.1-2a; 11.10), modifies it (11.2b; 11.11a; 13.1-2), and then refers to an external authority in justification of the modification (11.11b; 13.3a, 5-7). An identical pattern of modification also occurs in *Did.* 1.5b-6:

AFFIRMATION OF THE HOST TEXT:
1.5b Blessed is the one who gives according to the commandment, for he is guiltless.

MODIFICATION OF THE HOST TEXT:
1.5c Woe to the one who receives. For if he receives because he has need, he is guiltless, but if he does not have need, he shall stand trial as to why he received and for what, and being put in prison he will be examined about what he has done, and he will not come out of it until he pays the last penny.

EXTERNAL JUSTIFICATION FOR THE MODIFICATION:
1.6 But of this it was also said, 'Let your charitable gift sweat in your hands until you know to whom you give'.

Also observing some of these features of *Did.* 1.5b-6 Niederwimmer (1998: 86) writes:

> One receives the impression that the Didachist wanted, by quoting this aphorism, to restrict the appeal to unconditional almsgiving that existed in his tradition. He affirms the tradition. Indeed, blessed is the one who gives! But at the same time he warns against giving too quickly.

This pattern of affirmation, modification and justification points towards the teacher who wrote *Did.* 11.1-2, 10-11; 13.1-7 as also responsible for *Did.* 1.5b-6.

5. Didache *14.1–15.2*

Did. 14.1–15.2 has a number of points of contact with the body of material that has so far been attributed to the modifying teacher.

Did. 14.1-3 includes the pattern, 'affirm, modify, justify'. Thus, 14.1 affirms the host text by instructing its readers to continue meeting for the eucharist (cf. *Did.* 9 and 10) and confessing their faults publicly (cf. 4.14). *Did.* 14.2 then modifies this tradition by introducing an exception to this pattern for members who are in dispute (14.2). This modification is then justified, in 14.3, by means of an appeal to the external authority of Mal. 1.11.

Did. 15.1-2 shows parallels to the language of 11.10-11 and 13.1-7 in shared references to the concept of testing and truth (11.11 and 15.1), and the pairing of prophets and teachers (13.1-2 and 15.1-2). Further, there is an interest in money that extends from 1.5b-6 through 11.10-11; 13.1-7 to the call for the appointment of those who are not greedy for money in 15.1.

Some scholars are reluctant to see a direct follow through from *Did.* 13 to 14 because, as Schöllgen (1996: 59) observes, 'Ch 14…does not stand in close relation to what precedes'.[4] However, this apparent distance is caused by the integration of a previously existing tradition in 13.3a, 5-7 and so should not be mistaken for a change of author. Further, Kraft (1965: 173) sees an associative relation between the firstfruits of *Did.* 13 and the sacrificial thought of *Did.* 14. In both of these chapters there is a

---

4.   So also Knopf (1920: 35).

transfer of imagery from a Jewish context to a Christian one. Thus, in *Did.* 13 the Jewish high priest becomes the Christian prophet, while in *Did.* 14 the Jewish sacrifice becomes the Christian eucharist.

In conclusion then, *Did.* 14.1–15.2, by virtue of its parallel rhetorical structure, vocabulary and use of imagery appears to be the work of the same modifying author who also added 1.5b-6; 11.1-2, 10-11; 13.1-7 to the *Didache*.

6. Didache *7.1(c)^{5}d, 2-3, 4b*

In the preceding discussion of the extent of the Peri layer (cf. Chapter 5, section 1) it was noted that an external baptismal tradition appears to have been introduced into the baptismal instructions of the Peri layer. Certain features of this addition suggest that this may have been the work of the modifying teacher.

First, the tradition presented in 7.1(c)d, 2-3, 4b shows some similarities to the tradition used by the modifying teacher in 13.3a, 5-7. As well as addressing the second person singular, both insertions adopt a similar structure. Thus, both traditions begin with a general statement that might be taken as covering every eventuality:

> 7.2a If you do not have running water, however, baptize in other

> 13.3a Therefore, when you take any firstfruits of what is produced by the wine press and the threshing floor, by cows and by sheep, you shall give the firstfruits to the prophets,

This is then filled out with paired considerations of further eventualities:

> 7.2b (i) if you cannot in cold,
> 7.2b (ii) then in warm.

> 13.5 (i) If you make bread, take the firstfruits and give them according to the commandment.
> 13.6 (ii) Likewise, when you open a jar of wine or oil, take the firstfruits and give them to the prophets.

Finally, there is a further statement that accounts for any other unconsidered eventuality:

---

5.   The bracketing of 7.1c is intended to indicate that 7.1c may have appeared in *both* the host text (7.1a, c, e) and the interpolated tradition (7.1c, d and possibly 7.1e). The dimensions of the host and the inserted text in *Did.* 7 were discussed in Chapter 5, § 1.

7.3 But if you have neither, pour water on the head three times in the name of Father, Son, and Holy Spirit.

13.7 Take the firstfruits of money and clothing and whatever you own as you think best and give them according to the commandment.

Similarities of grammar and structure do not, in themselves, provide compelling evidence of a common interpolator. However, it is significant that these two traditions were used to modify the base text in similar ways. The insertion of 7.1(c)d, 2-3, 4b shifts the *Didache* from being a text that shows no distinct or profound break with the theology or practice of established Judaism, to one that is indisputably Christian. This change is effected by the (proposed) replacement of baptism in the name of the Lord (cf. 9.5) with baptism in the name of Father, Son and Holy Spirit. The original formula shows continuity with the 'yoke of the Lord' in *Did.* 6.3. The 'Lord' in this case may be readily understood as referring to the One God, and so baptism into his name could represent an initiation from Paganism into a form of Judaism. With the introduction of the threefold formula, however, the initiation can no longer be seen as bringing the baptized person into the fold of Judaism. Thus the new formula creates a shift away from established Judaism towards a distinctively Christian initiation. This shift is also illustrated by a willingness to depart from the traditional Jewish requirement of living water, although this method is still preferred.

The effect of the baptismal insertion is similar to that created by the insertion of the firstfruits tradition (13.3a, 5-7) because of the modifying teacher's interpretative comment regarding the identity of the prophets, '...for they are your high priests' (13.3b). This remark casts the interpolator's readers as belonging to an institutional structure that is parallel to, but certainly separate from, that of established Judaism. Thus, what was due to the leaders of the old institution, the Jewish high priests, is now due to the Christian prophets, the leaders of a new institution.

This pattern of endorsing or setting up a practice that is parallel to that of established Judaism, at the same time as being distinctively different from it, is characteristic of other elements of the modifying teacher's contribution. Thus, in 14.1 the teacher instructs the congregation to meet on the Sunday of the Lord, rather than the Sabbath; in 14.2, 3 certain rules governing the sacrifice of the Old Testament are still to be kept (hence the reference to Mal. 1.11), but are now to be applied to the eucharist.

Thus, while it is possible that the baptismal insertion could have been made at almost any point in the text's history, it is most likely that it was inserted by the modifying teacher. This is suggested by a parallel instance of the modifying teacher's willingness to use an external tradition (13.4a, 5-7) to modify the text, and by the separating effect (with respect to mainstream Judaism) that this insertion shares with the modifying teacher's other contributions.

7. Didache *8.1-2a, 2c-3*

Before attempting to argue that *Did.* 8.1-2a, 2c-3 was added to the *Didache* by the modifying teacher it is necessary to confirm the separate nature of *Did.* 8 with respect to the preceding and following text. Draper (1996b: 85) expresses an uncontroversial view when he observes:

> *Did.* 8 appears to be a later addition to the earliest text of the *Didache*. It is inserted after the reference to the baptismal fast in 7:4, but it has quite a different reference to 'stationary fasts' and daily prayer. It breaks up the natural flow in the catechetical manual from baptism to the eucharist. Moreover, it is not introduced by the formula which characterizes the liturgical sections of the *Didache* (περὶ δέ), and in the Ethiopian version it is set after 11:3-13.

Given that *Did.* 8.1-3 is a later addition to the text, what features does this insertion share, if any, with the contributions of the modifying teacher? Neither a pattern of affirmation, modification and justification, nor a separate appeal to an external authority are to be found here. (That the appeal to 'the gospel' is a later addition will be argued in Chapter 8, section 2, below.) However, Draper in his article, 'Christian Self-Definition against the 'Hypocrites' in *Didache* VIII' (1996c), argues convincingly that the function of *Did.* 8 is to create a publicly perceivable distance between traditional Jews and converts to Christianity. Thus, he concludes (1996c: 243):

> This study of the redactional process at work in the *Didache* has revealed a community which started by defining itself primarily against the Gentiles. The material was originally collected for the catechesis of Gentile converts. Differentiation of the Christian community from the pagan world was a key part in preparation for initiation. However, the lack of clear differentiation from other Jewish groups seems to have caused problems for the community at a later stage, perhaps under attack from the Pharisees...the instructions [of *Did.* 8] provide for Christian behaviour in the crucial public areas of fasting and prayer which would differentiate them from their opponents.

The effect of *Did.* 8 is, therefore, to create a readily perceptible difference between Christians and Jews. Thus, while (Pharisaic) Jews fast publicly on Mondays and Thursdays, Christians can demonstrate their membership of a distinctly different group by fasting publicly on Wednesdays and Thursdays (Draper 1996c: 233–35). In the same way Christians can be identified as such by their audible and possibly public recitation of the Lord's Prayer three times a day, instead of praying the traditional *Shema* or *Shemoneh Esreh* of Judaism (1996c: 235–36).

These acts of self-definition against Judaism are almost exactly similar to the 'parallel but different' practices advocated elsewhere by the modifying teacher: from high priest to prophet (13.3b), from Sabbath to Sunday of the Lord (14.1), from sacrifice to eucharist (14.1-3). It may therefore be observed that 8.1-3 shows signs of having been added to the *Didache* by the modifying teacher.

Before moving on, one additional observation needs to be made. While the teacher may have been responsible for the insertion of 8.1-2a, 2c-3 this should not be taken as implying that this modifier was also responsible for the creation of the Lord's Prayer as found in 8.2d. The purpose of the prayer in this context is to create public differentiation between Christian and Jew. This means that in place of the thrice-daily recitation of a distinctively Jewish prayer a distinctively Christian prayer is required. Thus, whatever its original context,[6] the prayer at 8.2c must have had an established and distinctive life in the Christian community.

8. Didache *9.5b*

The quotation offered at the end of *Did.* 9.5 is so brief that it is impossible to offer a conclusive assessment of the redactional layer to which it belongs. However, two features of this line do suggest, on balance, that it is likely to belong to the additions made by the modifying teacher.

The content of the quotation at *Did.* 9.5b may be credibly attributed to the modifying teacher, inasmuch as, like other elements of the teacher's contribution, it serves to emphasize the differentiation between acceptable and unacceptable members of the community.[7] However, this is also an

---

6. The Lord's Prayer (especially the version in Lk. 11) shares a number of characteristics with the eucharistic prayers recorded in *Did.* 9 and 10. It is possible, therefore, that this prayer is distinctively Christian because it derives from early eucharistic prayers.

7. Revelation shows a similar pattern to that exhibited in *Did.* 9.5 in that 'dogs' are barred from the heavenly city (22.15). These persons are not necessarily non-Jews, since 'those who practice falsehood' may also include the traditional Jews who are condemned in Rev. 2.9 and 3.9. If the reference to 'dogs' in *Did.* 9.5b was intended in the same sense as its use in Rev. 22.15, then the differentiating force of *Did.* 9.5b is consistent with the differentiating force of other elements of the Modifying Teacher layer, such as are noted in §§ 6 and 7, above.

interest of the author of the Peri layer (in 9.5a at least) and so particular weight may not be placed on this point.

Perhaps more significantly, the author of the Peri layer (to whom *Did.* 9.1-5a is attributed) does not otherwise use quotation formulae, unlike the modifying teacher. Further, the quotation formula used in *Did.* 9.5b is very similar to that used by the modifying teacher in *Did.* 1.6:

1.6	ἀλλὰ	καὶ		περὶ	τούτου δὲ	εἴρηται...
9.5b		καὶ	γὰρ	περὶ	τούτου	εἴρηκεν ὁ κύριος...

Thus Niederwimmer (1998: 45) may well be justified in expressing the opinion, 'I consider 9.5 redactional. In καὶ γὰρ περὶ τούτου εἴρηκεν ὁ κύριος…, the Didachist [modifying teacher] betrays his presence (cf. 1.6)'.[8]

While recognizing the limited evidence available *Did.* 9.5b will be treated, on the strength of the similarity between *Did.* 1.6 and 9.5b, as part of the modifying teacher's work in the following discussion. However, it should be noted that the attribution of this line to the Peri layer would make only a negligible difference to the later discussions with regard to the relationship between the *Didache* and Matthew's Gospel.

9. *Additional Minor Contributions by the Modifying Teacher*

In addition to the more major additions made, according to this proposal, by the modifying teacher two further additions may also be attributed to this redactor.

The linking line 'ταῦτα πάντα προειπόντες', at 7.1b, is sometimes identified as a later addition. It bears a strong resemblance to 11.1 and so may be the work of the modifying teacher. However, this does not change the status of the relationship between *Did.* 1–5 and the Peri layer. The addition of 7.1b, at whatever stage it was made, merely serves to make plain the service rendered to 7.1 by *Did.* 1–6. This addition clarifies rather than modifies.

A similar clarifying instinct may perhaps be found in *Did.* 5.2b. It was argued in Chapter 6, section 6. that this line was inserted after the addition of *Did.* 6.1 to 5.2 to make plain what was already clearly implied by 6.1.

---

8.   Niederwimmer attributes the whole of 9.5 to the 'Didachist' (the final redactor). However, this would be a very curious interpolation given the confusing arrangement of *Did.* 9 and 10 as they currently stand. Further, the parallel between *Did.* 9.5 and 10.6 suggests that some form of prohibition against the unworthy is likely to have stood in the original eucharist at *Did.* 9.1-5.

Inasmuch as this type of clarification is close to that performed by the addition of 'ταῦτα πάντα προειπόντες' in 7.1, then the addition 5.2b may also be seen as the work of the modifying teacher.[9]

10. *Summary and Conclusion: The Modifying Teacher Layer*

The work of the modifying teacher leaves an intermittent trail across the extant text of the *Didache*. However, these contributions are linked by a common method of modification[10] and by a common interest in two distinctive and related priorities: the rewards due to teachers and the need to achieve institutional separation from traditional Judaism.

The subject of the honouring and payment of teachers is addressed in the instruction to equate teachers with prophets and high priests, and to reward them on the basis of that equation (11.10-11 and 13.1-7). A similar focus appears in the call to receive 'as the Lord' those whose teaching leads to an increase in righteousness, even if their doctrine is at variance with that of the *Didache* itself (11.1-2). The instruction to appoint bishops and deacons who are 'not greedy for money' (15.1) may reflect a desire to ensure that funds to itinerant teachers are not curtailed by local leaders. While securing the teacher's income the modifier's insertions also limit their potential outgoings. Thus, 1.5b-6 offers a defence against the expectation that a teacher should lead by example in giving 'to anyone who asks you, and do not ask for it back'. It is perhaps also significant that the honour due to teachers and prophets is set as the standard for the regard in which bishops and deacons should be held (15.2), since this encourages local leaders to uphold the honour of itinerants.

Passages concerned to achieve institutional separation from Judaism include: the threefold baptismal rite (7.1b-3, 4b), which offers a distinctively Christian pattern of initiation, in contrast to the more ambiguous baptism 'in the name of the Lord' likely to have preceded it in the Peri/Base layer (cf. 9.5a). A similar effect is achieved by the modifier's teaching on fasting and prayer, in contradistinction to the practice of the

9.   None of the following arguments for Matthew's use of the *Didache* depend on an accurate assessment of the redactional location of *Did.* 5.2b or 7.1b. These assessments are made for the sake of completeness.

10.   The teacher adopts the practice of affirming the existing text, offering a modification of that text and then justifying that modification by means of appeal to an external authority. This pattern occurs in response to the *Didache*'s teaching on unconditional giving (1.5b-6), the payment of prophets and teachers (11.1-2, 10-11; 13.1-7), and the celebration of the eucharist (14.1-3).

'hypocrites' (8.1-2a, 2c-3). Separation is also expressed by the replacement of Jewish priests with Christian prophets and teachers (11.10-11; 13.1-3), the Jewish Sabbath with the Christian Sunday of the Lord (14.1) and the Jewish sacrifice with the Christian eucharist (14.3).

The two strands of the status of teachers and separation from Judaism are interwoven in the modifier's contributions and intersect, for example, in *Did.* 13.1-3. Here the teacher equates prophets with teachers, and then prophets (and thus teachers) with high priests. The result is a rationale for the financial support of prophets (and teachers) but it is one that requires the institutional separation of the Christian movement from Judaism.

In conclusion, the passages considered in this chapter (*Did.* 1.5b-6; 5.2b; 7.1b, d, 2-3, 4b; 8.1-2a, 2c-3; 9.5b; 11.1-2; 11.10-11; 13.1–15.2) display a consistency of method, vocabulary and purpose that is suggestive of a single redactor.[11]

---

11. It is not crucial, for the purposes of the argument in Part II, that one redactor was responsible for the insertion of all of these passages. Indeed, this ensuing argument depends on the presence of multiple contributors to the *Didache*, and so would benefit from arguments to suggest that these additions were made by more than one contributor. That said, such a conclusion would adversely affect my later arguments if it could be shown that elements attributed to the modifying teacher were in fact added after the insertion of the four references to 'the gospel'. This is not possible, however, in the crucial case of *Did.* 8. because the references to 'the gospel' within this chapter could not have been made in the absence of 8.1-2a, 2c-3. Similarly, the 'gospel' references in 15.3-4 are unlikely to have been added to a text in which the instructions of 14.1–15.2 were not already present. Given the threads of connection that bind 8.1-2a, 2c-3 and 14.1–15.2 to the other verses considered in this chapter, it is unlikely that any of these passages were added after the insertion of the 'gospel' references.

Chapter 8

THE GOSPEL LAYER:
8.2b; 11.3b; 15.3-4

The *Didache*'s four references to 'the gospel' have, as noted in Chapter 1, profoundly influenced perceptions of the whole text's relationship to Matthew's Gospel.

The following chapter challenges the assumption that these verses demonstrate the post-Matthean composition or compilation of the *Didache*, arguing instead that 8.2b; 11.3b and 15.3-4 are best understood as a distinct and final[1] contribution to the host text.

Prior to any attempt to assess the relationship of *Did.* 8.2b; 11.3b and 15.3-5 to the rest of the *Didache* it is necessary to consider a number of preliminary issues.

1. *Preliminary Issues*

1.1. *The Redactional Unity of* Didache *8.2b; 11.3b and 15.3-4*
This point is best considered in the light of a direct comparison of the passages in question.

> 8.2b ὡς ἐκέλυεσεν ὁ κύριος ἐν τῷ εὐαγγελίῳ αὐτοῦ (followed by the Lord's Prayer).
> 11.3b καὶ προφητῶν, κατὰ τὸ δόγμα τοῦ εὐαγγελίου οὕτω ποιήσατε (followed by rules for behaviour towards itinerant teachers).
> 15.3 ἐλέγχετε δὲ ἀλλήλους μὴ ἐν ὀργῇ, ἀλλ᾽ ἐν εἰρήνη, ὡς ἔχετε ἐν τῷ εὐαγγελίῳ· καὶ παντὶ ἀστοχοῦντι κατὰ τοῦ ἑτέρου μηδεὶς λαλείτω μηδὲ παρ᾽ ὑμῶν ἀκουέτω, ἕως οὗ μετανοήσῃ.
> 15.4 τὰς δὲ εὐχὰς ὑμῶν καὶ τὰς ἐλεημοσύνας καὶ πάσας τὰς πράξεις οὕτω ποιήσατε, ὡς ἔχετε ἐν τῷ εὐαγγελίῳ τοῦ κυρίου ἡμῶν.

Niederwimmer (1998: 49) comments with respect to these passages:

---

1.   With the exception of the Jerusalem addition, *Did.* 16.7.

What is immediately obvious is the symmetry of the diction:

ἐν τῷ εὐαγγελίῳ αὐτοῦ (8.2)
ἐν τῷ εὐαγγελίῳ (15.3)
ἐν τῷ εὐαγγελίῳ τοῦ κυρίου ἡμῶν (15.4)
ὡς ἐκέλευσεν ὁ κύριος (8.2)
κατὰ τὸ δόγμα τοῦ εὐαγγελίου[2] (11.3)
οὕτω προσεύχεσθε[3] (8.2)
οὕτω ποιήσατε (15.4).

All these formulations express the same concept, and it should be obvious
that all of the texts can be traced to one and the same author.

Despite the unity of these sayings not every scholar has attributed them
to the same author. For example, Audet (1958), because of his understanding of the redactional history of the *Didache*, attributes different significance to the use of 'gospel' in 8.2 and 11.3; 15.3-4 (he believes them to
have been written by the same author, but at different times).[4] Rordorf and
Tuilier (1978: 87-88) also perceive the references to 'the gospel' in 8.2;
11.3 and 15.3-4 as belonging to two different redactional layers. However,
these conclusions should be treated with caution because they are influenced by wider decisions regarding the redactional history of the larger
blocks of text within which these references fall. This method of redactional analysis is not sensitive to the possibility that one interpolator could
make several small insertions across the spread of a text. At this stage in
the analytical process, therefore, it is preferable to recognize that the conceptual similarity of these four references to 'the gospel' suggests that they
were all written by one author. This consideration must then be taken into
account in any larger conclusions regarding the redactional history of the
whole text.

1.2. *The Form of the* Didache*'s 'Gospel'*
Does an oral or written gospel lie behind the *Didache*'s references to 'the
gospel'? The blame for the considerable scholarly confusion over this

2.   Niederwimmer, surprisingly, elects to exclude οὕτω ποιήσατε from this version of *Did.* 11.3, even though he considers this to be characteristic of the author of
Did. 15.4.

3.   In his commentary, originally written in German in 1989, Niederwimmer includes οὕτω προσεύχεσθε as part of the insertion containing a reference to the 'gospel'.
However, in a later article (1995: 29) he appears to locate this phrase in the tradition to
which the gospel reference was subsequently added.

4.   Audet's general understanding of the *Didache*'s compositional history of the
Didache is outlined in the introduction to Part I. His position regarding the gospel references is criticized by Nautin (1959: 195–96).

issue may perhaps be laid at Köster's door. His approach to this question was to treat each mention of 'the gospel' on its own merits. This approach is commendable at a certain stage in the analytical process, but it runs the risk of missing the wood for the trees if individual results are not also viewed against a broader backcloth. That Köster has failed in this regard is illustrated by his extraordinarly complex conclusion (1957: 240):

> An einigen weiteren Stellen aber [in contrast to *Did.* 1.3-6] war die Wahrscheinlichkeit sehr groß, daß sie vom Kompilator der *Did.* nicht unbewußt innerhalb größerer Komplexe übernommen, sondern von ihm bewußt aus eigener Kenntnis synoptischer Überlieferung in sein Werk eingefügt wurden (*Did.* 7,1; 8,2; 9,5; 15,3). In der unmittelbaren Nachbarschaft gerade solcher Stellen fanden sich auch die Hinweise auf das εὐαγγέλιον, das zwar *Did.* 8,2 auch die mündliche Predigt bezeichnen könnte, aber in *Did.* 15,3.4 doch wohl ein schriftliches Evangelium meint. Dennoch stammen *Did.* 7,1; 8,2; 9,5; 15.3 nicht aus einem schriftlichen Evangelium sondern aus der freien Überlieferung.[5]

The difficulty with Köster's position is that it requires the author of 8.2b; 11.3b and 15.3-4 to behave in an extraordinary manner. Thus, according to Köster, the reader is expected to recognize a *written* authority concerned with every aspect of Christian behaviour (including a specific mention of prayer) in 'the gospel of our Lord' (15.4), and a *different* oral authority, which also carries instructions regarding prayer 'as the Lord directed in his gospel' (8.2b). If one author was responsible for both appeals to the Lord's gospel, then it is highly unlikely that two different gospels are in mind in both cases.

Despite the inherent difficulties resulting from the bringing together of Köster's carefully considered individual conclusions, the influence of his work is clearly demonstrated in Niederwimmer's (1998: 51) presentation of the possible permutations in the oral/written gospel debate:

> (a) All four passages refer to oral tradition (but can 15.3-4 be understood in this way?). (b) Εὐαγγέλιον refers to different things in the four passages: in 8.2, and perhaps in 11.3 as well, we are still dealing with the older usage

5. 'However, in the case of a few more verses [in contrast to *Did.* 1.3-6], the probability was very high that the compiler did not unconsciously include them as part of larger sections, but inserted them consciously in his work from his own knowledge of the synoptic tradition (*Did.* 7.1; 8.2; 9.5; 15.3). In the immediate context of these verses in particular we found the references to the εὐαγγέλιον, which in *Did.* 8.2 could denote oral preaching, but which in 15.3, 4 refers more likely to a written Gospel. Nevertheless, *Did.* 7.1; 8.2; 9.5; 15.3 do not come from a written Gospel, but from free tradition.'

(meaning the 'living voice of the good news' [*viva vox evangelii*]); in contrast, εὐαγγέλιον in 15.3 and 4 (but also 11.3?) already refers to a gospel in written form (*evangelium scriptum*): thus Koester. Audet adopted a similar opinion, seeing in 8.2 and 9.5 reference to an oral gospel, and in 11.3 and 15.3-4 to a written gospel. Rordorf and Tuilier employed this notion to distinguish a hypothetical second layer of redaction: only the second redactor could have understood εὐαγγέλιον in 15.3-4 as *evangelium scriptum*. But not only is this hypothesis of a double redaction questionable, in my opinion; the conceptual consistency of the clauses in which the key word 'gospel' appears does not suggest such an idea. Finally, we cannot completely exclude (c), the possibility that the redactor means the same thing in all four passages, namely, a written gospel, known to him and his readers and, because it preserves the words of Jesus, serving as a norm of faith and life. Koester also accepted this construal for 15.3-4, and considered it possible for 11.3; even for 8.2 he did not wish to exclude it absolutely.

If one author is likely to have been responsible for all four of the *Didache*'s references to 'the gospel' (as argued above), then it is also highly likely that this author had one authoritative 'gospel' in mind in each case. The question of whether an oral or written tradition is referred to thus becomes a question of which type of source sits most easily with all four references to this 'gospel'.

The reference to the gospel in *Did.* 15.3-4 indicates the presence of an external authority, in the possession of the readers, which may be consulted by them for final guidance with respect to church discipline, prayer, alms and all aspects of Christian behaviour. Scholars are in general agreement that *Did.* 15.3-4 probably refers to a written gospel.[6]

The reference to the gospel in 11.3b is followed by a set of instructions which, by virtue of their complex redactional history, are sometimes far from clear or self-consistent. This invites the possibility that the purpose of 11.3b was to point the reader to a more coherent and authoritative set of instructions on the subject of visitors and teachers. This suggests that the 'gospel' in view was at a more advanced state of stabilization than the text of the *Didache* itself. This is suggestive of a written text.

Of the four references to 'the gospel' the only instance where an appeal to a written text is problematic is 8.2b. The difficulty is twofold. First, and less significantly, the phrase 'as the Lord commanded in his gospel' could be taken as referring either to the spoken instructions of the Lord which have been passed on orally, or to a written account of those spoken instruc-

---

6.   Niederwimmer (1998: 50–51) cites Audet, Köster and Wengst, in addition to himself, as in favour of a written gospel at 15.3, 4. I am not aware of any scholar who sees a reference to an oral gospel in 15.3, 4.

tions. However, since this formula may be taken either way it poses no obstacle to understanding 'the gospel' as a written text which reports the spoken directions of Jesus, as occurs in all our extant gospels. The second difficulty is that the version of the Lord's Prayer recorded in *Did.* 8.2c does not appear in this precise form in any written gospel now known. It was Köster's (1957: 203-209) careful observation of this fact which caused him to consider the possibility that an oral tradition is referred to here. However, this does not exclude the possibility that an unknown written gospel is in view, or, as is argued below, that the mention of 'the gospel' in 8.2b serves a function other than to introduce a quotation from that written text.

In conclusion, since only one entity is likely to be behind the *Didache*'s repeated use of the term 'gospel', and since a written text is possible in all four instances, and preferable in three of those four, then it may be concluded that a written, rather than an oral, authority is likely to be indicated in each case.

1.3. *The Identity of the Written Gospel*

Given the written form of the *Didache*'s 'gospel', there are two possible texts to which it could refer; either the Gospel of Matthew, or some other gospel that is now lost. Matthew's Gospel is the only possible candidate among the extant texts because it is the only one that carries instructions for every dimension of behaviour mentioned by the *Didache* in connection with 'the gospel'; namely, prayer (Mt. 6.9-13; *Did.* 8.2b), prophets and visitors (Mt. 10.10, 40-42; *Did.* 11.3b), church discipline (Mt. 18.15-17; *Did.* 15.3) and almsgiving (e.g. Mt. 5.42; 6.1-4; *Did.* 15.4).

A further point in favour of the identification of Matthew's Gospel with the *Didache*'s 'gospel' may be found in *Did.* 15.3. This verse is interesting because, unlike 15.4, it does not simply refer to the 'gospel' and expect the reader to find all that they need to know on the subject in this external and superior text. Instead, 15.3 adds the detail, 'and let no one speak to anyone who wrongs another, let him not hear from you until he has repented' (15.3). If Matthew's instructions (18.15-17) are referred to in *Did.* 15.3, then a motive for the addition of this explanatory note may be offered. Matthew's reference to treating someone 'as a pagan or tax collector' may have seemed obscure or outdated to the person responsible for *Did.* 15.3. This could explain the inclusion of the supplementary note that to treat someone in this way meant to refuse to talk to them.

Given that Matthew's Gospel is the only extant gospel which contains teaching on church discipline, and given that this teaching also provides an explanation for the additional note in *Did.* 15.3, it may be concluded that Matthew's Gospel is a strong candidate for the text behind the *Didache*'s references to 'the gospel'.

The piece of evidence that causes the greatest difficulty for the straightforward identification of the *Didache*'s 'gospel' with Matthew's text is the conundrum posed by *Did.* 8.1-3. Here, *Did.* 8.2b calls upon its readers to pray 'as the Lord directed in his gospel' but the prayer that follows is not a quotation from any extant version of Matthew's Gospel. There is one particular variation that exemplifies the problem.[7] The *Didache*'s prayer has 'Πάτερ ἡμῶν ὁ ἐν τῷ οὐρανῷ', while all known manuscripts of Matthew's Gospel read 'Πάτερ ἡμῶν ὁ ἐν τοῖς οὐρανοῖς'. This means either that the author of *Did.* 8.2c quoted from an eccentric version of Matthew's Gospel which has now been lost, or that *Did.* 8.2c is not a quotation from Matthew's Gospel at all. The former possibility cannot be completely discounted but it does require a curious set of circumstances. First, there is no evident reason why a copyist should have introduced 'τῷ οὐρανῷ' for 'τοῖς οὐρανοῖς', since this change carries no theological significance and such a change disrupts a passage likely to be widely known in another form. Second, if such a variant did arise it is unlikely to have been preserved by later copyists because of the tendency to assimilate variant versions of the Lord's Prayer to the mainstream Matthean text (seen, for example, in manuscripts of Lk. 11.1-4). This means that, if *Did.* 8.2c derives from Mt. 6.9-14, then a very unusual version of Matthew's Gospel must have been used. Further, the author who used that unusual version must also have assumed that the Lord's Prayer was not already well known to the *Didache*'s potential audience in its standard Matthean form.

The difficulties associated with seeing *Did.* 8.2c as a direct quotation from Matthew's Gospel led Köster (1957: 240) to a new position:[8]

> Es ergibt sich also, daß der Kompilator der *Did.* wohl schon ein schriftliches Evangelium kannte, aber nicht selbst benutzte, sondern nur auf dasselbe verwies.[9]

7.   Other variations are noted and further discussed below. See also Niederwimmer (1998: 135, Table 9 and 136–37).

8.   Prior to Köster (1957) it was fairly common for scholars to see Matthew's Gospel behind 8.2b, so e.g. Schaff (1885: 188) and Massaux (1993: 154–55). See also Wengst (1984: 26–27). Köster (1957: 203–209) presented a powerful case for the non-quotation of Matthew's Gospel in *Did.* 8.2c. Köster's line has also been taken by Audet (1958: 171–73); Giet (1970: 200); Rordorf and Tuilier (1978: 86).

9.   'Thus, the result is that the compiler of the *Didache* is likely to have known a written gospel, but he himself did not use it; he only referred to it.'

Niederwimmer (1998: 51) follows this lead when, at the end of the passage quoted at length above, he adds the observation: 'Nota bene: This understanding does not mean that the author also *quotes* this gospel'. Thus Köster and Niederwimmer imagine that the Didachist could have referred to a written gospel at 8.2b, *while not quoting from that gospel at 8.2c*. This is an extraordinary position. It requires that an author who regards the Lord's gospel as normative for every aspect of Christian behaviour (15.4) including, specifically, prayer (8.2b; 15.4), should immediately turn aside from that gospel to quote a *different* tradition as exemplary for Christian practice (8.2c). If one author was responsible for 8.2b and 8.2c, then it is hard to believe that the latter is not a quotation taken from the gospel mentioned in the former. Herein lies the difficulty for the view that 'the gospel' is that according to Matthew, since *Did.* 8.2c appears *not* to be a direct quotation of Matthew's Lord's Prayer.

This raises a further possibility, that Matthew's Gospel is not in mind in *Did.* 8.2b and that another 'lost' gospel, containing this similar but different version of the Lord's Prayer, is directly quoted instead. Technically this is always a possibility, but it is not one without difficulties. In this case it is necessary to hypothecate a gospel that shares Matthew's otherwise unique combination of teaching on prayer, visitors, discipline and alms. In addition it is necessary to hypothecate the loss, without further trace, of a text that had sufficient authority and availability to be simply deferred to as a guide (without quotation) 'in everything that you do' (15.4).[10] Hypotheses of this kind must always be considered, but perhaps only as a last resort. This invites discussion of a fourth possible explanation for the pattern of *Did.* 8.1-3.

The potential contradiction within *Did.* 8.1-3 could be reconciled if this passage was in fact laid down in two separate stages. Thus, if *Did.* 8.1-2a, 2c-3 were composed as an act of Christian self-definition by the modifying teacher (cf. Chapter 7, section 7), then it need not have been taken from Matthew's Gospel. The subsequent publication of Matthew's Gospel and its rise to authoritative status might, however, have created a motive for the later insertion of the instruction to pray 'as the Lord directed in his

10. This position also requires that 8.2b serves as a formula designed to introduce a quotation from 'the gospel'. However, this cannot be the function of the reference to the gospel in either 11.3b or 15.3-4. In the case of 11.3b this is because this verse is followed by a multilayered text which cannot have been lifted in this form from another text. In the case of 15.3-4 there is an indication of the gospel's content in 15.3, but 15.4 is far from a quotation formula in that the reader is here invited to consult the gospel without any further indication of the precise content of that authority.

gospel'. This is the case because a discrepancy between the versions of the Lord's Prayer in *Did.* 8 and Mt. 6 could have caused confusion in later liturgical practice.[11] This circumstance invites one of two responses. Either the text of *Did.* 8.2c could have been altered to make it match the Matthean tradition, or instruction could have been given to guide the reader's perception of the *Didache*'s version of the Lord's Prayer in relation to that provided by Matthew. The eccentricities of the *Didache*'s prayer mean that it is highly unlikely that the first option was taken. This leaves the possibility that 8.2b was designed to subordinate the *Didache*'s prayer to the 'superior' version in Matthew's Gospel, while preserving the established text of the *Didache* as it had been received.[12]

The interpretation of 'gospel' in *Did.* 8.1-3 is far from straightforward. However, a reading which sees this term as part of a redactor's attempt to subordinate the *Didache* to the superior authority of Matthew's Gospel has two points in its favour. First, it does not require the hypothecation of a definitive 'gospel', remarkably similar to Matthew's, which has now disappeared. Second, a subordinating function for 'gospel' in *Did.* 8.2b is fully consistent with the way in which this term is used in *Did.* 15.3-4. In the latter instance the Christian is directed to this external source for ultimately authoritative advice regarding every aspect of Christian behaviour, including a specific reference to prayer.

With regard to the identity of the 'gospel' referred to in the *Didache*, therefore, it may be concluded that the strongest candidate is Matthew's Gospel. The popularity of this gospel in the early Church makes it compatible with the role of 'the definitive gospel'. Matthew's Gospel addresses all the issues mentioned in the *Didache* in connection with the gospel, and does so in a way which makes sense of the explanatory comment in *Did.* 15.3. The mention of the gospel at 8.2b creates a difficulty for this view if this line is seen as introducing a quotation from that gospel, which appears not to be Matthew's, in 8.2c. However, the possibility that 8.2b was *not* intended to serve as part of a quotation formula is suggested by the fact that, in *Did.* 11.3b and 15.3-4, appeals to the 'gospel', far from introducing quotations, are used to subordinate the *Didache* to an external authority. A similar function is attributable to *Did.* 8.2b if it was an insertion designed

11. In Chapter 11, § 3 it will be argued that Matthew directly quoted from the modifying teacher's work in *Did.* 8. This offers an explanation for the very close relationship between the two texts.

12. Examples of the common technique of altering the force of a text by means of interpolation, rather than by direct alteration, may be found in the contributions of the modifying teacher.

to subordinate the *Didache*'s prayer to a version that was understood to be the directly expressed 'instructions of the Lord'. The Lord's Prayer in Matthew's Gospel is presented in precisely these terms. I conclude, therefore, that the 'gospel' appealed to in the *Didache* was in fact that according to Matthew.

2. *The 'Gospel' References and the Modifying Teacher Layer*

So far I have argued that *Did.* 8.2b; 11.3b and 15.3-4 were all contributed by someone who used the term 'gospel' to refer to the Gospel of Matthew. If this is the case, then what implications follow for the redactional status of these insertions?

The relationship of *Did.* 8.2b; 11.3b and 15.3-4 to the rest of the text boils down to the question of whether or not these verses could have been written by the modifying teacher. This is the case because 8.2b and 15.3-4 both presuppose the presence of the Modifying Teacher layer and so could not have been added to the whole in its absence. The following analysis will concentrate, therefore, on each of the 'gospel' verses in turn and will ask whether they could have been written by the modifying teacher.

2.1. Didache *15.3-4*

To suggest that *Did.* 15.3-4 was written by the modifying teacher is to claim that the section 14.1–15.4 was penned as a continuous whole. The first indication that this might not be the case is provided by the eccentric order in which subjects are addressed. Thus, the issue of discipline is mentioned in 14.1-3, and also in 15.3, but advice on the appointment of bishops and deacons intervenes in 15.1-2. This arrangement causes Knopf (1920: 38) to suggest that 15.3 should be attached to 14.2 so that 'If the case in 14.2 occurs, and those concerned cannot be reconciled with one another, the other members of the community should intervene and gently put them right'.[13]

Knopf's attempt to reconstruct the text in this way is understandable but difficult to justify. There is good reason to suppose that *Did.* 14.1–15.2 was written by one author because these verses all show a consistency with the interests or compositional techniques of the modifying teacher (cf. Chapter 7, section 5). The return to the subject of discipline in 15.3 may therefore be attributed, either to this author's return from a digression to readdress the subject after realizing that it had been incompletely

---

13. This translation of Knopf is from Niederwimmer 1998: 203 n. 1.

considered three verses earlier, or to the work of a new and separate author who wished to supplement the teacher's earlier contribution.

That two separate authors were responsible for *Did.* 14.1–15.2 and *Did.* 15.3-4 is also suggested by the fact that the 'gospel' is appealed to in one case but not in the other. This is significant because the gospel is presented in 15.4 as an ultimate authority, beyond even the authority of the preceding text, for 'all that you undertake'. If the author who held this view of the gospel in 15.4 was also responsible for writing 14.1-3, then why was the gospel not mentioned in support of the instruction to 'be reconciled' in 14.2? This is particularly surprising if the gospel in question is that of Matthew, since Mt. 5.23-24 reads:

> 5.23 So if you are offering your gift at the altar, and there remember that your brother has something against you, 5.24 leave your gift there before the altar and go; first be reconciled to your brother, and then come and offer your gift (RSV).

This text offers much more direct support for the instruction 'be reconciled before sacrificing' (14.2) than does the somewhat oblique appeal to Mal. 1.11 actually used in *Did.* 14.3. The fact that Malachi 1.11 was preferred to Mt. 5.23-24 invites an explanation. If one author was responsible for the whole of 14.1–15.4, then it must be supposed that Malachi was preferred in 14.3 because its superior authority made even oblique support for the instruction in 14.2 preferable to that offered by the gospel. This explanation is difficult to sustain under a 'one author' hypothesis, however, because the author of *Did.* 15.4 evidently understands the gospel to be a text with ultimate authority in the direction of Christian behaviour. An alternative explanation for the use of Malachi at *Did.* 14.3 is that 'the gospel' was not known to, or understood as authoritative by, the author of 14.1-3. In this case the author of *Did.* 14.1-3 cannot also have composed *Did.* 15.3-4.

The case for the separation of 15.3-4 from the immediately preceding text is further supported by the observation that these appeals to 'the gospel' ultimately undermine the efforts of the modifying teacher. That is to say, the effect of 15.3-4 is to send the reader to consult the gospel, whose authority is to be accepted even over the careful modifications of the teacher. This would be like my including advice that a better study of Matthew's relationship to the *Didache* can in fact be found elsewhere. I might make such a statement when the alternative study contains an argument with which I agree, but not when it proposes an opposing view. It is true that Matthew's Gospel is essentially in accordance with the line taken by the modifying teacher in *Did.* 14.1-3; however, as will be considered in the following sections, this is not the case with all the teacher's instructions.

In summary, *Did.* 15.3-4 does not stand in continuity with the work of the modifying teacher in 14.1–15.2 for three reasons. First, the single topic of church discipline is considered in two separate places. Second, the teacher's failure to appeal to the gospel in 14.3 suggests that an authoritative gospel to which readers could be referred was not available in this case, while such was available to the author of 15.3-4. Third, the efforts of the teacher to explain the need for reconciliation between church members was perhaps unnecessary if this same author was immediately willing to subordinate this teaching to the superior authority of the gospel.

2.2. Didache *8.2b*

The problem of a contributor who immediately subordinates their additions to the superior authority of the gospel is again raised by the idea that the whole of *Did.* 8.1-3 was composed by one person. If the gospel referred to was Matthew's, then it must be proposed that this author demanded one action in 8.2b (pray as Jesus commands, as reported in Matthew's Gospel), and another in 8.2c (pray according to the slightly different wording set out below). Köster (1957: 209, 240) attempts to sidestep this difficulty by proposing that a not fully authoritative gospel is referred to in *Did.* 8.2b. This position is, however, very difficult to sustain. The text refers to the personal directions of the Lord, and this suggests that the author of 8.2b believed the gospel to be an authentic conduit of the teaching of Jesus. It is difficult to suppose that such a text could have been understood as only partially authoritative by author or readers. The treatment of the gospel in *Did.* 15.4 adds to the impression that this 'gospel of the Lord' was an ultimate authority. Thus, the problem remains. Why does 8.2b point the reader to the directions of the Lord in the gospel, while 8.2c appears to carry a version of that prayer that does not come from any known gospel?[14] The answer to this question may be that 8.2b was inserted into the *Didache* by the same person who also wrote 15.3-4, and for the same reason; namely, as a means of subordinating the teaching of the *Didache* to the authority of Matthew's Gospel, especially where the two texts are at variance.

In summary, those who see *Did.* 8.1-3 as the work of one author must explain why the direct speech of Jesus in Mt. 6 appears to be appealed to in 8.2b, but is not adhered to in 8.2c. Given the difficulties of this position

14. § 1.3, above, concluded that 'gospel' is likely to refer to Matthew's Gospel rather than a lost text.

it is perhaps preferable to suppose that the function of *Did.* 8.2b was to assure the reader that Matthew's version of the prayer was the one to be followed. This solution coheres with the apparently similar function of *Did.* 15.3-4, where the gospel is appealed to as an external authority without further quotation.

2.3. Didache *11.3b*

In Chapter 7 it was concluded that the Modifying Teacher layer included, among other verses, *Did.* 8.2a, 2c-3; 11.1-2, 10-11; 13.1–15.2. Given that 8.2b and 15.3-4 could only have been added to the *Didache* alongside or after the addition of this layer, and given that 11.3b was added by the same hand as 8.2b and 15.3-4, it follows that 11.3b must have been added either alongside or after the modifying teacher's addition of 11.1-2, 10-11; 13.1–15.2. This section considers which of these two alternatives is the more likely.

The *Didache*'s rules for the treatment of church leaders provokes the most substantial bout of activity on the part of the modifying teacher. An initial attempt to establish the legitimacy of the modifier's alterations is presented in 11.1-2; insertions that gainsay the previously existing version of the *Didache* are then made in 11.10-11 and 13.1-7; and additional instructions regarding the selection of leaders offered in 15.1-2. Is it likely that the person responsible for these alterations should, at the same time, undermine their efforts by referring the reader to the external authority of the 'gospel'? Such an act of self-abrogation would be required if the modifying teacher were also responsible for the appeal to the 'gospel' in 11.3b.

Another factor draws a question mark over the modifying teacher's authorship of *Did.* 11.3b. The modifier appeals to the practice of the ancient prophets in 11.11 and an otherwise unknown text quoted at 13.3a, 5-7. If this teacher also knew and was prepared to point to the 'gospel' at 11.3b, then why was this authority not directly employed in the defence of the wider position? That is to say, the attribution of 11.3b to the modifying teacher requires that this author ranked the practice of the ancient prophets and the text quoted at 13.3a, 5-7 in higher esteem than the gospel. Such a conclusion is at odds with the description of the gospel as that 'of the Lord' which provides guidance for all aspects of Christian behaviour. If this authority was so satisfactory, then why was it not quoted? If it was not agreeable, then why is it mentioned at all?

These difficulties are multiplied if the gospel in question is that according to Matthew. The instructions for travelling disciples in Mt. 10.5-15, and for those who receive them in Mt. 10.40-42, do not support the modifier's contention that prophets, teachers and workers should receive the community's firstfruits (*Did.* 13.1-7). For example, Mt. 10.8 explicitly states that: 'You received without payment; give without payment'. It is unlikely, therefore, that the modifying teacher would have included a cross-reference to this gospel in 11.3b.

In summary, the proposal that the modifying teacher was also responsible for the inclusion of the appeal to the gospel at 11.3b is difficult to sustain because it requires the immediate subordination of this author's own extensive emendations of the host text to a separate, and not necessarily agreeable, authority.

3. *Summary and Conclusion: The Gospel Layer*

This chapter began with an attempt to establish some preliminary questions. It was concluded that 8.2b; 11.3b and 15.3-4 were all written by the same hand, all referred to the same 'gospel' and in doing so very probably referred to the Gospel of Matthew. It was then noted that, according to the results of the preceeding redactional survey, these lines could only have been added alongside or after the addition of the Modifying Teacher layer. The possibility that these lines formed part of this teacher's work was then considered, but was rejected for three reasons. First, because of discontinuities in the treatment of subject matter in *Did.* 14.1–15.4. Second, the teacher's failure to appeal to the gospel when this would have forcefully supported the modifications being made. Third, it was considered unlikely that the teacher would have made careful modifications of the host text while then immediately pointing readers to the superior authority of the (not always agreeable) gospel.

Having concluded that *Did.* 8.2b; 11.3b and 15.3-4 were not composed by the modifying teacher, and given that these lines could not have been added prior to the addition of the Modifying Teacher layer, it follows that these verses constitute a separate redactional layer.

Chapter 9

THE FULL EXTENT OF THE PERI LAYER

In Chapter 5 I began to consider which elements of the *Didache* were added to the whole at the same time as *Did.* 9.1-5, and therefore formed part of the Peri layer. This discussion did not consider the possibility that the Peri layer also extended into *Did.* 1–5. I introduced this delay because the subsequent identification of *Did.* 1.5b-6 as part of the Modifying Teacher layer considerably simplifies the analysis of the relationship between the Peri layer and the various elements of *Did.* 1–5; the subject of this short chapter.

1. *The Peri Layer and* Didache *1.3-5a*

Did. 1.3-5a contains 'Q' sayings. This makes the redactional status of these verses a matter of particular interest. Many scholars assume that, because these lines are so close to Matthew's and Luke's Gospels, this section must have been added to the *Didache* alongside other additions where an explicit reference to 'the gospel' is made, or at least that these lines belong to one of the final redactional layers of the text.[1] These con-clusions are called into question, however, by the previously unrecognized change of redactional layer between *Did.* 1.3-5a and 1.5b-6.

In Chapter 7, section 4, above, it was noted that *Did.* 1.5b-6 exhibits the distinctive characteristics of the modifying teacher: an affirmation of the preceding teaching, the modification of that teaching and a justification of the modification by reference to an alternative tradition. *Did.* 1.5b-6 modifies 1.3-5a, and 1.3-5a must predate its own modification. Therefore, 1.3-5a must have been part of the *Didache* prior to the addition of the Modifying Teacher layer.

1.   For example, Draper (1996b: 76); Jefford (1989: 52–53); Audet (1958: 261–80) and Wengst (1984: 66).

Of the layers that predate the Modifying Teacher, the Peri layer stands out as a likely location for *Did.* 1.3-5a. This is the case negatively in that the sayings in 1.3-5a have no affinity with the subject matter, form or style of the Prophet layer, and sit uneasily within the flow of the Two Ways/ Teknon material. On the other hand a positive connection may be found between 1.3-5a and the Peri layer in their shared use of the concept of 'becoming perfect' in 1.4b(r) (καὶ ἔσῃ τέλειος) and 6.2 (τέλειος ἔσῃ). As already noted in Chapter 5, section 4, this term represents a standard of behaviour in accordance with the *halakah* of a particular group. The concept of perfection appears twice in the Peri layer: it is set as the ultimate goal for initiates (6.2) and is required of all at the final test (16.2). Given the importance of acquiring 'perfection', a description of this behavioural standard may be expected. The addition of καὶ ἔσῃ τέλειος to the set of sayings at 1.3-5a, suggests that these verses offer the relevant information.[2]

As noted in Chapter 4, section 3 the collection of individual sayings in 1.3-5a appears to have been formed prior to its inclusion within the *Didache*. However, καὶ ἔσῃ τέλειος disrupts the symmetry of these sayings and thus suggests that this line was added to the collection at a later date. If the function of this addition was to make clear that the instructions of 1.3b-5a epitomize the standard of perfection held up in 6.2 and 16.2, then it is likely that 6.2, 16.2 and 1.4b(r) were all added to the *Didache* at the same time. With 6.2 and 16.2 identified as elements of the Peri layer, then 1.4b(r), and hence the rest of 1.3-5a, may be attributed similarly.[3]

2. *The Peri Layer and the Title of the* Didache

The title of any text has a profound influence on the way it is read. It is necessary, therefore, to consider the place of the title in the formation of the *Didache*.

---

2.   Beyond the use of τέλειος, *Did.* 1.3-5a has two other features in common with other elements of the Peri layer. First, parallel transitional phrases occur at 1.3a, 6.1 and, more elaborately, 16.1-2. Second, both 1.3-5a and *Did.* 16 use other traditions to expand or illustrate an idea. This use of other traditions is dissimilar to the practice of the modifying teacher because these traditions are used to build up, rather than undermine, the existing text.

3.   It is, of course, possible that 1.4b(r) was added to 1.3-5a *after* these sayings had already been added to the *Didache*. However, this would merely have the effect of further increasing the antiquity of this group of sayings. Note: '(r)' refers to a redactional insert in the midst of 1.4b.

2.1. *The Puzzle of the Double Title*

The Jerusalem manuscript preserves a coloured sequence at the opening of the *Didache*. The superscribed title is written in red ink, the body of the text in black.[4]

διδαχὴ τῶν δώδεκα ἀποστόλων
Διδαχὴ κυρίου διὰ τῶν δώδεκα ἀποστόλων τοῖς ἔθνεσιν· ὁδοὶ δύο
εἰσί, μία τῆς ζωῆς καὶ μία τοῦ θανάτου, διαφορὰ δὲ πολλὴ ...

The latter of these two titles forms the first line of the main body of the text and continues into *Did.* 1.1 without a break. Why does the text have a double title?

Scholars commonly view the double opening of the *Didache* as the presentation of two alternative titles. Rordorf (1979: 106) says that the short title refers to Acts 2.42 and the long title to Mt. 28.19. Kleist (1948: 153 n. 1) suggests that the short title was written on the outside of the scroll and the long one at the start of the text itself and was thus copied twice by Leon (the scribe responsible for the Jerusalem manuscript). These solutions, however, introduce unnecessary complication.

It has long been recognized that ancient authors did not use superscribed titles. Their texts simply began at the beginning and continued to the end. This is not to say that the opening lines of a text might not have contained vital information for appreciating the subject and genre of the text; it is simply to observe that it was usual for texts to be given a title by *later* readers who needed a handle by which to refer to them. The title 'Διδαχὴ τῶν δώδεκα ἀποστόλων' is an uncontroversial choice in the case of a text beginning, 'Διδαχὴ κυρίου διὰ τῶν δώδεκα ἀποστόλων τοῖς ἔθνεσιν'.

An almost identical process of titling may be found, for example, in the case of the book of Revelation. In the several manuscripts of this text the occurrence of a double title is entirely standard. Thus the introductory lines provided by the author himself: 'The Revelation of Jesus Christ which God gave him to show his servants what must soon take place; and which he made known by sending his angel to his servant John' (Rev. 1.1), are commonly abbreviated and superscribed as 'The Revelation of John', or some such.

The doubling of the title in the Jerusalem manuscript provides good evidence for the antiquity of the long title (the first line of the text) relative

---

4.   A (black and white) photograph of the manuscript is provided in van de Sandt and Flusser (2002: 7).

to the superscribed title. The earliest students of the text were convinced of this position.[5] However, more recent scholarship has tended to see the long title as a later addition.[6]

The sole reason, as far as I can establish, for this latter position is the supposition that the *Didache* depends upon the *Doctrina apostolorum*. The *Doctrina* begins with a short title, 'The Teaching of the Apostles', and opens with the line 'There are two ways in the world...' On the basis of this evidence Niederwimmer (1998: 56–57) asserts, 'There is very good reason to suppose that, at a relatively early period, this was the title of the Christianized Two Ways tractate, and that this title then transferred to the *Didache*'. This position is, however, difficult to sustain.

First, and most importantly, as argued in the excursus in Chapter 4, the dependence of the *Didache* on the *Doctrina* is extremely doubtful.

Second, the pre-Christian origin and widespread occurrence of the Two Ways tradition provides no clear reason as to why the title 'The Teaching of the Apostles' should have attached to yet another version of the Two Ways, such as appears in the *Doctrina*. However, if the *Doctrina* depended on the *Didache*, rather than the reverse, then attribution to the apostles would be entirely understandable.[7]

Third, if the original title of the *Didache* was 'The Teaching of the Apostles', then it is very difficult to see why the long title should ever have been created and inserted under the short title. What purpose could such an operation serve? By contrast, the abbreviation and superscription of the

---

5. This was the view of Harnack (1884: 24–37); Bryennios (1883: 3) and Knopf (1920: 3).

6. Variations on this view are expressed by Audet (1958: 91–103, 247–54) and Niederwimmer (1998: 56–57).

7. Something of which Niederwimmer seems unaware is that the *Doctrina* and the *Didache*'s sharing of the same title is a problem that must be *overcome* by those who espouse the relative antiquity of the *Doctrina*. Audet (1996: 135) does detect this problem and attempts to addresses it as follows: 'Moreover, the title *Doctrina apostolorum*, which the *Duae viae* of Schlecht carries, does not present any serious difficulty [for Audet's view that the *Doctrina* predates the *Didache*]. Because, on the one hand, the *Duae viae* designated in this way by Rufinus did not have its own title, and because on the other hand, it appeared in almost identical form at the beginning of a writing bearing the title Διδαχή τῶν ἀποστόλων, it could have been enough that the two writings intersected in the course of their distribution in the same milieu for the title of the *Didache* to have passed to the Greek *Duae viae* and then, naturally, to its Latin version.' Thus, Audet implicitly admits that his view requires that the Two Ways *did not* originally bear its present title.

long title to form the short title is entirely logical and is paralleled in numerous other texts.

In conclusion, if the *Doctrina apostolorum* is not relevant to discussion of the *Didache*'s history, then there is every reason to suppose that the long title appeared first, and that the superscribed title was added later as a short-hand means of referring to the text we now describe as 'the *Didache*'.

2.2. *The Redactional Location of the Long Title*

Having concluded that the long title is the more original, it is possible to consider its redactional location. This is a two step process. First, it is necessary to identify the function of the long title. Then it will be possible to ask when this function is most likely to have been employed.

The function of the title, in this case, is not simply to attribute the text to an authoritative author, but also to specify that the teaching is directed 'τοῖς ἔθνεσιν'. This ambiguous term may be interpreted as referring either to nations in general, or to non-Jewish nations in particular, that is, Gentiles. A reason for preferring 'to the Gentiles' in this case is that 'τοῖς ἔθνεσιν' acts as a qualification of the initial statement. An author who sought to widen, rather than limit, the applicability of the teaching, might have done better to omit 'τοῖς ἔθνεσιν' altogether, or at very least to have used 'τοῖς πᾶσι ἔθνεσιν'.[8]

If the function of the title was to indicate the applicability of the teaching to the situation of Gentiles, then when is this title likely to have been introduced? The Modifying Teacher layer is a poor candidate since this layer appears to assume a Jewish background among his readers (cf., for example, 13.3). The Prophet layer is also unattractive since there is nothing here to suggest a Gentile audience. The Peri layer, on the other hand, does show signs of having been addressed to the situation of Gentiles. The central concern of the Peri layer is the question of who may be admitted to table fellowship at the community's eschatological meal. The answer given is that those who accept the Two Ways[9] as a declaration of the community rule, and who do their best to keep the food laws and the

---

8.   Translations of the New Testament usually interpret 'τά ἔθνη' as 'the Gentiles' and 'πάντα τά ἔθνη' as 'all the nations'. Bauer *et al.* (1957) state that 'τά ἔθνη' is usually used of foreigners, rather than every nation.

9.   'The precepts envisaging pederasty, magic, abortion, and exposure of babies, which are opposed to the commandments of the Decalogue, are more comprehensible if they are addressed to ancient Pagans' (Rordorf 1996a: 156). See also Audet (1958: 286).

whole 'yoke of the Lord'[10] (6.2-3) may be baptized (7.1), and thus entitled to share in the eschatological meal (9.5a). This initiation seems specifically designed for Gentiles who wish to join a form of Christianity governed by ethnic Jews. Certainly *Did.* 6.2-3 gives the impression that it was written by Jews consciously conceding to the moral inferiority and ignorance of incoming Gentiles.

> 6.2 If you can bear the entire yoke of the Lord, you will be perfect, but if you cannot, do what you can. 6.3 As for food, bear what you can, but be very much on your guard against food offered to idols, for it is worship of dead gods.

The Peri layer's interest in the initiation of Gentiles makes it an ideal redactional location for the long title of the *Didache*.

3. *The Peri Layer and the Two Ways Material*

Chapter 4 identified a number of separate elements within *Did.* 1–5. It is important to note, however, that the identification of separate elements does not necessarily equate to the identification of separate redactional layers. This is the case because an older tradition, or collection of traditions, may be incorporated into a younger base text. For example, if an artist composes a collage entitled 'Autumn' and incorporates within it an older picture called 'October' the compositional history of 'Autumn' may only be traced back to the single point at which 'Autumn' was created. It is not correct to say that 'October' represents an earlier stage in the history of 'Autumn' (even though it is an older composition), because 'Autumn' is not a development in the history of 'October'; it is the creation of a new and separate piece of art.

In seeking the base layer of the *Didache*, therefore, it is not necessarily the case that the oldest tradition represents the foundational layer. Rather the base layer may be identified as coinciding with the point at which the *Didache* distinctively became the *Didache*.

The identity of a text is crucially determined by its title. Thus, in the same way that 'Autumn' became 'Autumn' at the point where it was so named, the *Didache* became the *Didache* at the point when the long title was added. This teaching to the Gentiles happened to incorporate some older traditions, but its history is not the history of those incorporated units. From a redaction history point of view, therefore, the base of the *Didache*,

---

10. Flusser (1996: 199) and Draper (1995: 290) take 'yoke of the Lord' to refer to the Torah.

to which later developments were added, is the text originally following the title 'The Teaching of the Lord, by the Twelve Apostles, to the Gentiles'.

It was concluded, in Chapter 4, that *Did.* 1.3-5a must have been inserted into an form of the Two Ways that already included 1.2b and 2.1. Further, since 1.3-5a has been identified as part of the Peri layer, it may be concluded that the Peri layer consisted of the long title followed by a version of the Two Ways (already including the Law Summary and possibly also the Teknon material) which was further augmented by the addition of 1.3-5a. This whole collection of ethical teachings was then presented as a pre-baptismal rule by which Gentiles might be admitted to baptism, and thence to the eucharist.

The relationship of the Two Ways, Law Summary and Teknon material to the Peri layer may therefore be seen as akin to the relationship of 'October' to 'Autumn'. These ancient, combined traditions were taken and incorporated into a new document entitled 'The Teaching of the Lord, by the Twelve Apostles, to the Gentiles'.

4. *The Peri Layer and* Didache *16.1-6, 8-9*

In Chapter 5, section 4. it was noted that *Did.* 16.1-2 has certain affinities with *Did.* 6.1-3: both warn against deception while recommending the goal of perfection, and both have the form of linking material which affirms the preceding text. On this basis *Did.* 16.1-6, 8-9 was preliminarily linked with the Peri layer.

At this stage it is possible to observe an additional feature of *Did.* 16.1-6, 8-9 which points to its membership of the Peri layer. During the course of this chapter it has been argued that the Peri layer was in fact the base layer, or the original version, of the *Didache*. This document describes a system of initiation whereby a version of the Two Ways, variously augmented, was presented as a standard of moral perfection (1.4b and 6.2). Those who wished to enter the community were required to recognize this standard and to aspire to complete conformity with it, even if such had not yet been attained (6.2-3). Once initiation had occurred then participation in the community's meal, which presaged the eschatological ingathering, could take place (9.5a).[11] *Did.* 16.1-6, 8-9 serves as a suitable conclusion[12]

---

11. Additional instructions regarding the management of apostles are also included at 11.3a, 4-6.

12. Jefford observes (1989: 113–14): '...there can be little question that one finds here [in *Did.* 16] a typical, early Jewish-Christian tendency to conclude important writings with the promise and threat of an eschatological warning'.

to this document because it traces the fate of the initiate along similar lines. Thus, the community member is urged to conform completely to the established standard of perfection (16.1-2). Success in this regard allows entry, after the final judgment, to the complete eschatological reward (16.9; cf. 16.2).

In summary, *Did.* 16.1-6, 8-9 may be seen as a suitable conclusion to the Peri document because it reinforces the earlier parts of that document in warning against deceivers (6.1; 16.4b), in setting the goal of perfection (1.4b; 6.2; 16.2) and in looking forward to the heavenly destination of those who truly belong to the community (9.4-5a; 16.2, 9).

5. *Conclusion: The Full Extent of the Peri/Base Layer*

On the basis of the preceding considerations, the full extent of the Peri layer, which was also, I propose, the Base layer (and thus the original text of the *Didache*), may be identified as: long title; 1.1-5a; 2.1–5.2a; 6.1– 7.1a, c, e, 4a; 9.1-5a; 11.3a, 4-6; 16.1-6, 8-9.

Chapter 10

The aim of Part I has been to show that the *Didache* is not a unified whole, but is made up of different redactional layers which themselves incorporate barely adapted, previously existing traditions. Five stages in the composition of the *Didache* have been identified.

1. *The Peri/Base Layer Consisting of:*
The Long Title; 1.1-5a; 2.1–5.2a; 6.1–7.1a, c, e, 4a;
9.1-5a; 11.3a, 4-6; 16.1-6, 8-9.

At the foundation of the whole lies the Peri/Base layer. This composition provides a base for the later insertions. From this analysis it is apparent that the author of the Peri/Base layer was concerned to provide instruction regarding baptism, eucharist and apostles. A version of the ancient Jewish Two Ways teaching was used as a baptismal rule, expanded by the Teknon unit (3.1-7), the Law Summary unit (1.2b, c; 2.1) and a further sayings collection (1.3-5a), itself comprising five originally independent sayings. The resultant community code was then commended as a whole to those who sought baptism (6.1) and certain other legal details and attitudes added in 6.2-3. A description of the baptismal rite and accompanying fast followed in 7.1a, c, e, 4a, and the eucharist that the initiates were consequently entitled to join (cf. 9.5a) was ordered in 9.1-5a. The Peri/Base layer goes on to consider the management of apostles and then concludes, in traditional style, with an eschatological warning (16.1-6, 8-9) that incorporates a previously existing 'apocalypse' (16.3-6, 8-9).

The practice of incorporating whole sections of previously existing tradition, which themselves had incorporated or gathered further originally separate traditions/sayings, means that the Peri/Base layer includes (excluding the redactional comments of the compiler) nine previously separate units of tradition.

2. *The Prophet Layer: 10.1-7; 11.7-9, 12; 12.1-5*

The creation of the Prophet document appears to have been precipitated by the base document's limitations with regard to the ministry of prophets. This was the case in that the original teaching on the eucharist (9.1-5a) took no account of the practice of prophesying over the eschatological meal and so failed to regulate this behaviour. Further, the Peri document, if its teaching on apostles was applied to wandering prophets, was in danger of extinguishing the prophetic ministry altogether. Thus, it appears that, in response to the need for fuller teaching on prophets, the Prophet document was written. This document remained faithful to the teaching of the Peri/Base document where practicable, but re-framed conditions for wandering prophets so that they did not have to be forever on the move to avoid accusations of falsity.

While the Prophet document was initially independent of the Peri/Base document, the similarities of subject and language between these two texts appear to have prompted the later insertion of the Prophet text into the original version of the *Didache*. The common subject matter and language of *Did.* 9 and 10 provided a basis for the juxtaposition of the two eucharistic prayers, and the remainder of the Prophet text, concerning the testing and reception of prophets, was considered suitable for insertion after the Base layer's parallel teaching on the reception of apostles (11.3a, 4-6).

The Prophet document, which became the Prophet layer upon incorporation into the *Didache*, is thus a unified text. Although it appears to have been written under the influence of the Peri/Base layer it does not incorporate (unchanged) any previously existing units of tradition.

3. *The Modifying Teacher Layer:*
1.5b-6; 5.2b; 7.1b, d, 2-3, 4b; 8.1-2a, 2c-3;
11.1-2, 9-10; 13.1–15.2

The contribution of the modifying teacher is tied, by definition, to the text that it modifies. On this basis it can be confidently concluded that this layer was added to a version of the *Didache* to which the Prophet document had already been added, since this layer is modified by the teacher's material. A desire for financial stability appears as a central motivation for the teacher's modifications. This may be seen directly in the modifications regarding giving (1.5b-6) and support for prophet/teachers (13.1-7), and indirectly in the teacher's desire to create institutional differentiation between traditional Judaism and Christianity (7.1d, 2-3, 4b; 8.1-2a, 2c-3; 14.1). This had financial implications for the modifier because institutional separation brings with it a channelling of resources away from the old hierarchy and towards the new one (cf. 13.3).

The modifying teacher's efforts to re-draw the rulings of the *Didache* show a respect for the existing text, inasmuch as orthodoxy is demonstrated by endorsing the existing instructions. However, a desire to challenge the thrust of the basic Teaching prompts the quotation of three alternative traditions (at 1.6; 13.3a, 4-7 and 14.3). The modifier's desire to create institutional separation between Christians and Jews provides a motive for introducing two further traditions, regarding baptism (7.1c, 2-3, 4b) and prayer (8.2c). Consequently, besides the modifying teacher's own contributions, six additional authors are also quoted.

4. *Gospel Layer: 8.2b; 11.3b; 15.3-4*

The raw addition of the Prophet document to the Peri/Base text, combined with the subversive activities of the modifying teacher, created a text that was sometimes unclear or self-contradictory. In addition to these difficulties the appearance of Matthew's record of the direct speech of Jesus created a situation where contradictions were not only internal, but also external in relation to Matthew's work. The inclusion of the Gospel layer suggests that an interpolator, recognizing the authority of the *Didache* but also its conflict with Matthew's Gospel, chose to preserve the text of the *Didache* at the same time as ultimately subordinating it to the authority of the gospel. Thus, where there is a conflict between the *Didache* and the gospel regarding prayer (8.2b; 15.4), prophets (11.3b), discipline, almsgiving or any other matter (15.3-4), the authority of the gospel is ultimately upheld.

5. *The Jerusalem Addition: 16.7*

With the addition of the Gospel layer the history of the basic text comes to a close. Following Matthew's presentation of the teaching of Jesus there was no need for further additions to be made to the *Didache*. However, in the particular version of the *Didache* preserved in the Jerusalem manuscript, there was at least one further twist in the tail. The loss of the ending of *Did.* 16, after verse 8, created an apparent ambiguity as to who would participate in the resurrection. With the loss of a final judgment scene the resurrection appeared to function as an indiscriminate final reward. Using a thread of information remaining from the quotation of Zech. 14.5 in 16.8, a later scribe chose to indicate, by inserting 16.7, that the resurrection of 16.6 was selective, and that therefore only the 'holy ones' would receive this final benefit.

6. *Essential Conclusions from Part I*

For the sake of completeness, Part I attempted to present a full analysis of the compositional history of the *Didache*. This is a complex task and one that is unlikely to be correct in every detail. Progress towards Part II, however, requires the tenability of just two of these conclusions.

First, it is vital that the *Didache* should be seen as containing at least two units composed by different authors at different times.[1] The foregoing analysis goes well beyond this basic requirement in that it identifies four different redactional layers, of which the first three were said to contain a total of sixteen previously existing units of tradition. This means that my method for establishing Matthew's dependence on the *Didache* includes, in this regard at least, a substantial margin for error.

One other, more specific, conclusion from the preceding Part is also essential to the following discussion. This is the view, put forward in Chapter 8, that references to the 'gospel' were added after earlier layers of the text had been laid down. On this basis, all parts of the text that predate these additions may theoretically have been available to Matthew. If, as argued in detail above, *Did.* 8.2b, 11.3b and 15.3-4 represents the full extent of the 'Gospel layer', then Matthew's use of every other part of the text (besides 16.7) cannot be ruled out. By the same token, however, should the Gospel layer be shown to include more text than I have allowed, then any parts so included could not have been used by Matthew.

To sum up, if the diagram overleaf represents an even approximately accurate assessment of the compositional history of the Didache, then the ground is prepared for Part II.

---

1.   This is vital for the effectiveness of the arguments offered in Part II. A summary of this mode of argument was offered in Chapter 1.

7. *Summary Diagram*

The results of Part I are summarized in Figure 1, opposite. The *Didache*'s chapter numbers, alongside indications of major subject areas, are arranged across the top of the page (note that the long title is included before *Did.* 1.1). In the body of the diagram the redactional layers rise from the oldest to the youngest.

Patterned blocks indicate sayings and traditions which existed prior to their incorporation into the *Didache*. A pattern that recurs in two or three places signifies the same tradition on each occasion.

Each incorporated tradition has a two letter label. These correspond to labels used in column B in the text of the *Didache* at the beginning of this volume. These letters have the following meanings:

Within the Peri/Base layer:

LS = Law Summary unit (*Did.* 1.2b, d-e; 2.1)
SO = Sayings Onion (*Did.* 1.3-5a)
[within the Sayings Onion, a = 1.3b; b = 1.3c; c = 1.4a; d = 1.4b; e = 1.5a]
TK = Teknon unit (*Did.* 3.1-7)
TW = Two Ways (*Did.* 1.1-2a; 2.2-7; 3.8-5.2a)
AP = Apocalypse (*Did.* 16.3-6, 8-9)

The Prophet layer consists of one originally external tradition:

PR = The Prophet Document (*Did.* 10.1-7; 11.7-9, 12; 12.1-5)

Within the Modifying Teacher layer:

GV = 'Let the gift sweat in your hand' (*Did.* 1.6)
BP = Threefold baptismal tradition (*Did.* 7.1d, 2-3, 4b)
LP = Lord's Prayer (*Did.* 8.2c)
DG = 'Do not give what is holy to dogs' (*Did.* 9.5b)
FF = Firstfruits tradition (*Did.* 13.3a, 5-7)
ML = Malachi 1.11 (*Did.* 14.3)

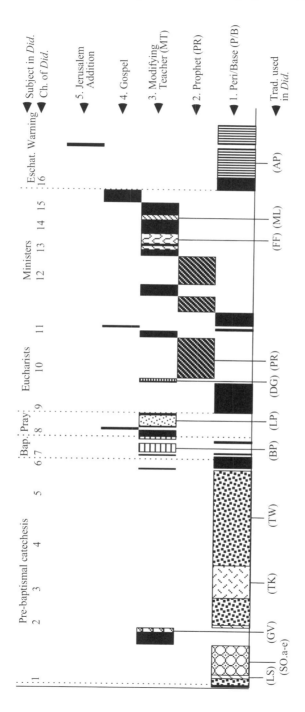

Figure 1: *The layers of the* Didache *with incorporated/quoted traditions*

7. *Essential Conclusions from Part I*

For the sake of completeness, Part I attempted to present a full analysis of the compositional history of the *Didache*. This is a complex task and one that is unlikely to be correct in every detail. Progress towards Part II, however, requires the tenability of just two of these conclusions.

First, it is vital that the *Didache* should be seen as containing at least two units composed by different authors at different times.[2] The foregoing analysis goes well beyond this basic requirement in that it identifies four different redactional layers, of which the first three were said to contain a total of sixteen previously existing units of tradition. This means that my method for establishing Matthew's dependence on the *Didache* includes, in this regard at least, a substantial margin for error.

One other, more specific, conclusion from the preceding Part is also essential to the following discussion. This is the view, put forward in Chapter 8, that references to the 'gospel' were added after earlier layers of the text had been laid down. On this basis, all parts of the text that predate these additions may theoretically have been available to Matthew. If, as argued in detail above, *Did.* 8.2b, 11.3b and 15.3-4 represents the full extent of the 'Gospel layer', then Matthew's use of every other part of the text (besides 16.7) cannot be ruled out. By the same token, however, if the Gospel layer could be shown to include more text than I have allowed, then any parts so included could not have been used by Matthew.

If it may be accepted that various diverse elements of the *Didache* were composed by more than one author at one time, and that references to 'the gospel' appear in one of the text's later redactional layers, then the ground is prepared for Part II.

---

2.   This is vital for the effectiveness of the arguments offered in Part II. A summary of this mode of argument was offered in Chapter 1.

Part II

THE POINTS OF CONTACT BETWEEN THE *DIDACHE* AND
MATTHEW'S GOSPEL

The introductory chapter observed that, if the *Didache* is a multi-layered document, then the presence of four references to 'the gospel' cannot be taken as proving a post-Matthean date for the whole text. It is now possible to add detail to this general observation in the light of Part I.

The foregoing analysis of the *Didache*'s composition concludes that the four appeals to 'the gospel' are restricted to a final redactional layer (the Gospel layer 8.2b; 11.3b; 15.3-4). This means that the use of 'gospel' in these verses may not be taken as requiring a similar knowledge of Matthew's Gospel by the rest of the *Didache*. Indeed the opposite implication might almost be taken, in that the need to subordinate the earlier layers of the *Didache* to the gospel implies that they were somehow out of tune with that text; a feature which may have arisen through ignorance of Matthew's work. Be that as it may, if 8.2b; 11.3b and 15.3-4 form a final and self-contained layer of the *Didache*, then references to 'the gospel' in this layer need not be taken as indicating a post-Matthean date for the other layers of the *Didache* (less the Jerusalem addition at 16.7).

If the references to 'the gospel' do not demonstrate that the earlier layers of the *Didache* were composed after the writing of Matthew's Gospel, then Matthew's direct dependence upon the first three layers of the *Didache* becomes a live possibility. Indeed, if the conclusions of Part I are even approximately correct, then it becomes possible to present a positive argument for Matthew's direct dependence on the *Didache*.

Part I identified 18 separate direct and indirect contributions to the first three layers of the *Didache*. These are listed below in Table 1 (alongside the two letter codes also used with the text of the *Didache* at the beginning of this volume). Alongside each of these elements are listed points in Matthew's Gospel commonly observed as having a link with the *Didache*.[1]

This table (opposite) shows that 14 of the 18 direct and indirect contributions to the *Didache* have one or more points of contact with Matthew's Gospel. Taken at face value, this pattern of connection is most readily explained if the diverse elements of the *Didache* were brought together by the creators of the first three layers, and the resulting composite document was then used by the author of Matthew's Gospel.

---

1.   See, for example, links examined and/or listed in, Jefford (1989: esp. 160-61); Court (1981: 111); Massaux (1993: esp. 181-82); Tuckett (1996) and Köster (1957).

Table 1: *Elements of the* Didache *and links with Matthew's Gospel*

Contributions to Did.		Location of contacts in Matthew's Gospel
Peri/Base Layer	P/B	25.8, 13; 28.16, 19-20
Two Ways	TW	5.7, 21, 27, 33; 7.13-14; 15:19; 19.18
Law Summary	LS	7.12; 22.38-39
Sayings Onion	SO.a	5.44
	SO.b	5.46-47
	SO.c	
	SO.d	5.39
	SO.e	5.42, 45
Teknon unit	TK	5.5, 21, 22, 27, 28
Apocalypse	AP	16.27; 24.10-12, 30-31; 25.31, 34, 46
Prophet Layer	PR	12.31
Mod. Teacher Layer	MT	5.19, 24, 26; 6.2, 5, 16; 10.10
'Let the gift sweat'	GV	
Threefold baptism	BP	28.19
Lord's Prayer	LP	6.9-13
'Do not give to dogs'	DG	7.6
Firstfruits tradition	FF	
Malachi 1.11	ML	

Alternative explanations for the pattern of connections between the two texts face considerable difficulties. For example, if the earlier layers of the *Didache* all used Matthew's Gospel, then numerous direct and indirect contributors must all be supposed to have used Matthew's Gospel, and in a remarkably similar way.[2]

Even greater complexities arise for the view that the *Didache* and Matthew's Gospel both depend on common traditions. In this case it must be supposed that numerous direct and indirect contributors to the *Didache* each happened to use, over a period of time, the same traditions that were coincidentally also gathered, at one time, by Matthew.

Having noted, on the basis of macro-level observation, that the simplest explanation for the pattern of contacts illustrated in Table 1 is that Matthew

---

2. Two points of similarity are noteworthy. First, with the exception of *Did.* 9.5b = Mt. 7.6 and *Did.* 13.1 = Mt. 10.10, none of the points of similarity are exactly identical; even the two Lord's Prayers differ slightly. Second, the majority of material shared by the two texts is, as Court (1981: 111) puts it, 'from Matthew's special material or from the synoptic traditions at points where Matthew's distinctive reading is preferred'. Thus, if the *Didache* is dependent on the gospel, then several of the *Didache*'s diverse contributors must all have had an uncanny ability to select Matthew's special material.

depended directly on the first three layers of the *Didache*, it is appropriate to test this hypothesis at the micro-level. In testing whether or not each individual point of contact may be credibly understood as due to Matthew's direct use of the *Didache* it is *not* necessary to show that this is the only possible explanation for a particular parallel between the two texts. That is to say, the implications of the macro-level observation will only be undermined if, for some reason, the micro-level investigation reveals that Matthew *cannot* have depended upon the *Didache* in a particular instance. Thus, the following studies need only show that Matthew's direct use of the *Didache* is feasible in each case. However, in the interests of thoroughness, I shall attempt to show that Matthew's direct use of the *Didache* is probable, and not merely possible, at the majority of their individual points of contact.

Chapter 11

MATTHEW'S GOSPEL AND THE MODIFYING TEACHER LAYER

As noted above, the aim of this chapter, and of the next four chapters, is to show that each point of contact between Matthew's Gospel and the *Didache* may be explained by Matthew's direct dependence upon the *Didache*. Beyond this efforts will also be made, where possible, to show that such dependence is not only possible but probable.

It is worth noting, in the case of points of contact within the Modifying Teacher layer, that success in demonstrating Matthew's knowledge of any part of this layer indicates Matthew's knowledge of the whole of the rest of the *Didache* (less, of course, the Gospel layer and Jerusalem addition). This is the case inasmuch as the Modifying Teacher layer cannot, by definition, have been composed apart from the two earlier layers that it modifies.

1. *Be Reconciled: Matthew 5.24 and* Didache *14.2*

Massaux (1993: 156–57) assesses the relationship between these two passages thus:

> These words [*Did.* 14.2] recall Mt. 5:23-24... This passage is peculiar to Mt. The presence of the word διαλλάγωσιν in this text of the Teaching suggests a literary contact with Mt., which has the same verb διαλλάγηθι, a verb which is found only here in the New Testament. Let me add that the general idea is identical to that in Mt.: do not offer any sacrifice – compare θυσία (*Did.*) with δῶρον ... ἐπὶ τὸ θυσιαστήριον (Mt.) – to the Lord before being reconciled to your neighbour.

Massaux is justified in pointing out the noteworthy similarities between *Did.* 14.2 and Mt. 5.23-34. However, this does not provide a basis for concluding that the former necessarily recalls the latter.

In Chapter 7 it was argued that *Did.* 14.1-3 exhibits the modifying teacher's mode of operation whereby the host text is affirmed (14.1), modified (14.2) and the modification justified by appeal to an external authority, in this case Mal. 1.11 (14.3). If this author were in possession of

Matthew's Gospel, then the pattern of argument used in these verses is somewhat surprising. In this case it must be supposed that, in an effort to teach reconciliation prior to sacrifice, an allusion to the specifically relevant words of Jesus (Mt. 5.23-24) is made in *Did.* 14.2, but without any attempt to remind the reader that these are the words of the Master. Indeed, rather than claim authority for these words on the basis that they are those of Jesus, the teacher finds their justification in a partially relevant quotation from Mal. 1.11. In this vein Niederwimmer (1998: 198), without further comment, remarks:

> The verb διαλλάσσεσθαι...recalls the dominical saying in Matt 5:23-24... Strikingly enough, however, the Didachist supports his demand not by appealing to the Lord's words in Matt 5:23-24, but by means of an Old Testament quotation.

Rather than supposing that the teacher knew Mt. 5.23-24, but chose not to directly invoke it, it is preferable to suppose that Matthew's record of Jesus' words is not referred to because it was not known by the modifying teacher.

The only difficulty with this conclusion is that, at some point, the tradition of Jesus' teaching reconciliation prior to sacrifice did emerge. If Matthew believed that Jesus used these words, then from where did he gain this impression, and why was this information not used by the modifying teacher? An answer to these questions may be provided if the modifying teacher was responsible for composing *Did.* 14.2, and if this verse was then found by Matthew in its present context.

A feature of *Did.* 14.1-3 suggestive of the modifying teacher's directly responsibility for the composition of 14.2, is the use of the sequence: affirmation of the existing text (14.1), modification of the existing text (14.2), justification of this modification by appeal to external authority (14.3). This pattern suggests that the purpose of the whole unit was to introduce new material into the standing text, and that the nub of that new material is contained in the central modificatory passage, in this case 14.2. Crucially, the fact that the teacher felt it necessary to appeal to an external authority to support the force of *Did.* 14.2 suggests that the statements within this verse did not already have a firmly established pedigree in the Christian tradition.

If the modifying teacher was originally responsible for the wording of *Did.* 14.2, then there is no difficulty in understanding why this teaching is not directly attributed to Jesus. At the same time, if Matthew came upon *Did.* 14.2 in its present context, then his direct attribution of this teaching to Jesus also becomes explicable. This is the case because *Did.* 14.2 stands within a text entitled, 'The Teaching of the Lord, by the Twelve Apostles, to the Gentiles'.[1] If Matthew knew this text, then it is possible that he treated its entire contents, including the contributions of the modifying teacher, as the teaching of Jesus.

This point of contact between the *Didache* and Matthew's Gospel is an important one for the claim that Matthew depended directly on the first three layers of the *Didache*. If the modifying teacher composed *Did.* 14.2, then neither theories of a shared root tradition, nor of the *Didache*'s use of Matthew's Gospel, can explain the connection between the two texts. The case for Matthew's knowledge of *Did.* 14.2 in the context of 'The Teaching of the Lord' also challenges the possibility of Matthew's indirect dependence on the *Didache*. This means that Matthew's direct knowledge of *Did.* 14.2 is not only feasible, it is also considerably more probable than the available alternatives. Further, if the observations made in Part I are accurate, then it follows that, if Matthew knew *Did.* 14.2, then he must also have known the rest of the Modifying Teacher layer, and, consequently, the two preceding layers that it modifies.

2. *The Last Penny: Matthew 5.26 and* Didache *1.5c*

Mt. 5.26 and *Did.* 1.5c have a striking phrase in common in their shared reference to the paying of the last penny. At the same time these passages are distinctly different inasmuch as *Did.* 1.5b-6 is concerned with combating abuses of the command to give without expecting a return, while Mt. 5.26 continues to deal with the subject of anger that runs throughout Mt. 5.21-26. These passages also differ in that *Did.* 1.5b-6 does not refer to the words of Jesus, while Matthew's discourse is placed on Jesus' lips.

A number of scholars note that some form of literary connection between the two texts is likely because of the unique shared use of 'ἀποδῷς/ ἀποδῷ τὸν ἔσχατον κοδράντην'.[2] However, it is unlikely that *Did.* 1.5c represents a conscious allusion to, or quotation from, Mt. 5.26 because such an invocation would not altogether serve the thrust of *Did.* 1.5b-6. That is to say, these verses are concerned to combat the abuse of free generosity by presenting the threat of gaol to potential offenders. The force of Mt. 5.26, on the other hand, is directed towards the promotion of reconciliation, a more eirenic outcome than that envisaged by the *Didache*. The

1.　For a discussion of the redactional location of this title see Chapter 9, § 2.2.
2.　For example, Massaux (1993: 151–52) and Jefford (1989: 48–49).

case against a direct appeal to Matthew's Gospel is also supported by the fact that no reference to the gospel is made in this passage. Indeed, rather than appeal to Jesus' words in the gospel, the authority of the teacher's remarks are supported, in *Did.* 1.6, by the quotation of a saying of unclear origin.[3]

While it is unlikely that *Did.* 1.5c represents a deliberate attempt subtly to invoke the authority of Mt. 5.26, it is possible that the teacher, having soaked up the language of Matthew's Gospel, unconsciously spoke in Matthean idiom at this point.[4] However, this explanation requires a considerable level of unconscious coincidence.[5] Of course this solution is always theoretically possible, but it should be treated with caution while less tenuous explanations are also on offer.

An appeal to unconscious coincidence is not required by the proposal that Matthew depended directly on *Did.* 1.5c. As with the call for reconciliation prior to sacrifice (*Did.* 14.2), the threat of having to pay back the last penny occurs within a unit in which the modifying teacher affirms the host text (1.5b), modifies that text (1.5c) and then justifies this modification by appeal to an external authority (1.6). As noted above, this pattern suggests that the central modificatory section is the original work of the modifier, hence the need to support this view by appealing to an external authority. If this is the case, then the wording of *Did.* 1.5c may be seen as original to this setting and its reappearance in Mt. 5.26 as due to Matthew's presupposition of *Did.* 1.5c. More than that, the fact that Matthew presents these words as the direct speech of Jesus, while the teacher does not, suggests that Matthew knew them in a context suggestive of this exalted origin. The title of the *Didache* creates a setting for *Did.* 1.5c which would allow Matthew to see the contribution of this modifying teacher as part of 'The Teaching of the Lord'.

Having considered the case for the *Didache*'s conscious or unconscious use of Mt. 5.26, and for Matthew's direct use of *Did.* 1.5c, it is appropriate

---

3.   The quotation offered at 1.6 is commonly identified as originating from a translation of Sir. 12.1. However, Niederwimmer (1998: 84–85) suggests that it has not yet been possible to give a secure demonstration of its source.

4.   Tuckett (1996) does not specifically address the connection between *Did.* 1.5c and Mt. 5.26. However, he is anxious elsewhere in his discussion (e.g. 1996: 102) to point out that he perceives the *Didache*'s allusion to, rather than direct quotation of, Matthew's Gospel.

5.   An appeal to coincidence, even on one occasion, is never entirely satisfactory. However, it must be remembered that every time this type of explanation is offered the level of coincidence rises accordingly.

to give some attention to the possibility that both texts shared a common tradition. This type of understanding is offered by Jefford (1989: 51), who declares the *Didache*'s reference to paying the last penny is 'a blatant quotation of the material that appears in the Sayings Gospel Q'.

There are two difficulties with this position. First, if, as seems likely, *Did.* 1.5c is the original work of the modifying teacher, then there is no basis for supposing that this line relies on some earlier tradition. Second, if *Did.* 1.5c consciously alluded to any other text, then it is surprising that this fact is not mentioned in support of the authority of the teacher's modificatory idea. Further, such a tradition may be expected to preserve the words of Jesus (hence Matthew's placement of the relevant phrase on Jesus' lips), but no mention of such an authoritative origin is mentioned by the modifying teacher.

The primary objective of this section has been to show that Matthew's direct use of *Did.* 1.5c is feasible. There is certainly no obstacle to this conclusion and so the observations made in the introduction to Part II hold good at this point. Beyond this minimum requirement I have also sought to present positive evidence for Matthew's direct use of the *Didache*.

3. *Fast and Pray: Matthew 6.5-16 and* Didache *8.1-2a, 2c-3*

There are striking similarities between *Did.* 8.1-2a, 2c-3 and Mt. 6.5-16. Both texts teach a practice of fasting and prayer that is self-consciously distinct from the discipline of 'the hypocrites', and both texts include very closely related versions of the Lord's Prayer.

Alongside these strong similarities, however, these texts exhibit some distinctive differences. With regard to fasting, the *Didache* teaches that Christians should demonstrate their differentiation from 'the hypocrites' by publicly fasting on different days (Draper 1996c: 233–35). Matthew, on the other hand, condemns the public piety of the hypocrites and teaches that fasting should be done without any public show at all. A similar pattern occurs in the case of prayer. The *Didache* expects its readers to demonstrate their difference from the hypocrites by publicly praying a different prayer from that used by 'the hypocrites' (Draper 1996c: 234–38). This demand is quite different from that required by Matthew, where the emphasis is once again on the value of private over public piety.

The versions of the Lord's Prayer provided by each text are also slightly different: Matthew has the plurals τοῖς οὐρανοῖς and τὰ ὀφειλήματα, while the *Didache* has these words in the singular; forgiveness is a present event in Matthew but a past one in the *Didache*; the *Didache* explicitly expects thrice daily repetition of the prayer, whereas Matthew's Gospel does not; the *Didache* includes a closing doxology, while the more widely favoured manuscripts of the gospel do not. Matthew, on the other hand, includes features that do not occur in the *Didache*: a reference to differentiation from the practice of Gentiles (before the Lord's Prayer), a reinforcement of the importance of forgiveness (after the Lord's Prayer), and a rule for private piety in almsgiving.

The verbal similarities between these two texts are so extensive as to make some form of literary relationship between them extremely likely, and this is a universal opinion amongst scholars.[6] Three types of relationship are logically possible. Either the *Didache* is directly dependent on Matthew,[7] or both texts depend on another unknown written/oral source,[8] or Matthew is directly dependent on the *Didache*.[9] The most credible option will be the one that provides the best explanation for the *differences*, as well as the similarities, between the two texts.

---

6.   'There is clearly a close relationship between these two texts. The question of literary dependence cannot easily be settled, since the great verbal similarity is accompanied by a difference of ethos. The direction of dependence between two such texts will depend on prior assumptions' (Draper 1996c: 242). See also Draper (1996b: 85–86) and nn. 7 and 8 below.

7.   Massaux (1993: 154–55) sees the sequence of the whole block of Jesus material in *Did.* 8.1-2 as proof of such dependence. Streeter (1924: 508): 'The relationship of this passage [*Did.* 8.1] to Matt 6.5-16, is clear. It is an interpretation according to the letter, but in flagrant discord with the spirit, of the Sermon on the Mount.'

8.   Köster (1957: 203) favours the view that the *Didache* here refers to the oral preaching of the Lord, although he does not rule out a reference to a written gospel. Difficulties with this position were raised in Chapter 8, § 2. Niederwimmer (1998: 136) states that the deviations between the two versions of the Lord's Prayer mean that 'It is hard to suppose that the *Didache* quotes directly from Matthew's Gospel. The agreements would rest on a common liturgical tradition.' Glover (1958: 18–19), responding to the quotation from Streeter noted in the footnote immediately above, writes: 'The Didachist's interpretation is *not* according to the letter of the Sermon on the Mount. The letter of Matt 6.16-18 is defied as flagrantly as the spirit. The *Didache* may indeed have found the first part of Matt's text "in some recognised official document": but it is hard to believe that the document was our gospel since an author with Matthew's interpretation before him could scarcely venture to substitute the extraordinary alternative found here.'

9.   Draper (1996c: 243) says: 'If there is a schema underlying Matthew's choice of material, which is not unlikely, then it is not unlikely that it would resemble *Didache* 8!' In making this statement Draper comes close to saying that Matthew is directly dependent on the *Didache*. However, he does not actually take this step, preferring instead to see both texts as dependent on a common source (cf. Draper 1996b: 85–86).

In seeking to explain the differences between *Did.* 8.1-2a, 2c-3 and Mt. 6.5-16, it is necessary to recognize that any number of hypothetical circumstances might be devised for this purpose. This means that the issue here is one of probability rather than necessity. I shall begin, therefore, by presenting my favoured explanation for the differences between the two texts. The relative merits and deficiencies of this hypothesis will then be compared with the main alternatives.

3.1. *Matthew Conflates Mark 12.40-44; 11.25 with* Didache *8*

I propose that the differences between Mt. 6.1-18 and *Did.* 8.1-2a, 2c-3 are best accounted for as the product of Matthew's conflation of these verses from *Did.* 8 with the teaching of Jesus recorded in Mk 12.40-44.

Mk 12.40-44 is generally assumed, by those who accept Markan priority,[10] to have been omitted by Matthew in his use of Mark's Gospel. To argue that these verses were in fact used in the construction of Mt. 6.1-16 it is necessary to show, first of all, that there is nothing about Mk 12.40-44 that requires its complete omission by Matthew. In addition, I aim to show that this supposed omission is so surprising that an alternative explanation for the apparent disappearance of these verses from Matthew's Gospel is invited.

It is commonly recognized that Matthew's Gospel incorporates a very high percentage of Mark's Gospel. Stanton (1989: 63) says that 'Only about 50 of Mark's 662 verses are not found in Matthew'. Goulder (1974: 34) goes further and suggests that

> The things which Matthew felt called to omit were…: The Young Man in the Sheet (Mark 14.51f) as being of dubious relevance; the Widow's Mite (Mark 12.41-4) probably as breaking the thread of the Woes discourse in 23; the Strange Exorcist (Mark 9.38f) as bringing discredit on John – but the logia at the end of the unit find a place elsewhere in Matthew; and a general statement at Mark 3.20, which disappears in Matthew's reformation of the Beelzebub incident. This gives a total of nine verses which have disappeared without trace, 1½ per cent of Mark. This figure is noticeably less than those customarily suggested, because we are accounting for such passages as the Seed Growing Secretly, or the coming of Jesus' relatives to lay hold of him, as being altered, and not omitted.

Whatever criteria are employed for measuring Matthew's faithfulness to Mark there can be little dispute that Matthew includes the vast majority of Mark's Gospel. In particular, a comparison of Mk 10.1–16.8 and Mt. 19.1–28.5 shows that Matthew preserves, in order, every element of Mark's text

---

10. Markan priority is assumed for the whole of this section.

almost without exception. The two omissions being the young man in a sheet (14.51-52), the loss of which is not surprising, and the lines including the widow's mite (12.40-44).

Goulder's explanation for Matthew's omission of the widow's mite, quoted above, is standard but inadequate. As Goulder admits in relation to the logia in Mk 9.39-42 (and as occurs on numerous other occasions), Matthew is perfectly capable of rearranging his sources to suit his own structure. The complete omission of Mk 12.40-44 suggests, therefore, that Matthew singularly objected to the content of these verses and not just their location in Mark's Gospel. West (1967–68: 80-83) proposes that the righteous widow did not fit in with Matthew's attitude to women, or that Matthew fought shy of the widow's willingness to give all that she had. However, this does not provide a motive for leaving these verses out *altogether*. That is to say, lessons may be gleaned from these verses other than that a woman may be especially commended, or that the giving of every possession is required of Christians.

Matthew's seemingly complete omission of Mk 12.40-44 is particularly startling when it is observed that these verses include one of the very rare occurrences where the teaching of Jesus is actually recorded by Mark, rather than merely commented on in retrospect. Matthew's interest in the teaching of Jesus is made plain by the length and prominence of the Sermon on the Mount, where other loose[11] fragments of Jesus' teaching supplied by Mark are included. It is striking, therefore, that one of Matthew's most significant omissions from Mark's Gospel should consist of material that is both rare in Mark and particularly precious to Matthew.

Two observations, therefore, suggest that Matthew is highly likely to have included Mk 12.40-44, in some form, in his gospel: Matthew includes almost every element of Mark's work and he shows a particular interest in the teaching of Jesus. That the widow's mite is not readily detectable in Matthew's Gospel may, therefore, be due to the alteration of these verses in some way, rather than their complete omission. The conflation of Mk 12.40-44 with *Did.* 8.1-2a, 2b-3 would provide an explanation for this type of alteration.

At the heart of the case for Matthew's conflation of Mk 12.40-44 and *Did.* 8.1-2a, 2b-3 is the observation that the influence of Mk 12.40-44, combined with Matthew's compositional strategy, may credibly account for almost every difference between *Did.* 8.1-2a, 2b-3 and Mt. 6.1-18.

---

11. By the term 'loose', I mean fragments of teaching that are not parables, or otherwise tied to an event in the narrative.

Before attempting to demonstrate this point in detail it is appropriate to identify a particular element of Matthew's compositional technique that appears to be at work in his construction of Mt. 6.1-18.

Matthew is a thematizer and collator who tends to group and conflate similar materials together. For example, his parables, healings and discourses are often arranged in blocks of similar kind or subject. In the Sermon on the Mount (a thematized discourse on Jesus' ethical teaching) Matthew arranges his material, where possible, within a wider organizational framework. As Draper (1996d: 347) remarks: 'The Sermon on the Mount is [Matthew's] own creation, ordering originally independent material (found partially scattered in Luke) according to a grand design'.

This technique may be seen particularly clearly in the antitheses (Mt. 5.21-48). H.D. Betz (1995: 201) comments:

> There clearly appears to be a rationale behind the six antitheses and their arrangement in the SM [Sermon on the Mount], but that rationale has so far eluded scholarship; few scholars have even discussed the question. A number of possibilities might be taken to provide an answer to each problem of the arrangement, but at closer inspection, each turns out to be a false lead.
>
> Can the arrangement of the antitheses in the SM be explained on the basis of the Decalogue (Exod 20:2-17)? The answer is negative because only the first two offenses, murder and adultery, follow each other in the Decalogue as well...

A possible explanation for the arrangement and content of the antitheses is that their *content* was determined by the resources available to Matthew, while their *form* was determined by his interest in presenting Jesus as giver of the true Law. According to this theory the Decalogue may be maintained as the organizing principle, while the deviation of the antitheses from the substance of these commandments may be attributed to the failure of Matthew's resources to supply further examples of their representation by Jesus.[12] Faced with this situation, it is possible that Matthew chose to continue his new version of the commandments by creating headings, or 'theses', related to the teaching of Jesus that *was* available to him. For example, it is apparent (by virtue of Luke's and Matthew's shared knowledge of a group of sayings expressed in Lk. 6.27-30 and Mt. 5.39-42, respectively) that Matthew had access to a saying of Jesus regarding non-retaliation. The thesis that precedes this antithesis is therefore selected by virtue of its appropriateness to the saying in hand, not because the *lex*

---

12. Certainly, no further examples of such teaching may be found in Matthew's resources so far as they are represented by Mark's and Luke's Gospels.

talionis is part of the ten commandments scheme that Matthew initially appears to be using (Mt. 5.21, 27). The same pattern occurs in Matthew's section on the love of enemies (5.43-48), and so may be suspected in the case of the other antitheses. This observation is supported by the absence of any of Matthew's sectional headings (the 'theses') in Luke's Sermon on the Plain. It appears, therefore, that Matthew gathered the teaching of Jesus pertaining to the Law, from whatever sources he had available, and arranged this material under suitable headings drawn from traditional sources.[13]

Matthew's policy of collating and organizing his resources according to a wider organizational framework may also be seen in Mt. 6.1-18, where, instead of creating a new rendering of 'the Decalogue', Matthew offers a new version of a Three Rules saying. The 'Three Rules' form has already been mentioned in Chapter 4, section 3 in connection with the three rules, 'bless, pray and fast' for your enemies in *Did.* 1.3. Jefford (1989: 44) claims that 'There is no question that the assemblage of the Three Rules derives from Jewish tradition'. He goes on to cite examples from *Tobit* 12.8 and *Gospel of Thomas* 6a, 14a. It is possible, therefore, that Matthew used this organizational scheme to manage the teaching on fasting, praying and almsgiving that he found in *Did.* 8 and Mk 12.

The distinctive of Jesus' Three Rules, as presented by Matthew, is his emphasis on the virtue of private piety and the heavenly reward that this will bring. The privacy aspect of this theme was, I suggest, taken by Matthew from the teaching of Jesus as presented in Mk 12.38-44. The placing of the account of the widow's offering immediately after Jesus' condemnation of those who exercise an ostentatious piety invites the possibility that Matthew saw Jesus' commendation of the widow as associated with the humility and privacy of her offering.

The 'hope of a future reward' motif is, I suggest, taken up and repeated according to the pattern of the Three Rules in a manner similar to Matthew's threefold expansion of the concept of reward in Mt. 10.40-42 = Mk 9.41.

These ideas of privacy and reward are then combined in Matthew's introduction to his Three Rules teaching:

> 6.1 Beware of practicing your piety before others in order to be seen by them; for then you have no reward from your Father in heaven.

---

13.   In the antitheses, Matthew's headings are not always entirely apposite. However, the antithetical form placed a constraint on the wording of the headings because they had to appear as traditional sayings that were then intensified by the teaching of Jesus.

This combined principle is then applied individually to almsgiving, prayer and fasting. Matthew's framework employs a repeated pattern whereby public righteousness leads only to earthly reward, while private righteousness leads to a heavenly reward.

> ACT: 6.2 So whenever you give alms
> PUBLIC: do not sound a trumpet before you, as the hypocrites do in the synagogues and in the streets, so that they may be praised by others.
> EARTHLY REWARD: Truly I tell you, they have received their reward.
> PRIVATE: 6.3 But when you give alms, do not let your left hand know what your right hand is doing, 6.4 so that your alms may be done in secret;
> HEAVENLY REWARD: and your Father who sees in secret will reward you.

> ACT: 6.5 And whenever you pray
> PUBLIC: do not be like the hypocrites; for they love to stand and pray in the synagogues and at the street corners, so that they may be seen by others.
> EARTHLY REWARD: Truly I tell you, they have received their reward.
> PRIVATE: 6.6 But whenever you pray, go into your room and shut the door and pray to your Father who is in secret;
> HEAVENLY REWARD: and your Father who sees in secret will reward you.

> ACT: 6.16 And whenever you fast,
> PUBLIC: do not look dismal, like the hypocrites, for they disfigure their faces so as to show others that they are fasting.
> EARTHLY REWARD: Truly I tell you, they have received their reward.
> PRIVATE: 6.17 But when you fast, put oil on your head and wash your face, 6.18 so that your fasting may be seen not by others but by your Father who is in secret;
> HEAVENLY REWARD: and your Father who sees in secret will reward you.

This regular framework is fleshed out with detail provided by both Mk 12 and *Did.* 8. Thus, the teaching on alms is provided by Mk 12.41-44, prayer comes from both Mk 12.40 and *Did.* 8.2, while fasting comes from *Did.* 8.1 alone. Opposition to hypocrisy is taken from *Did.* 8.1-2a and applied to all three actions. Similarly the virtue of private piety is taken from Mk 12.38-44 and applied to each case.

Into this basic and regular framework Matthew includes further instructions on the subject of prayer. The possibility that these additions were taken from a previously existing source is heightened by the fact that the neat pattern of the Three Rules structure is disrupted by these expansions. Almost all of these additions regarding prayer may be traced to either Mark's Gospel or the *Didache*.

> 6.7 When you are praying, do not heap up empty phrases as the Gentiles do; for they think that they will be heard because of their many words.

This phrase echoes the condemnation of the scribes' lengthy prayers for show recorded in Mk 12.40. In changing the culprits from scribes to Gentiles, Matthew extends his response to the hypocritical practice of those who 'pray in the synagogues' and so on (6.5), to include Gentiles who exercise an ostentatious piety.

> 6.8 Do not be like them, for your Father knows what you need before you ask him.

This line does not appear in Mark or the *Didache*. However, there is a parallel in Mt. 6.32b, which may suggest that Matthew has incorporated this line from teaching on prayer provided by the source that is also used in Mt. 6.32.

> 6.9 Pray then this way:
> Our Father in heaven (ἐν τοῖς οὐρανοῖς)
> hallowed be your name.
> 6.10 Your kingdom come.
> Your will be done,
> on earth as it is in heaven.
> 6.11 Give us this day our daily bread
> 6.12 And forgive us our debts (ὀφιελήματα),
> as we also have forgiven (ἀφήκαμεν) our debtors.
> 6.13 And do not bring us to the time of trial,
> but rescue us from the evil one.

The above version of the Lord's Prayer, as already noted, is very close to that found in *Did.* 8.2. There are, however, four differences between the two texts: the *Didache* has ἐν τῷ οὐρανῷ instead of Matthew's ἐν τοῖς οὐρανοῖς; the *Didache* has ὀφειλήν instead of Matthew's ὀφιελήματα; the *Didache* has ἀφίεμεν instead of Matthew's ἀφήκαμεν; and the *Didache* preserves a doxology whereas the most widely favoured manuscripts of Matthew's Gospel do not. The first of these differences is perhaps the most noteworthy. No known manuscript of Matthew's Gospel contains a reference to heaven in the singular at this point. This means that, if the teacher was quoting Matthew's Gospel, then it is highly unlikely that the version used contained the singular form. If the teacher knew Matthew's prayer, therefore, it is necessary to suggest a reason why Matthew's version is altered at this point. However, such a change carries no obvious theological significance, and so a motive for this change is not apparent. On the other hand, reference to heavens in the plural form is a widely recognized feature of Matthew's redactional activity.[14] In this vein, if

---

14. So Draper (1996b: 86). Examples of occasions where Matthew introduces a

Matthew depended on the *Didache*'s version of the prayer a change from singular to plural heavens may be simply and credibly attributed to Matthew's redactional activity.[15] The other differences between the two prayers offer less clear advice since, as is so often the case, arguments for the direction of dependence are open to reversal.[16] What may be said, however, is that there is no obstacle to supposing that Matthew may have used the *Didache*'s version of the prayer, even if other alternatives are also possible. This much is all that is required for the defence of the larger argument currently in progress.

> 6.14 For if you forgive others their trespasses, your heavenly Father will also forgive you; 6.15 but if you do not forgive others, neither will your Father forgive your trespasses.

A final difference between Mt. 6.1-18 and *Did.* 8.1-2a, 2c-3 is the presence of a re-emphasis of the importance of forgiveness immediately after Matthew's version of the Lord's Prayer (6.14-15). This passage was, I propose, taken from the minimal teaching on prayer to be found in Mk 11.25. As noted above, Matthew is willing to draw snippets of Jesus' loose teaching in Mark's Gospel for inclusion in the Sermon on the Mount. Mk 11.25 is the only instruction regarding prayer that Mark preserves; it is credible, therefore, that Matthew should incorporate this verse in his section on Jesus' teaching on prayer.

Before moving on to consider alternative explanations for the similarities between Mt. 6.1-16 and *Did.* 8.1-2a, 2c-3, it is worth recalling the strengths of the above 'conflationary' hypothesis in response to the challenge in hand. Of first importance is a recognition that Mt. 6.1-16 and *Did.* 8.1-2a, 2c-3 not only contain a large number of words in common, but also exhibit

---

reference to plural heavens where they do not appear in Luke/Q or Mark include, for example: Mt. 7.21 = Lk. 6.46; Mt. 11.12 = Lk. 16.16; Mt. 13.31 = Mk 4.30. Within Matthew's 'Special Material' plural heavens are referred to in, for example: 18.23; 23.9; 25.1. In all, Matthew refers to heaven using the plural on 56 occasions, and in the singular 27 times.

15. Köster (1957: 206) seriously entertains the possibility that the *Didache*'s version of the prayer is the older and suggests specifically that the singular form ἐν τῷ οὐρανῷ may be original.

16. Niederwimmer (1998: 136–38) offers a detailed discussion of the various possibilities. While firm conclusions are not easily drawn regarding the significance of the differences between the two prayers, Niederwimmer (1998: 136) expresses the opinion that 'It is hard to suppose that the *Didache* quotes directly from Matthew's Gospel'. Niederwimmer favours the view that both versions rely on a common liturgical tradition. This possibility will be addressed in due course.

three types of difference: Matthew emphasizes a private piety, while the *Didache* is concerned with public acts of prayer and fasting; Matthew includes additional Markan teaching on prayer and almsgiving which is absent from the *Didache*; and Matthew's version of the Lord's Prayer differs slightly from that recorded in the *Didache*. A satisfying explanation for the similarities between the two texts must also explain these dissimilarities.

The hypothesis of Matthew's conflation of Mk 12.40-44; 11.25 with *Did.* 8.1-2a, 2c-3 has three specific points in its favour. First, the influence of Mk 12.40 offers an explanation for Matthew's emphasis on private piety over against the *Didache*'s interest in public expressions of Christian identity. Second, this theory explains the absence, from *Did.* 8, of all the Markan elements within Mt. 6. Third, the slight differences between the two Lord's Prayers, especially the variation in the first line, are accounted for as being consistent with similar examples of Matthew's redactional activity.

It is also noteworthy that the conflationary and organizational programmes demanded by this hypothesis are consistent with several examples of this type of activity elsewhere in Matthew's work.[17] In addition, this hypothesis offers an explanation for Matthew's apparent omission of Mark's account of the widow's mite. According to the above, Matthew did include this teaching (in 6.1-18) but chose to interpret the significance of the widow's offering in the light of the condemnation of ostentatious piety that immediately precedes it.

The next stage in the defence of this hypothesis is to measure its benefits against those of alternative explanations for the similarities and differences between *Did.* 8.1-2a, 2c-3 and Mt. 6.1-18.

3.2. Didache *8 is Directly Dependent on Matthew 6.5-16*

Streeter (1924: 508) suggests that *Did.* 8 depends directly upon Mt. 6. However, Glover (1958: 18-19) takes him to task for his over-simple assumption:

> On *Did.* viii.l Streeter comments, 'The relation of this passage to Matt. vi. 5-16, is clear. It is an interpretation according to the letter, but in flagrant discord with the spirit, of the Sermon on the Mount. Such interpretations

---

17. Since the development of the Four Source Hypothesis, Matthew has been widely regarded as a conflator of prior traditions. Several examples of Matthew's conflationary activity are presented in each of the following four chapters, especially Chapters 13 and 14.

only arise where there is a letter to misinterpret and would compel us to assume that the words stood in some recognised official document, even if the author did not expressly quote them as from "his (i.e. the Lord's) Gospel"'.

... Here one may observe that the Didachist's interpretation is *not* according to the letter of the Sermon on the Mount. The letter of Matt. 16-18 is defied as flagrantly as the spirit. The Didachist may indeed have found the first part of Matthew's text 'in some recognized official document'; but it is hard to believe that that document was our gospel since an author with Matthew's interpretation before him would scarcely venture to substitute the extraordinary alternative found here.

Glover's point, with regard to the *Didache*'s teaching on fasting, is essentially the same as that which has already been made regarding the distinct difference between the ethos of *Did.* 8 and Mt. 6.1-16.[18] This difference is so great that it cannot be explained by a simple copying of Matthew by the Didachist; it appears that some other factor must have been at work. It is possible that the differences between Mt. 6 and *Did.* 8 may be attributed to the expression of the Didachist's own concerns or the conflation of Matthew with some other hypothetical document.[19] However, hypothetical solutions are less satisfying than those, such as that offered in the immediately preceding section, which rely solely on extant sources.

A further difficulty for the view that *Did.* 8 used Mt. 6 is the fact that the *Didache* succeeds in *completely avoiding* every part of Matthew's text which may be seen as coming from Mk 12.40-44 or 11.25. This omission of Markan material in *Did.* 8 may be coincidental, but such coincidence need not be appealed to if, in fact, *Did.* 8 was composed separately and prior to the formation of Mt. 6.

In summary, those who claim the direct dependence of *Did.* 8.1-2a, 2c-3 on Mt. 6.1-16 must provide some explanation for the distinctive differences between these two texts. Such an explanation may theoretically be provided, but not without additional hypothecation and appeals to precise coincidence.

18. See Chapter 8, § 2.2. Draper (1996c: 242) notes: 'The great verbal similarity [between *Did.* 8 and Mt. 6.1-16] is accompanied by a different ethos'.

19. Such a hypothetical text would have to be conceived as accounting for every difference between *Did.* 8 and Mt. 6.5-16. Since every detail of *Did.* 8 has some element of difference from Mt. 6.5-16, it would be necessary to hypothecate a text with teaching on each aspect covered by *Did.* 8. Such a text would need to be extremely close to *Did.* 8 as it now stands. If *Did.* 8 were dependent on such a text, then there is little motive for the additional use of Mt. 6.

3.3. *Matthew 6.1-16 and* Didache *8.1-2a, 2c-3 Depend on Common Tradition*

Scholars such as Köster (1957), Glover (1958) and Niederwimmer (1998), who conclude that the differences between Mt. 6.5-16 and *Did.* 8.1-3 cannot be accounted for by the *Didache*'s dependence on Matthew, view the similarities between these two texts as the product of their shared dependence on a common tradition.

The hypothecation of common tradition is, of course, a possible means of explaining the relationship between these two texts but it is unsatisfactory for a number of reasons. A multiplication of entities is methodologically acceptable when no other more straightforward explanation of the evidence is available, as appeared to be the case for those scholars who assumed that the *Didache* must post-date Matthew's Gospel. As I have attempted to show, however, this assumption is unjustified. Further, Matthew's conflation of Mark's Gospel and *Didache* accounts for the differences and similarities between these texts to a high degree of completeness. In this circumstance it is unnecessary to appeal to yet another shared hypothetical tradition.

When the actual shape of a suitable hypothetical source is considered in detail a further difficulty arises. Draper (1996c) argues persuasively that the function of *Did.* 8 was to provide a means of public differentiation between Pharisaic Jews and emerging Christians. In this context he notes (1996c: 238):

> In both cases, of instructions on fasting and on prayer, it is clear that the practices are not new. The community was already fasting twice a week, in solidarity with other Jewish groups, or the Pharisees at least. The community was already using the Lord's Prayer liturgically, as the doxology and amen shows. What the instruction does is to use these two practices to differentiate between the Christian community and its opponents, Pharisaic Jews. The days are changed for fasting... The prayer to be recited daily three times to replace the prayers of Pharisaic Judaism in the Lord's Prayer, thus providing a daily re-affirmation of the community's difference from other Jewish groups.

Draper observes that the practice of fasting is not changed, merely the time at which fasting occurs. However, the *time* at which prayers are said is not changed, therefore the point of differentiation is the *content* of these prayers. Thus, although Draper is probably correct that the Lord's Prayer was already known in another context it is likely that this prayer had *never* been used before as the essential thrice-daily prayer of the individual.[20]

20. The Lord's Prayer (especially the version in Lk. 11) shares a number of

The differentiatory function of *Did.* 8 implies that this teaching on fasting and prayer had never previously been configured in this form. This severely limits the options for the shape of any earlier tradition supposedly shared by both Matthew and the Didachist. The only viable possibility is that the original version of this tradition was incorporated virtually unchanged into the *Didache* and was also used, with alterations, by Matthew.

3.4. *Conclusion*

The primary objective of this section has been to show that Matthew's direct use of *Did.* 8.1-2a, c-3 is feasible. There is certainly no obstacle to this conclusion and so the observation made in the introduction to Part II holds good at this point.

In addition, it has been observed that the similarities and differences between Mt. 6.1-18 and *Did.* 8.1-2a, c-3 are explained if, to create a new Three Rules saying, Matthew conflated the *Didache*'s teaching on fasting and prayer (*Did.* 8.1-2a, 2c-3) with Mark's teaching on prayer and alms (Mk 12.40-44; 11.25). In suggesting that Matthew did, after all, incorporate the record of Jesus' teaching preserved in Mk 12.40-44, this proposal has the additional advantage of explaining the apparent omission of this passage in Matthew's otherwise (almost entirely) faithful preservation of Mk 10.1–16.8. These factors combine to suggest that Matthew's direct use of the *Didache* is, at this point at least, not only possible but probable.

4. *Preservation of Teaching: Matthew 5.17-20 and* Didache *11.1-2*

The numerous points of contact between these two passages suggest that there may be a literary dependence between them.[21]

In addition to elements of vocabulary shared by both passages (particularly the uncommon word καταλῦσαι in relation to teaching on the Law; cf. Draper 1996d: 349), there are also four points of conceptual similarity.

First, there is a common understanding that a body of teaching is to be retained unchanged (*Did.* 11.1) and preserved from destruction (Mt. 5.17).

characteristics with the eucharistic prayers recorded in *Did.* 9 and 10. It is possible that this prayer, distinctive to Christian worship, was taken and converted into a 'Christian *Shema*' as an act of community self-definition.

21. Draper (1996d: 346–52) draws attention to this similarity and concludes that it is the result of Matthew's direct dependence on the *Didache*. I have not repeated his reasoning here because it is coloured by the agenda of his wider argument.

The *Didache* seeks to preserve *Did.* 1–10 (which, in *Did.* 1–6, contains a summary of the community's understanding of the Law); in Matthew the teaching that is not to be destroyed is, once again, the Law.

Second, there is a common disapproval of those who destroy (*Did.* 11.2) or relax (Mt. 5.19a) the teaching. In the *Didache* these people are not to be listened to; in Matthew they are the least in the kingdom.

Third, there is a common commendation of those who preserve the teaching (*Did.* 11.1) and/or commandments in question (Mt. 5.19b). In the *Didache* these are to be received in the community; in Matthew those who do and teach the commandments are greatest in the kingdom.

Fourth, there is a common perception that it is possible to add to the righteousness of the Law. *Did.* 11.2b allows that a new teaching may come which leads to an increase in righteousness and knowledge of the Lord; Mt. 5.20 teaches that such an increase in righteousness, beyond the practice of the Scribes and Pharisees, is necessary for those who wish to enter the kingdom.

The verbal and conceptual similarities between *Did.* 11.1-2 and Mt. 5.17, 19-20 suggest the possibility of some literary link between the two texts. Draper (1996d: 348) remarks concerning the vocabulary, 'The wording is so close that some kind of literary relationship between the two writings seems to be required'.

It is unlikely that the *Didache* depended directly on Matthew at this point for two reasons. First, if it is accepted that *Did.* 11.1-2 belongs to the Modifying Teacher layer, then these verses form part of the teacher's characteristic pattern of affirming the host text (11.1-2a) and modifying it (11.2b), before justifying these subsequent modifications by appeal to various external authorities (cf. Chapter 7, section 3). On this basis *Did.* 11.1-2 may credibly be attributed to the original creativity of the modifier and so dependence on another text is unnecessary. Second, it is noteworthy that although Mt. 5.17-20 contains a number of elements in common with Lk. 16.16-17, *none* of these shared elements also appear in *Did.* 11.1-2. This means that any proposal of the Didachist's supposed use of Mt. 5.17-20 must include an explanation as to why only 'non-Lukan' elements of that passage were chosen/alluded to.

The case for Matthew's direct use of *Did.* 11.1-2 is less difficult to defend. First, if *Did.* 11.1-2 represents the original work of the modifying teacher, then any literary link with another text may be taken as demonstrating that text's presupposition of these verses of the *Didache*. Second, the fact that, once again, Matthew places this common material on the lips of Jesus, while the modifying teacher does not, suggests that Matthew found these words in a context where they could be taken as belonging to Jesus himself. Such a context is provided if Matthew found these words inserted into a text entitled 'The Teaching of the Lord, etc.'.[22] Third, if Matthew depended on *Did.* 11.1-2, then his conflation of this text with Lk./Q 16.16-17[23] could account for the absence of any Lk./Q material within *Did.* 11.1-2.

In the light of these factors it is possible to conclude, not only that Matthew's direct use of *Did.* 11.1-2 is feasible, but also that such a dependence is positively supported by the available evidence. Thus, the micro-level analysis of the link between *Did.* 11.1-2 and Mt. 5.17-20 coheres with the macro-level observation made in the introduction to Part II.

5. *Threefold Baptism: Matthew 28.19 and* Didache *7.1c, d, e*

The majority of scholars account for the close connection between the baptismal formulae in Mt. 28.19[24] and *Did.* 7.1 by supposing that they both rely on common liturgical practice (cf. Niederwimmer 1998: 127). Even Massaux, who detects the *Didache*'s direct dependence on Matthew's Gospel at almost every opportunity,[25] believes that the *Didache*'s direct literary dependence on Matthew's Gospel is, in this case, doubtful (Massaux 1993: 174-75). The case for the *Didache*'s direct dependence on Mt. 28.19 is made all the more dubious if the observations made in Chapter 5, section 1 are accepted. Here it was concluded that *Did.* 7.1d, 2-3, 4b has the character of a previously existing tradition that has been inserted into the base layer of the *Didache*. This separate tradition shows little sign (other than the shared baptismal formula) of connection with Matthew's Gospel, being principally concerned with practicalities such as the types of water that may be used and the length of the pre-baptismal fast.

At first sight, the view that *Did.* 7.1d, 2-3, 4b existed as a separate tradition prior to its insertion into the body of the *Didache* adds weight to the

---

22. See Chapter 9, § 2 for a discussion of the redactional location of the *Didache*'s long title.

23. In Chapter 14 I shall present a side argument suggesting that Matthew depended directly on Luke's Gospel. However, if Matthew depended on Q for the material also preserved in Lk. 16.16-17, then Mt. 5.17-20 may equally be seen as the conflation of *Did.* 11.1-2 with Q 16.16-17.

24. 'The suggestion that these verses are later additions to the Gospel seems to go too far, and the evidence adduced in support is rather flimsy' (Hartman 1997: 148).

25. The only other passage that Massaux places in this 'doubtful' category is *Did.* 2.1-3.

possibility that such traditions were common in the milieu of early Christianity.[26] If this were the case, then it is not impossible, as most scholars suppose, that Matthew and the *Didache* were both dependent on a common tradition in their use of the threefold formula. However, there is an important feature of Matthew's text which militates against the use of a common source and suggests, instead, Matthew's direct dependence on the *Didache*.

A consideration of the wider context of Mt. 28.19 introduces the possibility that Mt. 28.16-20 was, at least in part, directly inspired by Matthew's knowledge of a version of the *Didache* which included both the long title and the threefold baptismal formula.

> Mt. 28.16, Now the <u>eleven disciples</u> (ἕνδεκα μαθηταὶ) went to Galilee, to the mountain to which Jesus had directed them. 16.17 When they saw him, they worshipped him; but some doubted. 16.18 And Jesus came and said to them, 'All authority in heaven and on earth has been given to me. 16.19 Go therefore and make disciples of all <u>nations</u> (πάντα τὰ ἔθνη), <u>baptizing them in the name of the Father and of the Son and of the Holy Spirit,</u> (Βαπτίζοντες αὐτοὺς εἰς τὸ ὄνομα τοῦ πατρὸς καὶ τοῦ υἱοῦ καὶ τοῦ ἁγίου πνεύματος) 16.20 and <u>teaching</u> them (διδάσκοντες αὐτοὺς) to <u>obey everything that I have commanded you</u>. And remember, I am with you always, to the end of the age.'
>
> *Did.*long title, The <u>Teaching</u> (Διδαχὴ) of the Lord, by the <u>Twelve Apostles</u> (δώδεκα ἀποστόλων), to the <u>Gentiles</u> (τοῖς ἔθνεσιν) ... [followed in 1.1–6.3 by <u>an exposition of the commandments</u> in preparation for baptism] ... 7.1c, d <u>Baptize in the name of the Father and of the Son and of the Holy Spirit</u> (βαπτίσατε εἰς τὸ ὄνομα τοῦ πατρὸς καὶ τοῦ υἱοῦ καὶ τοῦ ἁγίου πνεύματος).

A version of the *Didache* that began with the long title and incorporated 7.1d, 2-3, 4b, would have included: an instruction by the Lord, via his twelve apostles, to teach Gentiles his interpretation of the commandments prior to their baptism in the name of the Father, the Son and the Holy Spirit.

These characteristics also appear in Mt. 28.16-20: Jesus commissions his eleven disciples to make disciples of all nations, to baptize them in the

---

26. In terms of extant texts the *Didache* and Matthew's Gospel represent the only two occasions when the threefold baptismal formula is used prior to Justin Martyr. This does not preclude the possibility that it was a common rite; however, the fact that, elsewhere, the New Testament frequently refers to baptism 'into the Lord Jesus' but never mentions the threefold formula, does not encourage the view that the latter was common liturgical practice.

name of the Father, the Son and the Holy Spirit, and to teach them to obey his commandments.

This level of connection is particularly striking because, according to the redactional study in Part I (Chapters 5, section 1 and Chapter 7, section 6) the tradition containing the threefold formula was not added to the *Didache* at the same time as the long title and the exposition of the commandments in *Did.* 1–6. This means that, if the *Didache* was directly dependent on Mt. 28.16-20, then two or more separate authors would have had to return to the same passage of Matthew to recreate, in stages, a text reflecting this commission by Jesus.

This difficulty does not arise if Matthew was inspired to compose the Great Commission by his knowledge of a version of the *Didache* that included the long title, an exposition of the commandments (1–6), and the threefold baptismal formula (7). With such a text in front of him, Matthew could have surmised that the very existence of the *Didache* provided evidence of an occasion in Jesus' life when he commissioned his twelve apostles to teach the nations his interpretation of the commandments, and to baptize them in the name of the Father, the Son and the Holy Spirit. The final verses of Matthew's Gospel thus records Jesus' direct speech in commissioning the eleven disciples[27] (28.16) to make disciples of all nations (28.19), to baptize them in the name of the Father, Son and Holy Spirit (28.19), and to teach them to obey his commandments (28.20).

In conclusion, the connection between Mt. 28.16-20 and the long title of the *Didache, Did.* 1–6 and *Did.* 7.1c, d is most adequately explained by Matthew's direct knowledge of a version of the *Didache* in which all these elements had already been gathered.

6. *Giving What is Holy to Dogs: Matthew 7.6 and* Didache *9.5b*

The apparently proverbial nature of the saying, 'Do not give what is holy to dogs' suggests at the outset that its appearance in both Mt. 7.6 and *Did.* 9.5 may be due to their shared and independent knowledge of a common

---

27. The change from Twelve Apostles to eleven disciples is typical of Matthew's redactional activity. The change from twelve to eleven is consistent with Matthew's special interest in the fate of Judas (e.g. 27.3-10). The change from Apostles to disciples is consistent with Mt. 10.1; 11.1 and 20.17 where the twelve are described as the twelve *disciples* against the witness of Mark and Luke. Matthew only uses the term Twelve Apostles once, at their commissioning, and consistently avoids it thereafter.

tradition. A difficulty with this view, however, is that this proverb does not appear in this form in any other known text.[28]

The similarities between the two texts extend beyond their content and the speaker to whom they are attributed in that both texts bear a connection to the eucharist.[29] It is generally overlooked that Mt. 7.9-10 has fish and bread as the desired elements, rather than fish and egg, as in Lk. 11.11-12. It is possible, given the eucharistic flavour of other fish and bread meals in the gospels,[30] that Matthew made this change to improve the connection between the saying used in Mt. 7.6 (if it was known to have a eucharistic origin) and Mt. 7.7-11.

Given the three points of similarity between Mt. 7.6 and *Did.* 9.5b, there are grounds for suggesting that a direct link of some kind exists between them. However, the direction of that link, when taken in isolation, is difficult to determine. There is strong evidence that both texts quote from another source. In *Did.* 9.5 the quotation formula makes this self-evident. In Mt. 7.6 the saying is so odd in its context that it is highly unlikely to be due to Matthew's redaction.[31] That is to say, it appears directly to contradict the sense of the preceding verses (do not judge) and the

28. Massaux (1993: 156) notes that the Talmud contains no trace of a proverb of this kind. Moreover, the fact that Jesus/the Lord is presented as the author of this saying in both cases renders unlikely the suggestion of Bultmann (1972: 107) that a stock secular proverb lies behind the quotations. One possible origin for a Lord's saying of this kind may be found in Rev. 22.15, where 'dogs' are excluded from the holy city, within which the final messianic banquet may be expected to take place. In Garrow (1997: 52–53) I note the possibility that Revelation was designed to be performed in a eucharistic context. If this was the case, then the prohibition of dogs from the city may reflect the prohibition of the unworthy from the eschatological feast of the eucharist. However, even if Matthew and the teacher did derive their saying from Revelation, it is unlikely that they both independently re-shaped this saying so as to arrive at identical renderings. It is, of course, possible that another eucharistic prophecy contained the exact words used by both Matthew and the teacher. However, the fact that no record of such a prophecy survives means that such a proposal requires the creation of another hypothetical entity. The relationship between the *Didache* and Matthew's Gospel creates considerable scope for the proposal of such entities, but their multiplication ultimately leads to a requirement for untenable levels of coincidental sharing by both Matthew and the diverse contributors to the *Didache*.

29. Massaux (1993: 156) overstates the case when he says that 'It is certainly *undeniable* that the "thing to preserve" in Mt. is not the Eucharist' [emphasis added].

30. Fish and bread eucharists are commonly depicted in catacomb and sarcophagus art of the early Christian centuries. See Heidenreich (1962).

31. Tuckett (1996: 108) concurs that 'Do not give what is holy to dogs', is not clearly MattR.

following (give to those who ask). If Matthew had wanted to balance the teaching on judging and giving with some redactional remark, then he could surely have managed something a little smoother than the famously awkward Mt. 7.6.[32]

Since both texts quote from another source, and both texts quote an identical proverb attributed to Jesus, there is little scope for pinning down the direction of the dependence between them. Therefore, it must be concluded that, when taken in isolation, this parallel may be equally well attributed to Matthew's direct dependence on the *Didache*, or to the *Didache*'s direct dependence on Matthew.[33]

7. *The Worker's Food: Matthew 10.10 and* Didache *13.1-2*

That there is likely to be some form of literary link between these two passages is suggested by the fact that they preserve an identical saying that is distinct from similar sayings found elsewhere. As Massaux (1993: 166) notes, regarding *Did.* 13.1-2:

> There is an exact verbal coincidence with Mt. (ἄξιος γὰρ ὁ ἐργάτης τῆς τροφῆς αὐτοῦ), and it is all the more discernible that in Lk. and 1 Tim., τροφῆς is replaced with μισθοῦ.

Beyond this it is difficult to draw firm conclusions regarding the relationship between the two texts because it is not possible to demonstrate that the saying was originally composed by either author.

It is highly unlikely that the modifier is responsible for the creation of the saying as it stands in *Did.* 13.2. The rights of teachers and prophets, rather than 'workers' *per se*, are the prime concern of the modifier. Thus, the additional mention of workers makes most sense if the teacher attempted to apply a generally accepted principle, 'the worker deserves his food', to the particular situation of those working as prophets and teachers. Taken in isolation, therefore, there is no reason why the modifier could not have taken this saying from Mt. 10.10.

To observe that the *Didache*'s use of Mt. 10.10 is possible is not, by any means, to say that such dependence is necessary. Matthew's Mission Discourse, in common with the Sermon on the Mount, shows signs of

---

32. Goulder (1974: 265): 'This is the most difficult text in the Gospel on any account'. H.D. Betz (1995: 493): 'The saying in 7:6 has always been known for its obscurity...'

33. Van de Sandt (2002) argues in some detail that the *Didache* is unlikely to have borrowed from Matthew's Gospel in this instance.

having been conflated from a collection of related sources.[34] If Matthew used a prior source in this case, then there is no reason why that source could not also have been quoted by the modifying teacher in *Did.* 13.2. At the same time there is no specific obstacle to the possibility that *Did.* 13.2 was one of the resources upon which Matthew drew in the creation of his Mission Discourse.

Ultimately there is not enough evidence to pin down the exact nature of the relationship between Mt. 10.10 and *Did.* 13.2. The fact that Matthew presents this saying as the direct speech of Jesus, while the *Didache* does not, might possibly be taken as pointing towards Matthew's knowledge of this saying in the context of 'The Teaching of the Lord, etc.'. At the same time, however, alternative explanations for the shared use of this saying are also viable.

8. *Conclusion: Matthew's Gospel and the Modifying Teacher Layer*

The introduction to Part II observed that the simplest explanation for the presence of so many points of contact between the first three layers of the *Didache* and Matthew's Gospel is that Matthew found and used the diverse traditions previously gathered together in this layered document.

The purpose of this chapter has been to test this hypothesis by examining whether or not Matthew's direct dependence on the *Didache* is credible at each of seven proposed points of contact between Matthew's Gospel and the Modifying Teacher layer.

Having conducted individual studies of the relevant parallels it is possible to conclude that there is no obstacle to the feasibility of Matthew's direct dependence on the *Didache* at any of the seven points of contact considered. More than that, it has been argued that Matthew's direct use of the *Didache* provides the fullest and simplest explanation for the similarities and the differences between the two texts in the case of: 'be recon-

---

34. Since the development of the Four Source Hypothesis, Matthew has been widely regarded as a conflator of prior traditions. Examples of Matthew's conflationary activity are presented in each of the following four chapters, especially Chapters 13 and 14. Dungan (1971: 51–63) argues, against majority opinion, that Matthew's Mission Discourse is not a conflation of Luke/Q, Mark and Special Matthew. Dungan's arguments are reversible and so it remains likely that Matthew does here conflate a set of related traditions. However, even if Dungan's thesis were correct, this could not be taken as in any way demonstrating that 'the worker deserves his food' is original to Matthew.

ciled' (*Did.* 14.2 = Mt. 5.23-24), 'the last penny' (*Did.* 1.5c = Mt. 5.26), 'pray and fast' (*Did.* 8.1-2a, c-3 = Mt. 6.1-16), 'preservation of teaching' (*Did.* 11.1-2 = Mt. 5.17-20) and 'threefold baptism' (*Did.* long title + 7.1d = Mt. 28.16-20).

Chapter 12

MATTHEW'S GOSPEL AND THE PROPHET LAYER

At the start of the following discussion of the single link between the Prophet layer and Matthew's Gospel (*Did.* 11.7 = Mt. 12.31) two preliminary points may be recalled. First, as noted in the introduction to Part II, Matthew's direct knowledge of the first three layers of the *Didache* provides the simplest explanation for the pattern of contacts between the two texts. Second, the Prophet layer (10.1-7; 11.7-9, 12; 12.1-5) is, according to the analysis offered in Part I, modified by the Modifying Teacher layer (at 11.1-2, 10-11 and 13.1–15.2). If, as argued in the preceding chapter, Matthew knew the Modifying Teacher layer, then it follows that he must also have known that which it modified, including the Prophet layer. These two initial points set up the hypothesis of Matthew's direct knowledge of *Did.* 11.7, which this short chapter is designed to test.

1. *The Unforgivable Sin: Matthew 12.31 and* Didache *11.7*

Synopsis 1 (on p. 188) illustrates the verbal and conceptual similarities between Mt. 12.31 and *Did.* 11.7, and thus suggests that there is likely to be a literary connection between the two. Three types of explanation for this relationship are logically possible. Either, the *Didache* presupposes/ depends upon Matthew's Gospel, or Matthew presupposes/depends upon the *Didache* or both texts refer to a common source.

The most recent and exacting exponent of the view that the *Didache* presupposes Matthew's Gospel is Christopher Tuckett (1996).[1]

At the heart of Tuckett's case for the *Didache*'s knowledge of Matthew's Gospel is his application of Köster's method for establishing the dependence of one text on another.

Tuckett (1996: 95), who describes this method as 'exemplary', explains its mechanics as follows:

---

1. Tuckett's article first appeared in 1989.

If material which owes its origin to the redactional activity of [one author] reappears in another work, then the latter presupposes the finished work of [the former].

Tuckett (1996: 95) goes on to warn that

one must not rule out the possibility that a feature could have been added to the tradition by two independent redactors. Nor should one assume that any dependence which is established on the basis of this criterion is necessarily direct: the later document may be several stages removed from the earlier one.

In the final analysis, however, Tuckett (1996: 95) concludes that

this criterion is really the only one which ultimately can determine whether [one text presupposes another].

The application of this method to the particular instance in hand means that, if Tuckett is able to identify examples of Matthew's redaction of Mark, which also appear in the *Did.* 11.7, then his case is made. To this end Tuckett (1996: 104–105) observes that 'the *Didache*'s wording agrees exactly with Matthew's redaction of Mark in Mt 12.31/Mk 3.28'.

This bold statement prompts one obvious question: is the non-Markan material in Mt. 12.31 *necessarily* original to Matthew, that is, MattR?

There is nothing in Matthew's additions to Lk./Q 12.10 and Mk 3.28-29 which could be described as necessarily Matthean. Further, there is no clear motive for the creation of such additions since Matthew appears to have conflated the parallel traditions preserved by Mark and Luke,[2] and thus has twice as much material as he needs to express the essential thrust of this passage already. The additional material does nothing to clarify, modify or otherwise enhance the (somewhat obscure) point being made, and so sits uneasily under the description 'MattR'.

If Matthew's inclusion of these additional elements is unlikely to have been driven by a clarifying or modifying motive, then it is possible that some other factor was at work. An author who sought to conflate Mk 3.28-29 and Lk./Q 12.10 with some other source might reasonably be expected to create a long-winded discourse such as Mt. 12.31-32. It is plausible, therefore, that what Tuckett ascribes to MattR is in fact the product of Matthew's attempt to be faithful to an additional source.

---

2.   Köster (1957: 216) expresses the confident belief that Matthew combines the Markan and Q versions of this saying.

Synopsis 1: *The unforgivable sin*

Did.	Mt.	Mk.
11.7 καὶ πάντα προφήτην λαλοῦντα ἐν **πνεύματι** οὐ πειράσετε οὐδὲ διακρινεῖτε·	12.31 Διὰ τοῦτο <u>λέγω ὑμῖν</u>,	3.28 Ἀμὴν <u>λέγω ὑμῖν</u> ὅτι πάντα
πᾶσα γὰρ **ἁμαρτία**	**πᾶσα ἁμαρτία** καὶ βλασφημία	
ἀφεθήσεται, αὕτη δὲ ἡ	<u>**ἀφεθήσεται** τοῖς ἀνθρώποις</u>, ἡ δὲ τοῦ	<u>ἀφεθήσεται τοῖς</u> υἱοῖς τῶν <u>ἀνθρώπ</u>ων,
ἁμαρτία	πνεύματος βλασφημία	τὰ ἁμαρτήματα καὶ αἱ <u>βλασφημ</u>ίαι ὅσα ἐὰν
οὐκ **ἀφεθήσεται**.	οὐκ **ἀφεθήσεται**.	βλασφημήσωσιν·

Lk.		
12.10 *καὶ πᾶς ὃς* ἐρεῖ *λόγον* εἰς *τὸν υἱὸν τοῦ ἀνθρώπου, ἀφεθήσεται αὐτῷ·* τῷ δὲ εἰς	12.32 *καὶ ὃς* ἐὰν εἴπῃ *λόγον* κατὰ *τοῖ υἱῷ τοῦ ἀνθρώπου, ἀφεθήσεται αὐτῷ*	
		3.29
	<u>ὃς δ' ἂν</u> εἴπῃ κατὰ τοῦ <u>*πνεύμ*</u>ατος τοῦ <u>*ἁγί*</u>ου,	<u>ὃς δ' ἂν</u> βλασφημήσῃ εἰς τὸ <u>πνεῦμ</u>α τὸ <u>ἅγιον</u>
τὸ ἅγιον *πνεῦμα* βλασφημήσαντι οὐκ ἀφεθήσεται.	οὐκ ἀφεθήσεται αὐτῷ οὔτε ἐν τούτῳ τῷ <u>αἰῶν</u>ι οὔτε ἐν τῷ μέλλοντι.	οὐκ ἔχει ἄφεσιν εἰς τὸν <u>αἰῶν</u>α, ἀλλὰ ἔνοχός ἐστιν αἰωνίου ἁμαρτήματος 3.30 ὅτι ἔλεγον, Πνεῦμα ἀκάθαρτον ἔχει.

These observations suggest that the non-Markan material in Mt. 12.31 is *not* necessarily MattR. This renders Tuckett's method for establishing the *Didache*'s dependence on Matthew unsafe at this point.

Further uncertainty surrounds Tuckett's conclusion in that it requires the Didachist to extract from Matthew's Gospel only those elements (with the exception of ἀφεθήσεται and οὐκ ἀφεθήσεται, which are essential to any discourse on the subject) that are not common to either Mark or Luke. If the whole of Mt. 12.31-32 was available, then why did the Didachist avoid, to such a large extent, words in Mt. 12.31-32 drawn from either Lk./Q 12.10 or Mk 3.28-29?

An alternative explanation for the presence of non-Markan elements in Mt. 12.31 is that Matthew included another source in his conflation of Mk 3.28-29 with Lk./Q 12.10. An entirely suitable candidate for such an additional source is *Did.* 11.7, a text that shows signs of independent origin,[3] addresses the subject in hand, and contains almost every word that Matthew cannot have derived from either Mark or Luke/Q.

Before rushing to conclude, on this basis, that Mt. 12.31 depends on *Did.* 11.7 one further possible explanation for their similarities must be noted. Köster (1957: 216) observes that Mark's version of the unforgivable sin is almost entirely different from that in Luke. He takes this, with some justification, as showing that a saying of this type circulated in various forms in early Christianity. This makes it possible that Matthew and the *Didache* both had independent access to a saying, or similar sayings, of this type. Taken in isolation Köster's argument is feasible. However, this explanation for the similarities between Mt. 12.31 and *Did.* 11.7 requires the hypothecation of yet another lost tradition of which Matthew and the *Didache* are the sole surviving representatives.

In conclusion, the view that the *Didache* here presupposes Matthew's finished Gospel, while not impossible, requires superfluous redactional activity on the part of Matthew and remarkably exact selection of those redactional elements by the Didachist. Köster's proposal of a shared common tradition is also technically feasible, but multiplies the hypothecation of lost sources. By contrast, the view that Mt. 12.31 conflates related teaching preserved in Mk. 3.28-29, Lk./Q 12.10 and *Did.* 11.7 is consistent with Matthew's conflationary practice,[4] does not require the additional hypothecation of lost sources, and plausibly explains the shape of Matthew's long-winded treatment of the subject of the unforgivable sin. Of the available options, therefore, the most probable is that Matthew knew and used *Did.* 11.7.

---

3.   Köster (1957: 216–17) argues that the *Didache* contains a more original version of the saying than does any of the Synoptic Gospels. While this type of argument is fraught with difficulty, Köster makes a reasonable case.

4.   For scholars who accept the Two Source Hypothesis it is conventional to see Matthew as an author who conflates 'Q' with Mark's Gospel. For further examples of Matthew's conflationary activity see Chapter 11, § 3.1. and Chapters 13, 14 and 15.

Chapter 13

MATTHEW'S GOSPEL AND *DIDACHE* 16

Having considered the contacts between Matthew's Gospel in the Modifying Teacher and Prophet layers, attention now turns to the earliest layer of the *Didache*, the Peri/Base layer. The number and complexity of the points of contact within this layer invites their treatment in three separate chapters. The first of these concerns the parallels between *Did.* 16 and certain elements of Matthew's Gospel.

The version of *Did.* 16 preserved in the incomplete Jerusalem manuscript is widely regarded as sharing some form of link with Mt. 24. The present chapter begins with a critique of Christopher Tuckett's view that this connection is due to the *Didache*'s presupposition of Matthew's Gospel. This is then followed by the presentation of a case for the direct dependence of Mt. 16.27; 24.10-12, 30-31; 25.31-34, 46 on *Did.* 16.3-6, 8-9.

1. Didache *16's Presupposition of Matthew 24*

Tuckett (1996: 95), the principal proponent of the view that *Did.* 16 presupposes Mt. 24, notes that

> Did 16 is widely recognized as containing a significant cluster of links with the synoptic tradition and it may be regarded as an important test case in the discussion of the problem of synoptic tradition in the *Didache*.

Tuckett's method for establishing the *Didache*'s dependence on Matthew's Gospel (see Chapter 12, section 1) requires a single instance where *Did.* 16 preserves Matthew's redaction of Mark's Gospel. He finds what appears to be a suitable example in *Did.* 16.8:

> The most significant connection between the *Didache* and material in both Matthew and Mark occurs in Did 16:8 (Τότε ὄψεται ὁ κόσμος τὸν κύριον ἐρχόμενον ἐπάνω τῶν νεφελῶν τοῦ οὐρανοῦ). The allusion to Dan 7:13 here is very similar to that in Mt 24:30 (cf. Mk 13:26). The very close relationship between the *Didache* and Matthew has often been noted. In particular the *Didache* shares with Mark and Matthew the use of

ὄψεται/ ὄψονται and the inversion of the order of 'coming' and 'clouds' as compared with Dan 7. Further, the *Didache* agrees with Matthew's redaction of Mark in using ἐπάνω (Matthew ἐπί) for Mark's ἐν with the 'clouds', and adding τοῦ οὐρανοῦ. A priori there is a strong case here for seeing the *Didache* reflecting MattR of Mark and hence presupposing Matthew's finished gospel. (1996: 98–99)

So far as it goes Tuckett's assertion is entirely correct. That is to say, if *Did.* 16.8 reproduces Matthew's alterations of Mark's Gospel, then *Did.* 16.8 must presuppose Matthew's Gospel. The critical flaw in Tuckett's case is that it rests on the untested assumption that Mk 13.26 is not dependent on *Did.* 16.8. This assumption must be tested because if, in fact, Mk 13.26 knows/presupposes *Did.* 16.8, then (assuming Markan priority) Matthew must also presuppose *Did.* 16. Under these circumstances the shape of Mt. 24.30 may be accounted for as the result of Matthew's conflation of Mk 13.26 and *Did.* 16.8 (cf. section 2.2 below).

Excursus: The Relationship Between Mark 13 and Didache *16*

The possibility that Mark's little apocalypse might in any sense be dependent on *Did.* 16 has never been addressed. It is appropriate at this stage, therefore, to challenge the consequent untested assumption that Mk 13 does not know *Did.* 16. I aim to show that there is one particular indicator of Mk 13's knowledge of *Did.* 16 which accords with Köster's method for establishing literary dependence. Tuckett (1996: 95) expresses this method as follows:

> If material which owes its origin to the redactional activity of [one author] reappears in another work, then the latter presupposes the finished work of [the former].

This method for establishing literary dependence may be applied in the case of *Did.* 16 and Mk 13 because both texts use a similar redacted form of Dan. 7.13 (LXX).

> Dan. 7.13 (LXX):
> ...ἐπὶ τῶν νεφελῶν τοῦ οὐρανοῦ
> ὡς υἱὸς ἀνθρώπου ἤρχετο, ...

> *Did.* 16.8:
> Τότε ὄψεται ὁ κόσμος τὸν κύριον
> ἐρχόμενον ἐπάνω τῶν νεφελῶν τοῦ οὐρανοῦ,
> καὶ πάντες οἱ ἅγιοι μετ᾽ αὐτοῦ

Mk 13.26:
καὶ τότε ὄψονται τὸν υἱὸν τοῦ ἀνθρώπου
ἐρχόμενον ἐν νεφέλαις
μετὰ δυνάμεως πολλῆς καὶ δόξης.

The alterations made to Dan. 7.13 that are common to both Mk 13.26 and *Did.* 16.8 include: the addition of τότε; the addition of ὄψεται/ὄψονται; a rearrangement of the word order so that instead of Daniel's, 'on the clouds, the Son of man, coming', the *Didache* and Mark share the word order, 'Son of man/Lord, coming, with/on the clouds'; a change in the direction of travel of Son of man/Lord (from heaven to earth rather than towards the Ancient of days).

These common redactional changes suggest that one text's redaction of Dan. 7.13 reappears in the other. This means that, according to Köster's criteria, either *Did.* 16.8 presupposes the existence of Mk 13.26, or the reverse. To determine the direction of dependence it is necessary to establish, if possible, the origin of the redactional changes common to both texts. If they originate with the Didachist, then Mk 13.26 presupposes *Did.* 16.8, and vice versa.

The likely origin of each of the redactional changes may be considered in turn. First, τότε is not a favourite word of Mark's. It occurs only six times in his gospel, four of which are in Mk 13. Mark uses καὶ very much more frequently to denote 'then'; it is therefore unlikely that the inclusion of τότε was the original work of the gospel writer. By contrast, τότε is the means by which the Didachist introduces each paragraph of the apocalypse (with the exception of the opening paragraph). There is therefore no difficulty in seeing the *Didache* apocalypse as responsible for the introduction of this change to Dan. 7.13.

Second, the introduction of ὄψεται/ὄψονται. As noted in Chapter 3, section 4.3, the addition of ὄψεται in the *Didache*'s allusion to Dan. 7.13 assists the creation of an oppositional parallel between the appearance of the world-deceiver (16.4b) and the being seen by the world of the Lord (16.8):

16.4b καὶ	τότε	φανήσεται	ὁ κοσμοπλανὴς	ὡς υἱὸς θεοῦ
16.8	τότε	ὄψεται	ὁ κόσμος	τὸν κύριον

The structural benefit derived from this change suggests that it may credibly be seen as the original work of the author of the *Didache*'s apocalypse. By contrast, the use of ὄψονται in Mk 13.26 is inconsistent with its context. Thus Hooker (1991: 319) notes that these words [ὄψονται and following] are no longer addressed to the disciples, perhaps because this saying or section was originally independent. It is by no means clear who the people referred to as 'they' are.

This lack of clarity is explicable if Mk 13.26 presupposes the *Didache*'s independent vision in which the 'they' referred to are ὁ κόσμος. The reverse view, that *Did.* 16.8 here presupposes Mk 13.26, requires Mark to make redactional changes to Dan. 7.13 that create ambiguity in his own text, but which happened to create a neat oppositional parallel when incorporated into the *Didache*'s apocalypse.

Similar observations may be made with regard to the common changes in Daniel's word order. It is possible that Mark made these changes, but if so, then they were highly convenient to the *Didache*'s structural programme. It is more likely, therefore, that the changes in word order were made by the Didachist to conform the text to the structure of the apocalypse, and that Mark then absorbed these changes.

Finally, the common change in the direction in which the Lord/Son of man travels. That Mk 13 apparently depicts the Son of man as travelling from heaven to earth, despite the fact that Daniel's text portrays this figure as travelling towards the Ancient of Days, is a point that is passed over without elaboration by some commentators. For example, Hooker (1991: 319) writes:

> Mark does not tell us in what direction he moves: in Daniel, the one like a son of man comes to God, and in isolation the saying here could have the same meaning; in the context Mark gives it, however, it is natural to think that they will see the Son of man coming *towards* them.

This change of direction invites an explanation. It is, of course, possible that Mark independently chose to interpret Dan. 7.13 in this way, despite the fact that this source does not directly invite such a change. Alternatively, the origin of such an alteration may be located in the *Didache*'s combination of Dan. 7.13 with Zech. 14.5. As discussed in Chapter 3, section 4.3, *Did.* 16.8-9 appears to have combined some of the rare Old Testament references to God's personal inbreaking to earth from heaven. Thus, *Did.* 16.8 opens with Zechariah's image of the Lord coming as judge and king and conflates it with Daniel's vision of one like a son of man coming on the clouds of heaven. The *Didache* then returns to Zech. 14.5 to note that the Lord is accompanied by all his holy ones.

Zech. 14.5
Καὶ ἥξει <u>κύριος</u> ὁ θεός μου,
<u>καὶ πάντες οἱ ἅγιοι μετ᾽ αὐτοῦ</u>

Dan. 7.13
... ἐπὶ τῶν νεφελῶν τοῦ οὐρανοῦ
ὡς υἱὸς ἀνθρώπου ἤρχετο,

Did. 16.8
τότε ὄψεται ὁ κόσμος
τὸν <u>κύριον</u> *ἐρχόμενον ἐπάνω τῶν νεφελῶν τοῦ οὐρανοῦ,*
<u>καὶ πάντες οἱ ἅγιοι μετ᾽ αὐτοῦ</u>

According to this arrangement Zechariah's vision provides the narrative base, while Dan. 7.13 provides a descriptive detail. Thus, the Lord's direction of travel is taken, without alteration, from Zechariah. This means that Mark's estimate of the Son of man's movements may credibly be explained if Mk 13.26 relies on *Did.* 16.8 and has sought to emphasize the eschatological role of Jesus by exchanging 'the Son of man' for 'the Lord'. Alternatively, to argue that *Did.* 16.8 presupposes (however indirectly) Mk 13.26 requires that the Didachist changed 'the Son of man' to 'the Lord'; changed 'in clouds with great power and glory' to 'upon the clouds of heaven'; and added, 'and all his holy ones with him', in order to introduce an allusion to Zech. 14.5. This is an unnecessarily complex explanation of *Did.* 16.8, which may be understood as a conflation of Old Testament texts without any reference to Mark's Gospel. It is preferable, therefore, to see the Lord/Son of man's direction of travel as determined by the *Didache*'s version of Zech. 14.5, which then provided a basis for Mk 13.26.

Thus, the addition of τότε, the addition of ὄψεται/ὄψονται, the rearrangement of Daniel's word order, and the direction of travel of the Lord Son of man, all appear to have their origin in the work of an author who quarried Old Testament references to God's personal inbreaking from heaven and conformed them to a carefully structured oppositional narrative. The reappearance in Mark's Gospel of these elements of the Didachist's redactional activity suggests that Mk 13.26 presupposes the finished *Didache* apocalypse.

Most dependency arguments are reversible and strongly susceptible to subjective bias. It is therefore worth recalling and re-examining Köster's method with respect to the above conclusion.

First of all Tuckett (1996: 95), following Köster, stated that

> if material which owes its origin to the redactional activity of [an author] reappears in another work, then the latter presupposes the finished work of [the former].

A potential difficulty in the application of this criterion can be that it is not always possible to state with confidence that a piece of redactional activity is *original* to a particular author. The viability of the argument presented above depends crucially, therefore, on the quality of the evidence that suggests the unique hand of the author of the *Didache*'s apocalypse in the creation of the version of Dan. 7.13 now found in *Did.* 16.8.

It was further noted that Tuckett (1996: 95) warns:

> Such a criterion must of course be applied with care, and one must not rule out the possibility that a feature could have been added to the tradition by two independent redactors.

The level of coincidence required for the independent redaction of Dan. 7.13 in both Mk 13.26 and *Did.* 16.8 is unusually high because of the four redactional steps involved: the addition of τότε, the addition of ὄψεται/ ὄψονται, the rearrangement of Daniel's word order, and the direction of travel of the Lord/Son of man. It is unlikely, therefore, that the similarities between these two versions of Dan. 7.13 were created by changes made by two independent redactors.

Tuckett (1996: 95) finally cautions that

> Nor should one assume that any dependence which is established on the basis of this criterion is necessarily direct: the later document may be several stages removed from the earlier one.

Once again, this is a warning that must be heeded. All that can be concluded on the basis of the evidence considered above is that Mk 13.26 appears to presuppose the existence of *Did.* 16.3-9 at some remove or other.

Tuckett (1996: 95) sums up this methodological discussion by stating that

> Nevertheless, this criterion is really the only one which ultimately can determine whether [one] text...presupposes [another text].

This observation is important because too often dependency arguments are constructed on the basis of the possibility that general similarities and differences between two texts may be accounted for by the dependence of one text upon the other. Such arguments are close to worthless because they are almost always reversible. Thus, although a line of development from *Did.* 16 to Mk 13 could certainly be drawn[1] the reverse is also

---

1. For example, there is no difficulty in reading Mk 13.13, 'ὁ δὲ ὑπομείνας εἰς τέλος οὗτος σωθήσεται', as a redactional development of *Did.* 16.5, 'οἱ δὲ ὑπομείναντες ἐν τῇ πίστει αὐτῶν σωθήσονται ὑπ' αὐτοῦ τοῦ καταθέματος',

conceivable, with the notable exception of the relationship between *Did.* 16.8 and Mk 13.26.

In conclusion, Mk 13.26 appears to have known a version of Dan. 7.13 redacted by the author of *Did.* 16.8. On the basis that *Did.* 16.3-6, 8-9 is a unified text (cf. Chapter 3), it may be concluded that whoever penned Mk 13.26 (and the other verses that form a unity with this verse) knew the whole of *Did.* 16.3-6, 8-9.[2]

I now return to the question of the relationship between Mt. 24 and *Did.* 16. If *Did.* 16.8 was a source, at whatever remove, for Mk 13.26, and if Mk 13 was a source for Matthew's eschatological discourse, then it is a logical impossibility that *Did.* 16.3-6, 8-9 could presuppose the existence of Matthew's Gospel. This argument, if cogent, removes the centrepiece of Tuckett's case for the *Didache*'s presupposition of Matthew's Gospel.

The remainder of Tuckett's argument regarding the relationship between *Did.* 16 and Mt. 24 runs as follows. First, he notes that

> Many who have argued against any dependence of the *Didache* on Matthew's gospel have appealed to the peculiar pattern in the parallels between the *Didache* and the synoptic gospels. It is said that Did 16 only shows links with material peculiar to Mt 24 in the synoptic tradition: the *Didache* does not have any links with material from Mt 24 which Matthew has derived from Mark. Hence, it is argued, the *Didache* is more likely to be dependent on the source(s) which lie behind Mt 24 and which were available to Matthew alone; if the *Didache* were dependent on Matthew, one would expect some of Matthew's Markan material to be reflected as well. Such an argument is in danger of ignoring some of the evidence of Did 16 itself. For the text of Did 16 contains possible allusions to synoptic

and so on. However, it is also possible to conceive of circumstances under which the direction of development between these two texts might be reversed.

2.   Additional support for Mark's knowledge of *Did.* 16.3-6, 8-9 may be found in a further indicator of the extreme antiquity and importance of the *Didache* apocalypse. In Chapter 3, § 4.3 it was argued that the rendering of Isa. 64.4 in *Did.* 16.9 was created by the Didachist so as to complete the sense and structure of the closing apocalypse. It is noteworthy therefore that in 1 Cor. 2.9 Paul quotes an identical version of this verse. It is unlikely that the various redactional changes involved were found by the Didachist 'ready made' for insertion into the apocalypse, so it is probable that *Did.* 16.9 represents the first occurrence of this rendering of Isa. 64.4. Paul's quotation therefore implies that the *Didache*'s apocalypse predates the writing of 1 Corinthians, and thus is highly likely to predate the composition of Mark's Gospel. The issue of Paul's relationship to the *Didache* is beyond the scope of this project. I aim to publish further research on this subject in due course.

material in four verses common to Matthew and Mark (and which Matthew presumably derived from Mark). (1996: 96)

Tuckett then goes on to consider, in turn, those occasions where the *Didache* contains material common to Matthew and Mark. With reference to *Did.* 16.4 he writes:

Did 16:4 mentions the κοσμοπλανής who, it is said, will do (ποιήσει) signs and wonders (σημεῖα καί τέρατα) and will perform iniquities ἃ οὐδέποτε γέγονεν ἐξ αἰῶνος. The language used is similar to that of Matthew and Mark. Mk 13:22/Mt 24:24 refers to the coming of false messiahs and false prophets who will perform σημεῖα καί τέρατα, 'leading astray' the elect; and in Mk 13:19/Mt 24:21 the coming tribulation is said to be such as never has been (οὐ γέγονεν) since the creation of the world. (1996: 96)

These overlaps do not carry the significance attributed to them by Tuckett when the unjustified assumption of Markan priority relative to the *Didache*'s apocalypse is removed. Thus, if *Did.* 16 is presupposed by Mk 13, then it is unsurprising that the *Didache*'s expectations about the coming world-deceiver should be picked up by Mark, and subsequently, by Matthew. Ironically, Köster (1972: 182) comes close to this explanation when he argues that, since Mk 13.19, 22 come from the *Vorlage* used by Mark in Mk 13, the *Didache* here shows contact only with Mark's source and not with Mark's Gospel itself.

Köster has been justly criticized for taking this route because of the lack of evidence for the form of Mark's *Vorlage*. However, if Mark's source was in fact *Did.* 16, or some derivative of that text, then Köster's case need only be amended to the extent that, since Mk 13.19, 22 come from *Did.* 16, it is logically impossible that *Did.* 16 could be dependent on either Mark or Matthew (assuming Markan priority).

The next instance where Tuckett notes a possible link between the *Didache* and Markan material used by Matthew is in the phrases, 'οἱ δέ ὑπομείναντες ἐν τῇ πίστει αὐτῶν σωθήσονται ὑπ' αὐτοῦ τοῦ καταθέματος' in *Did.* 16.5, and 'ὁ δὲ ὑπομείνας εἰς τέλος οὗτος σωθήσεται' in Mk 13.13/Mt. 24.13; 10.22. The connection between Mk 13.13 and *Did.* 16.5 is entirely to be expected if Mk 13 depends on the *Didache* apocalypse. This enigmatic line of the *Didache* is pivotal to the structure and perlocutionary force of that discourse (cf. Chapter 3, section 1) and so may be expected to recur in later versions of this eschatological scheme. Mark's simplification and interpretation of the line (in making the perseverence to the 'end' and through the omission of the enigmatic reference to 'the curse itself') suggests, although it does not compel, development from *Did.* 16.5 to Mk 13.13. Further, as Tuckett (1996: 98) notes, 'Many regard the verses [Mk 13.13] as pre-Markan and it is certainly not easy to point to any clear Markan characteristics'. If Mk 13.13 is indeed pre-Markan, and derives in the first instance (like Mk 13.26) from the *Didache*'s apocalypse, then the reappearance of Mark's version of this line in Mt. 24.13; 10.22 serves only to demonstrate a relationship between Matthew and Mark and nothing more.

It is at this stage in Tuckett's programme that he addresses the important case of the use of Dan. 7.13 in *Did.* 16.8, Mk 13.26 and Mt. 24.30. As argued above, the relationship between these four texts points to *Did.* 16.8 as the source of the redacted form of Dan. 7.13 which reappears in Mark and Matthew. As such this instance points to Mark's presupposition of the *Didache* and not, as Tuckett proposes, to the *Didache*'s presupposition of Matthew.

Tuckett concludes this section with the following rebuttal to those who claim that the *Didache* cannot have known Matthew because it appears only to know that in Matthew which is not common to Mark:

> Thus Did 16 has links not only with Matthew's special material, but also with material common to Matthew and Mark and, in the last instance considered, presupposes Matthew's redaction of Mark (1996: 101).

Tuckett's response to his opponents is justified inasmuch as they claim too much and so invite Tuckett's correction. However, as Tuckett himself would attest, the crucial piece of evidence is contained in 'the last instance'; if the *Didache* presupposes Matthew's redaction of Mark, then Tuckett's case is as good as sealed. However, if, as argued above, Matthew shows knowledge of *Mark's redaction of the Didache*, then the centrepiece of his case is removed.

Tuckett's argument continues with a consideration of those passages where *Did.* 16 reflects material that is peculiar to Matthew in the synoptic tradition. Here Tuckett attempts to continue the application of Köster's method by considering first of all whether or not the material peculiar to Mt. 24 is, by origin, Matthean redaction. If he can prove that it is, then its reappearance in *Did.* 16 will provide almost certain evidence of the *Didache*'s presupposition of Matthew's Gospel.

Tuckett's progress in this line of argument is obstructed by his inability to prove that the material peculiar to Matthew in Mt. 24.10-12 and 24.30a, 31 is original to that writer. Tuckett bases his case for the MattR status of these verses entirely on the fact that 'Within Matthean scholarship there is widespread agreement that [Mt. 24.10-12] are due to MattR' (1996: 101–102),[3] and with reference to Mt. 24.30a, 31 (1996: 104), 'Again many would ascribe this material to MattR in Matthew, though the limited extent makes any certainty impossible'.[4] The fact that a number of scholars have decided that these verses are MattR is not sufficient to make Tuckett's case. What is required is convincing evidence that these verses are entirely Matthew's work. Such evidence cannot be provided, and so this section of Tuckett's article does not further his overall thesis.

Tuckett's argument for the direct dependence of *Did.* 16 on Mt. 24 closes at this point. Although he succeeds in exposing the inaccuracy of the claim of his dialogue partners (that the *Didache* and Matthew only share material peculiar to Matthew), he fails to show that the *Didache* presupposes Matthew's redaction of Mark. This means that the case for *Didache* 16's use of Matthew has not been made and alternative explanations for their relationship remain worthy of exploration.

2. *Matthew's Gospel Depends Directly upon* Didache *16*

The commonly proposed alternative to the view that *Did.* 16 directly depends on, or presupposes, Mt. 24 suggests that both texts draw on a hypothetical common tradition. This particular view will be examined more closely at the close of this chapter. The other possible alternative, that Mt. 24 depends directly on *Did.* 16, has not previously been considered; an omission which may be attributed to the commonly held belief that *Did.* 16 must post-date Mt. 24. However, as the earlier excursus sought to demonstrate, this assumption is far from soundly based. There is therefore no obstacle to the possibility that Matthew used *Did.* 16. directly.

The case for Mt. 24's direct dependence on *Did.* 16 requires the defence of four propositions:

---

3.   Tuckett (1996: 102 n. 43) lists Lambrecht, Didier, Kilpatrick, Burnett, Kühschelm and Gundry as proponents of this view. A trawl through these authors will produce a collection of arguments for proposing Matthew's originality in these verses. However, it is extremely difficult to identify Matthew's original creation with any real confidence because he so clearly relied on written sources. Thus, that which may appear characteristic of Matthew may simply be characteristic of one of his sources.

4.   In this case (1996: 104 n. 48) Lambrecht and Gundry are cited. The note continues, 'Clearly Matthew is using traditional ideas and phraseology so that in that sense Matthew's language is traditional; the question is whether Matthew himself has supplied this traditional language'. This is, of course, an impossible question to answer, and so it can make no contribution to the debate in hand.

1. There is a definite connection of some kind between the two texts.
2. That connection cannot be due to the *Didache*'s direct or indirect dependence on Matthew's Gospel.
3. Direct dependence by Matthew upon *Did.* 16 is plausible or probable.
4. Matthew's Gospel and *Did.* 16 are unlikely to have shared a common tradition.

The density of parallels between *Did.* 16.3-6, 8 and Mt. 24.10-12, 30a, 31 means that the first of these propositions creates no difficulties. Tuckett (1996: 101) is correct in asserting that 'The existence of links between Did 16 and material peculiar to Mt 24 is accepted by all'.[5]

The second proposition was defended in this chapter's excursus, where it was argued that *Did.* 16.3-6, 8-9 contains an original redaction of Dan. 7.13, which then reappears in Mark's and Matthew's Gospels. If this observation is correct, then both gospels must presuppose the existence of *Didache*'s eschatological discourse. Further points in support of this proposition are contained in the following section.

What follows addresses the third proposition. (The fourth will be considered in section 4, below.) This entails the examination of individual points of contact between the two texts to consider whether Matthew's direct use of *Did.* 16 is plausible or probable in each case.

2.1. *Matthew 24.10-12 and* Didache *16.3-5*

Synopsis 2 shows that Mt. 24.9b follows Mk 13.13a almost verbatim. Matthew then abruptly breaks off from Mk 13 and immediately introduces material parallel to *Did.* 16.3-5. Mt. 24.13 then continues with verbatim use of Mk 13.13b.

Synopsis 2: *Events endured before the end*

Mk	Mt.	Did.
13.12 καὶ παραδώσει ἀδελφὸς ἀδελφὸν εἰς θάνατον καὶ πατὴρ τέκνον, καὶ ἐπαναστήσονται τέκνα ἐπὶ γονεῖς καὶ θανατώσουσιν αὐτούς·	24.9 τότε παραδώσουσιν ὑμᾶς εἰς θλῖψιν καὶ ἀποκτενοῦσιν ὑμᾶς,	

5. Scholars such as Kloppenborg (1979); Köster (1957) and Glover (1958) see the link as an indirect one, but detect it nonetheless.

Mk	Mt.	*Did.*
13.13a <u>καὶ ἔσεσθε μισούμενοι ὑπὸ πάντων</u> <u>διὰ τὸ ὄνομά μου.</u>	καὶ ἔσεσθε μισούμενοι ὑπὸ πάντων τῶν ἐθνῶν διὰ τὸ ὄνομά μου. 24.10 καὶ **τότε** [4]**σκανδαλισθήσονται** **πολλοὶ** καὶ ἀλλήλους	16.3 ἐν γὰρ ταῖς ἐσχάταις ἡμέραις **πληθυνθ**ήσονται οἱ [1]**ψευδοπροφῆται** καὶ οἱ φθορεῖς, καὶ στραφήσονται τὰ πρόβατα εἰς λύκους καὶ ἡ **ἀγάπη** στραφήσεταιμ εἰς μῖσος 16.4 αὐξανούσης γὰρ τῆς **ἀνομιας**,
	[3]**παραδώσουσιν** καὶ [2]**μισήσουσιν ἀλλήλους·**	[2]**μισήσουσιν ἀλλήλους** καὶ διώξουσι καὶ [3]**παραδώσουσι**... ... 16.5 **τότε** ἥξει ἡ κτίσις τῶν ἀνθρώπων εἰς τὴν πύρωσιν τῆς
	24.11 καὶ πολλοὶ [1]**ψευδοπροφῆται** ἐγερθήσονται καὶ πλανήσουσιν πολλούς· 24.12 καὶ διὰ τὸ **πληθυνθ**ῆναι τὴν **ἀνομίαν** ψυγήσεται ἡ **ἀγάπη** τῶν πολλῶν.	δοκιμασίας, καὶ [4]**σκανδαλισθήσονται** **πολλοὶ** καὶ ἀπολοῦνται,
13.13b <u>ὁ δὲ ὑπομείνας</u> <u>εἰς τέλος οὗτος</u> <u>σωθήσεται.</u>	24.13 <u>ὁ δὲ **ὑπομείνας** εἰς</u> <u>τέλος οὗτος</u> <u>**σωθ**ήσεται.</u> 24.14 καὶ κηρυχθήσεται τοῦτο τὸ εὐαγγέλιον τῆς βασιλείας ἐν ὅλῃ τῇ οἰκουμένῃ εἰς μαρτύριον πᾶσιν τοῖς ἔθνεσιν, καὶ τότε ἥξει τὸ τέλος.	οἱ δὲ **ὑπομείναντες** ἐν τῇ πίστει αὐτῶν **σωθ**ήσονται ὑπ᾽ αὐτοῦ τοῦ καταθέματος.
13.14 <u>Ὅταν δὲ ἴδητε τὸ</u> <u>βδέλυγμα τῆς</u> <u>ἐρημώσεως</u>...	24.15 <u>Ὅταν οὖν ἴδητε</u> <u>τὸ βδέλυγμα τῆς</u> <u>ἐρημώσεως</u>...	

This pattern is consistent with Matthew's conflation of Mk 13 and *Did.* 16 according to the following sequence:

Matthew decides to gather signs of the end of the age to create a teaching discourse on this subject. He begins, in Mt. 24, by following Mk 13 very closely. At Mk 13.9 he finds a reference to persecution that he has already used in Mt. 10. Being unwilling to make a direct link between his audience's current experience and the end of the age Matthew summarizes this section with simple references to betrayal, eschatological tribulation and execution in Mt. 24.9 (cf. Mk 13.12). Matthew then continues with the things that must be endured by those who, by their steadfastness, shall be saved. The first of these comes naturally from his next verse in Mark, that is, Mk 13.13a. However, Matthew is aware that *Did.* 16 also has a similar reference to endurance before salvation. Matthew therefore turns to the *Didache* for supplementary information. He finds the reference to steadfastness in 16.5 and then works backwards through *Did.* 16.3-5 to pick out further details of this stage of history. He omits reference to persecution because that has already been covered by the 'tribulation' mentioned in 24.9; he omits reference to the antichristian figure (*Did.* 16.4b) because this is duplicated in the abomination of desolation in Mk 13.14;[6] he omits the sheep and wolves because they have already appeared in Mt. 7. However, he does include, in reverse order, the causing of many to stumble, betrayal, hatred and the rising of many false prophets. He then summarizes the *Didache*'s contribution by pulling together references to multiplication, wickedness and reversal of love (Mt. 24.12). Matthew then rejoins Mk 13 at precisely the point where he left off in Mt. 24.9. Thus, Mt. 24.13 uses Mk 13.13b verbatim.[7]

This reconstruction has the advantage of explaining all the *differences* between Mt. 24.10-12 and *Did.* 16.3-5, as well as their similarities. If the direction of dependence were reversed, then it would be difficult to explain why the *Didache* expresses such a dense interest in these two verses of Matthew while there is hardly a point of contact between the two texts for the next seventeen verses of Matthew's Gospel. Further, it would be difficult to explain why *Did.* 16.3-5 might have reversed the order of Mt. 24.10-22 if there were direct dependence by the former on the latter. Tuckett attempts to explain the inexact quotations of Matthew by the

6.   Balabanski (1997: 192) also notes this correspondence.

7.   In this process Matthew follows what Vokes (1938: 111) describes as 'the custom of all apocalyptic writers, of stringing together old materials in a new form'. Vokes curiously attributes this activity to the composer of the remarkably unified *Didache* apocalypse, whom he sees as reusing Matthew – however eclectically or eccentrically.

Didache by claiming that the *Didache* is in the habit of alluding to Matthew, without quoting directly. The image he conjures is of the *Didache* breathing the atmosphere of Matthew's Gospel. Henderson (1995: 182) notes:

> That individuality which asserts itself wherever the *Didache* resembles the synoptics is so pronounced that Tuckett must remind the reader at least eight times about the freedom with which the *Didache* appropriates material which is in synoptic styles.[8]

This appeal to free allusion could explain the differences in the wording between Matthew's Gospel and the *Didache*, but it makes the extreme localization of these allusions all the more puzzling. What Tuckett proposes in the end is that the *Didache* breathes the atmosphere of Matthew, but is careful only to inhale almost exclusively non-Markan air. Given that twenty-nine verses of Mt. 24.1-36 appear to derive from Mk 13, it is remarkable that almost all of these so-called allusions should be densely located in five of the seven non-Markan verses.

In summary, the relationship between *Did.* 16.3-5 and Mt. 24.10-12, may be understood most plausibly as the product of Matthew's conflation of teaching on 'what must be endured prior to salvation' from both Mk 13.1-13 and *Did.* 16.3-5.

2.2. *Matthew 24.30-31 and* Didache *16.6, 8*

As Tuckett (1996: 103) observes, 'Parallels between Did 16.6 and Mt 24.30a, 31 are also widely recognised'. Here several features of the relationship between Mt. 24.10-12 and *Did.* 16.3-5 are repeated. Once again, as can be seen in Synopsis 3 (opposite), there is a strong relationship between the *Didache* and the non-Markan material in Matthew. Once again, a motive for the inclusion of this material at this particular point may be found in Matthew's desire to supplement Mark's material with information on a closely related subject to be found in the *Didache*.[9]

---

8.   Henderson (1995: 182 n. 11) cites the page numbers for these eight occasions from the 1989 version of Tuckett's article. These are: 1989: 198–99 and n. 11, 201 n. 19, 207–208, 211 n. 68, 212 and n. 71, 222 n. 108 and 226.

9.   It is not within the scope of this project to consider Matthew's relationship with the book of Revelation. However, Matthew's inclusion of the further detail 'καὶ τότε κόψονται πᾶσαι αἱ φυλαὶ τῆς γῆς' may indicate his knowledge of the account of the coming of the Son of man in Rev. 1.7.

Synopsis 3: *Signs of the Lord's coming*

Mk	Mt.	Did.
13.24 Ἀλλὰ ἐν ἐκείναις ταῖς ἡμέραις μετὰ τὴν θλῖψιν ἐκείνην ὁ ἥλιος σκοτισθήσεται, καὶ ἡ σελήνη οὐ δώσει τὸ φέγγος αὐτῆς. 13.25 καὶ οἱ ἀστέρες ἔσονται ἐκ τοῦ οὐρανοῦ πίπτοντες, καὶ αἱ δυνάμεις αἱ ἐν τοῖς οὐρανοῖς σαλευθήσονται.	24.29 Εὐθέως δὲ μετὰ τὴν θλῖψιν τῶν ἡμερῶν ἐκείνων, ὁ ἥλιος σκοτισθήσεται, καὶ ἡ σελήνη οὐ δώσει τὸ φέγγος αὐτῆς, καὶ οἱ ἀστέρες πεσοῦνται ἀπὸ τοῦ οὐρανοῦ, καὶ αἱ δυνάμεις τῶν οὐρανῶν σαλευθήσονται.	
	24.30 **καὶ τότε φανήσεται** τὸ **σημεῖον** τοῦ υἱοῦ τοῦ ἀνθρώπου **ἐν οὐρανῷ,** *καὶ τότε κόψονται πᾶσαι αἱ φυλαὶ τῆς γῆς*	16.6 **καὶ τότε φανήσεται** τὰ σημεῖα τῆς ἀληθείας· πρῶτον **σημεῖον** ἐκπετάσεως **ἐν οὐρανῷ,** εἶτα σημεῖον φωνῆς **σάλπιγγος,** καὶ τὸ τρίτον ἀνάστασις νεκρῶν· [Rev. 1.7[9] *καὶ κόψονται ἐπ' αὐτὸν πᾶσαι αἱ φυλαὶ τῆς γῆς*]
13.26 καὶ τότε ὄψονται τὸν υἱὸν τοῦ ἀνθρώπου ἐρχόμενον ἐν νεφέλαις μετὰ δυνάμεως πολλῆς καὶ δόξης. 13.27 καὶ τότε ἀποστελεῖ τοὺς ἀγγέλους καὶ ἐπισυνάξει τοὺς ἐκλεκτοὺς αὐτοῦ ἐκ τῶν τεσσάρων ἀνέμων ἀπ' ἄκρου γῆς ἕως ἄκρου οὐρανοῦ.	καὶ ὄψονται τὸν υἱὸν τοῦ ἀνθρώπου **ἐρχόμενον ἐπὶ τῶν νεφελῶν** τοῦ οὐρανοῦ μετὰ δυνάμεως καὶ δόξης πολλῆς· 24.31 καὶ ἀποστελεῖ τοὺς ἀγγέλους αὐτοῦ μετὰ **σάλπιγγος** μεγάλης, καὶ ἐπισυνάξουσιν τοὺς ἐκλεκτοὺς αὐτοῦ ἐκ τῶν τεσσάρων ἀνέμων ἀπ' ἄκρων οὐρανῶν ἕως ἄκρων αὐτῶν.	16.8 τότε ὄψεται ὁ κόσμος τὸν κύριον **ἐρχόμενον ἐπάνω τῶν νεφελῶν τοῦ οὐρανοῦ**

Thus, while following Mark's Gospel, Matthew finds a reference to the appearance of the Son of man in the clouds. He is aware that *Did.* 16.6, 8 also contains a reference to this point in history. If the sequence of events in the two accounts are set side by side then it is possible to see the information potentially available to Matthew.

Synopsis 4: *Two sets of signs accompanying the Lord's coming*

Mk	*Did.*
(13.9-23 persecution)	(16.5 Testing fire of persecution)
13.24 But in those days after that suffering,	16.6a And then shall appear the signs of truth
the sun will be darkened,	16.6b first the sign of extension in
and the moon will not give its light,	heaven
13.25 and the stars will be falling from heaven, and the powers in the heavens will be shaken.	16.6c next the sign of the trumpet call
	16.6d and third the resurrection of the dead
13.26 **Then they will see 'the Son of man coming in clouds'** with great power and glory.	16.8 Then the world will see **the Lord coming upon the clouds** of heaven,
13.27 Then he will send out the angels, and gather his elect from the four winds, from the ends of the earth to the ends of heaven.	

Matthew is faced with something of a puzzle here. Clearly, both texts refer to the same point in history, but they do not exactly agree because the events presaging the arrival of the Lord/Son of man are different: the moment of resurrection precedes the coming of the Lord in the *Didache*, but appears to follow it in Mark.

Matthew's version of the events surrounding the coming of the Judge may credibly be interpreted as his conflation of these two slightly different accounts. A possible conflationary programme may be reconstructed as follows:

Matthew decides to follow Mark's order and to use the *Didache*'s material as a supplement to Mark's scheme. Thus, Mark's signs of the coming Judge, following the tribulation, are preserved by Matthew. Rather than then going on to list the *Didache*'s version of these signs Matthew elects to meld the last two signs of truth with events that occur (according to Mark's account) after the coming of the Judge. Thus, Mark's angels use the *Didache*'s trumpet (sign two) to gather the elect. This gathering may be seen as equivalent to the *Didache*'s resurrection of the dead (sign three), and so the *Didache*'s version of this event is omitted to avoid dupli-cation. This leaves Matthew with the puzzle of the *Didache*'s first sign of truth, the enigmatic 'sign of the extension'. He elects to interpret this as a more general 'sign of the Son of man' and allows it to remain as one of the events preceding the coming of the Judge. All that remains for Matthew to do now is to conflate the common material concerning the coming of the Judge himself. He takes the first line from Mark (they will see the Son of man), the second line from the *Didache* (coming on the clouds of heaven), and the third line from Mark (with great power and glory).

This conflationary process is illustrated below. Here the text of Mk 13.24-27 and the re-ordered text of *Did.* 16.6, 8 are set alongside one another. The text of Mt. 24.29-31 may be almost exactly recreated by selecting the underlined words while reading from left to right across the whole page. **Note:** Italicized words indicate Matthew's deviations from the exact text of Mark and the *Didache*.

Synopsis 5: *The creation of Mt. 24.29-31 from Mk 13.24-27 and* Did. *16.6, 8*

Mk	*Did.*
(13.9-23 Persecution) 13.24 But in those days after that suffering, the sun will be darkened, and the moon will not give its light, 13.25 and the stars will be falling from heaven, and the powers in the heavens will be shaken.	(16.5 Testing fire of persecution) 16.6a And then shall appear the signs of truth 16.6b first the sign of *the Son of Man* in heaven [Rev. 1.7 and *then* all the tribes of the earth will mourn.]
13.26 And then they will see 'the Son of man coming in clouds' with power and great glory. 13.27 And he will send out the angels, and gather his elect from the four winds, from *one* end of heaven *to another.*	16.8 Then the world will see the Lord coming *on* the clouds of heaven, 16.6c next the sign of the *with a loud* trumpet call 16.6d and third the resurrection of the dead.

Matthew's text may, therefore, plausibly be explained as a conflation of Mk 13.24-27 and *Did.* 16.6, 8. By contrast, the *Didache*'s text is difficult to account for on the basis of its supposed dependence on Mt. 24.

First, there is the outstanding problem of the redacted version of Dan. 7.13 which is found in Mk 13.26, Mt. 24.30 and *Did.* 16.8. As noted in the excursus above, these redactional changes create a snug fit between Dan. 7.13 and the structure of the *Didache*'s apocalypse. If the Didachist inherited this version of Dan. 7.13 from Matthew, then it is a remarkable coincidence that the redactional activity of Mark and Matthew should have prepared Dan. 7.13 so neatly for its insertion into the *Didache*'s closing eschatological discourse.

Second, those who propose the *Didache*'s dependence on Mt. 24 must explain how the Didachist 'alluded' to Matthew, while so heavily favouring those parts of that gospel which do not come from Mark. This is true to the extent that all the parallels between *Did.* 16.6, 8 and Mt. 24.30-31 occur in Matthew's non-Markan material, with the single exception of the redacted version of Dan. 7.13.

Third, there is the puzzle of the relative order of the signs of the Judge's arrival in Matthew's Gospel and the *Didache*. If the *Didache* depended on Matthew, then it is extraordinary that the three signs of truth, which announce the coming of the Judge, should be constructed out of non-Markan elements of Matthew's text which both precede and *follow* the coming of that Judge in Matthew's account. If signs of the Judge's coming were sought by the *Didache* from Matthew's text, then it is hard to explain why the large collection of signs listed in Mt. 24.29-30a (parallel to those in Mk 12.24-25 and Rev. 1.7) were not quarried for this purpose.

In summary, the relationship between *Did.* 16.6, 8 and Mt. 24.30-31 may credibly be understood as the product of Matthew's conflation of teaching on 'the coming of the Judge' from both Mk 13.24-27 and *Did.* 16.6, 8. By contrast, it is difficult to reconstruct circumstances under which the *Didache*'s text could have arisen from a dependence on Mt. 24.

2.3. *Matthew 16.27 and* Didache *16.8-9*

The lost ending of the *Didache*'s apocalypse was reconstructed in Chapter 3, where it was concluded that a line with a similar function to that of 'reward each according to his deeds' (16.8) is likely to have formed part of the *Didache*'s original text (Chapter 3, section 4.4). It was also noted at that point, however, that the similar wording of both *Did.* 16.8-9 and Mt. 16.27 may have been created by the later assimilation of the *Didache*'s text to that of Matthew. This brief section will consider the further possibility that Mt. 16.27 depends directly on the original text of *Did.* 16.8-9.

Synopsis 6: *Judgment according to deeds*

Mk	Mt.	Did.
8.35 <u>ὃς γὰρ ἐὰν θέλῃ</u> <u>τὴν ψυχὴν αὐτοῦ σῶσαι</u> <u>ἀπολέσει αὐτήν· ὃς δ'</u> <u>ἂν ἀπολέσει τὴν ψυχὴν</u> <u>αὐτοῦ ἕνεκεν ἐμοῦ</u> καὶ τοῦ εὐαγγελίου σώσει <u>αὐτήν.</u>	16.25 <u>ὃς γὰρ ἐὰν θέλῃ</u> <u>τὴν ψυχὴν αὐτοῦ σῶσαι</u> <u>ἀπολέσει αὐτήν· ὃς δ'</u> <u>ἂν ἀπολέσῃ τὴν ψυχὴν</u> <u>αὐτοῦ ἕνεκεν ἐμοῦ</u> εὑρήσει <u>αὐτήν.</u>	
8.36 <u>τί γὰρ</u> <u>ὠφελεῖ</u> <u>ἄνθρω</u>πον <u>κερδῆσαι τὸν</u> <u>κόσμον ὅλον</u> καὶ <u>ζημιωθῆ</u>ναι <u>τὴν ψυχὴν</u> <u>αὐτοῦ;</u>	16.26 <u>τί γὰρ</u> <u>ὠφελη</u>θήσεται <u>ἄνθρωπος</u> ἐὰν <u>τὸν</u> <u>κόσμον ὅλον</u> <u>κερδήσῃ τὴν δὲ ψυχὴν</u> <u>αὐτοῦ ζημιωθῇ;</u>	
8.37 τί γὰρ <u>δοῖ</u> <u>ἄνθρωπος ἀντάλλαγμα</u> <u>τῆς ψυχῆς αὐτοῦ;</u>	ἢ τί <u>δώσει</u> <u>ἄνθρωπος ἀντάλλαγμα</u> <u>τῆς ψυχῆς αὐτοῦ;</u>	
8.38 ὃς γὰρ ἐὰν ἐπαισχυνθῇ με καὶ τοὺς ἐμοὺς λόγους ἐν τῇ γενεᾷ ταύτῃ τῇ μοιχαλίδι καὶ ἁμαρτωλῷ, καὶ <u>ὁ υἱὸς τοῦ ἀνθρώπου</u> ἐπαισχυνθήσεται αὐτὸν ὅταν ἔλθῃ <u>ἐν τῇ</u> <u>δόξῃ τοῦ πατρὸς αὐτοῦ</u> <u>μετὰ τῶν ἀγγέλων</u> τῶν ἁγίων.	16.27 μέλλει γὰρ <u>ὁ υἱὸς τοῦ ἀνθρώπου</u> ἔρχεσθαι <u>ἐν τῇ</u> <u>δόξῃ τοῦ πατρὸς αὐτοῦ</u> <u>μετὰ τῶν ἀγγέλων</u> αὐτοῦ, καὶ **τότε** ἀ**πο**δώσει ἑκάστῳ κατὰ τὴν πρᾶξιν αὐτοῦ. 16.28	16.8 **τότε** ὄψεται ὁ κόσμος τὸν κύριον **ἐρχόμενον** ἐπάνω τῶν νεφελῶν τοῦ οὐρανοῦ, καὶ πάντες οἱ ἅγιοι μετ' αὐτοῦ ἐπὶ θρόνου **βασιλείας** κατακρῖναι τὸν κοσμοπλάνον καὶ ἀ**πο**δοῦναι ἑκάστῳ κατὰ τὴν πρᾶξιν αὐτοῦ.
9.1 Καὶ ἔλεγεν αὐτοῖς, Ἀμὴν λέγω <u>ὑμῖν ὅτι εἰσίν τινες</u> ὧδε <u>τῶν</u> ἑστηκότων <u>οἵτινες</u> <u>οὐ μὴ γεύσωνται</u> <u>θανάτου ἕως ἂν ἴδωσιν</u> τὴν βασιλείαν τοῦ θεοῦ ἐληλυθυῖαν ἐν δυνάμει.	<u>ἀμὴν λέγω</u> <u>ὑμῖν ὅτι εἰσίν τινες τῶν</u> <u>ὧδε ἑστώτων οἵτινες</u> <u>οὐ μὴ γεύσωνται</u> <u>θανάτου ἕως ἂν ἴδωσιν</u> τὸν υἱὸν τοῦ ἀνθρώπου **ἐρχόμενον** ἐν τῇ βασιλείᾳ αὐτοῦ.	

Synopsis 6 shows that Mt. 16.25-28 follows Mk 8.35–9.1 very closely. Only two significant deviations from Mark's text are made and in both cases a parallel may be found in *Did.* 16.8.

If *Did.* 16.8 were dependent on Mt. 16 then, once again, the Didachist would have to be credited with a very particular ability to allude to non-Markan elements of Matthew. It is perhaps simpler to suppose that Matthew has once again conflated Mark's Gospel and the *Didache* at a point where they both address the subject of the coming Judge.

Thus, Matthew deviates from Mark's account of the coming Judge to include a reference to 'his' angels rather than Mark's 'the' angels. This may indicate the influence of *Did.* 16.8, which (in the reconstructed version) states that the Lord comes with all *his* holy ones.

Matthew distinctly deviates from Mark to include a reference to repaying each according to their deeds. This happens to match the record of an event which, according to *Did.* 16.8, also follows the arrival of the Judge.

Matthew further deviates from Mark in changing 'before they see that the kingdom of God has come with power' to, 'before they see the Son of man coming in his kingdom'. This change might also be under the influence of the *Didache*'s (reconstructed) vision of the returning Lord, which has him coming 'on his kingly throne'.

It would be unwise to rest too much on a proposed reconstruction of the lost ending of the *Didache*. However, the pattern of parallels between these three texts is remarkably similar to those considered earlier in this chapter. As such these parallels point towards Matthew's conflation of Mk 8.34–9.1 with *Did.* 16.8, rather than to the *Didache*'s selective dependence on the non-Markan material in Matthew.

2.4. *Matthew 25.31-46 and* Didache *16.8-9*

A notable feature of Matthew's eschatological discourse is that a very high proportion of its narrative elements has some parallel, however distant, with material also to be found in Mark's Gospel, Luke's Gospel and (in the above-mentioned instances) the *Didache*. The largest exception to this rule may be found in Matthew's final judgment scene where the sheep are separated from the goats. Following the reconstruction of *Did.* 16.8-9, however, some distinctive parallels between this final element of Matthew's discourse and the *Didache* may also be found.

Synopsis 7: *Arrival for judgment*

Mk	Mt.	Did.
8.38 ὃς γὰρ ἐὰν ἐπαισχυνθῇ με καὶ τοὺς ἐμοὺς λόγους ἐν τῇ γενεᾷ ταύτῃ τῇ μοιχαλίδι καὶ ἁμαρτωλῷ, καὶ <u>ὁ υἱὸς τοῦ ἀνθρώπου</u> ἐπαισχυνθήσεται αὐτὸν <u>ὅταν ἔλθῃ ἐν τῇ</u> <u>δόξῃ</u> τοῦ πατρὸς <u>αὐτοῦ</u> μετὰ τῶν <u>ἀγγέλων</u> τῶν ἁγίων.	25.31 "<u>Οταν</u> δὲ <u>ἔλθῃ ὁ</u> <u>υἱὸς τοῦ ἀνθρώπου ἐν</u> <u>τῇ δόξῃ αὐτοῦ</u> καὶ πάντες οἱ <u>ἄγγελοι</u> μετ' αὐτοῦ, τότε καθίσει ἐπὶ θρόνου <u>δόξης</u> <u>αὐτοῦ</u>·	16.8 Τότε ὄψεται ὁ κόσμος τὸν κύριον ἐρχόμενον ἐπάνω τῶν νεφελῶν τοῦ οὐρανοῦ, καὶ πάντες οἱ ἅγιοι μετ' αὐτοῦ, ἐπὶ θρόνου βασιλείας
9.1 Then he said to them, 'Truly I say to you, there are some standing here will not taste death defore they see the kingdom of God come in power'. (9.2-8 The transfiguration.)	25.32-46 **Scene of final judgment**	16.9 **Scene of final judgment**

Synopsis 7 shows that the event-line and wording of both passages are closely related. Thus a judge comes, accompanied by others and seated on a throne, to separate all people according to their actions; rewarding the righteous with an inheritance prepared for them and eternal life, while sending the wicked to eternal punishment. This collection of points of contact suggests a literary relationship of some kind between these two passages.

The *Didache*'s dependence on Mt. 25.31 is unlikely, however, because, as Synopsis 7 illustrates, this relationship would require the Didachist to change *every* element of Matthew which also agrees with Mark. Thus, Matthew and Mark's 'ὁ υἱὸς τοῦ ἀνθρώπου' becomes 'τὸν Κύριον' in the *Didache*; Matthew and Mark's 'ὅταν ἔλθῃ' becomes 'ἐρχόμενον' in the *Didache*; Matthew and Mark's 'ἐν τῇ δόξῃ (τοῦ πατρὸς) αὐτοῦ' becomes 'ἐπάνω τῶν νεφελῶν τοῦ οὐρανοῦ' in the *Didache*; and Matthew and Mark's 'ἄγγελοι' become 'ἅγιοι' in the *Didache*.

　　The pattern of relationship between these three texts is more easily explained if Matthew's Gospel here conflates Mk 8.38 and *Did.* 16.8. In this case Matthew may be seen as leading into an expansion of the *Didache*'s judgment scene by combining the *Didache*'s vision of the coming Judge with a parallel scene in Mark's Gospel. This pattern accounts for all of Matthew's deviations from Mark (with the exception of the detail that the Judge 'shall sit' on the throne), including the fact that, like the *Didache*, Matthew includes a scene of universal judgment, where this is absent from Mark.[10]

　　If Mt. 25.31 is most readily understood as a conflation of Mk 8.38 and *Did.* 16.8, then it follows that the small similarities between the scene of judgment in *Did.* 16.8-9 and Mt. 24.32–25.45 (see Synopsis 8) may also be seen as due to Matthew's dependence on the *Didache*. Matthew's judgment scene may be either an imaginative expansion on the idea of repayment for actions (*Did.* 16.8) and the virtue of being a 'sheep' (*Did.* 16.3), or a conflation of the *Didache* with some other vision of judgment.

Synopsis 8: *The universal judgment*

Did.	Mt.
16.8 τότε ὄψεται ὁ κόσμος τὸν κύριον ἐρχόμενον ἐπάνω τῶν νεφελῶν τοῦ οὐρανοῦ,	25.31 Ὅταν δὲ ἔλθῃ ὁ υἱὸς τοῦ ἀνθρώπου ἐν τῇ δόξῃ αὐτοῦ
καὶ πάντες οἱ ἅγιοι μετ' αὐτοῦ, ἐπὶ θρόνου βασιλείας κατακρίναι τὸν κοσμοπλάνον	**καὶ πάντες οἱ ἄγγελοι μετ' αὐτοῦ**, τότε καθίσει **ἐπὶ θρόνου** δόξης αὐτοῦ· 25.32 καὶ συναχθήσονται ἔμπροσθεν αὐτοῦ πάντα τὰ ἔθνη, καὶ ἀφορίσει αὐτοὺς ἀπ' ἀλλήλων, ὥσπερ ὁ ποιμὴν ἀφορίζει τὰ πρόβατα ἀπὸ
καὶ ἀποδοῦναι ἑκάστῳ κατὰ τὴν πρᾶξιν αὐτοῦ.	τῶν ἐρίφων, 25.33 καὶ στήσει τὰ μὲν πρόβατα ἐκ δεξιῶν αὐτοῦ τὰ δὲ ἐρίφια ἐξ εὐωνύμων. 25.34 τότε ἐρεῖ ὁ βασιλεὺς τοῖς ἐκ δεξιῶν αὐτοῦ, Δεῦτε, οἱ
16.9b **κληρονομοῦντες** ἐκεῖνα, ἃ ὀφθαλμὸς οὐκ	εὐλογημένοι τοῦ πατρός μου, **κληρονομήσατε** τὴν **ἡτοιμασμένην ὑμῖν βασιλείαν ἀπὸ**

　　10.　Certainties in this matter are even less readily available than usual, given that the lines 'καὶ πάντες οἱ ἅγιοι μετ' αὐτοῦ' and 'ἐπὶ θρόνου βασιλείας' are part of my reconstruction of the lost ending of the *Didache*. However, some additional support may be found for this reconstruction inasmuch as it accounts for almost every element of Matthew's text which is non-Markan. If the reconstruction were merely an assimilation to Matthew's text, then the complete omission of the Markan material in Matthew would require a high level of coincidence.

Did.	Mt.
εἶδεν καὶ οὓς οὐκ ἤκουσεν καὶ ἐπὶ καρδίαν ἀνθρώπου οὐκ ἀνέβη, ἃ ἡτοίμασεν ὁ θεὸς τοῖς ἀγαπῶσιν αὐτόν.	καταβολῆς κόσμου· 25.35 ἐπείνασα γὰρ καὶ ἐδώκατέ μοι φαγεῖν, ἐδίψησα καὶ ἐποτίσατέ με, ξένος ἤμην καὶ συνηγάγετέ με, 25.36 γυμνὸς καὶ περιεβάλετέ με, ἠσθένησα καὶ ἐπεσκέψασθέ με, ἐν φυλακῇ ἤμην καὶ ἤλθατε πρός με. 25.37 τότε ἀποκριθήσονται αὐτῷ οἱ δίκαιοι λέγοντες, Κύριε, πότε σε εἴδομεν πεινῶντα καὶ ἐθρέψαμεν, ἢ διψῶντα καὶ ἐποτίσαμεν; 25.38 πότε δέ σε εἴδομεν ξένον καὶ συνηγάγομεν, ἢ γυμνὸν καὶ περιεβάλομεν; 25.39 πότε δέ σε εἴδομεν ἀσθενοῦντα ἢ ἐν φυλακῇ καὶ ἤλθομεν πρός σε; 25.40 καὶ ἀποκριθεὶς ὁ βασιλεὺς ἐρεῖ αὐτοῖς, Ἀμὴν λέγω ὑμῖν, ἐφ' ὅσον ἐποιήσατε ἑνὶ τούτων τῶν ἀδελφῶν μου τῶν ἐλαχίστων, ἐμοὶ ἐποιήσατε.
	25.41 Τότε ἐρεῖ καὶ τοῖς ἐξ εὐωνύμων, Πορεύεσθε ἀπ' ἐμοῦ οἱ κατηραμένοι εἰς τὸ πῦρ τὸ αἰώνιον τὸ ἡτοιμασμένον τῷ διαβόλῳ καὶ τοῖς ἀγγέλοις αὐτοῦ· 25.42 ἐπείνασα γὰρ καὶ οὐκ ἐδώκατέ μοι φαγεῖν, ἐδίψησα καὶ οὐκ ἐποτίσατέ με, 43 ξένος ἤμην καὶ οὐ συνηγάγετέ με, γυμνὸς καὶ οὐ περιεβάλετέ με, ἀσθενὴς καὶ ἐν φυλακῇ καὶ οὐκ ἐπεσκέψασθέ με. 25.44 τότε ἀποκριθήσονται καὶ αὐτοὶ λέγοντες, Κύριε, πότε σε εἴδομεν πεινῶντα ἢ διψῶντα ἢ ξένον ἢ γυμνὸν ἢ ἀσθενῆ ἢ ἐν φυλακῇ καὶ οὐ διηκονήσαμέν σοι; 25.45 τότε ἀποκριθήσεται αὐτοῖς λέγων,
16.9a τότε ἀπελεύσονται οἱ μέν πονηροὶ εἰς αἰώνιον κόλασιν, οἱ δὲ δίκαιοι πορεύσονται εἰς ζωὴν αἰώνιον,	Ἀμὴν λέγω ὑμῖν, ἐφ' ὅσον οὐκ ἐποιήσατε ἑνὶ τούτων τῶν ἐλαχίστων, οὐδὲ ἐμοὶ ἐποιήσατε. 25.46 καὶ ἀπελεύσονται οὗτοι εἰς κόλασιν αἰώνιον, οἱ δὲ δίκαιοι εἰς ζωὴν αἰώνιον.

The concluding verse of Matthew's judgment scene, and of the whole eschatological discourse (25.46), is closely related to *Did.* 16.9. These verses are so similar that, taken in isolation, it would be difficult to establish the direction of dependence. In context, however, the evidence for the dependence of Mt. 25.31 on *Did.* 16.8 points towards Matthew's continued dependence on the *Didache* in Mt. 25.46. This view is perhaps further supported by the observation that the construction of *Did.* 16.9 conforms to the structural priorities of the composer of the *Didache*'s apocalypse (see Chapter 3, section 4.2).

3. *A Further Challenge to* Didache *16's Direct Use of* Matthew's Gospel

Following the completion of the immediately preceding section, it is possible to offer a further challenge to the case for *Did.* 16's direct use of Matthew's Gospel.

It was noted in Chapter 3 that the eschatological discourse recorded in *Did.* 16 is a tightly structured and balanced whole (cf. Chapter 3, section 4.8). The view that this discourse was directly inspired by Matthew's Gospel requires that its author chose to create this discourse by working together Mt. 16.27; 24.10-12, 30, 31; 25.31-46. This arrangement requires, not only the taking of inspiration from dispersed elements of Matthew's work, but also the taking of elements from passages that, almost exclusively, occur at points where Matthew deviates from an otherwise close following of Mark's Gospel.

All things are theoretically possible, but this explanation for the creation of the *Didache*'s eschatological discourse stretches credulity to its limit.

4. *Conclusion: Matthew's Gospel and* Didache *16*

I mentioned earlier that the case for Matthew's direct dependence on *Did.* 16 requires the defence of four propositions. First, that there is a definite connection of some kind between the two texts. Second, that that connection cannot be due to the *Didache*'s direct or indirect dependence on Matthew's Gospel. Third, that direct dependence by Matthew upon *Did.* 16 is plausible or probable. Fourth, that Matthew's Gospel and *Did.* 16 are unlikely to have shared a common tradition. A defence has now been offered for the first three propositions (the fourth will be considered shortly).

First, it has been noted that there is wide evidence for, and universal acceptance of, a connection of some kind between *Did.* 16 and Mt. 24.

Second, the presence, in *Did.* 16.8, of an original redaction of Dan. 7.13, which then reappears in Mark's and Matthew's Gospels, suggests that the *Didache* cannot depend on either of these texts. Further, the creation of the closely tailored eschatological discourse in *Did.* 16.3-6, 8-9 via allusion to, or straightforward dependence on, Mt. 16.27; 24.10-12, 30-31; 25.31-32 was shown to require eccentric selections from Matthew's non-Markan material on the part of the Didachist.

Third, it has been shown, in section 2 above, that the relationship between Mark's Gospel, *Did.* 16 and Mt. 16, 24 and 25 may plausibly be explained by Matthew's conflation of Mark's Gospel and the *Didache* where they address similar subjects.

At this stage, therefore, it is possible to observe that there is no obstacle to the view that Matthew depended directly on the unified discourse preserved in *Did.* 16.3-6, 8-9. Indeed, the proposal that Matthew conflated related material from Mark's Gospel and *Did.* 16 provides an explanation for both the similarities and the differences between Mt. 24.10-12 = *Did.* 16.3-5; Mt. 24.30-31 = *Did.* 16.6, 8; and Mt. 16.27 = *Did.* 16.8. An explanation for Matthew's deviations from his otherwise largely faithful use of Mk 8.34–9.1 and 13.1-32 is also offered by this hypothesis.

The case for Matthew's direct use of *Did.* 16 is further supported by the conclusions drawn in Chapters 11 and 12, above; if Matthew knew the Modifying Teacher layer and/or the Prophet layer, then there is every reason to suppose that he also knew the Peri/Base layer. In addition, Matthew's direct knowledge of *Did.* 16 is consistent with the observation made in the introduction to Part II, where it was noted that Matthew's knowledge of the *Didache* provides the simplest explanation for the spread of contacts between the first three layers of the *Didache* and Matthew's text.

Having said all this, there is one further possible explanation for the presence of material held in common by Matthew's Gospel and *Did.* 16. This is the widely held view that Mt. 24 and *Did.* 16 depend on common tradition.[11] This hypothesis was developed by scholars who considered it unlikely, for some of the reasons discussed above, that *Did.* 16 depended directly on Mt. 24. This belief, combined with the assumption that *Did.* 16 cannot pre-date Matthew's Gospel, led to the proposal that both texts depend on a common source(s) or tradition(s).

This view has two important weaknesses. First, the assumption that *Did.* 16 could not pre-date Matthew's Gospel (and thus could not be a direct source for it) is without foundation. Not only is there no positive basis for such an assumption,[12] but there are strong indications of the extreme antiquity of the *Didache*'s eschatological discourse (see the excursus earlier in this chapter). Second, if the case for Matthew's direct use of *Did.* 16 is plausible, then the introduction of further hypothetical entities is unneces-

11. This is the view expressed by: Köster (1957: 173–90); Audet (1958); Glover (1958: 21–25) and Kloppenborg (1979).

12. Possible bases for this assumption are noted in the introductory chapter, and an attempt to expose their weaknesses is offered in the course of Part I.

sary. Not only that, but it is extremely difficult to reconstruct a suitable tradition/source for such a role. This is the case because *Did.* 16.3-6, 8-9 shows every sign of being an original work inspired by a number of different ideas and sources.[13] It is highly unlikely, therefore, that Matthew should happen to have supplemented his Markan source with material similarly, but independently, formed. A more realistic possibility is that *Did.* 16.3-6, 8-9 was known by Matthew as a separate discourse prior to its incorporation into the *Didache*. However, in view of the numerous other points of contact between the rest of the *Didache* and Matthew's Gospel[14] it is more likely that Matthew knew *Did.* 16.3-6, 8-9 as the conclusion of 'The Teaching of the Lord, by the Twelve Apostles, to the Gentiles', and thus used it to supplement Mark's words of Jesus with regard to the events of the End.

13. Old Testament sources for this discourse appear to include Dan. 7.13, Zech. 14.5 and Isa. 64.1-4 (Chapter 3, § 4.3.)

14. In addition to the points of contact noted above and below in Chapters 11 to 15, there is also a possible link between *Did.* 16.1 and Mt. 24.42 and 25.1-13 as noted, for example, by Court (1981: 113) and Tuckett (1996: 108). This contact is not considered in full because the clarity of any link with Matthew's Gospel is blurred by similarities between *Did.* 16.1, Mk 13.35 and Lk. 12.35. However, two observations may be made regarding this point of connection. First, there is no indication that *Did.* 16.1 must presuppose the existence of Matthew's Gospel. To this effect Tuckett (1996: 108) admits: 'Certainty is not possible... There is nothing here that is so clearly MattR that it could only have derived from Matthew's gospel.' This point having been noted, it is also interesting to observe that *Did.* 16.1-6, 8-9 (as a whole) contains a number of the elements seen by Wenham (1984) as likely to have appeared in an eschatological scheme known by Matthew, Mark, Luke and Paul. Wenham (1984: 365) offers the concluding observation: 'If anything, Matthew appears from our study as the evangelist who most often and most fully reproduces the pre-synoptic form of the tradition'. This conclusion chimes with evidence gathered from elsewhere in the present volume. For example, the excursus in this chapter argues that *Did.* 16.8 is presupposed by Mk 13.26. It is significant, therefore, that an *additional* parallel between Mark's little apocalypse and *Did.* 16 occurs at Mk 13.35 = *Did.* 16.1. This is suggestive of Mark's knowledge of the tightly structured apocalypse quoted in *Did.* 16.3-6, 8-9 in its present context. If this is the case, then there is no possibility (assuming Markan priority) that *Did.* 16.1 was written after the creation of Matthew's Gospel. Under these circumstances it is most likely that Matthew knew the *Didache*'s apocalypse in its present context, rather than as an independently existing tradition.

Chapter 14

MATTHEW'S GOSPEL AND *DIDACHE* 1.1-6

The sayings source 'Q' has commanded keen scholarly interest over the last century. Catchpole (1993: 23-25) suggests that one of the best arguments for the existence of a tradition shared by Matthew and Luke may be found in the slight differences between Matthew's and Luke's renderings of 'turn the other cheek' and 'give your cloak/tunic as well'. He suggests that the tradition behind these sayings was concerned with insults and so probably contained Matthew's version of 'turn the other cheek' and Luke's version of 'give your tunic as well'. Thus he states (1993: 25):

> The content of the first part of the bipartite saying in Matthew matches the content of the second part of the comparable saying in Luke. Both Matthew and Luke have in different ways marred it… [it is] likely that we have chanced upon an original saying which was concerned with the subject of insult and treated it by focussing on two of the most damaging forms that insult might take.

It is striking that Catchpole's reconstruction of this element of 'Q' is remarkably similar to *Did.* 1.4b:

> If someone strikes you on your right cheek, turn your other to him also, …
> If someone takes your coat, give him your shirt also.

Given this similarity it is surprising that there is no mention of *Did.* 1.4 in Catchpole's discussion. This raises the further question of why so few of the resources expended in the pursuit of 'Q' have overflowed into the study of the extant sayings in *Did.* 1.3-5a. Once again, the assumption that these sayings post-date the gospels is the likely cause. One of the aims of this chapter is to challenge that assumption.

At the start of an analysis of the cluster of connections between Matthew's Gospel and *Did.* 1.1-6, three points may be recalled. As noted in the introduction to Part II, Matthew's direct knowledge of the first three layers of the *Didache* (and the various complete traditions and quotations incorporated therein) provides the simplest explanation for the spread of contacts between the two texts. Second, *Did.* 1.1-5a is modified by a contribution of the modifying teacher at 1.5b-6. If, as argued in Chapter 11, Matthew knew *Did.* 1.5c, then it is highly likely that he also knew the preceding verses thereby modified. Third, according to the compositional analysis offered in Part I, *Did.* 16 and *Did.* 1.1-6 both belong to the same redactional layer. On this basis, Matthew's direct knowledge of *Did.* 16, as argued in the preceding chapter, implies his knowledge of the rest of the Peri/Base layer, including *Did.* 1.1-6.

These initial points serve as a reminder of the working hypothesis that this chapter will explore and test; contacts between *Did.* 1.1-6 and Matthew's Gospel are best explained by the direct dependence of the latter on the former.

Before entertaining the possibility that Matthew directly depended upon *Did.* 1.1-6 it is necessary to begin with an important ground-clearing exercise. Thus, section 1, below, will consider the feasibility of Matthew's dependence on the *Didache* in each individual case. Section 2 will then argue that the clustering within *Did.* 1.1-6 of contacts with Matthew's Gospel indicates Matthew's direct knowledge of this passage. Third, by way of support for this conclusion, sections 3 and 4 offer an explanation for the differences, as well as the similarities, between parallel passages in Matthew's Gospel and *Did.* 1.1-6.

1. *The Points of Contact between Matthew's Gospel and* Didache *1.1-6*

The purpose of this section is to show that Matthew's direct use of the various elements of *Did.* 1.1-6 is possible at each point of contact, even if other dependency relationships are also, at this stage at least, comparably feasible. This programme requires the demonstration that no part of *Did.* 1.1-6 *demands* the prior existence of Matthew's Gospel. If this much may be achieved, then Matthew's use of *Did.* 1.1-6 remains a possibility and the programme of this chapter may continue.

1.1. *The Two Ways Saying and the Golden Rule: Matthew 7.12, 13-14 and* Didache *1.1, 2e*
While the two ways saying and the golden rule are not especially rare teachings, two features of their use in Matthew's Gospel and the *Didache* suggest a link between the two texts. First, the two sayings are closely, and unusually, juxtaposed in both cases (Massaux 1993: 147). Second, they share a common appreciation of the golden rule as a summary of the Law (Jefford 1989: 36-37). This is expressed explicitly in Mt. 7.12 and is

implicit in the *Didache* inasmuch as *Did.* 1.2 provides a summary of the Law that is then expanded in the teaching that follows (cf. 1.3a and 2.1).

Taken in isolation, there is no basis for determining the direction of any dependence between *Did.* 1.1 and Mt. 7.13. The two ways saying was widespread in both Christian and Jewish circles, and so it is not possible to determine whether the *Didache* or Matthew preserves an older form. So far as this saying is concerned, therefore, there is no reason to suppose that the *Didache* must have taken this concept from Mt. 7.13, or vice versa. This means that Matthew's use of the *Didache* remains possible at this point, as does the *Didache*'s use of Matthew's Gospel.

Tuckett argues that the appearance of the golden rule in both *Did.* 1.2b and Mt. 7.12 may be accounted for as the product of the *Didache*'s direct dependence on Matthew. He writes (1996: 107): 'The version of the golden rule in *Did.* 1.2d may also be derived from Matthew. It is true that the version given here uses the negative form which is found elsewhere in Jewish sources.' It should be recognized, however, quite how unusual is the positive form of the golden rule. Its appearance in Matthew's and Luke's Gospels represent its earliest known occurrence.[1] Even the Western text of Acts 15, despite the positive version in Luke's Gospel, has the rule in its negative form. By contrast the negative form was, as Tuckett notes, available in Jewish sources. This means that the *Didache*'s version of the golden rule need not depend on Matthew's. Consequently there is, once again, no obstacle to the possibility that Matthew here presupposes the *Didache*'s version.

1.2. *The Double Love Command: Matthew 22.37-40 and* Didache *1.2b-d*

The command to love God and love your neighbour is by no means uniquely shared by Matthew's Gospel and the *Didache*. However, the use of πρώτη...δευτέρα in connection with this type of double love command is an unusual feature shared by both texts. Mk 12.28, 31 also uses πρώτη...δευτέρα, but the emphasis on two requirements to love is less marked in this version because of Mark's inclusion of the *Shema* as the headline of the first command. Matthew's omission of the *Shema* means that his first command is, primarily, to love God. This increases the parallel between the double love commands in Mt. 22.37-39 and *Did.* 1.2b-d, which in turn suggests that some form of relationship between the two texts is possible at this point.

---

1.   Köster (1957: 168–69) refers to the rarity of the positive golden rule. *1 Clement* 13.2c and Justin, *Dial.* 93.1. contain the only other occurrences in early Christian literature. Köster notes that the positive form appears to have been introduced by the gospels.

Köster's (1972: 172) observations regarding the pre-redactional nature of the *Didache*'s double love command (relative to Matthew) may point towards the *Didache* as the source of this formation. However, the direction of any dependence cannot be more firmly established with the evidence currently in hand. This means that *Did.* 1.2b-d need not presuppose the existence of Mt. 22.37-39, and thus Matthew's use of the *Did.* 1.2b-d remains a viable possibility.

1.3. Lex talionis *and Love for Enemies: Matthew 5.38-48 and* Didache *1.3b-5a*

Tuckett's analyses of the various points of connection between Mt. 5.38-48 and the *Did.* 1.3-5a are characterized by scholarly caution regarding the weight that should be placed on each piece of evidence. In fact there are almost no points where Tuckett declares with any force that the *Didache* must presuppose Matthew's Gospel. The occasion when Tuckett is prepared to express most confidence is in his observation that *Did.* 1.3b uses διώκω in agreement with Mt. 5.44b against Lk. 6.28b. Thus, he argues (1996: 116):

> The word may well be a Matthean favourite (cf. the use in the penultimate beatitude Mt 5:10, which is widely regarded as due to MattR). Hence the likelihood is that it is due to MattR here. One could argue that the word is too general to carry much weight here; but against this is the fact that the motif of persecution is not one that really dominates this, or any, section of the *Didache*. It is therefore unlikely to have been added by the Didachist himself. This small agreement between the *Didache* and Matthew may thus be an instance where the *Didache* presupposes MattR and hence Matthew's finished gospel.

By Tuckett's own confession the only factor that lends support to his case here is the *Didache*'s supposed general lack of interest in persecution, with the exception of this instance. This observation is not quite correct, nor would it be relevant if it were correct. The element of inaccuracy lies in the recurrence of an important reference to persecution in *Did.* 16.4-5. On the evidence of Chapter 3, section 1 the Christian's response to persecution is a determining factor of their ultimate fate, and, according to the layer scheme presented in Part I, *Did.* 16 formed part of the same layer as *Did.* 1.3b. On this basis responses to persecution may be seen as being of continued interest to the original author of the text.

The more important weakness in Tuckett's case is that it assumes that the author of 1.3b was also the author of the rest of the *Didache*, or at least some significant portion of that text. However, the Three Rules saying in

which διώκω appears is likely to have been already independently formed
prior to its incorporation into the collection of sayings in *Did.* 1.3b-5a (cf.
Chapter 4, section 3). For Tuckett's argument to carry any weight, therefore, he must show that persecution is a motif that is recognizably alien to
the Three Rules saying in *Did.* 1.3b. However, as Rordorf (1991: 402)
notes:

> In fact the verb διώκω can scarcely carry the weight given it by Tuckett;
> on the contrary, I believe precisely that the specifically *Didache* expression
> '*fast* for those who persecute you' presupposes a concrete background of
> persecution from the Jewish side.[2]

Not only is there a lack of any concrete evidence that *Did.* 1.3-5a must
presuppose the existence of Matthew's Gospel, but there is also evidence
that the *Didache* here preserves sayings that are more ancient than those
found in either Matthew's or Luke's Gospels. As noted at the start of this
chapter, Catchpole's (1993: 23-25) reconstruction of the tradition behind
Matthew's and Luke's versions of 'turn the other cheek' and 'give your
cloak/tunic as well' is remarkably similar to *Did.* 1.4b. This suggests either
a knowledge of the evangelists' source on the part of the Didachist, or that
the *Didache* was used and adapted by both Matthew and Luke.

Further details of the case for Matthew's use of *Did.* 1.3-5a will be set
out in due course. In the meantime it need only be noted that Matthew's use
of these verses remains a possibility, if only one possibility among others.

1.4. *The Last Penny: Matthew 5.26 and* Didache *1.5c*
An argument for Matthew's direct use of *Did.* 1.5c has already been
presented in Chapter 11, section 2.

2. *The Implication of Multiple Points of Contact within* Didache *1.1-6*

The discussion in section 1, above, set out to establish that there are
several points of contact between Matthew's Gospel and *Did.* 1.1-6 and
that none of these *requires* the *Didache*'s knowledge of Matthew's Gospel.
This means that Matthew's knowledge of *Did.* 1.1-6 remains a possibility.
The aim of this section is to go beyond this point and show that Matthew's
use of these verses is not merely possible, but probable.

To achieve this result it is necessary to recall observations made in Part
I regarding the compositional history of *Did.* 1.1-6. Here it was observed
that these verses became part of the whole in four separate stages:

2.   The article which I cite as Tuckett (1996) was first published in 1989.

TW: At the root of everything lies the original Two Ways document. This accounts for *Did.* 1.1-2a, c and 2.2-7; 3.8–5.2a.

LS: Prior to the incorporation of this Two Ways teaching into the *Didache* a Law Summary including the second half of the double love command and the golden rule was added (1.2b, d, e), along with a linking line to restore the flow of the text (2.1) (Chapter 4, section 6).

SO: Upon the creation of the Base layer of the *Didache* the Two Ways teaching was taken (already including 1.2b, d, e and 2.1) and a discreet collection of sayings (1.3b-5a) was inserted into it as a means of fleshing out the significance of the commands in 1.2. The creator of the *Didache* introduced this collection of sayings with 'Τούτων δὲ τῶν λόγων ἡ διδαχή ἐστιν αὕτη' (1.3a), and also inserted the comment 'καὶ ἔσῃ τέλειος' (1.4b(r)) (cf. Chapter 4, section 3).

MT: Some time later a teacher found it necessary to offer a modification of the rules for giving and generosity set out in *Did.* 1.4b-5a. To this end the modifying teacher added *Did.* 1.5b-6, which itself includes the quotation of an external authority in 1.6 (see Chapter 7, section 4).

Further, it was noted that *Did.* 1.3b-5a comprises a collection of separate sayings gathered around a central gnome. These sayings appear to have been formed independently of one another, and to have been virtually unaltered in the course of their collection (cf. Chapter 4, section 3).

> SO.a: 1.3b a Three Rules saying.
> SO.b: 1.3c a saying on making friends of enemies.
> SO.c: 1.4a a saying regarding fleshly passions.
> SO.d: 1.4b a set of sayings regarding response to insults.
> SO.e: 1.5a a saying regarding giving.

This compositional history means that the text of *Did.* 1.1-6 may be seen as ultimately deriving from ten originally separate points of origin: the Two Ways source, the Law Summary, an 'onion' of five originally separate sayings (with redactional comment at 1.3a and 1.4b(r)), and a later modification of those sayings, which itself included the quotation of an external authority.

By contrast, there is good evidence to suggest that Matthew's Sermon on the Mount, although dependent on various different sources, was created by one author at one time, and further, that this author reshaped his sources to create a text that conformed to a unified style and agenda.

Given the contrasting compositional histories of *Did.* 1.1-6 and Mt. 5–7 it is informative to note the pattern of contacts between the two texts. The lettering system relates to the separately conceived elements of *Did.* 1.1-6, as set out above:

The last penny:	Mt. 5.26 = *Did.* 1.5c	MT
Turn the other cheek:	Mt. 5.39 = *Did.* 1.4b	SO.d
Tunic and cloak:	Mt. 5.40 = *Did.* 1.4b	SO.d
The extra mile:	Mt. 5.41 = *Did.* 1.4b	SO.d
The request:	Mt. 5.42 = *Did.* 1.5a	SO.e
Response to enemies:	Mt. 5.44 = *Did.* 1.3b	SO.a
Character of Father:	Mt. 5.45 = *Did.* 1.5a	SO.e
As the Gentiles do:	Mt. 5.47 = *Did.* 1.3c	SO.b
Be perfect:	Mt. 5.48 = *Did.* 1.4b(r)	P/B
The golden rule:	Mt. 7.12 = *Did.* 1.2e	LS
The two ways:	Mt. 7.13 = *Did.* 1.1	TW

According to this analysis, Matthew's Sermon on the Mount exhibits contact with eight of the ten separate elements within *Did.* 1.1-6. This circumstance may be explained in one of three ways. Either eight individual, self-contained, direct and indirect contributions to *Did.* 1.1-6 were forged in consultation with Matthew's Gospel, or Matthew found *Did.* 1.1-6 as an already composed unit and used it to supplement his record of the teaching of Jesus, or the several contributors to *Did.* 1.1-6 all happened to share the same tradition(s) that were also used by Matthew.

The first of these options is difficult to sustain because it requires several separate units to be coincidentally created in consultation with Matthew's Gospel. Not only that, none of these units fully reproduces Matthew's version of the sayings concerned (despite their inherent authority as the reported words of Jesus). This means that each of the contributors to *Did.* 1.1-6 must be supposed to have had a motive for deliberately non-quoting or merely alluding to Matthew's Gospel.

The second option, Matthew's direct knowledge of *Did.* 1.1-6, creates no difficulties. The similar treatment of material from different layers of the *Didache* is to be expected if Matthew knew *Did.* 1.1-6 as a completed whole.[3] The elements of smoothing and development are also explicable if Matthew found this group of individual sayings and chose to iron out the redundancies and incongruencies among them.

---

3.   An explanation for the variation between parallel sayings in Matthew's Gospel and the *Didache* is offered in §§ 3 and 4, below.

Given that Matthew's direct knowledge of *Did.* 1.1-6 provides a satis-factory explanation for the relationship between these two texts, there is no particular reason to multiply entities by considering the possible inter-vention of a common tradition or traditions. However, this view is the-oretically possible and thus demands attention.

The theory that each contributor to *Did.* 1.1-6 referred to tradition(s) also used by Matthew is unlikely to be correct for one of two reasons. If a single common tradition is proposed, then the creation of *Did.* 1.1-6 must be seen as a piece-by-piece *reconstruction* of that original source. In the end this hypothesis suffers from very similar difficulties to the idea that the contributors to the *Didache* each faithfully consulted Matthew's Gospel and so built up a composite parallel to a unified whole. Alternatively, if more than one common tradition was involved, then it must be supposed that the direct and indirect contributors to the *Didache* each happened to consult and bring together the same separate traditions, at different times, that were also consulted and brought together by Matthew, at one time. The larger the number of shared traditions the more coincidence is required for the parallel collections in both Matthew's Gospel and *Did.* 1.1-6.

The shared tradition theory is thus in a cleft stick. A single common tradition requires the gradual reconstruction by the direct and indirect con-tributors to *Did.* 1.1-6 of their own source; multiple common traditions require the coincidental gathering of dispersed material by both Matthew and the various contributors to *Did.* 1.1-6. It is simpler, and very much more probable, therefore, to suppose that Matthew, in his search for exam-ples of the teaching of Jesus, found the sayings gathered in *Did.* 1.1-6 and incorporated them into his Sermon.

3. *A General Explanation for the Differences between* Didache *1.1-6 and its Contacts in Matthew's Gospel*

One point that the foregoing analysis of the relationship between *Did.* 1.1-6 and Matthew's Gospel did not consider is a possible explanation for the verbal differences between these two texts, despite their extensive concep-tual similarity. This does not mean that the above conclusion is invalid, since, even without this detail, Matthew's use of *Did.* 1.1-6 remains the simplest explanation for the connections between Matthew's unified Ser-mon and the composite teachings of *Did.* 1.1-6. However, these dissimi-larities in wording present a puzzle that is worthy of further exploration.

Before attempting to provide an explanation for the differences between *Did.* 1.1-6 and similar passages in Matthew's Gospel it is necessary to

consider the relationship of Luke's Gospel to *Did.* 1.1-6 and of Luke's
Gospel to Matthew's Gospel in connection with these passages.

3.1. *Luke's Gospel and* Didache *1.2-5a*

Tuckett (1996: 127-28) is representative of the common view that *Did.*
1.3-5a presupposes the existence of Luke's Gospel:

> The result of this detailed analysis of Did 1:3-5a in relation to the synoptic
> parallels in Mt 5 and Lk 6 shows that this section of the *Didache* appears
> on a number of occasions to presuppose the redactional activity of both
> evangelists, perhaps Luke more clearly than Matthew. This suggests very
> strongly that the *Didache* here presupposes the gospels of Matthew and
> Luke in their finished forms.[4]

Despite the widespread currency of this view, it is, once again, difficult
to sustain in the light of the compositional history of *Did.* 1.1-6 proposed
in Part I. Here it was argued that *Did.* 1.3b-5a is made up of five originally
separate sayings (cf. Chapter 4, section 3), and that *Did.* 1.2b, d-e was not
added to the *Didache* at the same time as this sayings collection. If these
suggestions are correct then *Did.* 1.2-5a may be said to contain material
from the six separate points of origin (labelled LS and SO.a-e).

Compared with the complex compositional history of *Did.* 1.2-5a, Lk.
6.27-38 has a strong structural and thematic unity. This whole unit is built
along similar lines to the collection of sayings in *Did.* 1.3b-5a, although
on a larger scale. Thus the positive golden rule at Lk. 6.31 serves as the
central gnome, which is then expanded and interpreted by the sayings set
on either side. As Kirk (1998: 163) notes: 'Verse 31…has long been a
bone of contention in exegesis of the passage, for it seems to advocate a
mild reciprocity ethic present in most everyday social relations and thus in
collision with the radical ethic of the sayings flanking it'. He goes on to
argue cogently that because the golden rule is hermeneutically open it is
interpreted in terms of the radical sayings with which it is juxtaposed.

A structural presentation of Lk. 6.27-36, illustrating its similarity to the
arrangement of the sayings collection in *Did.* 1.3b-5a, is set out below:

---

4.   The confident tone of this conclusion, with regard to *Did.* 1.1-6's presupposition of Matthew's Gospel, may suggest that I have failed to mention some important
element of Tuckett's case in my § 1, above. This is not the case. The presence of διώκω
in Mt. 5.44 and *Did.* 1.3b is indeed the centrepiece of Tuckett's argument. Its merits are
discussed in § 1.3, above.

6.27   But I say to you that hear,

      Love your enemies,
      do good to the ones hating you,

6.28   bless the ones cursing you.
      pray concerning the ones insulting you.

6.29   To the one striking you (sg) on the cheek, turn also the other;
      and from the one taking your (sg) cloak also the tunic do not prevent.

6.30   To every one asking you – give,
      and from anyone taking what is yours, do not ask back.

6.31   And as you wish that men may do to you, do to them the same.

6.32   And if you love the ones loving you, what thanks is to you?
      For even sinners love those who love them.

6.33   And if you do good to ones doing good to you, what thanks is to you?
      Even sinners do the same.

6.34   And if you lend from whom you hope to receive, what thanks is to you?
      Even sinners lend to sinners to receive as much again.

6.35   But love your enemies,
      and do good
      and lend, nothing despairing
      and your reward will be great,
      and you will be sons of the Most High
      because he is kind to the unthankful and the evil.

6.36   Be merciful just as your Father is merciful.

Above the central gnome at 6.31 (italicized) Luke has created four pairs of sayings. The first two pairs (6.27b, 28) are themselves pairs of opposed responses. The second two pairs (6.29, 30) are also linked in that they both respond to the actions of another, rather than their words or attitudes. The whole set of sayings is suitably headed by 'love your enemies' since all the following sayings may be seen as subordinate to that theme, and they all serve to radicalize the significance of the central golden rule.

In the next three verses (6.32, 33, 34) Luke then elaborates on three positive actions, 'love, do good, lend', that arise from the actions approved of in Lk. 6.27-31. These three actions are then reinforced once again, in this same order, in Lk. 6.35a. The theme of reward, which emerges in 6.32-34, then reappears once more in conjunction with 'love, do good, lend' in Lk. 6.35b. A summary statement, 'Be merciful, just as you Father is merciful', then rounds off the whole at Lk. 6.36.

Luke's discourse thus has a balance of sayings around the central gnome. This structure suggests that this arrangement has not been subsequently disrupted, but that it was put together by one person at one time.[5] The content of the 'onion' also has a unity in its repeated calls to love, do good, and give/lend; however, this unity is not so great as to imply that the whole passage was created independent of any prior sources. In 6.27-31, in particular, the differing structures of the first four pairs of sayings suggests that this group was forged from originally separate sayings.[6] On the basis of this analysis, Lk. 6.27-36 may be described as a unified discourse in that it was forged, by one author at one time, from prior sources.

Given the contrasting compositional histories of *Did.* 1.2-5a and Lk. 6.27-36 the pattern of contacts between the two texts is, once again, informative. The letter annotations relate to the separately conceived elements of *Did.* 1.2-5a, as set out above:

Love your enemies:	Lk. 6.27 = *Did.* 1.3c and 1.3b	SO.b and SO.a
Those hating you:	Lk. 6.27 = *Did.* 1.3c	SO.b
Blessing for curse:	Lk. 6.28 = *Did.* 1.3b	SO.a
The other cheek:	Lk. 6.29 = *Did.* 1.4b	SO.d
Cloak and tunic:	Lk. 6.29 = *Did.* 1.4b	SO.d
Give to all who ask:	Lk. 6.30 = *Did.* 1.5a	SO.e
Do not ask back:	Lk. 6.30 = *Did.* 1.5a	SO.e
Golden rule:	Lk. 6.31 = *Did.* 1.2e	LS
Love the loving ones:	Lk. 6.32 = *Did.* 1.3c	SO.b
What thanks due?:	Lk. 6.32, 33, 34 = *Did.* 1.3c	SO.b

According to this analysis Lk. 6.27-36 exhibits a dense concentration of contacts with five of the six separate elements within *Did.* 1.2-5a. This is more likely to be due to Luke's knowledge of the complex of separate sayings in *Did.* 1.2-5a, which he then forged into a unity, than to repeated homage to Lk. 6.27-36 by five separate and indirect contributors to *Did.* 1.2-5a.[7]

---

5.   This point is frequently disputed by commentators (e.g. Nolland 1989: 297). However, a forward glance to the table of connections between *Did.* 1.2-5a and Lk. 6.27-34 shows that every line of Lk. 6.27-34 is paralleled in *Did.* 1.2-5a. It would be remarkable, therefore, if part of Lk. 6.27-34 were a later interpolation, since neither the structure of the whole, nor the link with *Did.* 1, is disrupted by this putative insertion.

6.   For example, the change in the number of addressees in 6.29, compared with the other sayings in the group suggests that, at some point, this saying did not belong to the group in which it is now found. Incidentally, this variation also occurs in the parallel saying in the *Didache*.

7.   The proposal that *Did.* 1.2-5a depends on a gospel harmony does not ease this

The proposal of Luke's use of *Did.* 1.2-5a also serves to provide a possible explanation for the emergence of a positive form of the golden rule.[8] The *Didache* has a negative version of the rule (1.2d) which, by virtue of compositional history of *Did.* 1, is expanded by a set of positive instructions (1.3-5a). This curious arrangement need not persist if Luke was responsible for reworking the gathered elements of *Did.* 1.2-5a. To iron out this mismatch it is possible that Luke changed the golden rule to a positive form so as to make it consistent with the positive sayings by which it is expanded and interpreted.

In summary, the presence of a dense sequence of contacts between the non-unified text of *Did.* 1.2-5a and the unified text of Lk. 6.27-36 is explained most easily by Luke's reworking of the *Didache*'s separate sayings into an extended set of sayings arranged around a central gnome which he then used as exemplary of the teaching of Jesus in his Sermon on the Plain.

3.2. *Evidence for Direct Contact between Matthew's and Luke's Gospels*

If Luke's Gospel depended upon *Did.* 1.2-5a and Matthew's Gospel also depended upon *Did.* 1.1-6, then important implications follow for the relationship between Matthew's and Luke's Gospels. This is the case because of a number of instances of agreement between these gospels *against* the *Didache*. The texts overleaf show these agreements underlined and highlighted in bold.

The agreements between the gospels against the *Didache* can only be explained by one of three means. Either the collection of agreements is coincidental, or Matthew and Luke both made use of a text (now lost) that had previously gathered material from *Did.* 1.1-6, or Matthew knew Luke's Gospel directly (or vice versa).

The number of agreements against the *Didache* makes pure coincidence highly unlikely. Defence of the second option also incurs considerable complication. This is the case because any intermediate text supposed to have been used independently by both gospel writers must have contained all their points of exclusive agreement. This means ultimately that any proposed hypothetical text must be conceived as being remarkably similar to either Matthew or Luke's version of *Did.* 1. This situation is not impossible, but it does require an unnecessary multiplication of entities when a

---

difficulty. Here it must be proposed that separate contributions to *Did.* 1.2-5a were all made with reference to a gospel harmony in each individual case. Dependence on shared traditions is also problematic for the reasons initially outlined in Chapter 1.

8.   See n. 1 of this Chapter.

Mt. 5.38-48: agreements with Lk. 6.27-36 against Did. *1.1-6*

5.38 Ἠκούσατε ὅτι ἐρρέθη, Ὀφθαλμὸν ἀντὶ ὀφθαλμοῦ καὶ ὀδόντα ἀντὶ ὀδόντος. 5.39 ἐγὼ δὲ λέγω ὑμῖν μὴ ἀντιστῆναι τῷ πονηρῷ· ἀλλ᾽ ὅστις σε ῥαπίζει εἰς τὴν δεξιὰν σιαγόνα [σου], στρέψον αὐτῷ καὶ τὴν ἄλλην· 5.40 καὶ τῷ θέλοντί σοι κριθῆναι καὶ τὸν χιτῶνά σου λαβεῖν, ἄφες αὐτῷ καὶ τὸ ἱμάτιον· 5.41 καὶ ὅστις σε ἀγγαρεύσει μίλιον ἕν, ὕπαγε μετ᾽ αὐτοῦ δύο. 5.42 τῷ αἰτοῦντί σε δός, καὶ τὸν θέλοντα ἀπὸ σοῦ **δανίσασθαι** μὴ ἀποστραφῇς.

5.43 Ἠκούσατε ὅτι ἐρρέθη, Ἀγαπήσεις τὸν πλησίον σου καὶ μισήσεις τὸν ἐχθρόν σου. 5.44 ἐγὼ δὲ λέγω ὑμῖν,

ἀγαπᾶτε τοὺς ἐχθροὺς ὑμῶν καὶ προσεύχεσθε ὑπὲρ τῶν διωκόντων ὑμᾶς, 5.45 ὅπως γένησθε **υἱοὶ** τοῦ πατρὸς ὑμῶν τοῦ ἐν οὐρανοῖς, ὅτι τὸν ἥλιον αὐτοῦ ἀνατέλλει ἐπὶ **πονηροὺς** καὶ ἀγαθοὺς καὶ βρέχει ἐπὶ δικαίους καὶ ἀδίκους. 5.46 ἐὰν γὰρ ἀγαπήσητε τοὺς ἀγαπῶντας ὑμᾶς, τίνα

μισθὸν ἔχετε; οὐχὶ καὶ οἱ τελῶναι τὸ αὐτὸ ποιοῦσιν; 5.47 καὶ ἐὰν ἀσπάσησθε τοὺς ἀδελφοὺς ὑμῶν μόνον, τί περισσὸν ποιεῖτε; οὐχὶ καὶ οἱ ἐθνικοὶ τὸ αὐτὸ ποιοῦσιν;

5.48 Ἔσεσθε οὖν ὑμεῖς τέλειοι **ὡς ὁ πατὴρ ὑμῶν** ὁ οὐράνιος τέλειός **ἐστιν**.

direct connection between the two gospels provides a sufficient explanation of the facts.[9]

In sum, the gospels' agreements against the *Didache* mean that (according to Köster's method for establishing dependency, see Chapter 12 section 1), either Luke knows Matthew's redaction of the *Didache*, or Matthew knows Luke's redaction of the *Didache*. At this point, therefore, I venture the following general explanation for Matthew's inexact reproduction of material derived from *Didache* 1: Matthew conflated *Did.* 1 and Luke's Gospel[10] wherever these two texts present similar material. It is now appropriate to examine this hypothesis in greater detail.

9.   The introduction of a hypothetical source adds further complications to the relationship between Luke's Gospel and the *Didache* in that it requires either Luke to conflate this source with the *Didache* itself, or for this source to preserve a version of *Did.* 1.2-5a which preserves *both* that which is exclusively common to Luke's Gospel and the *Didache, and* that which is exclusively common to Luke's and Matthew's Gospels. In the latter case this hypothetical source would have to be remarkably similar to Lk. 6.27-36 itself.

10.   The possibility that Matthew directly depended on Luke's Gospel has not been widely explored – West (1967–68), Huggins (1992) and Hengel (2000: 169–207) represent notable exceptions to this rule. However, lack of activity in this direction cannot

Lk. 6.27-36: agreements with Mt. 5.38-48 against Did. *1.1-6*

6.27 Ἀλλὰ ὑμῖν λέγω τοῖς ἀκούουσιν,

ἀγαπᾶτε τοὺς ἐχθροὺς ὑμῶν, καλῶς ποιεῖτε τοῖς μισοῦσιν ὑμᾶς,

6.28 εὐλογεῖτε τοὺς καταρωμένους ὑμᾶς,

προσεύχεσθε περὶ τῶν ἐπηρεαζόντων ὑμᾶς.

6.29 τῷ τύπτοντί σε ἐπὶ τὴν σιαγόνα πάρεχε καὶ τὴν ἄλλην,

καὶ ἀπὸ τοῦ αἴροντός σου τὸ ἱμάτιον καὶ τὸν χιτῶνα μὴ κωλύσῃς.

6.30 παντὶ αἰτοῦντί σε δίδου,

καὶ ἀπὸ τοῦ αἴροντος τὰ σὰ μὴ ἀπαίτει.

6.31 καὶ καθὼς θέλετε ἵνα ποιῶσιν ὑμῖν οἱ ἄνθρωποι, ποιεῖτε αὐτοῖς ὁμοίως.

6.32 καὶ εἰ ἀγαπᾶτε τοὺς ἀγαπῶντας ὑμᾶς, ποία ὑμῖν χάρις ἐστίν;

καὶ γὰρ οἱ ἁμαρτωλοὶ τοὺς ἀγαπῶντας αὐτοὺς ἀγαπῶσιν.

6.33 καὶ [γὰρ] ἐὰν ἀγαθοποιῆτε τοὺς ἀγαθοποιοῦντας ὑμᾶς,

ποία ὑμῖν χάρις ἐστίν;

καὶ οἱ ἁμαρτωλοὶ τὸ αὐτὸ ποιοῦσιν.

6.34 καὶ ἐὰν **δανίσητε** παρ' ὧν ἐλπίζετε λαβεῖν, ποία ὑμῖν χάρις [ἐστίν]; καὶ ἁμαρτωλοὶ ἁμαρτωλοῖς **δανίζουσιν** ἵνα ἀπολάβωσιν τὰ ἴσα.

6.35 πλὴν **ἀγαπᾶτε τοὺς ἐχθροὺς ὑμῶν**

καὶ ἀγαθοποιεῖτε

καὶ **δανίζετε** μηδὲν ἀπελπίζοντες·

καὶ ἔσται ὁ **μισθὸς** ὑμῶν πολύς, καὶ ἔσεσθε **υἱοὶ** ὑψίστου,

ὅτι αὐτὸς χρηστός ἐστιν ἐπὶ τοὺς ἀχαρίστους καὶ **πονηρούς**.

6.36 Γίνεσθε οἰκτίρμονες καθὼς [καὶ] **ὁ πατὴρ ὑμῶν** οἰκτίρμων **ἐστίν**.

4. *Matthew's Conflation of* Did. *1.1-6 and Similar Material in Luke's Gospel: A Specific Explanation for Differences between Matthew's Gospel and* Did. *1.1-6*

That Matthew conflated his sources is widely accepted in contemporary Synoptic studies.[11] Matthew's conflationary practice has also been illustrated in earlier elements of this volume. For example, Matthew was described as conflating *Did.* 8 and Mk 12.40-44; 11.25 (Chapter 11,

---

be attributed to the identification of an inpenetrable obstacle to such a possibility, since such has never been established. A full discussion of the synoptic relationships is not within the scope of the present study. All that need be noted for the sake of the current argument is that there is no established reason why Matthew could not have known Luke's Gospel. Thus, there is no bar to an explanation of the differences between Matthew's Gospel and *Did.* 1.1-6 on the basis of Matthew's conflation of similar passages in both Luke's Gospel and the *Didache*.

11. See, for example, Sanders and Davies (1989: 78) and Downing (1980: 38).

section 3); Mk 3.28-29 and *Did.* 11.7 (Chapter 12, section 1); and Mk 13 and *Did.* 16 (Chapter 13, sections 2.1-4). It is therefore possible that Matthew here conflated *Did.* 1.1-6 with similar material that he also found in Luke's Gospel. This theory is now expounded, albeit briefly, in an attempt to provide a possible explanation for some of the differences between Matthew's Gospel and the material which, according to this hypothesis, he drew from *Did.* 1.1-6.

4.1. *Turn the Other Cheek, Tunic and Cloak, Extra Mile, etc.: Lk. 6.29-30 = Mt. 5.38-42* = Did. *1.4b*

Lk.	Mt.	Did.
	5.38 Ἠκούσατε ὅτι ἐρρέθη, Ὀφθαλμὸν ἀντὶ ὀφθαλμοῦ καὶ ὀδόντα ἀντὶ ὀδόντος. 5.39 ἐγὼ δὲ λέγω ὑμῖν μὴ ἀντιστῆναι τῷ πονηρῷ·	1.4b
6.29 τῷ τύπτοντί σε ἐπὶ τὴν <u>σιαγόνα</u> πάρεχε <u>καὶ τὴν ἄλλην,</u>	ἀλλ' ὅστις σε **ῥαπίζει** εἰς τὴν δεξιὰν <u>σιαγόνα</u> [σου], στρέψον αὐτῷ <u>καὶ τὴν ἄλλην·</u>	ἐάν τίς σοι δῷ **ῥάπισμα** εἰς τὴν δεξιὰν σιαγόνα, στρέψον αὐτῷ καὶ τὴν ἄλλην, καὶ ἔσῃ τέλειος·
καὶ ἀπὸ τοῦ αἴροντός σου <u>τὸ ἱμάτιον</u> καὶ <u>τὸν χιτῶνα</u> μὴ κωλύσῃς.	5.40 καὶ τῷ θέλοντί σοι κριθῆναι καὶ <u>τὸν χιτῶνά</u> σου λαβεῖν, ἄφες αὐτῷ <u>καὶ τὸ ἱμάτιον·</u>	
	5.41 καὶ ὅστις σε ἀγγαρεύσει μίλιον ἕν, ὕπαγε μετ' αὐτοῦ δύο.	ἐάν ἀγγαρεύσῃ σέ τις μίλιον ἕν, ὕπαγε μετ' αὐτοῦ δύο· ἐάν ἄρῃ τις τὸ ἱματιόν σου, δὸς αὐτῷ καὶ τὸν χιτῶνα·
6.30 παντὶ <u>αἰτοῦντί σε</u> δίδου, καὶ ἀπὸ τοῦ αἴροντος τὰ σὰ μὴ ἀπαίτει.	5.42 τῷ <u>αἰτοῦντί σε</u> <u>δός</u>, καὶ τὸν θέλοντα ἀπὸ σοῦ <u>δανίσασθαι</u> [cf. Lk. 6.35] μὴ ἀποστραφῇς.	ἐάν λάβῃ τις ἀπὸ σοῦ τὸ σόν, μὴ ἀπαίτει· οὐδὲ γὰρ δύνασαι.

If Matthew depended directly upon *Did.* 1.4b, then it is curious that he did not preserve the *Didache*'s order, 'cheek, mile, cloak', but has instead the order, 'cheek, cloak, mile'. However, if Matthew conflated the similar material in Lk. 6.29 with *Did.* 1.4b, then a possible explanation for this change presents itself.

Thus, Matthew begins his antithesis to *Lex Talionis* with *Did.* 1.4b. The *Didache*'s somewhat rough 'δῷ ῥάπισμα' is smoothed to 'ῥαπίζει' and Matthew changes 'ἐάν τίς' to 'ὅστις', but otherwise the two lines are almost identical.

Matthew, following a pattern of taking alternate lines from similar source texts, then switches to the similar text in Luke's Gospel where the line following Luke's version of the saying 'turn the other cheek' is, 'and from anyone taking away your cloak, do not withhold even your tunic' (Lk. 6.29). Matthew sets this saying in a legal context, rather than the context of insult that it has in Luke's text, and reverses the order of cloak and tunic accordingly.[12] Additional changes are made to Luke's vocabulary to fit Matthew's new setting for the saying.

Matthew then returns to the *Didache* for further examples of non-retaliation. He finds one in the *Did.* 1.4b that was omitted by Luke, namely the call to go an extra mile. This saying is then adapted to Matthew's structure by converting the 'ἐάν' to 'ὅστις', and is then taken over almost verbatim from the *Didache*.

Matthew closes his antithesis in 5.42 by returning, in his alternate fashion, to Lk. 6.30. This gives him instructions regarding giving to those who ask. However, Matthew takes a cue from Luke's triad of 'love, do good and *lend*' (cf. Lk. 6.34, 35) and completes his verse by interpreting Luke's 'καὶ ἀπὸ τοῦ αἴροντος τὰ σὰ μὴ ἀπαίτει' as 'καὶ τὸν θέλοντα ἀπὸ σοῦ δανίσασθαι μὴ ἀποστραφῇς'.

An explanation is thus provided for Matthew's change in the order of *Did.* 1.4b. The supposed conflation of Lk. 6.29-30, 34 and *Did.* 1.4b also goes some way to explaining the difference between the *Didache*'s stark instruction to 'give to all without expecting a return' and Matthew's call to 'give to those who beg and to lend to those who would borrow'.

---

12. Cf. Catchpole (1993: 23–25).

4.2. *Love for Enemies: Lk. 6.27-28, 32-35a = Mt. 5.44, 46-47 = Did. 1.3b-c*

Lk.	Mt.	Did.
	5.43 Ἠκούσατε ὅτι ἐρρέθη, Ἀγαπήσεις τὸν πλησίον σου καὶ		
6.27 Ἀλλὰ ὑμῖν λέγω τοῖς ἀκούουσιν, <u>ἀγαπᾶτε τοὺς ἐχθροὺς ὑμῶν</u>, καλῶς ποιεῖτε τοῖς μισοῦσιν ὑμᾶς, 6.28 εὐλογεῖτε τοὺς καταρωμένους ὑμᾶς, προσεύχεσθε περὶ τῶν ἐπηρεαζόντων ὑμᾶς. ...	μισήσεις τὸν ἐχθρόν σου. 5.44 ἐγὼ δὲ λέγω ὑμῖν, <u>ἀγαπᾶτε τοὺς ἐχθροὺς ὑμῶν</u> **καὶ προσεύχεσθε** **ὑπὲρ τῶν διωκόντων ὑμᾶς,** ...	1.3b εὐλογεῖτε τοὺς καταρωμένους ὑμῖν **καὶ προσεύχεσθε** ὑπὲρ τῶν ἐχθρῶν ὑμῶν, νηστεύετε δὲ **ὑπὲρ τῶν διωκόντων ὑμᾶς·**
6.32 καὶ εἰ <u>ἀγαπᾶτε τοὺς ἀγαπῶντας ὑμᾶς,</u> ποία ὑμῖν χάρις ἐστίν; καὶ γὰρ οἱ ἁμαρτωλοὶ τοὺς ἀγαπῶντας αὐτοὺς ἀγαπῶσιν.	5.46 ἐὰν γὰρ <u>ἀγαπ</u>ήσητε <u>τοὺς ἀγαπῶντας ὑμᾶς</u>, τίνα <u>μισ</u>θὸν ἔχετε; **οὐχὶ καὶ** οἱ τελῶναι τὸ αὐτὸ **ποιοῦσιν;**	1.3c ποία γὰρ χάρις, ἐὰν ἀγαπᾶτε τοὺς ἀγαπῶντας ὑμᾶς;
6.33 <u>καὶ</u> [γὰρ] <u>ἐὰν</u> ἀγαθοποιῆτε τοὺς ἀγαθοποιοῦντας ὑμᾶς, ποία ὑμῖν χάρις ἐστίν; καὶ οἱ ἁμαρτωλοὶ τὸ αὐτὸ ποιοῦσιν. ... 6.35 πλὴν ἀγαπᾶτε τοὺς ἐχθροὺς ὑμῶν καὶ ἀγαθοποιεῖτε καὶ <u>δανί</u>ζετε μηδὲν ἀπελπίζοντες· καὶ ἔσται ὁ <u>μισθ</u>ὸς ὑμῶν πολύς,	5.47 **καὶ ἐὰν** ἀσπάσησθε τοὺς ἀδελφοὺς ὑμῶν μόνον, τί περισσὸν ποιεῖτε; **οὐχὶ καὶ** οἱ ἐθνικοὶ **τὸ αὐτὸ ποιοῦσιν;**	**οὐχὶ καὶ τὰ ἔθνη** **τὸ αὐτὸ ποιοῦσιν;** ὑμεῖς δὲ ἀγαπᾶτε τοὺς μισοῦντας ὑμας καὶ οὐχ ἕξετε ἐχθρόν.

The shape of Mt. 5.44, 46-47 may be accounted for as the result of Matthew's conflation of Lk. 6.27-28, 32-35a and *Did.* 1.3b-5a. Here, however, the pattern of combination is more complex.

Mt. 5.43 states that 'hate your enemies' was an existing saying, but this is not attested in any extant piece of Jewish literature. It is likely, therefore, that Matthew appended this phrase to 'love your neighbours' so as to create a suitable setting for the teaching of Jesus that he found in

Lk. 6.27.[13] Thus 'love your enemies' is taken by Matthew from Luke's Gospel.

The immediately following 'pray for those who persecute you' in Mt. 5.44 is a combination of the last two lines of the Three Rules saying in *Did.* 1.3b.

Mt. 5.46-47 then reworks *Did.* 1.3c with reference to Lk. 6.32-35a. Matthew essentially follows *Did.* 1.3c, but imports the concept of 'reward' from Lk. 6.35a to replace the 'grace' of *Did.* 1.3c.

The *Didache*'s single warning against common reciprocity is presented in double form in Mt. 5.46-47, possibly a reflection of the triple form found in Lk. 6.32-34. In Matthew the two actions considered are 'love', taken from *Did.* 1.3c and 'greet', which is not found in either Luke's Gospel or the *Didache*. Common reciprocity is described by Matthew as exhibited by tax collectors (5.46) and Gentiles (5.47). The former is unique to Matthew; the latter may derive from *Did.* 1.3c.

In all, therefore, three of the differences between *Did.* 1.3b-c and Mt. 5.44, 46-47 may be accounted for by the hypothesis of Matthew's conflation of the *Didache* with Luke's Gospel.

4.3. *Sons of the Father: Lk. 6.35b = Mt. 5.45 =* Did. *1.5a*

Lk.	Mt.	*Did.*
6.35b καὶ ἔσεσθε <u>υἱοὶ</u> ὑψίστου, ὅτι αὐτὸς χρηστός ἐστιν ἐπὶ τοὺς ἀχαρίστους καὶ <u>πονηρούς</u>.	5.45 ὅπως γένησθε <u>υἱοὶ</u> τοῦ **πατρὸς** ὑμῶν τοῦ ἐν οὐρανοῖς, ὅτι τὸν ἥλιον αὐτοῦ ἀνατέλλει ἐπὶ <u>πονηροὺς</u> καὶ ἀγαθοὺς καὶ βρέχει ἐπὶ δικαίους καὶ ἀδίκους.	1.5a παντὶ τῷ αἰτοῦντί σε δίδου καὶ μὴ ἀπαίτει· πᾶσι γὰρ θέλει δίδοσθαι ὁ **πατὴρ** ἐκ τῶν ἰδίων χαρισμάτων.

Mt. 5.45 and *Did.* 1.5a share a conceptual similarity in that they both call for indiscriminate generosity (of different kinds) on the basis that such is consistent with the behaviour of the Father. Beyond this connection there are considerable differences between the two passages, a number of which may be accounted for if Matthew conflated Lk. 6.35b with *Did.* 1.5a. That is to say, the second part of Mt. 5.45 may be seen as an elaboration of Luke's description of God's generosity to all. Thus Matthew takes the single saying from Lk. 6.35b and works it into a pair of sayings

---

13. Chapter 11, § 3.1. includes a brief discussion of Matthew's method in the creation of the antitheses in Mt. 6.

(a similar pairing of parallel sayings also occurs in the immediately ensuing verses, Mt. 5.46, 47):

Lk. 6.35b	Mt. 5.45b
For he is kind to the ungrateful and the wicked	for he makes his sun rise on the evil and on the good,
	and he sends rain on the righteous and on the unrighteous

Once again, therefore, Matthew's use of Luke's Gospel may account for some of the differences between related texts in the *Didache* and Matthew's Gospel.

4.4. *Be Perfect: Lk. 6.36 = Mt. 5.48 =* Did. *1.4b(r)*

Lk.	Mt.	Did.
6.36 Γίνεσθε οἰκτίρμονες καθ<u>ὼς</u> [καὶ] <u>ὁ πατὴρ</u> <u>ὑμῶν</u> οἰκτίρμων <u>ἐστίν</u>.	5.48 Ἔσεσθε οὖν ὑμεῖς τέλειοι <u>ὡς ὁ πατὴρ</u> <u>ὑμῶν</u> ὁ οὐράνιος τέλειός ἐστιν.	1.4b(r) καὶ ἔσῃ τέλειος·

Mt. 5.48 shares an interest in human perfection with *Did.* 1.4b(r). However, unlike the *Didache*, Matthew makes his call for perfection on the basis that this is a quality of the Father. This difference between the two texts may be accounted for, with a remarkable degree of completeness, if Matthew conflated *Did.* 1.4b(r) with Lk. 6.36.

4.5. *The Golden Rule: Lk. 6.31 = Mt. 7.12 =* Did. *1.2d*

Lk.	Mt.	Did.
6.31 καὶ καθὼς <u>θέλ</u>ετε ἵνα <u>ποιῶσιν ὑμῖν</u> <u>οἱ ἄνθρωποι</u>, <u>ποιεῖτε αὐτοῖς</u> ὁμοίως	7.12 **Πάντα** οὖν **ὅσα ἐὰν** <u>θέλ</u>ητε ἵνα <u>ποιῶσιν ὑμῖν</u> <u>οἱ ἄνθρωποι</u>, οὕτως καὶ ὑμεῖς <u>ποιεῖτε αὐτοῖς</u>· οὗτος γάρ ἐστιν ὁ νόμος καὶ οἱ προφῆται.	1.2d **πάντα** δὲ **ὅσα ἐὰν** θελησῃς μὴ γίνεσθαί σοι, καί σὺ ἄλλῳ μὴ ποίει.

Mt. 7.12 differs from *Did.* 1.2d in that it contains a positive, rather than a negative, version of the golden rule. These texts, while conceptually similar, share an inconsistent pattern of verbal similarity. That is to say, their first lines are very similar but this commonality does not persist.

The pattern of relationship between Mt. 7.12 and *Did.* 1.2d is explained if, once again, Matthew referred to the *Didache* for the first part of his version of the golden rule, and then to Lk. 6.31 for its completion.

4.6. *The Two Ways: Lk. 13.23 = Mt. 7.13* = Did. *1.1*

Lk.	Mt.	Did.
13.23 εἶπεν δέ τις αὐτῷ, Κύριε, εἰ <u>ὀλίγοι</u> οἱ σωζόμενοι; ὁ δὲ εἶπεν πρὸς αὐτούς, 13.24 Ἀγωνίζεσθε <u>εἰσελθεῖν</u> <u>διὰ τῆς στενῆς</u> θύρας, ὅτι <u>πολλοί</u>, λέγω ὑμῖν, ζητήσουσιν εἰσελθεῖν καὶ οὐκ ἰσχύσουσιν.	7.13 <u>Εἰσέλθα</u>τε <u>διὰ τῆς</u> <u>στενῆς</u> πύλης· ὅτι πλατεῖα ἡ πύλη καὶ εὐρύχωρος ἡ <u>ὁδὸς</u> ἡ ἀπάγουσα εἰς τὴν ἀπώλειαν, καὶ <u>πολλοί</u> εἰσιν οἱ εἰσερχόμενοι δι᾽ αὐτῆς· 7.14 τί στενὴ ἡ πύλη καὶ τεθλιμμένη ἡ <u>ὁδὸς</u> ἡ ἀπάγουσα εἰς τὴν ζωήν, καὶ <u>ὀλίγοι</u> εἰσὶν οἱ εὑρίσκοντες αὐτήν.	1.1 Ὁδοὶ δύο εἰσί, μία τῆς ζωῆς καὶ μία τοῦ θανάτου, διαφορὰ δὲ πολλὴ μεταξὺ τῶ δύο ὁδῶν.

Matthew shares the concept of two widely contrasting ways of living with *Did.* 1.1. However, his ways are towards 'life' and 'destruction', rather than the *Didache*'s 'life' and 'death'. Matthew has gates to his 'ways', while the *Didache* has no equivalent, and he speaks of the numbers taking one way or the other, while the *Didache* does not.

Matthew's choice of 'destruction' rather than death is explicable in terms of an independent redactional decision. That is to say that 'death' is not a necessarily final destination in Matthew's Gospel; indeed it is a route that Christ himself must take. Thus it is possible that to convey the full negativity of the way of death, Matthew chose to describe it as leading to absolute destruction.

Some of the other conceptual differences between these versions of the two ways may be explained if Matthew conflated *Did.* 1.1 with Lk. 13.23-24. Luke refers to those who enter the narrow door. This could provide a basis for Matthew's description of his 'ways' as having a guarded entrance. However, Matthew's decision to refer to the *Didache*'s 'ways' means that he cannot simply adopt Luke's 'door', since doors are indoor features and ways are outdoor ones. Hence, Matthew has a possible motive for changing Luke's 'door' into 'gates' so as to remain consistent with the image of 'ways' taken from the *Didache*.

Luke also speaks of the number of those who will be saved, which, if taken up by Matthew, would explain the inclusion of this element in Mt. 7.13 despite its absence from *Did.* 1.1.

4.7. *The Last Penny: Lk. 12.59 = Mt. 5.26 =* Did. *1.5c*

Lk.	Mt.	*Did.*
12.59 <u>λέγω σοι, οὐ μὴ</u> <u>ἐξέλθῃς ἐκεῖθεν ἕως</u> καὶ τὸ <u>ἔσχατον</u> λεπτὸν <u>ἀποδῷς</u>.	15.26 ἀμὴν <u>λέγω σοι, οὐ</u> <u>μὴ ἐξέλθῃς ἐκεῖθεν ἕως</u> ἂν <u>ἀποδῷς</u> τὸν <u>ἔσχατον</u> κοδράντην.	1.5c καὶ οὐκ ἐξελεύσεται ἐκεῖθεν, μέχρις οὗ ἀποδῷ τὸν ἔσχατον κοδράντην.

Mt 5.25-26 has a number of parallels with Lk. 12.57-59. In the last line, however, Matthew differs from Luke in referring to 'the last κοδράτην', rather than the last 'λεπτὸν'. This divergence is explicable if, according to the present hypothesis, Matthew follows Luke's Gospel in the verses preceding Mt. 5.26 but in the final phrase conflates Luke's text with the similar line in *Did.* 1.5c.

4.8. *Summary: The Differences between* Didache *1.1-6 and Matthew's Gospel*
It is not within the scope of this volume to offer a full consideration of the relationship between the Gospels of Matthew and Luke. Nevertheless, it has been possible to demonstrate that the theory of Matthew's conflation of similar material in Luke's Gospel and the *Didache* does offer an explanation for the divergences between *Did.* 1.1-6 and parallel material in Matthew's Gospel. To this extent the preceding section may be seen as supportive of the primary hypothesis of this chapter; namely, that Matthew made direct use of *Did.* 1.1-6.

5. *Conclusion*

This chapter began with a ground-clearing exercise (section 1) which found no obstacle to Matthew's dependence on any element of *Did.* 1.1-6.

Section 2 then presented a positive case for such a dependence by focusing on the differing compositional histories of *Did.* 1.1-6 and Matthew's Gospel (and particularly the Sermon on the Mount). To put this in terms of an analogy, *Did.* 1.1-6 is something like a shelf full of ingredients; being made up of a sequence of separately composed elements. By contrast, Matthew's Sermon is more like a cake; having the character of a unified whole forged from disparate material. On the basis of this analogy, then, it is unlikely that the units within *Did.* 1.1-6 were independently created under the influence of Matthew's text. It is more credible to suppose that Matthew found the sequence of elements gathered in *Did.* 1.1-6 and combined them with one another, and with material from other resources, to create his Sermon.

In sections 3-4 an additional piece of evidence was considered in support of the above conclusion. Here it was suggested that the differences between *Did.* 1.1-6 and similar passages in Matthew's Gospel may be explained by Matthew's conflation of like material from both the *Didache* and Luke's Gospel. This latter suggestion has larger implications that cannot be explored in full in this monograph. However, so far as the issue may be taken, an explanation for the relationship between Matthew's Gospel, Luke's Gospel and *Did.* 1.1-6, simpler than the somewhat complex proposals usually offered,[14] may credibly be proposed on this basis.

In conclusion, the direct dependence of Matthew's Gospel on *Did.* 1.1-6 provides an explanation of the relationship between these two texts that is very much simpler than any of the alternatives, especially given the presence of material common to Luke's Gospel within *Did.* 1.1-6. The conclusion that Matthew directly depended upon *Did.* 1.1-6 has been arrived at without relying on observations made previously in Part II; however, it is a conclusion that is fully consistent with those findings.

14. Some scholars, e.g. Vokes (1938: 63); Robinson (1920: 50-58) and Layton (1968: 377) explain the triangular relationship between *Did.* 1.1-6 and Matthew's and Luke's Gospels by proposing that the *Didache* was dependent on *both* of the gospels or some later harmony of the two. This type of explanation further complicates the process by which, it must be proposed, each individual layer and unit within *Did.* 1.1-6 came to be formed.

Chapter 15

Having considered, in Chapters 13 and 14, the dense collection of contacts between Matthew's Gospel and *Did.* 16 and *Did.* 1, this short chapter now turns to examine links that occur at further points within the *Didache*'s Peri/Base layer.

At the outset it should be noted that, if these additional points of contact do indeed fall within the Peri/Base layer (as conceived in Part I), then evidence for Matthew's direct use of elements of this layer may be taken as evidence of Matthew's knowledge of the whole of that layer, including these additional elements. Beyond this point, however, the purpose of this chapter is independently to consider whether there is any feature of these contacts which demands that their author knew Matthew's Gospel. If no such feature can be identified, then the viability of the hypothesis proposed in the introduction to Part II is maintained.

1. *Vice List: Matthew 15.19 and* Didache *5.1*

Butler (1961: 33) suggests that the order of the vices in *Did.* 5.1 is explicable if the *Didache* were editing a list similar to that in *Barnabas* 20 in the light of the list in Mt. 15.19. Taken in isolation this is theoretically possible, although it does not immediately account for the *Didache*'s in-clusion of vices that appear neither in *Barnabas*, nor in Matthew's Gospel, for example ἐπιθυμίαι, αἰσχρολογία, ζηλοτυπία and ἀλαζονεία. At the same time, however, Butler's view is not the only viable explanation for the similarities between Mt. 15.19 and *Did.* 5.1; an alternative possibility is that Mt. 15.19 represents the conflation of the vice lists in *Did.* 5.1 and Mk 7.21, as set out below.

Did.	Mt.	Mk
	15.19 <u>ἐκ γὰρ τῆς καρδίας</u> ἐξέρχονται <u>διαλογισμοὶ</u> πονηροί,	7.21 ἔσωθεν <u>γὰρ ἐκ τῆς καρδίας</u> τῶν ἀνθρώπων οἱ <u>διαλογισμοὶ</u> οἱ κακοὶ ἐκπορεύονται,
5.1b φόνοι, μοιχεῖαι, ἐπιθυμίαι,	<u>φόνοι,</u> <u>μοιχεῖαι,</u>	
πορνεῖαι, κλοπαί, εἰδωλολατρίαι, μαγεῖαι, φαρμακίαι, ἁρπαγαί,	<u>πορνεῖαι,</u> <u>κλοπαί,</u>	<u>πορνεῖαι,</u> <u>κλοπαί,</u> <u>φόνοι,</u> 7.22 <u>μοιχεῖαι,</u> πλεονεξίαι, πονηρίαι,
ψευδομαρτυρίαι, ὑποκρίσεις, διπλοκαρδία, δόλος, ὑπερηφανία, κακία, αὐθάδεια, πλεονεξία, αἰσχρολογία, ζηλοτυπία, θρασύτης, ὕψος, ἀλαζονεία.	ψευδομαρτυρίαι, <u>βλασφημίαι.</u>	δόλος, ἀσέλγεια, ὀφθαλμὸς πονηρός, <u>βλασφημία,</u> ὑπερηφανία, ἀφροσύνη·

According to this theory *every* element of Matthew's list is sourced either from Mk 7.21 or *Did.* 1.5b. This is not to claim that Mt. 15.19 could only have depended on the *Didache* and Mark's Gospel, but it is to note that such dependence is feasible. To this extent the working hypothesis of Matthew's direct use of the *Didache* remains unchallenged at this point.

2. *The Meek and the Merciful: Matthew 5.5, 7 and* Didache *3.7, 8*

Tuckett (1996: 108) says of this relationship:

> The saying 'the meek shall inherit the earth' in Did 3:7 could derive from Mt 5:5, though the position and presence of that beatitude in Matthew is textually uncertain and common dependence of the Didache and Matthew on Ps 36.11 is equally likely.

Despite this apparently balanced assessment Tuckett is not justified in placing both options on an even footing. To say that *Did.* 3.7 is equally likely to have been derived from Ps. 36 or Mt. 5.5 is to neglect the very superior claim of Ps. 36. As discussed in Chapter 4, section 5, the whole of *Did.* 3.1-7 has the form of a piece of Jewish Wisdom literature based on an exposition of Ps. 36. It was also noted that the common reference to the inheritance of the meek in both Ps. 36 and *Barnabas* 19 may explain why the Teknon material was inserted into the Two Ways, and why it was inserted at precisely this point. Thus, there is every reason to suppose that *Did.* 3.7, like the verses that precede it, derives from Ps. 36. Under these circumstances there is no basis for supposing that Mt. 5.5 was anywhere in view.

Conversely, the close combination of references to the meek and the merciful in both *Did.* 3.7, 8 and Mt. 5.5, 7 provides evidence for Matthew's direct dependence on the *Didache*. In Part I it was noted that *Did.* 3.7 forms a part of the Teknon unit, an exposition of Ps. 36 inserted into the Two Ways tractate. *Did.* 3.8, on the other hand, does not fall within the Teknon unit, belonging instead to the Two Ways tractate. It is noteworthy, therefore, that elements from these originally separate traditions, closely juxtaposed in the *Didache*, should reappear in *similarly close combination* amongst Matthew's non-Lukan beatitudes. This circumstance can either be explained as the product of remarkable coincidence, or as the result of Matthew's conflation of Luke's beatitudes with the instructions to be meek and merciful in *Did.* 3.7 and 3.8.

3 *The Commandments:* Didache *1.2a, 4b(r); 2.2 and Matthew 19.17-21*

Matthew's version of Jesus' response to the rich young man is, in many ways, very similar to that recorded in Mk 10.17-22 (and Lk. 18.18-23). However, Matthew deviates from these accounts in four respects. First, he has Jesus preface the listing of the commandments with the phrase, 'If you wish to enter into life'. Second, he places the commandments themselves in the future, rather than the present tense. Third, he adds a call to 'love your neighbour as yourself' as an additional commandment. Fourth, he replaces Mark's 'one thing is lacking' with 'if you wish to be perfect (τέλειος)'.

Each of these changes could be explained if Matthew conflated Mk 10.17-22 with *Did.* 2.2-3. Thus, the *Didache*'s presentation of the commandments as part of the 'way of life' would account for Matthew's insertion of 'If you wish to enter into life'. The *Didache*'s placement of the commandments in the future tense then gives rise to the similar pattern in Matthew. The *Didache* maintenance of a close link between the command to love the neighbour (1.2) and the commandments that spell out the meaning of that command (cf. 2.1 leading into 2.2-3) would account for Matthew's inclusion of neighbour love as part of the essential list of commandments. Finally, the *Didache*'s presentation of 'τέλειος' as the goal of its ethical instructions (1.4b[r]; see also 6.2 and 16.2) would explain why Matthew replaced Mark's 'one thing is lacking' with 'if you wish to be perfect (τέλειος)'.

This is not to suggest that Matthew could only have adapted Mk 10.17-22 under the influence of *Did.* 2.2-3. However, the differences and similarities between the two texts are neatly accounted for by Matthew's use of the *Didache* at this point.

4. *The Commandments: Matthew 5.21, 27, 33 and* Didache *2.2-3*

The quotation of elements of the decalogue in Matthew's antitheses has never provoked particular comment because a source, for the first two at least, is so readily provided by the Old Testament. However, this ready source has blinded scholars to the curiosity of the prohibition 'You shall not swear falsely (οὐκ ἐπιορκήσεις)'. This extremely unusual Greek word for 'swear falsely' is not only a New Testament *hapax*, it does not appear in any contemporary Jewish or Christian text other than Mt. 5, *Did.* 2.3 and, in a different form, the Jewish *halakah* of *Pseudo-Phocylides*. This coincidence suggests a further point of connection between the *Didache* and Matthew's Gospel. If such does exist, then there is insufficient evidence to determine, in isolation at least, the direction of any dependence. To this extent, therefore, Matthew's direct use of the *Didache* remains feasible in this instance.

5. *Fencing the Law: Matthew 5.21, 22, 27, 28 and* Didache *3.2-3*

In terms of direct verbal parallels the connection between *Did.* 3.2-3 and Mt. 5.22, 28 is not especially strong. However, their similar understanding of the relationship between anger and murder, lust and adultery is striking and raises the possibility of a connection between the two texts.

As observed in Chapter 4, section 5, the 'Teknon unit' (*Did.* 3.1-7) has the character of an independently conceived Jewish Wisdom exposition of Ps. 36, which was later incorporated into the Two Ways tractate. This immediately suggests three reasons why it is unlikely to have been written in the light of Matthew's Gospel. First, all the raw material for this unit is available in Ps. 36 and so knowledge of Matthew's Gospel is unnecessary to explain its content. Second, the idea of a 'fence to the law' is characteristic of Jewish wisdom and so appeal to a Christian text need not be used to explain its form. Third, to maintain the theory that the *Didache* used Matthew's Gospel, the composer of the Teknon unit must be supposed to have had a particular, or coincidental, reason for making selections only from Matthew's special material.

Given that the direct dependence of the Teknon unit on Matthew's Gospel is highly unlikely, three other possible explanations for their similarity remain, besides appeal to sheer coincidence. It is possible that both Matthew and the composer of the Teknon unit made use of a common source, or that Matthew knew the Teknon unit before it was incorporated into the *Didache*, or that Matthew knew the Teknon unit in its present context. Of these options the first is unlikely since Ps. 36 appears to provide the inspiration for *Did.* 3.1-7, while this is very much less obviously the case for Matthew's text. The second option requires Matthew to use a tradition which, coincidentally, was later incorporated into a text with numerous other similarities to Matthew's work. The third option, by contrast, merely requires Matthew to draw material from the Teknon unit alongside his use of several other of the *Didache*'s diverse elements. This option is particularly attractive when it is observed that the direct speech of Jesus recorded in Mt. 5.21-28 includes points of similarity not only with *Did.* 3.2-3, but also with *Did.* 1.5b and 14.2 (cf. Chapter 11, sections 1 and 2).

In conclusion, there is nothing to suggest the *Didache*'s knowledge of Matthew's Gospel in this instance. Indeed, the similarities between the two texts at this point suggest Matthew's knowledge of the Teknon unit after it had been incorporated into the *Didache*.

6. *Summary: The Peri/Base Layer and Matthew's Gospel*

The last three chapters have sought to show that, taken in isolation, each point of contact between Matthew's Gospel and the Peri/Base layer may feasibly be explained as due to Matthew's direct knowledge of the *Didache*. Further, it has been noted that in most cases Matthew's knowledge of the *Didache* is not only feasible but probable.

This result offers piece-by-piece confirmation of the hypothesis proposed in the introduction to Part II; namely, that the several links between the first three layers of the *Didache* and Matthew's Gospel are most simply explained by Matthew's direct use of these layers of the *Didache* to supplement the words of Jesus available from other sources.

A table collating the individual findings of the last five chapters is set out below.

Directions of dependence between the Didache *and Matthew's Gospel: a summary of individual conclusions drawn in Chapters 11 to 15*

	Did.	Mt.	Mk	Lk.
Beatitudes	3.7,8 ———————➤	5.3-7 ◄——————————		6.20-21
Immutable teaching	11.1-2———————➤	5.19		
Be reconciled	14.2 ————————➤	5.24		
Commandments	2.2-3◄———————	5.21, 27, 33		
Fencing the Law	3.2-3 ————————➤	5.22,28		
Last penny	1.5b ————————➤	5.26 ◄——————————		12.58-59
Cheek, mile, coat	1.4b ————————➤	5.39 ◄——————————		6.29
Love your enemies	1.3b ————————➤	5.44 ◄——————————		6.27-28
As son of Father	1.5a ————————➤	5.45 ◄——————————		6.35b
Non-reciprocal love	1.3c ————————➤	5.46 ◄——————————		6.32-35
Be perfect as Father	1.4b ————————➤	5.48 ◄——————————		6.36
Alms, fast, pray	8.1-2 ———————➤	6.1-16 ◄———11.25; 12.40, 44		
Giving to dogs	9.5◄———————➤	7.6		
Golden rule	1.2d ————————➤	7.12 ◄——————————		6.31
Two ways	1.1 —————————➤	7.13 ◄——————————		13.23-24
Worker's food	13.2◄———————➤	10.10		
Unforgivable sin	11.7 ————————➤	12.31-32 ◄◄— 3.28-29———————		12.10
Vice list	5.1——————————➤	15.19 ◄— 7.21-22		
Judgment by deeds	16.8-9 ——————➤	16.27b		
The Commandments	1.2a; 2.2; 1.4b(r)➤	19.17-20 ◄—10.17-22		
Two loves	1.2b, d-e ————➤	22.37-39 ◄——————————		10.27
Signs of the End	16.3-5————————➤	24.10-12 ◄—13.13		
The coming Judge	16.6, 8 ——————➤	24.30-31 ◄—13.26-27		
Hour of Parousia	16.1 ————————➤	24.42; 25.13◄13.35		
Final judgment	16.8-9————————➤	25.31-46		
Great Commission	title + 7.1d——➤➤	28.19		

————➤ denotes where one particular direction of dependence was considered probable.

◄————➤ denotes where (taken in isolation) dependence in either direction, or upon a common source, was considered feasible.

Chapter 16

CONCLUSION

Bryennios's discovery of the *Didache* held out the tantalizing promise of new insight into little known aspects of early Christian belief and practice. However, ongoing failure to establish its location within the web of early Christian life and literature means that its full potential has yet to be realized.

The aim of this volume has been to secure one dimension of the *Didache*'s original context. I chose to examine its relationship to Matthew's Gospel because some form of connection with this gospel is all but undeniable. Of course, there is a world of difference between establishing 'some form of connection' and pinpointing a connection of a particular type. In this case, however, two factors promised to overcome the usual problem of perpetually reversible dependency arguments: Matthew's Gospel and the *Didache* share numerous unique similarities and the *Didache* is a distinctively composite creation. I use the term 'distinctively composite' to convey the sense, not only that the *Didache* was laid down in layers, but also that it contains previously existing elements that have maintained their prior form. To use a crude illustration, the *Didache* may be likened to a fish pie within which whole fish and substantial pieces of fish, of distinctly different types, may still be distinguished (for example, the Two Ways tractate, the Sayings Onion, the Teknon unit, the Prophet Document, the closing Apocalypse, and so on).

The composite character of the *Didache* promises to provide a means of establishing its relationship to Matthew's Gospel because points of connection between the two texts occur within so many of the separate elements incorporated into the *Didache*, as well as within the editorial comments of the *Didache*'s direct contributors. This combination of factors is best explained, I propose, if Matthew took small pieces from the variety of separate whole traditions within the *Didache*'s 'pie', as well as from the editorial comment that surrounds them, and mixed them, with related resources from elsewhere, to make a dish in which whole distinct traditions are no longer apparent. Rather, Matthew's creation is one in which elements from different resources are thoroughly mixed together to create a unified whole.[1]

While accepting the limitations of this analogy it succeeds in holding simultaneously in view the distinctively composite nature of the *Didache* as well as the presence of multiple contacts between the two texts. If my 'fish pie' analogy is even approximately correct, then the two mainstream explanations for the texts' relationship face considerable difficulties.

Take, to begin with, the idea that the *Didache* consistently depends upon Matthew's Gospel. This proposal requires the various creators of the whole traditions that ultimately became incorporated into the *Didache*, separately and in each case, to refer to fragments of Matthew's Gospel in the process of creating these whole and self-contained traditions. Not only that but they must also be supposed to have selected fragments that are often widely dispersed in Matthew's Gospel and closely conflated with material from other sources. In addition to the activity of these indirect contributors it is also necessary to propose a repeated homage to Matthew's Gospel by editors who directly contributed to the *Didache*, most particularly the editor of the third redactional layer.[2] As a result, therefore, it is necessary to imagine a queue of indirect contributors, each with diverse backgrounds, interests and styles, lining up over a period of time to draw inspiration from

---

1.   Analogies, while useful in some respects, are seldom capable of conveying the full complexity of the case. The analogy of the unified fish pie is, strictly speaking, most appropriate when applied to Matthew's teaching discourses, such as the Sermon on the Mount and the Apocalyptic Discourse. Most scholars recognize a combination of literary craftsmanship combined with a use of prior sources in the construction of Jesus' speeches. Carson, while arguing for the unity of the text, bears witness to a general recognition that this unity was forged, largely successfully, by the combination of prior sources. Carson (1984: 17) thus states: 'The question of the unity of Matthew's Gospel has little to do with source-critical questions. Instead it deals with how well the evangelist has integrated his material to form cohesive pericopes and a coherent whole. In sections very difficult to interpret (e.g., Matt 24), it is sometimes argued that the evangelist has sewn together diverse traditions that by nature are incapable of genuine coherence. Failing to understand the material, he simply passed it on without recognizing that some of his sources were mutually incompatible.

There are so many signs of high literary craftsmanship in this Gospel that such skepticism is unjustified.'

2.   Whether or not my analysis of the compositional history of the *Didache* is correct in detail, it remains the case that points of contact with Matthew's Gospel occur within parts of the *Didache* that may, with some confidence, be attributed to both direct and indirect contributors.

Matthew's Gospel. Their work must then be gathered by direct contributors who have a similar surgeon's instinct for selecting from the gospel material that is 'from Matthew's special material or from the synoptic traditions at points where Matthew's distinctive rendering is preferred' (Court 1981: 111). This picture is incredible. I conclude, therefore, that the first three layers of the *Didache* cannot have depended upon Matthew's Gospel.

The majority of scholars in the contemporary debate agree that the *Didache* did not directly depend on Matthew's Gospel.[3] They propose, instead, that both texts held a number of separate traditions in common. This approach overcomes two important difficulties. First, evidence to suggest the antiquity of the *Didache*'s traditions relative to Matthew's Gospel need not be over-ridden, since it is possible that the *Didache* preserves the sources it shares with Matthew more faithfully than did the evangelist. Second, this reading avoids the need for a row of direct and indirect contributors who each picked out fragments of Matthew's special material from Matthew's unified text. Instead, it may be imagined that Matthew and the Didachist both fished in the same pool of early traditions and gathered a number in common. Matthew, it may then be proposed, conflated these with other related material to create substantial discourses as well as shorter speeches of Jesus, while the Didachist preserved them more or less in their original state.

The shared use of common traditions provides an initially plausible explanation for the presence of similar material in both the gospel and *the Didache's whole incorporated traditions*. Even here, however, high levels of coincidence must be appealed to. The first of which is that Matthew and the *Didache* must have had access to a range of diverse traditions that are

---

3.   It is interesting to note that the line of approach used is not based on a compositional analysis. Instead, these scholars tend to prefer 'development' arguments. That is to say, evidence is found to suggest that Matthew's version of a particular saying is, for some reason or another, more developed than the similar saying found in the *Didache*. A small selection of these types of observation have been made in the preceding discussion. In most cases, however, I have favoured a compositional approach in the belief that this type of argument is less easily reversed than the tracing of supposed developments. Nonetheless, it is noteworthy that arguments in favour of the antiquity of the *Didache*, in relation to Matthew's Gospel, may consistently be made where they share similar material – even if, on occasion, such arguments are not the only possible explanation for the differences between the two texts. Scholars who detect ancient traditions in the *Didache*, relative to their counterparts in Matthew's Gospel include, amongst others, Köster (1957); Rordorf (1991); Kloppenborg (1979) and van de Sandt (2002).

distinctively similar to one another in comparison with those preserved in other early Christian documents. This implies, not only that they fished at the same lake, but that they fished the same part of that lake at a similar time (without drawing directly from one another's catch). Other factors suggest, however, that this is unlikely to have been the case. The compositional analysis in Part I noted that the *Didache*'s Base layer appears to have been written by a Jew to a Gentile audience and by someone with no identifiable interest in the ministry of prophets. The Prophet layer, by contrast, is solely concerned with regulating, protecting and making viable the prophetic ministry. Then again, the Modifying Teacher layer appears to have been written to an audience with a Jewish, rather than a Gentile, background. Furthermore, this author felt unable to modify the base text directly but was forced to recognize and accept its authoritative status; an authority likely to have been established over a period of time. These factors combine to suggest that these layers were contributed by different editors at different times and in different contexts. This observation decreases the likelihood that Matthew and the Didachists fished the same part of the lake at the same time, thus increasing the coincidence required to explain their shared knowledge of otherwise unknown forms of tradition. On the other hand, this difficulty does not arise if Matthew knew and used the *Didache*. In this case there would be nothing surprising about the reappearance in Matthew's Gospel of elements from several of the *Didache*'s diverse range of incorporated traditions.

The independent use of shared traditions requires an even greater level of coincidence when it is observed that these separate traditions are sometimes similarly juxtaposed by both Matthew and the *Didache*. For example, the concept of two ways is juxtaposed with the golden rule in *Did.* 1.1 (TW)[4] and 1.2e (LS); while a similar combination appears in Mt. 7.13 and 7.12. Instructions to be meek and merciful occur in *Did.* 3.7 (TK) and 3.8 (TW); and also in Mt. 5.5 and 5.7. A call for perfection is linked with loving beyond those who love you in *Did.* 1.4b(r) (P/B) and 1.3c (SO.b); and also in Mt. 5.46, 47 and 5.48. Separate traditions set alongside one another in the *Didache* also re-appear in similar juxtaposition in Matthew's account of Jesus' response to the rich young ruler. Thus, Matthew combines the idea of entering life (Mt. 19.17) with a keeping of the commandments

---

4.   The two letter codes used in this discussion refer to separate traditions identified as having been incorporated into the *Didache* during the process of its composition (cf. Part I). A key to these codes may be found in the introduction to the full text of the *Didache* at the beginning of this volume.

(Mt. 19.18), including love of neighbour (Mt. 19.19), to attain the goal of moral perfection (Mt. 19.21). A uniquely similar arrangement appears in the *Didache*'s combination of the 'way of life' (*Did.* 1.1 – TW) with a demand to love the neighbour (*Did.* 1.2d – LS) to attain moral perfection (*Did.* 1.4b[r] – P/B) and keep the commandments (*Did.* 2.2 – TW). On the other hand, complex coincidence need not be appealed to if Matthew knew and used the *Didache* directly. In this case the reappearance of separate traditions in similar juxtaposition is entirely to be expected.[5]

Although demanding high levels of coincidence, an appeal to the independent use of shared traditions provides a theoretically possible explanation for similarities to Matthew's Gospel that occur *within one of the Didache's incorporated units*. However, this explanation is very much more difficult to apply when the point of contact occurs within the *Didache*'s redactional material. For example, a point of contact falls within *Did.* 11.1-2 (= Mt. 5.17-20) which is highly likely to be an original creation of the modifying teacher (cf. Chapter 11, section 4 and Chapter 7, section 4). There are also strong reasons for supposing that *Did.* 1.5b is an original composition, crafted for this specific location, by the modifying teacher. First, it only makes sense in response to the preceding instructions regarding giving. Second, resort is made to an obscure proverb, in *Did.* 1.6, to support the authority of 1.5b. This suggests that 1.5b has no previous authoritative pedigree of its own and thus, that the reappearance of a reference to paying back the last penny in Mt. 5.26 is unlikely to be due to the shared use of a common tradition.[6] A very similar circumstance occurs in *Did.* 14.2, where the modifying teacher calls readers to be reconciled before making sacrifice. Support for this instruction is sought, in *Did.* 14.3, from the tangentially relevant Mal. 1.11. This suggests that *Did.* 14.2 did not have a prior pedigree of its own to which appeal could be made, a circumstance that sits at odds with Matthew's apparent knowledge of a saying of the Lord that directly addresses the relevant subject (Mt. 5.24). If both texts depended on a common source, then why does Matthew present it as a saying of Jesus, while the modifier mentions no authoritative source at all? This problem does not arise, however, if Matthew knew and used *Did.* 14.2. Under these circumstances the original contribution of

---

5.   Even though an extraordinary set of coincidences is required, it is still theoretically possible that Matthew and the Didachists made independent use of several previously existing traditions, perhaps already clustered in groups. However, to account for the spread of points of contact between the two texts any such clusters would need to be so large as to be all but indistinguishable from the *Didache* itself.

6.   For a full discussion of this point see Chapter 11, § 2.

the modifying teacher could be understood as a Lord's word because it stood within a text entitled 'The Teaching of the Lord, etc.'[7]

In all, therefore, an explanation for the several similarities between Matthew's Gospel and the *Didache* which proposes their independent use of common resources must overcome the following difficulties: the coincidental knowledge, at different times and circumstances, of several forms of tradition that are not known in any other text; the similar juxtaposition, on a number of occasions, of those separate traditions; and Matthew's consistent attribution of all this material to Jesus, even though the original creativity of one of the *Didache*'s redactors is evident on at least three occasions. On the other hand, if Matthew directly used the *Didache*, then none of these factors presents a difficulty. Under these circumstances it would be natural to expect redactional as well as traditional elements within the *Didache* to reappear in the gospel, sometimes in similar combination. Further, it would be unsurprising to find this material consistently treated as the direct speech of Jesus, since, from Matthew's point of view, it all appears under the title, 'The Teaching of the Lord, by the Twelve Apostles, to the Gentiles'.

So far I have pointed out complications facing the two mainstream explanations for the connections between the *Didache* and Matthew's Gospel, while at the same time seeking to show that these difficulties do not apply if Matthew depended directly on the *Didache*. If this latter solution is so simple, it may reasonably be asked, then why has it not been seriously considered in the past? I offered an initial response to this question in Chapter 1, but must now return to the crucial matter of the presence of four appeals to 'the gospel' in *Did.* 8.2b, 11.3b and 15.3-4.

These references to a 'gospel' present an obvious obstacle to the view that Matthew directly depended upon the *Didache*. If, as is highly likely, these lines were written with knowledge of Matthew's Gospel,[8] then a significant qualification must be added to any theory of Matthew's use of the *Didache*; namely, that the references to 'the gospel' were inserted after the *Didache*'s earlier layers had been made use of by Matthew.

---

7. For a full discussion of this point see Chapter 11, § 1. Additional points of contact that fall within direct contributions to the *Didache* (on the basis of the analysis presented in Part I) include: the long title, the call to be perfect (1.4b[r]), and the linking verses prior to the closing apocalypse (16.1-2).

8. Strictly speaking, if the 'gospel' referred to was an oral or lost gospel, then it would not follow that these references must have been written after the creation of Matthew's text. However, as discussed in Chapter 8, § 1, it appears highly likely that Matthew's Gospel is in view here.

At first sight, this assignment of the gospel references in *Did.* 8.2b; 11.3b and 15.3-4 to a wholly separate redactional layer may seem a rather lame attempt to sidestep evidence that is hostile to my overall thesis.[9] It is not the case, however, that these gospel references present a puzzle for my argument alone, or that they present fewer difficulties for the alternative hypotheses. This can be illustrated by the crucial example of the Lord's Prayer in *Did.* 8. What must be wrestled with here is that *Did.* 8.2b instructs its readers to pray 'as the Lord commanded in his gospel', but the immediately ensuing prayer is unlikely to have appeared in any manuscript of Matthew's work.[10] Those who propose the *Didache*'s dependence on Matthew at this point must provide some explanation for the absence of Matthew's version of the prayer. A related problem is posed for those who see the *Didache* as compiled by someone who sometimes reveals a direct knowledge of Matthew's Gospel, but who prefers to quote that gospel's sources, rather than the gospel itself.[11] These scholars must explain why Jesus direct instructions, as recorded in Matthew's Gospel, are set up as a standard in 8.2b and then set aside in 8.2c.

Since the combination of an appeal to the gospel in 8.2b and its non-quotation in 8.2c presents a puzzle for any theory that sees these two lines as composed by the same author, it may be preferable to see them as belonging to two different redactional layers. Under these circumstances the disjunction between 8.2b and 8.2c need not be due to editorial incompetence, but may be explained in terms of a later contributor's respect for the basic text. Thus, a later interpolator may have wished to point readers to Matthew's version of the Lord's Prayer, while at the same time being unwilling to make direct alterations to the established document. The insertion of 8.2b achieves this goal, even though the resulting text is somewhat awkward. A similar effect is created when the modifying teacher avoids direct revision of the host, but nonetheless manages to alter its force by inserting new material. Here again the reading that results is sometimes awkward and self-contradictory.

As well as providing an explanation for the disjunction between *Did.* 8.2b and 8.2c, two further factors favour the proposal that 8.2b; 11.3b and 15.3-4 were inserted to subordinate the *Didache* to Matthew's Gospel.

---

9.   Full details of my reasoning for the separation of *Did.* 8.2b; 11.3b and 15.3-4 from the rest of the *Didache*'s compositional history may be found in Part I, especially in Chapter 7, §§ 3, 5, 7; Chapter 8, and Chapter 11, § 3.

10.   See Chapter 11, § 3.1.

11.   See the comments of Niederwimmer and Köster quoted on pp. 134-35.

First, such an understanding allows each of the four references to 'the gospel' to perform a similar function; something which cannot be achieved if *Did.* 8.2b is seen as a quotation formula, since it is not possible for *Did.* 15.3, 4 to operate in this way. Second, this proposal presents a credible motive for the inclusion of appeals to 'the gospel'. Matthew's proposed conflationary practice results in divergences between his text and related teaching in the *Didache*, which in turn creates a need for guidance as to which set of instructions should be followed. Such guidance is provided by appeal to 'the gospel' at those points where the differences between the two texts are most likely to cause confusion (8.2b; 11.3b and 15.3) as well as a catch-all indication that Matthew's Gospel should be seen as having the final word (15.4). By contrast, it is difficult to detect a credible motive for the inclusion of references to 'the gospel of the Lord' by someone who also added the Lord's Prayer or, for example, rules regarding visitors. In this case the interpolator's additional contributions would be immediately undermined by their simultaneous recognition of the ultimate authority of Matthew's divergent instructions.

On closer inspection, therefore, the assignment of *Did.* 8.2b; 11.3b and 15.3, 4 to a separate redactional layer provides the only explanation for their inclusion that does not require inconsistent or eccentric behaviour on the part of their contributor. This in turn means that, while there are severe obstacles to the view that the *Didache* depended on Matthew's Gospel, or that both texts independently used common traditions, there is no barrier to the conclusion that Matthew knew and used the first three layers of the *Didache*. Indeed, the evidence points overwhelmingly in this direction. The preceding discussion identified 26 points of contact between the two texts (listed at the end of Chapter 15). Of this total, six fall within material attributed to the original creativity of the *Didache*'s redactors, while the remainder occur within 11 of the 15 passages identified as separate traditions incorporated into the *Didache*. Individual analyses of each of these points of contact found positive evidence for Matthew's knowledge of the *Didache* in 22 of the 26 instances, and found no evidence to preclude Matthew's direct knowledge of the *Didache* in the other four. Even if my specific identification of layers and incorporated traditions within the *Didache* is inaccurate or incomplete, it remains undeniable both that the *Didache* has a distinctively composite character, and that it contains widely dispersed and unique points of contact with Matthew's Gospel. I conclude that the only credible explanation for this combination of factors is Matthew's direct dependence on those elements of the *Didache* that pre-date the interpolation of the four appeals to external authority of 'the gospel'.

When Archbishop Bryennios stumbled across a manuscript of the *Didache* he came to believe that he had made a sensational find. However, ongoing failure to establish its location within the web of early Christian life and literature has severely weakened the impact of his discovery. The above case for Matthew's direct knowledge of the *Didache* will, I hope, lead to a secure appraisal of the *Didache*'s place within the life of the first Christians.[12] Once this location has been established, the frustrated potential of Bryennios's remarkable discovery may finally come to fruition.[13]

12. The hypothesis of Matthew's use of the *Didache* opens up a number of new questions, or places old questions in a new light. Among these are the nature of the *Didache*'s relationship to the several other texts of the New Testament with which it shares points of contact. A very partial exploration of this question has been undertaken above in relation to Luke's and Mark's Gospels and, to an even lesser extent, with regard to 1 Corinthians and Revelation. If the *Didache* is a pre-Matthean text, then studies of its relationship to other first-century texts should serve, not only to confirm this conclusion, but also to assist in the more specific identification of the *Didache*'s dates, authorships and provenances.

13. If Matthew knew the *Didache* then a great many implications follow, some of which are noted in the preceding discussion. One implication treated in partial detail is that the *Didache* provides evidence for a new solution to the Synoptic Problem; namely, that Matthew used Mark's Gospel to provide the spine of his account and supplemented this with relevant material from the *Didache*, Luke's Gospel (possibly Revelation) and other sources. This solution places the *Didache* in a 'Q-like' position in that there is evidence for Luke's and Matthew's combined knowledge of the Base layer of the *Didache*. However, the *Didache* also provides evidence for Matthew's direct knowledge of Luke's Gospel, thus obviating the need for a more extensive 'Q' to explain the remainder of the double tradition. This provides an example of how a new perspective on the *Didache* opens up the possibility of new solutions to otherwise unsolved puzzles. The *Didache*'s ability to answer this and other questions will provide its own means of further identifying and confirming its place amongst the documents of the first Christians.

BIBLIOGRAPHY

Aldridge, R.E.
    1999   'The Lost Ending of the *Didache*', *VigChr* 53: 1–15.

Alfonsi, L.
    1972   'Aspetti della struttura letteraria della Διδαχή', *Studi classici in onore de Q. Cataudella* 2: 465–81.

Alon, G.
    1996   'Halakah in the Teaching of the Twelve Apostles (*Didache*)', in Draper (ed.) 1996: 165–94.

Audet, J.-P.
    1952   'Affinités Littéraires et Doctrinales du "Manuel de Discipline"', *Revue Biblique* 59: 219–38.
    1958   *La Didachè. Instructions des Apôtres* (Études bibliques; Paris: Gabalda).
    1996   'Literary and Doctrinal Relationships of the "Manual of Discipline"', in Draper (ed.) 1996: 129–47.

Balabanski, V.
    1997   *Eschatology in the Making: Mark, Matthew and the Didache* (SNTSMS, 97; Cambridge: Cambridge University Press).

Bammel, E.
    1996   'Pattern and Prototype of *Didache* 16', in Draper (ed.) 1996: 364–72.

Barr, D.L.
    1986   'The Apocalypse of John as oral enactment', *Int* 40: 243–56.

Bartlet, J.V.
    1921   'The Didache Reconsidered', *JTS* 22: 239–49.

Bauer, W., W.F. Arndt and F.W. Gingrich
    1957   *A Greek–English Lexicon of the New Testament* (Chicago: Chicago University Press).

Benoît, A.
    1953   *Le Baptême Chrétien au Second Siècle: La Théologie de Pères* (Paris: Presses Universitaires de France).

Betz, H.D.
    1995   *The Sermon on the Mount: A Commentary on the Sermon on the Mount, including the Sermon on the Plain (Matthew 5:3–7:27 and Luke 6:20-49)* (Hermeneia; Minneapolis: Fortress Press).

Betz, J.
    1996   'The Eucharist in the Didache', in Draper (ed.) 1996: 244–75.

Boring, M.E.
    1982   *Sayings of the Risen Jesus: Christian Prophecy in the Synoptic Tradition* (SNTSMS, 46; Cambridge: Cambridge University Press).

Bouley, A.
1981   *From Freedom to Formula: The Evolution of the Eucharistic Prayer from Oral Improvisation to Written Texts* (Catholic University of America Studies in Christian Antiquity, 21; Washington, DC: Catholic University of America Press).

Bradshaw, P.F.
1981   *Daily Prayer in the Early Church: A Study of the Origin and Early Development of the Divine Office* (Alcuin Club Collections, 63; London: SPCK).

Brown, G., and G. Yule
1983   *Discourse Analysis* (Cambridge Textbooks in Linguistics; Cambridge: Cambridge University Press).

Bryennios, P.
1883   Διδαχὴ τῶν δώδεκα ἀποστόλων ἐκ τοῦ ἱεροσολυμιτικοῦ χειρογράφου νῦν πρῶτον ἐκδιδομένη μετὰ προλεγομένων καὶ σημειώσεων ἐν οἷς καὶ τῆς Συνόψεως τῆς Π. Δ., τῆς ὑπὸ Ἰωάνν, τοῦ Χρυσοστόμου, σύγκρισις καὶ μέρος ἀνέκδοτον ἀπὸ τοῦ αὐτοῦ χειρογράφου (Constantinople: Voutyra).

Bultmann, R.
1972   *The History of the Synoptic Tradition* (trans. J. Marsh; Oxford: Blackwell).

Butler, B.C.
1960   'The Literary Relations of *Didache*, Ch. XVI', *JTS* 11: 265–83.
1961   'The "Two Ways" in the *Didache*', *JTS* 12: 27–38.

Carrington, P.
1957   *The Early Christian Church*, I (2 vols.; Cambridge: Cambridge University Press).

Carson, D.A.
1984   'Matthew', in F.E. Gaebelein (ed.), *The Expositor's Bible Commentary*, VIII (Grand Rapids, MI: Zondervan): 1–599.

Catchpole, D.R.
1993   *The Quest for Q* (Edinburgh: T. & T. Clark).

Cody, A.
1995   'The *Didache*: An English Translation', in Jefford (ed.) 1995: 3–14.

Connolly, R.H.
1923   'The Use of the Didache in the Didascalia', *JTS* 24: 147–57.
1932   'The "Didache" in Relation to the Epistle of Barnabas', *JTS* 33: 237–53.

Court, J.M.
1981   'The Didache and Matthew's Gospel', *SJT* 34: 109–120.
1997   *Reading the New Testament* (New Testament Readings; London: Routledge).

Creed, J.M.
1938   'The Didache', *JTS* 39: 370–87.

Cullmann, O.
1953   *Early Christian Worship* (SBT, 10; London: SCM Press).
1963   *The Christology of the New Testament* (London: SCM Press).

Dehandschutter, B.
1995   'The Text of the *Didache*: Some Comments on the Edition of Klaus Wengst', in Jefford (ed.) 1995: 37–46.

Dibelius, M.
1938   'Die Mahl-Gebete der Didache', *ZNW* 37: 32–41.

Dix, G.
    1945   *The Shape of the Liturgy* (Westminster: Dacre).
Downing, F.G.
    1980   'Redaction Criticism: Josephus' *Antiquities* and the Synoptic Gospels',
                   JSNT 9: 29–48.
Draper, J.A.
    1983   *A Commentary on the Didache in the Light of the Dead Sea Scrolls and*
                   Related Documents (unpublished PhD dissertation, Cambridge University).
    1985   'The Jesus Tradition in the Didache', in D. Wenham (ed.), *Gospel Perspec-*
                   tives. V. *The Jesus Tradition Outside the Gospels* (5 vols.; Sheffield: JSOT
                   Press): 269–89.
    1991   'Torah and Troublesome Apostles in the Didache Community', *NovT* 33.4:
                   347–72.
    1992   'Christian Self-Definition against the "Hypocrites" in Didache 8', in E.H.
                   Lovering (ed.), *Society of Biblical Literature 1992 Seminar Papers* (Atlanta,
                   GA: Scholars Press): 362–77.
    1995   'Social Ambiguity and the Production of Text: Prophets, Teachers, Bishops,
                   and Deacons and the Development of the Jesus Tradition in the Community
                   of the *Didache*', in Jefford (ed.) 1995: 284–312.
    1996a   'The *Didache* in Modern Research: An Overview', in Draper (ed.) 1996:
                   1–42.
    1996b   'The Jesus Tradition in the *Didache*', in Draper (ed.) 1996: 72–91.
    1996c   'Christian Self-Definition against the "Hypocrites" in *Didache* VIII', in
                   Draper (ed.) 1996: 223–43.
    1996d   'Torah and Troublesome Apostles in the *Didache* Community', in Draper
                   (ed.) 1996: 340–63.
- Draper, J.A. (ed.)
    1996   *The* Didache *in Modern Research* (AGJU, 37; Leiden: E.J. Brill)
Drews, P.
    1904   'Untersuchungen zur Didache', *ZNW* 5: 53–79.
Dungan, D.L.
    1971   *The Sayings of Jesus in the Churches of Paul: The Use of the Synoptic*
                   Tradition in the Regulation of Early Church Life (Oxford: Basil Blackwell).
Ehrman, B.D.
    2003   *The Apostolic Fathers*, I (LCL, L24; Cambridge, MA: Harvard University
                   Press)
Finkelstein, L.
    1928–29   'The "birkat ha-mazon"', *JQR* 19: 211–63.
Flusser, D.
    1996   'Paul's Jewish-Christian Opponents in the *Didache*', in Draper (ed.) 1996:
                   195–211.
Funk, F.X.
    1887   *Doctrinae duodecim apostolorum, Canones ecclesiastici ac reliquae doc-*
                   trinae duarum viarum expositiones veteres (Tübingen: Henrici Laupp).
Garrow, A.J.P.
    1997   *Revelation* (New Testament Readings; London: Routledge).
Gero, S.
    1977   'The So-called Ointment Prayer in the Coptic Version of the Didache: A Re-
                   evaluation', *HTR* 70: 67–84.

256   *The Gospel of Matthew's Dependence on the* Didache

Giet, S.
1970   *L'Enigme de la Didachè* (Paris: Ophrys).
Glover, R.
1958   'The Didache's Quotations and the Synoptic Gospels', *NTS* 5: 12–29.
1985   'Patristic Quotations and Gospel Sources', *NTS* 31 (1985): 234–51.
Goodspeed, E.J.
1945   'The Didache, Barnabas and the Doctrina', *ATR* 27: 228–47.
Goulder, M.D.
1974   *Midrash and Lection in Matthew* (London: SPCK).
Halleux, A. de
1996   'Ministers in the *Didache*', in Draper (ed.) 1996: 300–320.
Harnack, A. von
1884   *Die Lehre der zwölf Apostel nebst Untersuchungenzur ältesten Geschichte der Kirchenverfassung und des Kirchenrechts* (Leipzig: Hinrichs).
Harnack, A. von and O. van Gebhardt
1886   *Texte und Untersuchungen zur Geschichte der altchristlichen Literatur* (Leipzig: Hinrichs).
Harris, J.R.
1887   *The Teaching of the Apostles (Διδαχὴ τῶν ἀποστόλων)* (London: Clay).
Hartman, L.
1997   *'Into the Name of the Lord Jesus': Baptism in the Early Church* (Studies in the NT and its World; Edinburgh: T. & T. Clark).
Heidenreich, A.
1962   *The Catacombs: Pictures from the Life of Early Christianity* (London: The Christian Community Press).
Henderson, I.H.
1995   'Style-switching in the *Didache*: Fingerprint or Argument', in Jefford (ed.) 1995: 177–209.
Hengel, M.
2000   *The Four Gospels and the One Gospel of Jesus Christ: An Investigation of the Collection and Origin of the Canonical Gospels* (Harrisburg, PA: Trinity Press International).
Hooker, M.D.
1991   *The Gospel According to St Mark* (BNTC; London: A. & C. Black).
Hruby, K.
1972   'La "birkat ha-mazon"', *Mélanges Liturgiques offerts au R. P. dom Bernard Botte: à l'occasion du cinquantième anniversaire de son ordination sacerdotale (4 Juin 1972)* (Louvain: Abbaye du Mont César).
Huggins, R.V.
1992   'Matthean Posteriority: A Preliminary Proposal', *NovT* 34: 1–22.
Hüntermann, U.
1931   'Ad cap. I Doctrinae XII apostolorum', *Antonianum* 6: 195–96.
Jefford, C.N.
1989   *The Sayings of Jesus in the Teaching of the Twelve Apostles* (VigChrSup, 11; Leiden: E.J. Brill).
1995   'Did Ignatius of Antioch Know the *Didache*?', in Jefford (ed.) 1995: 330–51.
Jefford, C.N. (ed.)
1995   *The* Didache *in context: essays on its text, history, and transmission* (NovTSup, 77; Leiden: E.J. Brill).

Jeremias, J.
1966   *The Eucharistic Words of Jesus* (London: SCM Press).
Jones, F.S., and P.A. Mirecki
1995   'Considerations on the Coptic Papyrus of the *Didache* (British Library
            Oriental Manuscript 9271)', in Jefford (ed.) 1995: 47–87.
Kelhoffer, J.A.
2000   *Miracle and Mission: The Authentication of Missionaries and their Message
            in the Longer Ending of Mark* (WUNT, 112; Tübingen: Mohr).
Kirk, A.K.
1998   *The Composition of the Sayings Source Q: Genre, Synchrony, and Wisdom
            Redaction in Q* (NovTSup, 91; Leiden: E.J. Brill).
Kleist, J.A.
1948   *The Didache, The Epistle of Barnabas, The Epistles and the Martyrdom of
            St. Polycarp, The Fragments of Papias. The Epistle to Diognetus* (Ancient
            Christian Writers, 6; Westminster, MD: Newman).
Kloppenborg, J.S.
1979   'Didache 16:6-8 and Special Matthean Tradition', *ZNW* 70: 54–67.
1995   'The Transformation of Moral Exhortation in *Didache* 1–5', in Jefford (ed.)
            1995: 88–109.
Knopf, R.
1920   *Die Lehre der zwölf Apostel. Die zwei Clemensbriefe* (HNT.E; Tübingen:
            Mohr).
Köhler, W.-D.
1987   *Die Rezeption des Matthäusevangelium in der Zeit vor Irenäus* (WUNT, 14;
            Tübingen: Mohr).
Köster, H.
1957   *Synoptische Überlieferung bei den apostolischen Vätern* (TU, 65; Berlin:
            Akademie-Verlag).
1972   Überlieferung und Geschichte de frühchristlichen Evangelienliteratur', in
            W. Haase (ed.), *Aufstieg und Niedergang der Römischen Welt: Geschichte
            und Kultur Roms im Spiegel der Neuern Forschung*, II.2 (Berlin: W. de
            Gruyter): 1463–1542.
Kraft, R.A.
1965   *Barnabas and the Didache: A New Translation and Commentary*, III (New
            York: Thomas Nelson).
Lake, K.
1912   *The Apostolic Fathers*, I (LCL; Cambridge, MA: Harvard University Press)
Layton, B.
1968   'The Sources, Dates and Transmission of Didache 1:3b–2:1', *HTR* 61:
            343–83.
Lietzmann, H.
1953–64   *Mass and Lord's Supper: A Study in the History of the Liturgy* (trans. D.H.G.
            Reeve; Leiden: E.J. Brill).
Lightfoot, J.B., and J.R. Harmer
1891   *The Apostolic Fathers* (London: Macmillan)
1998   *The Apostolic Fathers* (rev. and ed. M.W. Holmes; Grand Rapids, MI: Baker
            Book House, 2nd edn).
Lilje, H.
1956   *Die Lehre der Zwölf Apostel: eine Kirchenordnung des ersten christlichen
            Jahrhunderts* (Hamburg: Furche).

Luz, U.
1989   *Matthew 1–7: A Continental Commentary* (trans. W.C. Linss; Minneapolis: Augsburg).

Massaux, E.
1993   *The Influence of the Gospel of Saint Matthew on Christian Literature before Saint Irenaeus*, III (trans. N.J. Belvaland S. Hecht; 3 vols.; Macon, GA: Mercer University Press).

Mazza, E.
1995   *The Origins of the Eucharistic Prayer* (trans. R.E. Lane; Collegeville, MN: The Liturgical Press).
1996   'Elements of a Eucharistic Interpretation', in Draper (ed.) 1995: 276–99.

Mees, M.
1971   'Die Bedeutung der Sentenzen und ihrer Auxesis für die Formung der Jesuworte nach Didache 1:3b–2:1', *Vetera christianum* 8: 55–76.

Metzger, M.
1987   *Les Constitutions Apostoliques* (Sources chrétiennes; Paris: Cerf).

Middleton, R.D.
1935   'The Eucharistic Prayers of the Didache', *JTS* 36: 259–67.

Milavec, A.
1995   'The Saving Efficacy of the Burning Process in *Didache* 16.5', in Jefford (ed.) 1995: 131–55.

Mitchell, M.M.
1989   'Concerning PERI DE in 1 Corinthians', *NovT* 31: 229–56.

Mitchell, N.
1995   'Baptism in the *Didache*', in Jefford (ed.) 1995: 226–55.

Moule, C.F.D.
1961   *Worship in the New Testament* (Ecumenical Studies in Worship, 9; London: Lutterworth Press).

Nautin, P.
1959   'La composition de la "Didachê" et son titre', *Revue de l'histoire des religions* 78: 191–214.

Niederwimmer, K.
1989   *Die Didache* (KAV, 1; Göttingen: Vandenhoeck & Ruprecht).
1995   'Der Didachist und seine Quellen', in Jefford (ed.) 1995: 15–36.
1996   'An Examination of the Development of Itinerant Radicalism in the Environment and Tradition of the *Didache*', in Draper (ed.) 1996 : 321–39.
1998   *The Didache* (trans. L.M. Maloney; Hermeneia; Minneapolis: Fortress Press).

Nolland, J.
1989   *Luke 1–9:20* (WBC, 35a; Dallas: Word Books).

Pardee, N.
1995   'The Curse that Saves (*Didache* 16.5)', in Jefford (ed.) 1995: 156–76.

Patterson, S.J.
1995   '*Didache* 11-13: The Legacy of Radical Itinerancy in Early Christianity', in Jefford (ed.) 1995: 313–29.

Peterson, E.
1951   'Über einige Probleme der Didache-Überlieferung', *RivAC* 27: 37–68.

Quasten, J.
1975   *Patrology*. I. *The Beginnings of Patristic Literature* (3 vols.; Utrecht: Spectrum).

Riggs, J.W.
    1984   'From Gracious Table to Sacramental Elements: The Tradition-History of Didache 9 and 10', *Second Century* 4: 83–102.
    1995   'The Sacred Food of *Didache* 9-10 and Second-Century Ecclesiologies', in Jefford (ed.) 1995: 256–83.

Robinson, J.A.
    1920   *Barnabas, Hermas and the Didache: Being the Donnellan Lectures Delivered before the University of Dublin in 1920* (London: SPCK).

Rordorf, W.
    1972a   'Une chapitre d'éthique judéo-chrétienne: les deux voies', *Recherches* 60: 109–128.
    1972b   'Le Baptême selon la *Didachè*', *Mélanges Liturgiques offerts au R. P. dom Bernard Botte O.S.B.* (Louvaine: Abbaye du Mont César): 499–509.
    1979   'La tradition apostolique dans la Didachè', *L'Année canonique* 23: 105–114.
    1981   'Le problème de la transmission textuelle de *Didachè* 1.3b–2.1', in F. Paschke (ed.), *Überlieferungsgeschichtliche Untersuchungen* (TU, 125; Berlin: Akademie-Verlag): 499–513.
    1991   'Does the Didache Contain Jesus Tradition Independently of the Synoptic Gospels?', in H. Wansborough (ed.), *Jesus and the Oral Gospel Tradition* (JSNTSup, 64; Sheffield: Sheffield Academic Press): 394–423.
    1996a   'An Aspect of the Judeao-Christian Ethic: The Two Ways', in Draper (ed.) 1996: 148–64.
    1996b   'Baptism according to the *Didache*', in Draper (ed.) 1996: 212–22.

Rordorf, W., and A. Tuilier
    1978   *La doctrine des Douze Apôtres (Didachè)* (Sources chrétiennes, 248; Paris: Les Éditions du Cerf, 2nd edn, 1998).

Sabatier, P.
    1885   *ΔΙΔΑΧΗ ΤΩΝ ΙΒ ΑΠΟΣΤΟΛΩΝ: La Didachè ou L'Ensignement des Douze Apôtres* (Paris: Noblet).

Sanders, E.P., and M. Davies
    1989   *Studying the Synoptic Gospels* (London: SCM Press).

Sandt, H. van de
    2002   '"Do not give what is holy to days" (Did 9:5d and Matt 7:6a): The Eucharistic Food of the Didache in its Jewish Purity Setting', *VigChr* 56: 223–46.

Sandt, H. van de, and D. Flusser
    2002   *The Didache: Its Jewish Sources and its Place in Early Judaism and Christianity* (Compendia Rerum Iudaicarum ad Novum Testamentum, III, 5; Assen: Royal Van Gorcum).

Schaff, P.
    1885   *The Oldest Church Manual, Called the Teaching of the Twelve Apostles* (New York: Funk & Wagnalls, 2nd edn, 1886).

Schöllgen, G.
    1991   'Didache: Zwölf-Apostel-Lehre', in G. Schöllgen and W. Geerlings, *Didache. Zwölf-Apostel-Lehre/Traditio Apostolica. Apostolische Überlieferung* (Fontes christiani, 1; Freiburg: Herder): 23–139.
    1996   'The *Didache* as a Church Order: An Examination of the Purpose for the Composition of the *Didache* and its Consequences for its Interpretation', in Draper (ed.) 1996: 43–71.

Seelinger, H.R.
1996   'Considerations on the Background and Purpose of the Apocalyptic Final Chapter of the *Didache*', in Draper (ed.) 1996: 373–82.
Sperber, D., and D. Wilson
1986   *Relevance: Communication and Cognition* (Oxford: Basil Blackwell).
Stanton, G.N.
1989   *The Gospels and Jesus* (Oxford Bible Series; Oxford: Oxford University Press).
Streeter, B.H.
1924   *The Four Gospels* (London: Macmillan).
Talley, T.J.
1984   'The Literary Structure of Eucharistic Prayer', *Worship* 58: 404–420.
Taylor, C.
1886   *The Teaching of the Twelve Apostles, with Illustrations from the Talmud* (Cambridge: Deighton Bell).
Tuckett, C.M.
1989   'Synoptic Tradition in the Didache', in J.-M. Severin (ed.), *The New Testament in Early Christianity* (Leuven: Leuven University Press): 197–230.
1996   'Synoptic Tradition in the *Didache*', in Draper (ed.) 1996: 92–128.
Tuilier, A.
1995   'La *Didachè* et le Problème Synoptique', in Jefford (ed.) 1995: 110–30.
Vielhauer, P.
1965   'The Final Chapter of the Didache', in E.S. Hennecke and W. Schneemelcher (eds.), *New Testament Apocrypha II* (Philadelphia: Westminster Press).
Vokes, F.E.
1938   *The Riddle of the Didache: Fact or Fiction, Heresy or Catholicism?* (London: SPCK).
Vööbus, A.
1968   *The Liturgical Traditions in the Didache* (Stockholm: Estonian Theological Society in Exile).
Wedderburn, A.J.M.
1987   *Baptism and Resurrection: Studies in Pauline Theology against Its Graeco-Roman Background* (WUNT, 44; Tübingen: Mohr).
Wengst, K.
1984   *Didache (Apostellehre), Barnabasbrief, Zweiter Klemesbrief, Schrift an Diognet* (Darmstadt: Wissenschaftliche Buchgesellschaft).
Wenham, D.
1984   *The Rediscovery of Jesus' Eschatological Discourse* (Gospel Perspectives, 4; Sheffield: JSOT Press).
West, P.H.
1967–68   'A Primitive Version of Luke in the Composition of Matthew', *NTS* 14: 75–95.

INDEXES

INDEX OF REFERENCES

BIBLE

Old Testament		10.4	48	5.5	xviii, xix, 159, 239, 240, 247
Exodus					
13.21	48	*Daniel*			
19.9	48	7	191	5.7	xviii, xix, 159, 239, 240, 247
20.2-17	169	7.13	38, 48, 49, 52-54, 58, 190-96,	5.10	219
Deuteronomy				5.17-20	177-79, 185, 248
8.10	15		198, 200, 207, 213,	5.17	xxvi, xxvii, 177,
2 Samuel			215	5.17	178
22.10	48	*Nahum*		5.19-20	178
1 Kings		1.3	48	5.19	xxvi, xxvii, 159,
8.10	48	*Zechariah*			178, 243
Psalms		14.5	46, 49, 52-54, 153,	5.20	xxvi, xxvii, 178
18.9-12	48		193, 194,	5.21-48	169
36	xi, 84, 85, 240-42		215	5.21-28	242
36.9	84	*Malachi*		5.21-26	163
36.11	84, 239	1.11	xi, 121, 123, 138,	5.21	xvi, xvii, 159, 170,
36.18	84		161, 162,		241, 243
36.20	84		248	5.22	xvi, xvii, 159, 241,
68.4	48				243
104.3	48	*Tobit*		5.23-24	138, 161, 162, 185
Isaiah		12.8	80, 170	5.24	xxx, xxxi, 159, 161,
6.9-10	114	*Sirach*			243, 248
64.1-4	55, 215	12.1	xi, 76, 164	5.25-26	236
64.1-2	52, 55			5.26	xvi, xvii, 159, 163,
64.1	52, 55	New Testament			164, 185,
64.2-3	52, 55	*Matthew*			
64.4	51-55, 196	5	224, 241		
Ezekiel		5.3-7	243		
1.4	48				

Matthew (cont.)

5.27 — xvi, xvii, xviii, xix, 159, 170, 241, 243

5.28 — xviii, xix, 159, 241, 243

5.33 — xvi, xvii, 159, 241, 243

5.38-48 — 219, 227, 228

5.38-42 — 230

5.38 — 227, 230

5.39-42 — 169

5.39 — xiv, xv, 159, 222, 227, 230, 243

5.40 — xiv, xv, 222, 227, 230

5.41 — xiv, xv, 222, 227, 230

5.42 — xiv, xv, 133, 159, 222, 227, 230-32

5.42 — 159, 222, 227, 230-32

5.43-48 — 170

5.43 — 227, 232

5.44 — xiv, xv, 159, 219, 222, 224, 227, 232, 233, 243

5.45 — xiv, xv, 159, 222, 233, 234, 243

5.46-47 — 159, 232, 233

220, 222, 236, 243, 248

5.46 — xiv, xv, 228, 232-34, 243, 247

5.47 — xiv, xv, 222, 228, 232-34, 247

5.48 — xiv, xv, 222, 228, 234, 243, 247

6 — 136, 139, 174, 175, 233

6.1-18 — 167-70, 173, 174, 177

6.1-16 — 173, 175, 176, 185, 243

6.1-4 — 133

6.2 — xxii, xxiii, 159, 171

6.3 — 171

6.4 — 171

6.5-16 — 165-67, 174, 176

6.5 — xxii, xxiii, 159, 171, 172

6.6 — 171

6.7 — 171

6.8 — 172

6.9-14 — 134

6.9-13 — 5, 133, 159

6.9 — xxii, xxiii, 172

6.10 — xxii, xxiii, 172

6.11 — xxii, xxiii, 172

6.12 — xxii, xxiii, 172

6.13 — xxii, xxiii, 172

6.14-15 — 173

6.14 — 173

6.15 — 173

6.16-18 — 166

6.16 — xxii, xxiii, 5, 159, 171

6.17 — 171

6.18 — 171

6.32 — 172

7 — 73, 202

7.6 — xxiv, xxv, 5, 79, 159, 181-83, 243

7.7-11 — 182

7.9-10 — 182

7.12 — xiv, xv, 159, 217, 218, 222, 234, 235, 243, 247

7.13-14 — xiv, xv, 159, 217, 218, 222, 235, 236, 243, 247

7.13 — 235

7.14 — 235

7.21 — 173

10 — 202

10.1 — 181

10.5-15 — 140

10.6 — 35

10.8 — 141

10.10 — xxviii, xxix, 133, 159, 183, 184, 243

10.22 — 37, 197, 198

10.40-42 — 133, 140, 170

11.1 — 181

11.12 — 173

12.31-32 — 188, 243

12.31 — xxvi, xxvii, 5, 159, 186-89

12.32 — 187

13.10-17 — 114

13.31	173	202, 204,	25.31-34	190
14.19	25	213, 214,	25.31-32	213
15.19	xx, xxi,	243	25.31	xxxii,
	159, 238,	24.10		xxxiii,
	239, 243			159, 210-
15.24	35			12
15.36	25	24.11	xxx, xxxi,	25.32-46	210
16–18	175	201	25.32	211
16	209, 214	24.12	xxx, xxxi,	25.33	211
16.25-28	209	202	25.34	xxxii,
16.25	208	24.13	37, 197,		xxxiii,
16.26	208		198, 200-		159, 211
16.27	xxxii,		202	25.35	212
	xxxiii, 46,	24.14	201	25.36	212
	50, 56,	24.15-16	38	25.37	212
	159, 190,	24.15	201	25.38	212
	207, 208,	24.21	197	25.39	212
	213, 214,	24.23-24	38	25.40	212
	243	24.24	197	25.41	212
18.15-17	133	24.29-31	206	25.42	212
18.23	173	24.29-30	207	25.43	212
19.1–28.5	167	24.29	203	25.44	212
19.17-21	240	24.30-31	159, 190,	25.45	212
19.17-20	243		203, 207,	25.46	xxxii,
19.17	247		213, 214,		xxxiii, 46,
19.18	xvi, xvii,		243		50, 51,
	159, 248	24.30	39, xxxii,		159, 190,
19.19	248		xxxiii,		212
19.21	xiv, xv,		190, 198-	26	23
	248		200, 204,	26.64	38
20.17	181		207, 213	27.3-10	181
22.37-40	218	24.31	xxxii,	28.16-20	180, 181,
22.37-39	218, 219,		xxxiii,		185
	243		198-200,	28.16	xiv, xv,
22.38-39	159		204, 213		159, 180,
22.38	xiv, xv	24.32–25.45	211		181
22.39	xiv, xv	24.42	xxx, xxxi,	28.17	180
23.9	173		215, 243	28.18	180
24	190, 196,	25	214	28.19-20	159
	198-200,	25.1-13	215	28.19	xiv, xv,
	202, 207,	25.1	173		xxii, xxiii,
	213, 214,	25.8	159		144, 159,
	245	25.13	xxx, xxxi,		179-81,
24.1-36	203		159, 243		243
24.9	200, 202	25.31-46	39, 43,	28.20	xiv, xv,
24.10-22	202, 203		209, 213,		180, 181
24.10-12	159, 190,		243		
	198-200,				

Mark

3.20	167
3.28-29	188, 189, 230, 243
3.28	186, 188
3.29	187
4.10-12	114
4.30	173
6.41	25
7.21-22	243
7.21	238, 239
8.34–9.1	209, 214
8.35–9.1	209
8.35	208
8.36	208
8.37	208
8.38	208, 210, 211
9.1	208, 210
9.2-8	210
9.38	167
9.39-42	168
9.41	170
10.1–16.8	167, 177
10.17-22	240, 241, 243
11.25	167, 173-75, 177, 229, 243
12	170, 171
12.24-25	207
12.28	218
12.31	218
12.38-44	170, 171
12.40-44	167, 168, 174, 175, 177, 229
12.40	171, 172, 174, 243
12.41-44	167
12.44	243
13	39, 191-93, 195-97, 200, 202, 203, 230
13.1-32	214
13.1-13	203
13.9-23	205, 206
13.9-13	37
13.9	202
13.12	200, 202
13.13	37, 195, 197, 198, 200-202, 243
13.14-15	38
13.14	201, 202
13.19	197
13.21-22	38
13.22	197
13.24-27	206, 207
13.24	203, 205, 206
13.25	203, 205, 206
13.26-27	243
13.26	190-96, 198, 204-207, 215
13.27	204-206
13.35	215, 243
14	23
14.22	25
14.51-52	168
14.51	167
14.62	38

Luke

6	224
6.20-21	243
6.27-38	224
6.27-36	224, 226-29
6.27-34	226
6.27-31	225, 226
6.27-30	169
6.27-28	232, 243
6.27	225, 226, 228, 232, 233
6.28	219, 225, 226, 228, 232
6.29-30	230, 231
6.29	225, 226, 228, 230, 231, 243
6.30	225, 226, 228, 230, 231
6.31	78, 224-26, 228, 234, 235, 243
6.32-35	232, 233, 243
6.32-34	225, 233
6.32	225, 226, 228, 232
6.33	226, 228, 232
6.34	225, 226, 228, 231
6.35	225, 228, 230-34, 243
6.36	225, 228, 234, 243
6.46	173
10.27	243
11	176
11.1-4	134
11.11-12	182
12.10	187-89, 243
12.35	215
12.57-59	236
12.58-59	243
12.59	236
13.23-24	235, 243
13.23	235
13.24	235
15.4	35
15.6	35
15.24	35
16.16-17	178, 179
16.16	173
18.18-23	240
21.8	38
21.19	37
22.19	25
24.30	25

John
6   25
6.11   25
6.12   25, 35
6.53-58   25

Acts
2.42   144
15   218

1 Corinthians
2.9   30, 46, 50,
                      51, 55,
                      196
11   23
11.24   25
12.3   30, 31, 37

Galatians
3.13   30, 31

1 Thessalonians
4.14   47

2 Thessalonians
1.4-6   37
2.3-11   39
2.3   38, 39
2.8   39
2.12   39
2.13-14   39

Titus
2.12   78

1 Peter
2.11   78
4.12-13   36, 37
4.12   33, 36

Revelation
1.1   144
1.7   204, 206,
                      207
2.9   125
2.10   37, 47
3.9-10   37, 47

3.9   125
6.9-11   47
6.9-10   37, 47
7.9-17   47
7.14-17   37, 47
12.11   37, 47
13.5   47
13.6   47
13.7   38, 47
13.8   47
13.14   47
14.1-5   47
14.12   47
19.11   39
19.14   47
19.19-21   39
20.4   37, 47
20.11-15   39, 43
21.7   37, 47
22.3   31, 38
22.15   125, 182

OTHER ANCIENT REFERENCES

Qumran
1QS
3   74
4.3   84

Jewish Literature
Birkat Ha-Mazon
I   18
II   18
III   18

Christian Literature
Apostolic Constitutions
                      VII
17   58
32   50, 55
32.1-5   44
32.1   40, 50
32.2   40
32.3   41
32.4-5   56, 60
32.4   41, 48, 49,
                      55, 56, 64

32.5   41, 45, 50-
                      56

Epistle of Barnabas
18–20   5, 67, 72,
                      83, 84, 91
18   72, 84
19   240
19.2   86
20   88, 90,
                      238
21   74

Didache
1–13   10
1–10   178
1–6   5, 67, 126,
                      178, 181
1–5   29, 67, 71,
                      75, 78, 83-
                      85, 90, 92,
                      98-101,
                      126, 142,

                      147
1   29, 75,
                      226, 227,
                      229, 238
1.1–6.3   180
1.1–6.1   7, 99
1.1-6   216, 217,
                      220-24,
                      227-30,
                      236, 237
1.1-5   149, 150,
                      217
1.1-3   7, 10
1.1-2   90, 91,
                      153, 221
1.1   xiv, xv,
                      144, 153,
                      217, 218,
                      222, 235,
                      236, 243,
                      247, 248
1.2-6   224, 226,
1.2-5
3

Didache (cont.)

227, 229

1.2   xiv, xv,
          54, 69, 70,
          75, 85-87,
          90, 91,
          148, 150,
          153, 217-
          19, 221,
          222, 224,
          226, 227,
          234, 235,
          240, 241,
          243, 247,
          248

1.3–2.1   5-7, 10,
          67-71, 73-
          75, 82

1.3-6   3, 67-70,
          75, 77, 82,
          85, 87, 90,
          91, 131

1.3-5   75, 77-80,
          82, 83, 85,
          87, 91,
          142, 143,
          148, 150,
          153, 216,
          219-21,
          224, 227,
          232

1.3-4   75

1.3   xiv, xv,
          10, 67, 69,
          70, 79-83,
          86, 143,
          153, 170,
          218-22,
          224, 226,
          232, 233,
          243

1.4–5.2   81

1.4–2.1   10

1.4-5   81, 82,
          221

1.4   xiv, xv,
          10, 71, 75,
          76, 78, 79,

81-83,   2.2-3   240, 241,
143, 148,   243
149, 153,   2.2   xvi, xvii,
216, 220-   240, 243,
22, 226,   248
230, 231,   2.3   xvi, xvii,
234, 240,   241
241, 243,   2.4   xvi, xvii
247-49   2.5   xvi, xvii

1.5-6   71, 75-77,   2.6   xvi, xvii
          83, 85, 90,   2.7   85, xvi,
          91, 113,   xvii
          120-22,   3.1-7   73, 83, 85,
          127, 128,   90, 91,
          142, 151,   150, 153,
          163, 217,   240-42
          221   3.1-6   67, 83, 84

1.5   xiv, xv,   3.1   xvi, xvii,
          xvi, xvii,   73, 85
          70, 71, 73-   3.2-3   241-43
          77, 82,   3.2   xvi, xvii,
          120, 153,   73
          163-65,   3.3   xviii, xix,
          185, 217,   73
          220-22,   3.4   xviii, xix,
          226, 233,   73
          236, 242,   3.5   xviii, xix,
          243, 248   73

1.6   xvi, xvii,   3.6   xviii, xix,
          76, 77, 91,   73
          126, 152,   3.7   xviii, xix,
          153, 164,   84, 239,
          221, 248   240, 243,
          149, 150   247

2.1–5.2   90   3.8–5.2   90, 91,
2.1-7   179   153, 221
2.1-3   xvi, xvii,   3.8   xviii, xix,
2.1   69, 70, 75,   71, 239,
          86, 87, 90,   240, 243,
          91, 148,   247
          150, 153,   3.9   xviii, xix
          218, 221,   3.10   xviii, xix
          241   4.1   xviii, xix,

2.2–6.1   7   71, 73,
2.2–5.2   10   4.2   xviii, xix
2.2-7   69, 70, 75,   4.3   xviii, xix,
          85, 90, 91,   73
          153, 221   4.4   xviii, xix

4.5 xviii, xix
4.6 xviii, xix
4.7 xviii, xix
4.8 xx, xxi, 73
4.9 xx, xxi
4.10 xx, xxi
4.11 xx, xxi, 88
4.12 xx, xxi
4.13 xx, xxi
4.14 xx, xxi, 58, 121
5.1 xx, xxi, 238, 239, 243
5.2–6.2 73
5.2 xx, xxi, 73, 85, 87-90, 100, 126-28, 151
6.1–7.1 149, 150
6.1-3 7, 28, 93, 97, 101, 105, 106, 148
6.1 xxii, xxiii, 73, 87-90, 100, 101, 105, 126, 143, 149, 150
6.2–10.6 104
6.2-3 10, 100, 147, 148, 150
6.2 xxii, xxiii, 73, 74, 76, 100, 101, 105, 143, 147-49, 241
6.3 xxii, xxiii, 100, 101, 105, 123, 147
7–16 68, 71, 72
7–15 7
7–10 7

7 94, 95, 102, 122, 181
7.1-4 28
7.1-3 127
7.1 xxii, xxiii, 10, 20, 90, 93-103, 105, 106, 113, 122, 123, 126-28, 131, 147, 151-53, 179-81, 185, 243
7.2-4 xxiii, 10
7.2-3 10, 94-96, 113, 122, 123, 128, 151-53, 179, 180
7.2 xxii, xxiii, 94-96, 122
7.3 xxii, xxiii, 94-96, 123
7.4 xxii, xxiii, 10, 93-96, 101, 102, 105, 106, 113, 122-24, 127, 128, 149-53, 179, 180
8 3, 5, 6, 124, 136, 167, 170, 171, 174-77, 229
8.1–11.2 10
8.1-3 3, 96, 97, 124, 125, 134, 135, 136, 139, 176
8.1-2 113, 124, 125, 128,

8.1 xxii, xxiii, 5, 96, 97, 166, 171
8.2-3 113, 124, 125, 128, 135, 140, 151, 152, 165, 167, 168, 173-77
8.2 xxii, 2-5, 125, 129-35, 136, 137, 139-41, 152, 153, 155, 158, 171, 172, 249-51
8.3 xxii, xxiii
9–10 13, 14, 28, 92, 104
9 12-15, 17, 19-28, 31, 93, 102, 121, 125, 126, 151, 177
9.1-5 19-21, 93, 97, 101, 104-109, 111, 126, 142, 149-51
9.1 xxiv, xxv, 20, 26, 93, 97, 103
9.2-5 23, 24
9.2-4 14, 20, 21, 23, 25
9.2-3 24
9.2 xxiv, xxv, 13, 26

135, 151, 152, 165-68, 171, 173-77, 185, 243

Didache (cont.)					
9.3–10.5	16	10.5	xxvi, xxvii, 18, 19, 24, 27, 35	11.4-6	93, 101, 103, 105, 106, 109, 111, 148-51
9.3-4	13	10.6	xxvi, xxvii, 14-19, 21-23, 27, 28, 98, 108	11.4	xxvi, xxvii, 101, 103, 109
9.3	xxiv, xxv, 26	10.7	xxvi, xxvii, 102, 107-12, 118	11.5	xxvi, xxvii, 101, 107, 110
9.4-5	149	10.9	114	11.6	xxvi, xxvii, 101, 102, 107, 110, 111
9.4	xxiv, xxv, 22, 24, 27, 35	11–15	7	11.7-12	28, 101, 102, 104
9.5	xxiv, xxv, 5, 14, 17, 19, 21, 22, 27, 28, 93-95, 98, 108, 113, 123, 125-28, 131, 132, 147, 148, 150, 153, 159, 181, 182, 243	11–12	76	11.7-9	101, 103, 107-109, 111-14, 151, 153, 186
		11	110	11.7-8	113
		11.1-6	102	11.7	xxvi, xxvii, 5, 102, 107, 108, 110-12, 186-89, 230, 243
		11.1-2	33, 102, 104, 113, 118-22, 127, 128, 140, 151, 177-79, 185, 186, 243, 248	11.8-9	109, 111
10	12-15, 17-28, 31, 93, 121, 125, 126, 151, 177	11.1	xxvi, xxvii, 120, 126, 177, 178	11.8	xxvi, xxvii, 107, 108
10.1-7	28, 107-109, 111, 112, 151, 153, 186	11.2	xxvi, xxvii, 33, 120, 178	11.9-10	151
10.1-6	107, 108, 111	11.3–13.2	10	11.9	xxvi, xxvii, 108, 113, 115, 118
10.1	xxiv, xxv, 14, 15, 19, 21-23, 26, 27	11.3-13	124		
		11.3-6	28, 101-104	11.10-11	101, 108, 113-19, 121, 122, 127, 128, 140, 186
10.2-5	13, 14, 17, 19, 23, 24	11.3	xxvi, xxvii, 2-5, 93, 101-106, 109, 129-33, 135, 136, 137, 140, 141, 148-52, 155, 158, 249-51	11.10	xxviii, xxix, 113, 114, 116, 118-20
10.2-3	21				
10.2	xxiv, xxv, 18, 26				
10.3	xxiv, xxv, 18, 19, 21, 23, 24, 26				
10.4-5	21				
10.4	xxiv, xxv, 18, 27				

11.11	xxviii, xxix, 113, 115-18, 120, 121, 140	13.3-7	184, 243 116, 119	14.3	xxx, xxxi, 121, 123, 128, 138, 139, 152, 154, 162, 248
		13.3-4	116, 117		
		13.3	xxviii, xxix, 10, 116-23, 125, 140, 146, 152, 154		
11.12	xxviii, xxix, 101, 103, 107-109, 111-14, 151, 153, 186			15	3, 5, 6, 11
				15.1-2	121, 137, 140
		13.4-7	152	15.1	xxx, xxxi, 121, 127
12–15	103	13.4	xxviii, xxix, 10, 117, 124	15.2	xxx, xxxi, 127
12.1-5	107, 109, 111, 112, 114, 151, 153, 186	13.5-7	10, 116-24, 140, 154	15.3-4	3-5, 128-32, 135, 136-41, 152, 155, 158, 249, 250
12.1	xxviii, xxix, 109	13.5	xxviii, xxix, 116, 122		
12.2-3	109				
12.2	xxviii, xxix, 110	13.6	xxviii, xxix, 117, 122	15.3	xxx, xxxi, 2, 129-35, 136, 137, 251
12.3-5	110, 111				
12.3	xxviii, xxix	13.7	xxviii, xxix, 117, 123	15.4	xxx, xxxi, 2, 129-33, 135, 138, 139, 152, 251
12.4	xxviii, xxix	14	121		
12.5	xxviii, xxix, 118	14.1–16.8	10		
13–14	121	14.1–15.4	137, 138, 141	16	7, 29, 30, 35, 38-41, 43, 47, 50, 54, 55, 65, 92, 93, 104, 105, 143, 148, 152, 190, 191, 195-200, 202, 213-15, 217, 219, 230, 238
13	121, 122	14.1–15.2	121, 122, 128, 137-39		
13.1–15.2	113, 128, 140, 151, 186				
13.1-7	111, 116-19, 121, 122, 127, 140, 141, 151	14.1-3	121, 125, 127, 137-39, 161, 162		
		14.1-2	118		
13.1-3	128	14.1	xxx, xxxi, 121, 123, 125, 128, 152, 161, 162	16.1-6	93, 104-106, 148-50, 215
13.1-2	116-18, 120, 121, 183				
13.1	xxviii, xxix, 116-19, 159	14.2	xxx, xxxi, 121, 123, 137, 138, 161-64, 185, 242, 243, 248	16.1-2	65, 66, 104, 105, 143, 148, 149, 249
13.2	xxviii, xxix, 116-19, 183,				

Didache (cont.)
16.1   xxx, xxxi,
         65, 66,
         105, 215,
         243
16.2   xxx, xxxi,
         56, 65,
         105, 143,
         149, 241
16.3-9   195
16.3-8   56, 65
16.3-6   30, 36, 54,
         65, 66,
         104, 153,
         190, 196,
         200, 213-
         15
16.3-5   43, 200,
         202-204,
         214, 243
16.3-4   60
16.3   xxx, xxxi,
         40, 50, 58,
         60, 61,
         200, 211
16.4-5   57, 105,
         219
16.4   xxx, xxxi,
         xxxii,
         xxxiii, 36,
         40, 47, 53,
         57-60, 62,
         63, 149,
         192, 197,
         200, 202
16.5   xxxii,
         xxxiii, 29-
         39, 41, 46-
         49, 54, 56,
         59-62, 65,
         195, 197,
         198, 201,
         202, 205,
         206

16.6   xxxii,
         xxxiii, 41,
         43, 44, 46,
         53, 54, 59,
         60, 62, 63,
         153, 203-
         207, 214,
         243
16.7   xxxii,
         xxxiii, 3,
         11, 29, 43,
         44, 46, 49,
         64, 65,
         104, 129,
         152, 153,
         155, 158
16.8-9   xi, 30, 36,
         56, 59, 64-
         66, 93,
         104-106,
         148-50,
         153, 190,
         193, 196,
         200, 207-
         209, 211,
         213-15,
         243
16.8   xxxii,
         xxxiii, 35,
         36, 39-43,
         46, 48-50,
         52-55, 57,
         59-62, 64,
         65, 152,
         153, 190-
         96, 198,
         200, 203-
         15, 243
16.9   xxxii,
         xxxiii, 30,
         54, 55, 59-
         63, 149,
         196, 210-
         12

Doctrina Apostolorum
1.1   72
1.3   72
2.2   73
3.1   73, 74
4.8   70, 71, 74
4.13   74
6.1-4   73
6.1   73, 74
6.4   73

Gospel of Thomas
6a   80, 170
14a   80, 170

Justin Martyr
First Apology
65–66   93

Dialogue with Trypho
47.4.11 37
93.1   218
120   39

Q
12.10   188, 189
16.16-17 179

Classical References
Clement of Rome
*1st Epistle of Clement
to Corinthians*
13.2   218

Pliny the Younger
Letter to Trajan
10.96.7 98

Papyri
P.Oxy
xiv, 1782   78, 85

INDEX OF AUTHORS

Aldridge, R.E. 38, 39, 42, 44, 45
Alfonsi, L. 10
Alon, G. 25
Arndt, W.F. 20, 31, 146
Audet, J.-P. 2, 3, 10, 15, 22, 23, 38, 68,
    69, 72, 74, 84, 87, 89, 117, 130,
    132, 134, 142, 145, 146, 214

Balabanski, V. 202
Barr, D.L. 48
Bartlet, J.V. 66
Bauer, W. 20, 31, 146
Betz, H.D. 169, 183
Betz, J. 13-17, 20-24, 48
Boring, M.E. 118, 119
Bouley, A. 13-16, 22
Brown, G. 69, 97
Bryennios, P. 1, 3, 13, 32, 145, 244, 252
Bultmann, R. 182
Butler, B.C. 2, 238

Carrington, P. 4
Carson, D.A. 245`
Catchpole, D.R. 216, 220, 231
Connolly, R.H. 73, 78, 84
Court, J.M. 6, 69, 158, 215, 246
Creed, J.M. 13
Cullmann, O. 16

Davies, M. 229
Dibelius, M. 16, 22
Dix, G. 13
Downing, F.G. 229
Draper, J.A. 2-4, 7, 16, 17, 22, 32, 33, 38,
    68, 70, 72, 79, 84, 91, 94, 95, 99,
    100, 103-105, 110, 114, 115, 119,
    124, 125, 142, 147, 165, 166, 169,
    172, 175-78

Dungan, D.L. 184

Finkelstein, L. 19
Flusser, D. 1, 100, 144, 147
Funk, F.X. 32

Garrow, A.J.P. 47, 69, 182
Gebhardt, O. van 29
Gero, S. 13
Giet, S. 2, 29, 134
Gingrich, F.W. 20, 31, 146
Glover, R. 2, 13, 82, 91, 166, 174-76,
    200, 214
Goodspeed, E.J. 68
Goulder, M.D. 167, 168, 183

Halleux, A. de 10
Harnack, A. van 10, 29, 69, 145
Harris, J.R. 29
Hartman, L. 94, 179
Heidenreich, A. 182
Henderson, I.H. 203
Hengel, M. 229
Hooker, M.D. 192, 193
Huggins, R.V. 229
Hüntermann, U. 69

Jefford, C.N. 2, 3, 7, 80, 85, 86, 142, 148,
    158, 163, 165, 170, 217
Jeremias, J. 13, 17

Kirk, A.K. 76, 78, 81, 224
Kleist, J.A. 144
Kloppenborg, J.S. 2, 66, 68, 83, 87, 89,
    91, 200, 214, 246
Knopf, R. 10, 121, 137, 139, 145
Köhler, W.-D. 2
Köster, H. 2, 6, 7, 10, 131-35, 139, 158,

166, 173, 176, 187-89, 191, 192,
194, 197, 198, 200, 214, 218, 219,
246, 250
Kraft, R.A. 7, 100, 121

Layton, B. 2, 68, 76, 77, 91
Lietzmann, H. 14, 16, 21-23
Luz, U. 2

Massaux, E. 2, 5, 134, 158, 161, 163,
166, 179, 182, 183, 217
Mazza, E. 3, 13-15, 17, 19, 22, 26, 27
Mees, M. 2
Metzger, M. 40
Middleton, R.D. 13
Milavec, A. 29-37, 39
Moule, C.F.D. 16

Nautin, P. 10, 130
Niederwimmer, K. 10, 20, 29, 36, 43, 65,
67-73, 76-78, 81-83, 85-87, 89, 91,
93, 95, 99, 104, 115-17, 121, 126,
129-32, 134, 135, 137, 145, 162,
164, 166, 173, 176, 179, 250
Nolland, J. 226

Pardee, N. 32, 34-37
Peterson, E. 14

Quasten, J. 14

Riggs, J.W. 13, 17, 19, 23, 24
Robinson, J.A. 72, 76

Rordorf, W. 2, 4, 10, 30, 31, 38, 68, 75,
76, 87, 91, 94, 98, 99, 117, 130,
132, 134, 144, 146, 220, 246

Sabatier, P. 3
Sanders, E.P. 229
Sandt, H. van de 1, 5, 20, 144, 183, 246
Schaff, P. 1, 134
Schöllgen, G. 10, 29, 95, 115-17, 121
Sperber, D. 97, 98
Stanton, G.N. 167
Streeter, B.H. 3, 166, 174

Taylor, C. 29
Tuckett, C.M. 2, 4-6, 38, 158, 164, 182,
187, 188, 190, 191, 194-200, 202-
204, 215, 218-20, 224, 239, 240
Tuilier, A. 2, 10, 30, 31, 38, 117, 130,
132, 134

Vielhauer, P. 2
Vokes, F.E. 13, 71, 202
Vööbus, A. 23, 95

Wedderburn, A.J.M. 94
Wengst, K. 2, 10, 29, 38, 44, 132, 134,
142
Wenham, D. 215
West, P.H. 168, 229
Wilson, D. 97, 98

Yule, G. 69, 97